YEMEN

Other Titles in This Series

Oil, the Arab-Israel Dispute, and the Industrial World: Horizons of Crisis, edited by J. C. Hurewitz

The Persian Gulf: An Introduction to Its People, Politics, and Economics, David E. Long

The Middle East: Critical Choices for the United States, edited by Eugene V. Rostow

Westview Special Studies on the Middle East

Yemen: The Politics of the Yemen Arab Republic
Robert W. Stookey

The 1962 revolution in North Yemen and the international involvement in the ensuing ten-year civil war focused world attention on an ancient country then barely emerging from a centuries-long isolation. The imposing hydrological works built there in antiquity, the sophisticated network of international commerce that excited the envy of the Greeks and Romans, the many cultures and political regimes that succeeded one another over a turbulent 2,000-year history—these had been familiar to only a handful of specialists even in the Islamic world. And many aspects of the country's unique civilization remain to be explored in depth by Western scholars.

The past has left a deep and observable imprint on contemporary Yemen. Robert Stookey traces the distinctive features of present-day Yemeni society and politics to their remote origins, a task no previous Western work has attempted, and brings the country's political history up to date through 1976. In so doing he enables a better understanding of the international role of the Arabian Peninsula's most populous nation, a nation strategically situated at the mouth of the Red Sea and one whose labor force is essential to the economies of Saudi Arabia and other major oil-producing Arab states.

Robert Stookey's distinguished record as a foreign service officer has included many Arabic area assignments, among them posts in Yemen and Saudi Arabia. At present Dr. Stookey is a research associate at the Center for Middle Eastern Studies, University of Texas at Austin.

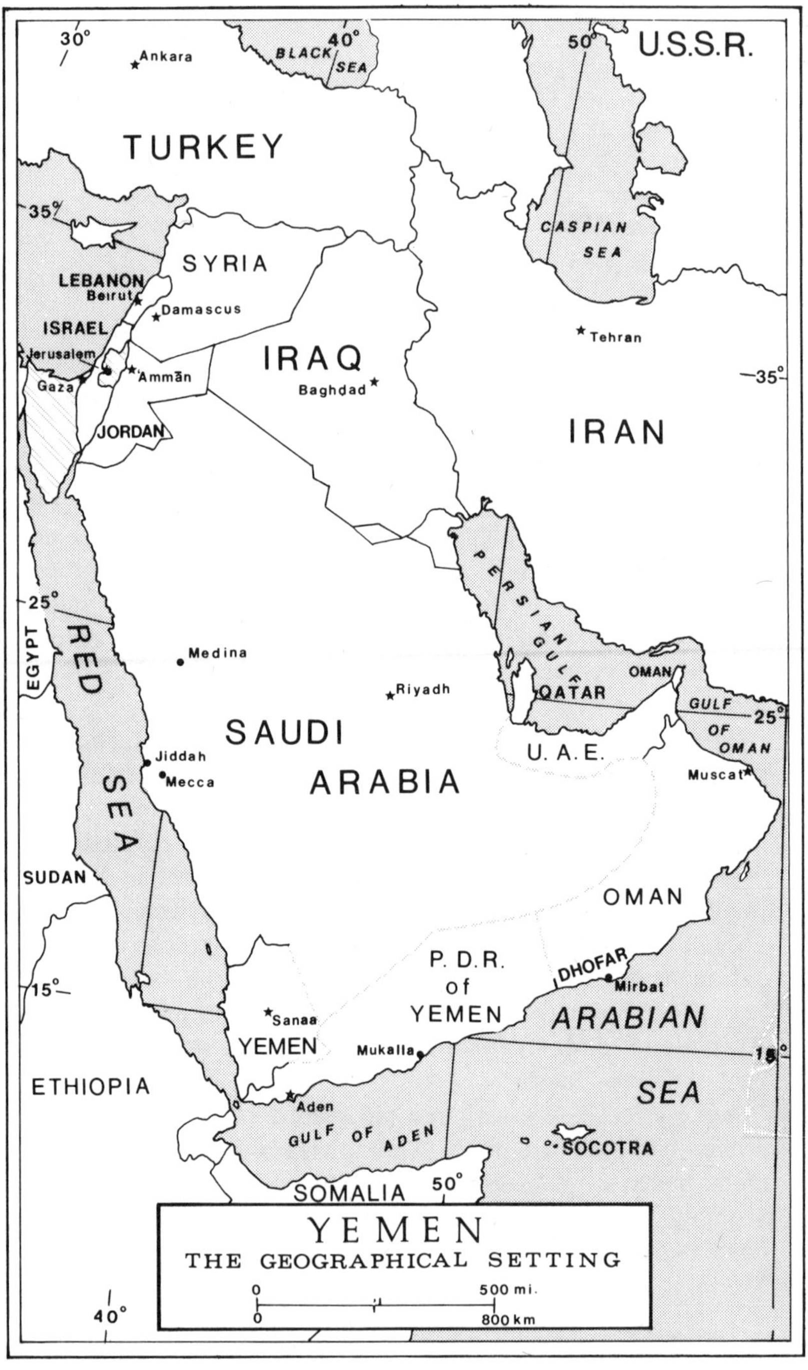

YEMEN
THE GEOGRAPHICAL SETTING

YEMEN

The Politics of the Yemen Arab Republic

Robert W. Stookey

Westview Press • Boulder, Colorado

Westview Special Studies on the Middle East

Published 1978 in the United States of America by
Westview Press, Inc.
5500 Central Avenue
Boulder, Colorado 80301
Frederick A. Praeger, Publisher and Editorial Director

Library of Congress Cataloging in Publication Data
Stookey, Robert W 1917–
Yemen: the politics of the Yemen Arab Republic.
(Westview special studies on the Middle East)
Bibliography: p.
Includes index.
1. Yemen—History I. Title.
DS247.Y45S76 953'.32 77-454
ISBN 0-89158-300-9

Printed and bound in the United States of America

This book is dedicated to the memory of some distinguished Yemenis of our time whose devoted service to their country has been tragically and prematurely terminated. The saddening roster begins with ‘Abd al-Raḥmān Abū Ṭalīb, followed by Muḥammad ‘Alī ‘Uthmān, Muḥammad Aḥmad Nu‘mān, ‘Abdullah al-Ḥajrī, and now Ibrāhīm al-Ḥamdī.

Among the marvels God has decreed is this: of the seven regions into which the inhabited one-fourth of the terrestrial globe is divided, rising above the sheath of water enveloping the Earth, each region is linked to one of the seven planets that journey nightly through the heavens. The region of Yemen is governed by Saturn. God Almighty has willed that Saturn's influence shall be a sinister one, inducing dissension, calamity, violent commotion, and the like. By virtue of this planetary influence, those parts are rarely free of civil strife. This is the ordinance of God, the Glorious, the Omniscient.

—Quṭb al-Dīn al-Nahrawālī,
al-Barq al-Yamānī

Contents

List of Figures

Preface

This book is concerned with the politics of the land known since September 1962 as the Yemen Arab Republic. Few visitors to that country, difficult of access until rather recently, escape the grip of an enduring fascination, whether with the aspect of its rugged, austere terrain, the distinctive virtuosity of its architecture and folk arts, or the engaging personality and customs of its people. Americans sensitive to the stark beauties of our own Southwestern deserts are stirred by many comparable Yemeni landscapes. The sentiment is reciprocated by the Yemenis; an excellent U.S. Information Agency documentary film on Arizona was a smash hit at the Ta'izz royal palace in 1961, and the eccentric old monarch, Aḫmad Ḥamīd al-Dīn, himself viewed it repeatedly.

Aside from the country's exotic appeal there are sound, if indirect, reasons for an American concern with Yemen and its role in the world community. In the material sense, the area is no longer Arabia Felix, as it was enviously termed by the classical Greeks and Romans, nor as verdant as it was reputed to be by northern Arabs in the early Islamic era. Its key role in international commerce ended centuries ago. It is situated on the wrong side of the Arabian Peninsula, judging from present geological knowledge, to be endowed with petroleum wealth.

On the other hand, its location on the Bāb al-Mandab Strait places it in a position to control maritime traffic to and from the Red Sea, the Gulf of Aqaba, and the Suez Canal. It is the most populous country on the Arabian Peninsula. The economies of several major Arab oil-producing states depend heavily on the labor of hundreds of thousands of temporary Yemeni migrants. The political outlook of the government and people of Yemen thus has important implications for the security and prosperity of the region. Recognizing this fact, Saudi Arabia, the United Arab Emirates, Kuwait, Iran, and Jordan have long striven to establish positions by which they may influence the policies and actions of the Yemen Arab Republic and defeat the attempts of the socialist powers, the neighboring People's Democratic Republic of Yemen, and other Arab states of the far left to lead the country in radical, disruptive directions.

The anxiety to promote stability in the region, rather than any direct stake in the country itself, has shaped United States policies toward Yemen. With America's steadily increasing dependence on the countries of the Arabian Peninsula and the Persian Gulf for its energy supply, this concern must inevitably persist and increase, and with it the need to understand the attitudes and past experiences underlying Yemeni political behavior.

In studying Yemeni affairs over a period of many years, this writer has been increasingly impressed by the deep roots underlying present-day attitudes and events, and the extent to which Yemen's national experiences, even those remote in time, illuminate its political actions. The present work is designed to identify and describe the major political and social configurations in the country's past, and to show how they have contributed to its present orientation and behavior. It is thus a political essay rather than a consecutive, narrative account. At the same time, it is hoped that the substantive material presented will serve to delineate the broad outline of Yemen's three-thousand-year history, thus offering a background that no single Western work has heretofore provided.

Yemeni, or South Arabian, studies comprise a broad, rich field as yet only partially furrowed by the scholarly plow. European savants of the nineteenth and early twentieth centuries made extensive collections of inscriptions in the ancient South Arabian script, revived knowledge of the language in which their messages were expressed, and endeavored to construct a picture of the pre-Islamic societies in the region. Clarification of the many important details that remain obscure awaits scientific excavation of key archaeological sites already identified. Present-day Yemeni officials are quite aware that excavation is a process of destruction, and are cautiously deferring large-scale "digs," awaiting the day when Yemenis will have the technical skills to act as equal participants in such operations. German and Dutch scholars of an earlier generation made considerable headway in analyzing the quality of Islam in Yemen, with particular reference to the Zaidi sect. British and other European orientalists, meanwhile, published some edited texts and translations of important historical documents. By and large, nevertheless, scholarly work on Yemen long remained the province of a relatively few specialists.

The revolution of 1962 and the ensuing civil war greatly stimulated interest in Yemen's politics and its culture, both in the West and in the Arab world. For the first time, serious efforts have been made to identify and inventory the wealth of material in Arabic concerning Yemen's history and civilization, much of it still in manuscript and widely dispersed in European and Middle Eastern capitals as well as in Yemen itself. The two principal resulting volumes are Ayman Fu'ād Sayyid, *Maṣādir Ta'rīkh al-Yaman* (Cairo: Institut français d'archéologie orientale, 1974), and 'Abdullah Muḥammad al-Ḥabshī, *Marāji' Ta'rīkh al-Yaman* (Damascus: Ministry of Culture, 1972). It is hoped that a comprehensive bibliography will soon become available of publications in Western languages regarding Yemen, as the result of a project instituted at Cambridge University by the eminent Professor R. B. Serjeant and carried forward at the American University of Beirut under the direction of Professor Maḥmūd Ghūl. Meanwhile, both Arab and Western scholars are publishing a modest flow of texts and translations, and of studies on specific junctures in Yemeni history.

Many important manuscripts remain to be published and more monographs written before a scholar can undertake with confidence the writing of a satisfactory general history of

Yemen, based on secure knowledge of the relevant cultural, economic, sociological, and political factors. It does seem feasible, however, to single out for consideration the data now accessible concerning the country's internal political character at various periods in its past, and to trace the origins of its distinguishing contemporary features. This is the purpose the present work is intended to fulfill. If it contributes to the reader's understanding of Yemen's current affairs and imparts some idea of the satisfactions to be gained through study of its long, turbulent, and varied past, the author's purpose will have been well served.

As will be apparent from the footnotes and bibliography, the work relies on primary Arab sources where these have become available in published form, upon a variety of secondary sources in both Arabic and Western languages, and upon first-hand experience. The author is indebted to the U.S. Department of State for permitting him to review the correspondence from the American diplomatic mission in Yemen during his incumbency as its chargé d'affaires (July 1961–March 1963), and to certain former Foreign Service colleagues for information imparted in conversation and in documents in their possession. Particular gratitude is due the Committee on International Exchange of Persons for a Fulbright-Hays Senior Research Scholar grant that made possible an extended sojourn in Yemen in 1973. Responsibility for the statements and judgments herein is, of course, the author's alone. Thanks, finally, are due to the Middle East Studies Center, University of Texas at Austin, for financing production of the maps and charts, which were drawn by Roxane Pierce.

Introduction

During the winter of 1959 the Legation of the Mutawakkilite Kingdom of Yemen in Washington startled officers of the State Department concerned with Arab affairs by sending out a handsome and unusual holiday greeting card. On an outline map of the Arabian Peninsula, the location of the traditional (not the then current) Yemeni capital, Sanaa, was represented by a small jewel, and a shaded area appeared to define the extent of the kingdom's putative territory. The shading encompassed, in addition to Yemen as delimited on conventional maps of the time, Aden and the entire Aden Protectorate, Dhofar, Muscat and Oman, and the Trucial Coast up to the eastern base of the Qatar Peninsula; a generous portion of the Empty Quarter, reaching approximately to the Wadi Dawāsir on the north; and Nejran and Asir on the northwest. The extent of Yemen conveyed by the legation's card was more faithful to Arab legend than to history or practical politics. The shaded area corresponded roughly to that populated, according to one school of Arab genealogy, by the descendants of Qaḥṭān (The Joktan of the Bible), son of Shem and grandson of Noah. While this family tree is doubtless partly invented, it is accepted among Arabs who live in South Arabia, or whose ancestors, however distant, were born there; they draw an ethnic distinction between themselves and their cousins in the northern portion of the Arabian Peninsula, descendants of ʻAdnān.

No historical instance exists of a distinct South Arabian state embracing this entire territory. The eleventh-century Ṣulayḥid kings had responsibility for Fatimid interests as far east as Oman, and even India. The Rasūlids held the province of Dhofar under loose suzerainty in the thirteenth and fourteenth centuries, and Zaidi imams later made forays into that area. Generally speaking, however, Yemeni authority has not normally extended eastward beyond Hadramaut, i.e., the Qu'aitī State of the former East Aden Protectorate. Nejran and Asir, on the other hand, were integral to Yemeni history for many centuries, until their conquest in 1934, confirmed by a treaty awarding them to the kingdom of Saudi Arabia.

The boundary between the two states now bearing the Yemeni name reflects the stalemate early in the present century between the energies of two intrusive, non-Arab empires: the Ottoman, then in occupation of Yemen, and the British, in Aden and the Protectorates; the fact that no Yemeni authority participated in establishing the line was of political import until 1967, when the United Kingdom withdrew from the region. The Anglo-Turkish line disappears south of the Yemeni town of Ḥarīb, and the present-day Yemen Arab Republic (Y.A.R.) has no eastern boundary, although some cartographers have improvised one, and some journalists greatly gifted in mathematics were able, during the civil war of the 1960s to calculate with precision the proportion of Yemeni territory held at any given time by Royalists and Republicans respectively.

There are no terms in which Yemen may reasonably be said to have had a single, continuous political regime during the past three millennia. Upon the collapse of the Sabean, or Ḥimyarite, state in the sixth century A.D., Yemen was occupied in turn by Ethiopia and Persia before it was converted to Islam and became first one province, then several provinces, of the Arab Empire. When Abbasid control of the remoter territories weakened, entities appeared in Yemen, as elsewhere, which may be taken as independent for purposes of analysis. Several such states often coexisted on the territory of the ancient Ḥimyarite state, and while the term "Yemen" came into general use, it designated a geographical region rather than a political entity. Some of these regimes were conquered by successive dynasties in the north: ʻAlid, Fatimid, Ayyūbid, Mameluke, and finally Ottoman. Over time, local independence periodically reasserted itself, whether through indigenous effort or through defiance of metropolitan authority by its appointed governors.

Of the many regimes that succeeded one another, or coexisted, in Yemen over the centuries, this study devotes particular attention to those whose imprint persists in present-day Yemen. Thus, as educated Yemenis are aware of, and take pride in, the civilization of their remote ancestors and as, furthermore, the general tribal pattern of Yemeni society was laid down in antiquity, the first chapter examines the evolution of the ancient Sabean state between its rise in the eighth century B.C. and its extinction in the sixth century A.D. As Yemen today is a self-consciously Islamic state, we need to consider the rise of Islam in the seventh century, and the Arab Empire, as they related to Yemen. At two periods between the ninth and eleventh centuries, states tributary to the Fatimid caliphs arose in Yemen which left a permanent mark in the Ismāʻīlī minority that still survives; these are discussed in Chapter 3. Basic to the study of current Yemeni politics is an understanding of the cleavage within the society between the Zaidi sect of Shīʻa Islam and the Shāfiʻī rite of Sunnī Islam; Chapter 4 explains the nature of Zaidism as a political system and the circumstances of its establishment in Yemen. The next chapter is devoted to the most successful and durable of the Sunnī regimes in Yemen, that of the Rasūlid sultans, from the thirteenth to the fifteenth century. Chapter 6 is concerned with the Zaidi imamate at the peak of its geographical extent, and with the external challenges it faced from the Mameluke and Ottoman states. The remainder of the study is devoted to twentieth-century Yemen. Chapter 7 examines the political aspects of the Mutawakkilite Kingdom (1919-1962) and describes the processes of change that culminated in the 1962 revolution. The following chapter treats the early years of the republican regime, the civil war, and outside intervention in Yemen's affairs. The concluding chapter follows the Yemeni political system as it evolved through the national reconciliation of

1970, the promulgation of the Permanent Constitution, the 1971 elections, the erosion of civilian, consultative government, and the inception of the current military regime.

In this discussion, the political aspect of a society is taken to consist of the processes and structures though which coercion may legitimately be exercised in pursuit of authoritatively established aims. Legitimacy refers to a conception, shared by rulers and subjects, of the proper locus of the right to coerce, the range of activities it ought to embrace, and the manner of its exercise. Most societies, including the Yemeni, are stratified by classes or groups with varying interests and outlooks; those in authority commonly face not one single public, but a variety of publics, which may hold differing conceptions of who has a right to govern, and for what purposes. Rulers must either devise some basis for their legitimacy vis-à-vis each major segment of the society, or expend resources to limit the ability of one or more to challenge or obstruct the exercise of authority. In each such dyadic relationship, legitimacy is defined in terms of those satisfactions, abstract or material, which rulers and ruled agree to be a proper motive of coercion. Where agreement is comprehensive, governments are likely to be strong and to exert highly centralized authority; if, on the other hand, opinion is divided from sector to sector of the society, government tends to be weak and authority is dispersed.

From such a viewpoint, political values and patterns of authority are major variables. It has been found useful to distinguish between *instrumental* values, which lead subjects or rulers to seek immediate gratification of material or status aspirations through political processes, and *consummatory* values which move men to forgo present worldly gratifications for the sake of more abstract aims that may include the propagation of a religious faith, proselytization for particular political or social institutions, economic modernization or industrialization, national prestige or power, and the like. A familiar three-way typology of authority patterns has been used. Where all significant choices are made at the apex of the polity and the officials who enforce them at all levels are in essence emanations of the sovereign, responsive to his will and subject to removal at his pleasure, we have a pure form of *hierarchical* authority. If decisions in certain fields only are centralized at the top, with the mode of execution subject to the discretion of subordinate officials, while choice in other matters is exercised by substructures, as is common in a federal system, we have a *pyramidal* pattern of authority. Where, finally, a central, institutionalized process for decision-making is absent, and ad hoc coalitions are created to formulate and execute each major decision, we have a *segmental* authority pattern, commonly (but not necessarily) based on kinship linkages.

Political change consists of an alteration of the value pattern in a society either by the re-ordering of priority among existing aims, or by the introduction of new values and abandonment of former aims. Where a change in emphasis takes place within a stable set of values, dramatic alterations may occur in the pattern of authority and in the ability of the society to pursue its political objectives; but such changes are reversible over a limited time span. On the other hand, where innovating values are introduced and effectively asserted, whether by newly formed social elements, by previously existing elements newly able to make demands on the political system, or by external influence, lasting political change has taken place. In the study of Yemeni politics under the Zaidi imams which is a major concern of this book, we encounter change of both types. The set of political values remained markedly stable over many centuries. Dramatic centralization of authority, expansion in the political system's capabilities, and decline in the need for actual coercion occurred when the rulers concentrated their energies on consummatory aims corresponding to values generally held by politically relevant segments of the society. These processes were reversed when such aims were achieved or subordinated to objectives instrumental principally for the imams themselves. Under the last imams, however, partly through their own policies and actions and partly through impingement of the external environment, attachment to some of the old values weakened or disappeared, and innovative ones appeared which appealed to groups increasingly able and determined to pursue their aspirations through the political system. These changes ultimately received expression in revolution, and the supplanting of a theocratic monarchy by a relatively secular republic.

For the transliteration of Arabic names and terms the writer has generally followed the Library of Congress system of romanization. For ease of reading, however, proper names reasonably current in journalistic or other writing addressed to a general public have been left without diacritical marks, (e.g., Hadramaut, Asir, Hijaz, Sanaa). Reputable authorities are not always agreed on the transliteration of some of the more obscure Yemeni proper names. The Arabic texts in which they occur are frequently unpointed; where the short vowels happen to be marked they often vary from author to author, and even from page to page within the same text. The present writer has sought competent authority for the vocalization of each name; he will nevertheless not be surprised if readers discover solid ground for some alternate renderings. In a few passages quoted from Arabic writers the English versions of earlier translators have been used for their particular flavor. Otherwise, translations from Arabic and other languages throughout are by the present author.

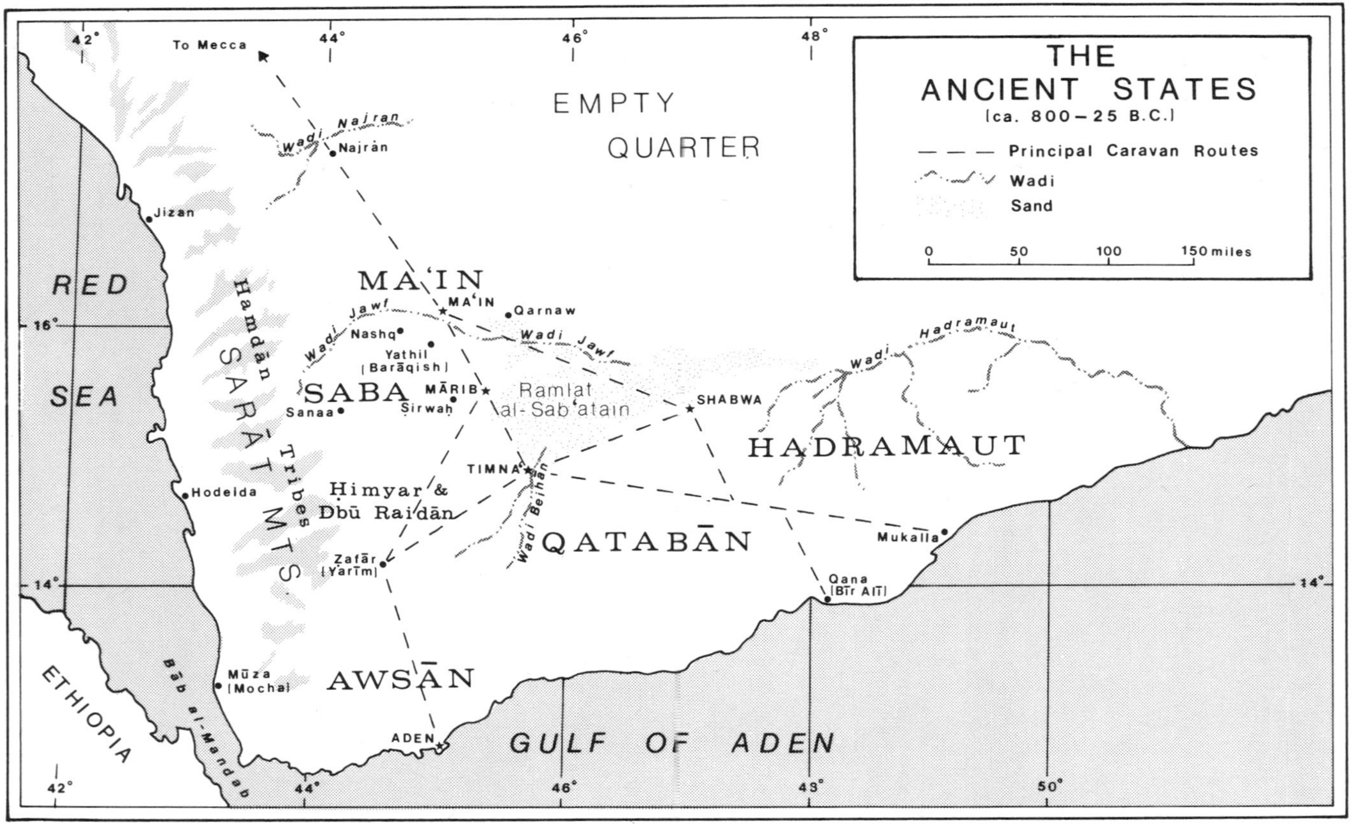
THE
ANCIENT STATES
(ca. 800–25 B.C.)
Principal Caravan Routes
Wadi
Sand
0
50
100
150 miles
EMPTY QUARTER
To Mecca
Wadi Najran
Najrān
Jizan
RED SEA
MA'IN
MA'IN
Qarnaw
Wadi Jawf
Nashq
Yathil (Barāqish)
SABA
MĀRIB
Sirwah
Sanaa
Hamdān Tribes
SARĀT MTS.
Ramlat al-Sab'atain
SHABWA
Wadi Hadramaut
HADRAMAUT
TIMNA
Wadi Beihan
Himyar & Dbū Raidān
Hodeida
QATABĀN
Mukalla
Zafār (Yarīm)
Qana (Bīr Alī)
Mūza (Mocha)
AWSĀN
ADEN
GULF OF ADEN
ETHIOPIA
Bāb al-Mandab
42°
44°
46°
48°
50°
16°
14°

Figure 1

1
The Ancient States

During the millennium preceding the Christian era, the geographical situation and natural resources of Southern Arabia (see figure 1) offered the potential for large-scale collective human enterprise, given effective political institutions. The records of the area's societies, scanty and at best of unsure interpretation, permit us to form only a general idea of how their affairs were ordered. Some of their brilliant achievements are not in doubt. For many centuries the Southern Arabs organized and administered the supply to Egypt, Mesopotamia, the Levant, and eventually Rome, of their own luxury products, as well as many from Africa, India, and China. They built some of the most imposing hydrological works of the ancient world, sustaining dense, prosperous populations in regions which now support merely a few nomadic herdsmen. The vigor of the political systems which made these feats possible declined, in part through the displacement of primordial values by new motives of a more abstract nature and of alien origin. Their capabilities at length became inadequate to maintain their economic strength and, finally, their independent identity.

The Incense Trade

The frankincense tree is native to the present Omani province of Dhofar. From early antiquity its resin was a precious necessity for religious ritual in Egypt and other cultures to the north. In the earliest periods of which we are informed, the produce was controlled by the rulers of Hadramaut, to the west of Dhofar, who required the bulk of it to be shipped by raft to the port of Qana (near the present Bīr ʻAlī), whence it was carried overland to Shabwa, the Hadrami capital. Control of the onward transport was the object of competition among several South Arabian states. More widely grown local products, such as myrrh and other aromatics, diversified the trade; there were also imports from Africa (ostrich feathers, ivory, etc.), India (spices, precious stones, sandalwood, and fine textiles), and China (notably raw silk). Monsoon winds facilitated maritime exchange over the Indian Ocean between the South Arabians and their trading partners in Africa and the Indian subcontinent. The Red Sea had no such dependable system of winds, few sheltered ports, and many navigational hazards. While the Egyptians and eventually the Romans learned to sail the Red Sea, the Southern Arabs usually preferred the land routes north. Overland transport was made technologically feasible by the camel, domesticated at an undetermined date, but in regular caravan use before 1000 B.C.[1] From Hadramaut it was necessary to avoid both the rugged Sarāt mountain chain to the west, and the waterless Empty Quarter to the east, in order to arrive at Wadi Nejran, an essential way station. It is in the transition zone between the Sarāt and the desert that the states arose, within the territory of present-day Yemen Arab Republic, which functioned as middlemen in the ancient trade: Saba (Sheba) and Maʻīn. Common commercial preoccupations intertwined their history with that of Hadramaut, Qatabān, and Awsān, their neighbors to the south.

Maʻīn and Saba

The origins and early movements of the Southern Arabs are still a matter of scholarly inquiry and speculation. Certainly, they had been in their historical locations several centuries before they began making durable written records. Linguistically they fell into two groupings: the first including the peoples of Hadramaut, Qatabān in the Wadi Beihan, and Maʻīn; and the second the Sabeans and their Hamdān cousins, whose language remained closer to Northern Arabic.[2] Social organization in both groupings was, and remained, tribal. Kinship solidarity was reinforced by common religious beliefs. The large tribal entities, which became coterminous with political units, were united by devotion to one or more deities, commonly a supreme god related to the moon or the sun, with whom might be associated secondary dieties, frequently connected with the planet Venus. Component tribes also worshiped local gods, often of an animistic or ancestral nature, some of which survived until the rise of Islam.

Both Maʿīn and Saba developed a prosperous agricultural base and built numerous irrigation works; as many as eighty ancient barrages were still remembered and listed in the tenth century A.D. by the historian Hamdānī.[3] It is the Sabeans, however, who developed the engineering and administrative skills necessary to construct and maintain the renowned ʻĀrim Dam at Mārib. The potential was provided by the local geography. The western slopes of the Sarāt are too precipitous, and their valleys too narrow, to offer practical sites for storage of large volumes of water. The slope to the east is gentle, and on the plateau near Mārib was found the combination of features needed for large-scale works: a watercourse, Wadi Adhana, carrying the seasonal run-off from a large section of the mountains; a spot where elevated ground on both banks made the construction of a barrage feasible; a capacious storage area upstream; and a large expanse of fertile soil downstream.

The supposition formerly held that these two states succeeded one another chronologically has given way, under rigorous analysis of the available evidence, to the recognition that they existed side by side for several hundred years, and that Maʿīn's historical period was entirely included in that of Saba. The latter had achieved sufficient stature to be mentioned in inscriptions of Sargon and Sennacherib of Assyria (in the late eighth and early seventh centuries B.C.), more than a hundred and fifty years before the first Minean king of record. The elaborate Hebrew and Arab legends of the visit to King Solomon (mid-tenth century B.C.) by a queen of Saba are undoubtedly rooted in historical incident.

The Mineans were settled in the Jawf region, to the northeast of present-day Sanaa. In addition to their capital at Qarnaw (also called Maʿīn, the site of contemporary al-Sudā), they built other urban centers, notably Nashq, and Yathil, whose impressive remains are now known as Barāqish. Practicable caravan routes to and from Hadramaut led either directly across the Ramlat Sabatain Desert or through the cultivated valleys of Saba and Qatabān. Maʿīn was well placed to control the northward commercial traffic. During its ascendancy it enjoyed control of Hijaz, and was thus in a position to regulate and protect the trade up to the caravan terminal at Gaza.

Minean society was composed of scattered city-states dependent upon agriculture and commerce, and of nomadic herdsmen. The people (except for slaves) were nevertheless members of the single tribe of Maʿīn, united not only by kinship, but also in devotion to the moon-god Athtar, the chief tribal diety. Social stratification was rigid. A king ruled by divine right, regularly associating his son and heir apparent in power during his own reign. Officials and civil magistrates were drawn from a landed aristocracy, and a numerous priestly class constituted a concurrent bureaucracy, collecting and administering temple revenues.

The principal motivations of Minean society appear to have been a consummatory concern for fulfilling the ritual requirements of the cult, and the more practical ambition to preserve Maʿīn's predominant position in the caravan trade. More than its neighbors, Maʿīn exhibits theocratic characteristics. Although there were parallel civil and religious tax systems, state property was considered that of the god, and the resources of the cult as well as of the state might be devoted to civil works such as defensive fortifications, which were dedicated to the god.

The pattern of authority in Maʿīn was markedly pyramidal. The monarch, though ruling by divine authority, was not an autocrat. He did not serve in the role of high priest, and it is not recorded that he fulfilled any priestly function. His power was moreover exercised in consultation with an advisory body, the General Council of Maʿīn, composed of members of the aristocracy and of the priesthood; decisions of sufficient importance to be recorded in inscriptions, including on one occasion the appointment of a tax gatherer, were issued jointly in the name of the king and the council. This consultative pattern extended to the towns, where mayors, elected to one-year terms, were assisted by councils of elders. Responsibility for major state enterprises was delegated to subordinate echelons of the society. Whereas few public works, such as fortifications, are attributed to the initiative of the king, many are ascribed to individual clans or subtribes, who undertook them in lieu of payment of taxes.

Such decentralization of authority would not appear to promote maximum mobilization of capabilities, and indeed the Maʿīn record is mixed in this respect. On the one hand, the Mineans apparently succeeded in organizing and defending the trade routes throughout their independent period. Traces of their activities have been turned up by archaeologists in localities as far afield as Ur in southern Iraq: along the principal route north through al-ʿUlā in present-day Saudi Arabia, where they maintained a major installation; at Maʿān in Transjordan; and in the Negev and the Sharon coast of Palestine.[4] On the other hand, Maʿīn was never a great military power, and at several periods was forced to submit to the suzerainty of its neighbors when these achieved, for a time, the requisite military capability. Thus Maʿīn was tributary to the first "mukarribs" of Saba beginning late in the fifth century B.C.; its kings were vassals of Qatabān in the second century A.D.; and the territory was finally absorbed in the Sabean state in the ensuing Ḥimyarite era.

Saba lay to the south of Maʿīn, with its capital at Mārib and a second urban center at Ṣirwāḥ. At the end of the sixth century B.C., when the earliest known Sabean inscriptions were carved, authority was ascribed to a trinity composed of a king, the tribe of Saba, and the tribal god, Ilmaqa.[5] While representative institutions were well established, with a tribal council fulfilling a distinct legislative function, administration was more centralized than in Maʿīn and salient public concerns more instrumental. The king typically took personal credit for public works brought to completion, and it was under his auspices that colonists were settled on land newly brought into production. The Sabeans were markedly development minded, and furthermore aspired to a major share in the caravan trade. Certainly, concentrated authority and a high degree of common purpose between rulers and subjects were required for the impressive engineering achievement represented by the Mārib Dam, built during successive reigns toward the end of the fifth century B.C. The Sabeans' political imagination transcended the tribe; they were able to conceive, and for a time to realize, a political structure embracing a number of diverse tribes under their leadership.

The first era of Saba's dominance over its neighbors dates from the reign of Karib'il Watar, toward the end of the fifth century B.C. By a skillful combination of diplomacy and military force this monarch forged a federation under Sabean rule extending over Hadramaut, Awsān, Qatabān, and Ma'īn. Symbolizing his rise in status, Karib'il Watar abandoned the title of king and took that of "mukarrib," which appears to denote the unifying and holding together of numerous peoples.[6] In the ensuing century of Sabean ascendancy, the great Mārib Dam was completed; commercial missions were dispatched across the Red Sea to gather aromatics and other valuable trade commodities; permanent colonies were established in Ethiopia contributing to an acculturation which, several centuries later, produced the kingdom of Aksum. The incense trade was firmly in Sabean hands. In 323 B.C. Alexander the Great sent Anaxicrates on his exploratory voyage around the Arabian Peninsula. As reported by Theophrastos, he found South Arabia unquestionably the land of the Sabeans; no mention is made of the tributary states. Incense and the other merchandise moving in international trade were deposited in the temple of Ilmaqa at Mārib, where the priests collected a tax of one third before releasing the goods for northward transport.

This South Arabian unity gradually dissolved. During the third century B.C., Hadramaut, Qatabān, and Ma'īn reasserted their independence. The Ptolemaic geographer Eratosthenes (ca. 273-192 B.C.) depicts the four kingdoms on an equal footing, all prosperous and well supplied with temples and royal palaces in their respective capitals. The transition is underscored by the fact that the rulers of Saba have abandoned the mukarrib title; in their inscriptions they are again simply kings. Qatabān, on the other hand, has become an expansionist state; it has taken possession of Awsān, and thus controls the Bāb el-Mandab; it has occupied Hadramaut for a time; and its monarchs now style themselves mukarrib. Ma'īn has reached the apogee of its commercial fortunes, with firm control of the caravan route as far as Palestine, and a major installation at al-'Ulā in Hijaz (the ancient Dadan).

The Ptolemies had meanwhile restored to Egypt the vigor and enterprise of a great maritime power in the Red Sea. Their effort was concentrated on the resources of the African shore: gold, ivory, elephants, rhinoceros horn, etc. Egypt did not attempt to occupy South Arabia, and posed at first only a potential threat to the caravan route and to the South Arabian monopoly of the entrepôt trade in Eastern products. It is nevertheless tempting to suppose some relationship between the appearance of an intrusive power and the contemporaneous political changes in Saba. Situated between Saba and the Red Sea, the Hamdān tribal federations, Ḥāshid and Bakīl, hitherto of minor relevance to Sabean politics, figure increasingly in the inscriptions. The centralized administrative institutions alter little by little. Subjected or recruited tribes are placed under the authority of a magistrate, *kabīr*, in whom land ownership is vested and whose office tends to become hereditary. The scope of action of the Sabean king narrows, although he remains the leader of important military operations. The trend is toward a pyramidal pattern of authority, and while Saba's wealth became legendary in the Mediterranean world, it was not, apparently, a major political or military power.

The absorption of Egypt by Rome in the middle of the first century B.C. introduced a more persistent, and eventually disastrous, challenge to the South Arabian commercial position. The expedition of Aelius Gallus, prefect of Egypt, in 24 B.C., to conquer Saba or ally it with Rome, was a failure. The Romans remained resentful of the outrageous prices charged by Arab traders for their merchandise, and of the fact that everything had to be paid for in cash, there being no Roman goods the Arabs needed in exchange. A momentous change occurred when a Roman ship, in the reign of the Emperor Claudius (41-54 A.D.), was by chance blown from the Bāb al-Mandab all the way to Ceylon. Rome thus learned fortuitously that many of the spices, textiles, and other products previously assumed to be produced in Arabia Felix actually originated far to the east. In the next generation Hippalus discovered the pattern of the monsoon winds, and Roman merchant ships began sailing directly to India, bypassing South Arabian ports such as Muza (Mocha), which declined in status to a local emporium of the incense traffic.

The Roman encroachment was followed by a long period of warfare among the South Arabian states, marked by shifting alliances in which the Ethopian state of Aksum, founded probably late in the first century A.D., assumed an increasing role. Although dates and details remain obscure, major changes were set in motion. Qatabān, in a renewed phase of vigor, overpowered the state of Awsān and extended its suzerainty over the last kings of Maʿīn. Growth of the maritime trade obliged Saba to turn its attention westward and to the south, in an effort to inhibit it or to share in it. The Hamdān tribes were fully incorporated into the political structure. Saba embarked upon a campaign of conquest against the Ḥimyarites, who occupied the crucially strategic southwest corner of the peninsula. By the time of the anonymous *Periplus of the Erythraean Sea*, well into the second century or perhaps even into the third,[7] Saba and Ḥimyar compose a dual kingdom, whose monarchs style themselves kings of Saba and Dhū Raydān.[8] The new orientation toward the sea is reflected in the fact that Ẓafār now serves concurrently with Mārib as capital, while Muza has recovered its position as an international entrepôt. Sabean authority extends over the island of Socotra, and over portions of the Horn of Africa. The king, Karib'il Watar Yuhanʿim, is in cordial contact with the emperors of Rome. Saba has, finally, conquered Qatabān, and only Hadramaut preserves a separate political identity.

Karib'il Watar was the last king of a Hamdānid dynasty which had replaced the indigenous Sabean royal house in circumstances which remain obscure. Without sons of his own, he named as co-regent a Ḥāshid chief, Yarim Ayman, who became the founder of a second Hamdānid line. In the next generation there appeared a royal dynasty of the Bakīl wing of Hamdān, inaugurated by Fari' Yanhub, who, with his sons Ilsharaḥ Yaḥḍub and Ya'zil Bayyin, reigned concurrently with the Ḥāshids. Curiously, the two dynasties appear to have been allies, not rivals. The inscriptions record no hostilities between them. Both invoked the Hamdān god, Ta'lab, as well as the traditional Sabean deities. They shared the royal palace, Salḥīn, at Mārib. According to later Arab tradition, Ilsharaḥ collaborated with his Ḥāshid contemporary, Sha'r Awtar, in constructing the fabled Ghamdān palace at Sanaa, a twenty-story tower roofed with alabaster, guarded at its four corners by hollow statues of lions so fashioned that they roared when the wind blew.

These two kings continued the expansionist policy by undertaking operations against Hadramaut, and sacked its capital, Shabwa. Saba had not, however, sufficiently absorbed its previous conquests. The Ḥimyarites rebelled under their chiefs Yasir Yuhan'im and his son Shāmir Yuhar'ish, seized control of the Tihama north to Nejran, and fought the royal forces already hard pressed by a revolt of the Khawlān, just north of the ancient Sabean heartland. Ethiopia, which had in the past supported Saba against Ḥimyar (its immediate commercial competitor), switched sides and allied itself with the Ḥimyarites against Saba, which had now become a maritime power menacing Ethiopian trade with Hadramaut and the East. With this support Shāmir embarked upon a campaign which enabled him to claim the throne for himself. The extent of his conquests is reflected in the title he eventually assumed: king of Saba, Dhū Raydān, Hadramaut, and Yamnat.[9] These events, which probably date from the last quarter of the third century, resulted in the first political unification of all South Arabia under a single ruler.

Impressive as this Ḥimyarite exploit undoubtedly was, the product was not a cohesive, unified nation with power equal to the sum of its parts. To judge from the sparse inscriptions of the period, the fragmentation already in process for several centuries has sapped the strength of the central authority. The king deals individually, by negotiation, with tribes and local magnates. Military operations are the only field in which the monarch's role is unquestioned. Incorporation of Hadramaut in the Sabean state was a challenge to the interests of Ethiopia, where Aksum had reached the peak of its vitality and imperial ambitions. South Arabia appears to have mounted only feeble resistance to an invasion which extinguished its separate identity for a time.

The political characteristics which made possible Saba's first territorial expansion had been altered by its very success. The rise in the state's fortunes in the fifth century B.C. can plausibly be attributed to a firm tribal cohesiveness and common purpose, marked under the first mukarrib by the withdrawal of local privileges from colonies on newly developed public lands. As Saba expanded, it encompassed other tribes with interests and outlooks differing from those of the Sabeans, tribes which had long enjoyed their own sovereignty, and which had been Saba's rivals and equals. Tribal diversity persisted in attachment to varied ways of ordering civil affairs, including the allocation and use of land. Gods were tribal deities, and while one tribe's recognition of, and respect for, the god of another might be recorded in inscriptions, the notion that one god might be worshiped by many or all tribes was not yet conceived. The religious component of legitimate authority gave way to secularism; the range of agreed values between ruler and subjects diminished, together with demands on the central political system. The evolution of the *kabīr* from a bureaucratic to a feudal institution created legitimate authorities at subordinate levels of the society, with their own values and interests. The transition affected Saba itself; the disappearance of the Sabean tribal council around the dawn of the Christian era implied a weakened central government. As movement toward a pyramidal authority pattern is commonly associated with decline in government capability, it is not surprising that the new Ḥimyarite dynasty proved unable to defend the hollow structure it had created against outside attack.

Ethiopian Invasion and the Rise of Monotheism

Annexation of Hadramaut placed the Sabean state in a

position to control the trade in South Arabia's incense and aromatics, and to threaten Ethopian access to the products of the East. In the absence of detailed historical records, we can only assume that commercial rivalry prompted Aksum to invade South Arabia and to annex it to her African empire. Although of less than four decades duration,[10] this first Ethopian occupation had far-reaching implications for the subsequent development of the South Arabian state. The success of the invasion cast discredit upon the numerous tribal gods, one of whose major functions was to safeguard the community and ensure victory in war. It lent credibility to the notion that there is but a single god, and encouraged the innovative idea that the coercive propagation of particular forms of worship is an appropriate function of the state. Finally, the occupation helped to make of South Arabia an object of concern to the two rival empires to the north, Byzantium and Sassanid Persia.

Quite probably, systematic monotheism first reached Yemen in the form of Judaism. No independent historical evidence confirms the ancient tradition among Yemeni Jews that their ancestors migrated to South Arabia before the destruction of the First Temple. More likely, the major Jewish settlements in Arabia followed upon the destruction of Jerusalem by the Emperor Titus in 70 A.D. Many Jews migrated to Yemen, where they proselytized with some success.[11] It is unclear to what extent the Yemeni Jews who moved en masse to Israel in 1948 were descendants of these early migrants, or of their indigenous converts. In any case, the first Christian missionaries in South Arabia found Judaic communities flourishing within the predominantly pagan environment.

Christianity gained a foothold in South Arabia during, but not as a consequence of, the occupation. The Aksumite king, 'Ela Amida, who conducted the invasion, was a pagan. His son and successor, Aizanas, was converted to Arian Christianity by a Christian captive, Frumentius, probably about the year 340, and made it the official religion of his domain. In the years 341-346 the Patriarch Theophilus dispatched a Syrian missionary to South Arabia who apparently converted the Sabean chief at Ẓafār, founded a see there of which he served as bishop, and planted several other churches in the region.[12]

Monotheistic principles were thus familiar to the South Arabians when they undertook to free themselves from foreign rule. The prince of the deposed Ḥimyarite dynasty, Malik-Karib Yuha'nim, who led the war of liberation, invoked a single deity, Dhū Samāwī, "Lord of the Heavens," who apparently had come to embody the virtues and attributes of all the old tribal gods. It has been suggested that Dhū Samāwī is to be identified with the God to whose worship Theophilus' missionary had converted the people of the Ḥimyarite capital and that Malik-Karib was thus a Christian.[13] Upon his death, however, his son and successor embraced a form of Judaism which remained for a century the established faith and an important animating force of the Ḥimyarite state. As'ad Ab-Karib is known to the later Arab annalists as a great conquerer by the name of As'ad Kāmil al-Tubba'.[14] He is credited with placing Nejd under Sabean suzerainty, and with an expedition against pagan Mecca, as well as with improbable ventures much further afield. Saba attained its greatest geographic extent under As'ad and his immediate successors, as is reflected in their inflated title, Kings of Saba, Dhū Raydān, Yamnat, and their Arabs[15] of the High Country and Tihama.

The most spectacular deeds attributed to this Judaizing dynasty were motivated by concern for the propagation of the faith. Instrumental concerns, at the same time, were not entirely lost sight of. As'ad's son, Sharaḥbi'il Yu'fir, exerted a major effort to repair damages to the Mārib Dam. A lengthy inscription records that one segment of the structure, and related masonry works, were rebuilt in 449. The following season's flood swept away the new construction, and the king mustered twenty thousand men of Ḥimyar and Hadramaut to restore it and strengthen the buttresses. (It is noteworthy that the tribe of Saba, diminished in number, cohesiveness, and vigor, was no longer equal to the task of maintaining the dam by itself.) There is, however, little evidence that commerce was a major concern of state policy. Events to the north and east were, in fact, reducing the importance of South Arabia in international trade.

In 330 the Emperor Constantine removed the capital of the

Mediterranean world from an insecure Rome to the Golden Horn. His successor, Theodosius, divided the beleaguered empire between his sons in 395. Constantinople replaced Antioch and Alexandria as the metropole of the eastern Mediterranean, concentrating its wealth and organizing its trade. With the rise of the Sassanids, Persia became a key factor in the Eastern trade. Most of the raw silk, textiles, jewels, spices, and perfumes required at Byzantium were now transshipped from Chinese or Indian to Persian caravans for overland carriage to the Eastern Roman Empire, or from Chinese junks to Persian vessels for shipment up the Persian Gulf and the Euphrates. Cargoes available for Egyptian mariners on the Red Sea and for Arab camel-drivers north through Hijaz were gradually reduced to local products, notably South Arabian incense and myrrh, which remained in demand. The shift in trade channels was bitterly resented by the Egyptians and Syrians, and intensified their sectarian quarrels with the Byzantine patriarchs. Chronically at war with Persia, Byzantium explored the possibility of reviving the former communication patterns, but without substantial result. South Arabia's prosperity declined, and with it the ability to mobilize resources in pursuit of political goals. The preoccupation of both rulers and people meanwhile shifted from worldly concerns to the issue of how the deity, acknowledged ever more generally as one and supreme, ought to be worshiped.

Extinction of the Sabean State

The last of the Judaizing kings of Saba, Yūsuf Ash'ar Dhū Nuwās, was a passionate defender and propagator of the state religion. He persecuted various Christian congregations in South Arabia, but is chiefly notorious for his campaign against the community at Nejran. Appearing before the town with a strong army, he demanded that the Christians choose between apostasy and death. Most remained steadfast in their faith, were cast into trenches in which great fires had been kindled, and thus perished. Memory of the incident is preserved in the Koran (Sura 85), as well as in contemporary Christian hagiographic writings.[16] Survivors spread news of the atrocity as far as Byzantium, which countenanced massacres of Christians only by other Christians of the established sect, and was horrified. The emperor urged the king of Aksum to intervene against Dhū Nuwās. In two successive attacks the Ethiopians completed the reoccupation of Yemen in 525. Dhū Nuwās was killed, apparently by his own subjects.

The history of Saba's last decades is obscured by a dense layer of hearsay and legend written down well after the rise of Islam. Modern study of the few surviving inscriptions[17] tends to credit the account of the Byzantine historian Procopius, according to which the Ethiopians, after defeating Dhū Nuwās, left garrisons in Saba to protect the Christian communities, and set up as puppet king a local notable, Sumyafa' Ashwa'. The Sabeans revolted under the leadership of Abraha, who took the throne in 535, acknowledging nominal Ethiopian suzerainty but repulsing successive expeditions mounted to restore direct Ethiopian rule.

A militant Christian, Abraha is known to Arab tradition as leader of an expedition, including an unlikely troop of elephants, aimed at destroying the pagan shrines at Mecca, a goal which was frustrated by divine intervention. Documentary evidence records a more successful enterprise of Saba and the prestige the state enjoyed even in its decline. A famous description commemorates the repair of the Mārib Dam; an international celebration in 543 marked the completion of the work, and was attended by the envoys of the Negus of Abyssinia, the emperor of Byzantium, the king of Persia, and the kings of Ghassān and Ḥīra. The great barrage had suffered a succession of breaches over a period of three centuries. Early in the third century the structure had been damaged so severely, perhaps by an earthquake or volcanic activity, that there was a large scale, permanent migration of the people whose lands were destroyed. Among these were the ancestors of the Ghassānids in Syria, the Lakhmids of Ḥīra, and the Aws and Khazraj tribes of Yathrib. In 449, as previously noted, a further major breach had been repaired. Symptomatic of the waning of Saba's power and influence is the fact that the damages repaired under Abraha's auspices were, at least in part, caused by sabotage perpetrated by tribes in rebellion against his rule. This was the last effort Saba could put forth to keep the great structure in serviceable condition. When next it was damaged, no effort at restoration was made; the people whose livelihood had depended upon it simply fled leaving their lands open to encroachment by the desert.

Arab tradition includes the final disaster at Mārib among three fateful events of the year 570, popularly named the "Year of the Elephant," after Abraha's campaign into Hijaz, supposed to have taken place that year. While the king was thus preoccupied, pagan notables of Ḥimyar appealed to the king of Persia to assist them in destroying Abraha's Christian regime and the influence of his Ethiopian suzerains. In 575 Chosroes I sent a force of malefactors released ad hoc from his prisons, under the command of Wahriz. They dealt the death blow to the Sabean state and made of South Arabia a province of the Sassanian Empire.

The third event of the Year of the Elephant is said to be the birth at Mecca of the Prophet Muḥammad, who in the following century was to give the world a new universal religion and to lay the foundations of one of the great empires of human history. Yemen and the rest of the Arab South were to pass directly from rule by a Persian governor to control from the Islamic capital at Medina.

Early Islam disparaged the preceding age as unenlightened and idolatrous, and discouraged attention to its history and culture except to enhance understanding of the Koran. Memory of the ancient South Arabian states nonetheless survived in oral tradition, with inevitable selectivity and embellishment. Recollection of Maʿīn and Saba virtually disappeared, and the age of ignorance in South Arabia was remembered simply as the time of the Ḥimyarites. The language of the Koran displaced the South Arabic of the inscriptions for all literary purposes. Knowledge of the ancient script, the *musnad*, did not die out entirely; Yemeni scribes faithfully recorded in their Arabic manuscripts its phonetic values. But the meaning of the carved texts became less and less clear. By the tenth century A.D., the time of the great Yemeni historian Ḥasan bin Aḥmad al-Hamdānī, the tribal names on the old monuments were taken to refer to individuals instead of peoples.[18] The creative art of genealogy made of Saba a grandson of Qaḥṭān and the ancestor not only of the extensive Hamdān, Azd, and 'Arīb groups of tribes but of all the Ḥimyarites as well. Two hundred years later, Nashwān bin Sa'īd al-Ḥimyarī crystallized the then surviving lore regarding the ancient kings and their exploits in his well-known epic.[19] Modern archaeology, drawing upon the literature of classical Greece and Rome as well as the South Arabian inscriptions and artifacts, has only begun to piece together a coherent account of ancient Yemeni civilization and its correlation with the traditions recorded in the Islamic era; it amply confirms, however, the accomplishments of the South Arabians and their prestige in the ancient world.

This heritage, whether based in tradition or in confirmable fact, is raw material for national myth and symbol, and could promote among modern Yemenis the same sense of national identity and pride as comparable legacies have fostered in Egypt, Iraq, and Syria. Leaders of the Yemen Arab Republic are aware of their country's distant past, and have taken pains to protect its archaeological remains. An able and learned director of antiquities (Qāḍī Ismā'īl bin 'Alī al-Akwa') working from the office of the president, is encouraging public awareness of the importance of ancient artifacts and their preservation. Detailed knowledge of the pre-Islamic era is as yet the property of a few scholars familiar with the *musnad* script, with the pertinent Greco-Roman writings, and with some work of contemporary Western archaeologists and historians. Their books are gradually disseminating knowledge of the distant past among the Yemeni public; and if the claims made for the achievements of their remote ancestors sometimes exceed what rigorous construction of the evidence might justify,[20] there is no lack of precedent.

2
The Islamic Background

Early Islam

As South Arabia's political capabilities declined, its role in such international commerce as persisted over the caravan routes along the Sarāt diminished. Way-stations and garrisons manned by Yemenis in Hijaz disappeared, and Hijazis themselves assumed a new role as middlemen between the southern entrepôts and the markets to the north. The people of this region consisted mainly of two groups: Arab tribes, mostly nomadic, chronically at war one with another; and settled artisans, cultivators, and traders subject to, but protected by, the tribes. Intertribal anarchy was mitigated to some degree by a general veneration for certain holy enclaves, often containing a stone or other natural object assumed to possess supernatural properties. On such neutral ground, and notably during the annual season designated by some cults for pilgrimage, mutually hostile Arabs could meet, perform religious rites, conduct commercial exchanges, and settle outstanding disputes. Temporal and spiritual authority within such precincts became hereditary in specific families which, over time, assumed the status of a priestly aristocracy with considerable moral influence over the turbulent tribes. Prominent among these sacred localities was the town of Mecca, the site of a cubical structure, the Ka'ba, containing a black stone around which centered a cult featuring the worship of a number of gods. Responsible for the conduct of religious ceremonies, the accommodation of pilgrims, and mediation among the tribes, was the clan of Quraysh, whose members were at the same time leading merchants. The measure of their influence is that caravans traveling between Mecca and Yemen or Palestine, provided with safe-conduct by Quraysh, passed unhindered through the territory of otherwise lawless and predatory Arab tribes.

The Prophet Muḥammad was born into Quraysh about 570. An orphan, his family ensured his livelihood by first arranging his employment by a rich widow and merchant, Khadīja, and later his marriage to her. He engaged in commerce until, at about the age of forty, he became convinced that God had chosen him as the final messenger in the long succession of those He had sent to warn men of the consequences of their evil conduct, and to exhort them to submit to His will.

Central to the revelation Muḥammad received piecemeal over two decades was the absolute one-ness of God and the sinfulness of attributing divine qualities to any except Him. His preaching purported to summon the Arabs not to a new religion but to the pristine faith of the Patriarch Abraham, from whom the pagan Arabs as well as their neighbors, the Jewish communities in the Peninsula, claimed descent. The Prophet's uncompromising monotheism nevertheless threatened to discredit and destroy the Mecca pantheon, and with it the political and economic power of its custodians. His message was therefore opposed by most chiefs of Quraysh. As the community of Muslims grew, recruited mainly from the disadvantaged classes and Muḥammad's immediate family, it came under increasing social pressure and ultimately the threat of physical danger. Muḥammad sought a more congenial field for the propagation of the faith, and found it in the town of Yathrib, where the leading tribes, Aws and Khazraj, were at swords' points and in need of an impartial mediator of high moral authority to keep peace between them. Their chiefs agreed to associate no other gods with Allah, and extended their protection to Muḥammad's band of believers, who migrated gradually from Mecca to Yathrib, where the Prophet himself moved in 622.

The Islamic era is dated from this event, which marked the beginning of the evolution of the new faith from simply a religious cult toward a system of community life embracing many aspects of social custom, government, civil status, commerce, and morals. Building upon the existing norms of ordering relations among the Arab tribes, supplemented by his continuing divine revelation, Muḥammad worked with great political skill to consolidate his authority within Yathrib or al-Medina, the City of the Prophet, as it came to be known. He attempted to supplant the influence of Quraysh, to gain control of Mecca's sacred enclave, and to incorporate all the Arabs of the peninsula in a single community whose affairs would be arranged in accord with the revealed word of God. The strength of the Muslim community grew steadily through its varied and judicious activities. Proselytizing for Islam went forward, enhanced by some adaptations from the pagan cults, such as belief in, and pilgrimages to, the Kaʻba. The unstable loyalties of the tribes were wooed by clever diplomacy. Lucrative raids were undertaken against Quraysh caravans and against Jewish communities which derided the new religion. Within eight years the Muslims were in secure possession of Hijaz, had gained adherents in most areas of the Peninsula, and were skirmishing with Byzantine border forces to the north. Yemen, the most populous region of Arabia and a key factor in its commerce, inevitably figured prominently among the Prophet's preoccupations, and its accession to Islam was facilitated by the decline of the Sassanian Empire, to which it was subject.

Under Chosroes II, Sassanid Persia, in a final burst of imperial vigor, moved against Byzantium, and in campaigns during the period 612-618 seized all Syria and Palestine, Egypt, and much of Anatolia. The Roman emperor Heraclius began the reconquest in 622, the year of Muḥammad's move to Medina, and by 628 Byzantine troops were invading Persia itself. The long struggle exhausted both empires, and their oppressive rule alienated large segments of their respective populations, thus easing the way for the Arab conquests soon to begin. The tyrannical Chosroes succumbed to a conspiracy led by his own son, and Persia lapsed into an anarchy in which a dozen pretenders, both male and female, grasped and lost the throne during the next fourteen years. Control over the governors of remote provinces such as Yemen became exceedingly tenuous.

Arab tradition, which perhaps owes something to imagination, relates that Muḥammad wrote to Chosroes in 628 enjoining him to embrace Islam. The king angrily tore the Prophet's message to bits and ordered Bādhān, his governor in Yemen, to send him the head of "that man in Hijaz." Bādhān sent two messengers to invite Muhammad to accompany them to Sanaa. The Prophet meanwhile received word from heaven that the king had been murdered by his son Shirawayh. The messengers told Muḥammad that they would inform Bādhān of this astonishing allegation; the Prophet concurred and added, "Tell him that my faith and my dominion will equal the possessions of Chosroes. Tell him furthermore that if he becomes a Muslim, I shall confirm him in his possessions and give him rule over his people, the Sons." The Sons (*Abnā'*) were descendants of the eight hundred Persian convicts who were sent, some seventy years before, to assist the Ḥimyarites against the Ethiopian occupation, and who annexed Yemen to the Sassanid empire. Upon receiving the Prophet's message, Bādhān said, "These are indeed the words of a king, and I believe he is a prophet. Let us see whether what he says is true. If so, he is a heaven-sent prophet; if not, we shall consider what to do about him." Shortly a letter arrived from Shirawayh stating that he had killed the king in order to spare the Persian aristocracy from further massacre at his hands. Convinced by this confirmation of Muḥammad's revelation, Bādhān at once became a Muslim, and placed Yemen at Muḥammad's disposition. Bādhān's act gave official sanction to propaganda for Islam which had already been conducted successfully for a number of years among Yemenis on their home ground, and among Yemeni residents of Hijaz, some of whom are reported to have embraced the new faith even before the Hegira. Fulfilling his promise, Muḥammad confirmed Bādhān in his governorship of Yemen.

The conversion of entire tribes recorded by the traditionists may be viewed by skeptics as reflecting somewhat shallow conviction. At the same time, there is no doubt that Muḥammad's appeal reached effectively into all corners of the Arabian Peninsula. Representatives of Yemeni tribes were conspicuous among the Arab delegations which traveled to Medina during the Prophet's last years (629-632) to make formal submission. Muḥammad was particularly solicitous of these recruits, and frequently praised the Yemenis. He told his entourage, "People have come to you from Yemen. They are the most amiable and gentlehearted of men. Faith is of Yemen, and wisdom is Yemeni."

The first mass conversion of an important Yemeni tribe was that of the Ashā'ira, in the Tihama. A large party, headed by their shaikh Abū Mūsā al-Ash'arī, traveled north by sea, arriving at Medina in 628, just as Muḥammad returned from plundering the wealthy Jewish community at Khaibar. The Prophet broke Arab precedent, and aroused his helpers' resentment, by including these Yemeni converts, who had not participated in the battle, in the division of the booty. He furthermore appointed Abū Mūsā governor on his behalf over the Tihama. The following year the crucial Hamdān group of tribes reportedly submitted in its entirety, under the personal influence of Muḥammad's cousin, 'Alī bin Abī Ṭālib, then on a mission to Yemen. Thenceforth tribal conversions proliferated, and delegations appeared in Medina from Aden, Hadramaut, Mahra, and the entire south. The Prophet took the occasion of these visits to establish the rudiments of an administrative structure. Bādhān having died, his son Shahr was named governor of the district of Sanaa. By the time of Muḥammad's demise in 632, South Arabia was apportioned among ten governors, the majority chosen from among the most trusted members of his entourage and the best versed in the tenets of the faith. Where a native notable was appointed, a missionary was usually provided to assist him in educating the people in their obligations as Muslims, including their function as taxpayers. In a further effort to ensure that Islamic injunctions were scrupulously applied by those in power and observed by the citizenry, he sent trustworthy individuals, well versed in the faith, on tours of Yemen as teachers, judges, or inspectors.

Idealized by later generations as the perfect society, governed in strict accord with divine precept, primitive Islam was in actuality a simple and fragile structure. The fundamentals of the faith, few in number and firmly rooted in already-current beliefs, attained a certain universality in Arabia. The totality of Muḥammad's revelation, on the other hand, could have been known to only a few close associates. The comprehensive systematizing of law, theology, and codes of conduct was the work of succeeding centuries.

In its political aspects the early Muslim community was the Prophet's personal handiwork, and peculiarly dependent upon his charisma. He emphasized to his converts that they were submitting to the will of God, not to his own will as a man. Instructed by his revelation, he sought the advice of the Muslims, and respected it in arriving at a number of significant decisions. Thus it was not a total theocracy. The fact that Muḥammad made no claims to infallibility apart from the content of his revelation lent some credibility to the rivals who asserted their prophethood and produced fissures within the Arabian polity during Muḥammad's lifetime.

These divisions were not reversions to idolatry and polytheism, but rather rejections of Medina's secular authority. Muḥammad's contemporary Musailima bin Ḥabīb, in Yamāma, also claimed to be a recipient of divine revelation; he gained an important popular following as spokesman for al-Raḥmān,[1] and proposed to Muḥammad that they divide the world between them. Comparable movements sprang up in other regions of the peninsula, including Yemen. The concept of Islam as a central authority sanctioned by God, ordering the temporal affairs of all believers, took root only slowly. The allegiance accorded to Muḥammad by the tribes was not, by Arab custom, final and irrevocable, nor did it pass without question to another. The assertion by force of arms of the spiritual and temporal unity of Arabia was the major preoccupation of the Caliph Abū Bakr, who fell heir to the Islamic leadership upon the Prophet's death.

The Yemeni Apostasy

The career of the false prophet al-Aswad Abhala bin Ka'b, of the ‘Ans section of the Madhḥij tribe, and the independence movement which survived him, are marked by a number of the abrupt shifts of loyalty which are a feature of all periods of Yemeni history. Al-Aswad attracted a certain following as a worker of marvels, and led credulous Yemenis to believe that a familiar spirit informed him of his enemies' plans and of the secret thoughts of men. He challenged Islam in the name of a deity peculiar to Yemen: Raḥmān al-Yaman. In Muḥammad's last year he recruited a military force sufficient to seize Nejran from Muḥammad's governor, Khālid bin Sa‘īd. This feat attracted additional recruits, and he turned south at the head of seven hundred mounted men. He stormed and took Sanaa, executed its governor, Shahr, dispersed the Persian troops, and forced Muḥammad's personal agent, Mu‘ādh bin Jabal, to flee to Medina. Tribal defections soon obliged Muḥammad's other governors in Yemen to retire to Hijaz, leaving al-Aswad in precarious control of much of Yemen. (The Hamdān tribes, however, preserved their loyalty to Islam.)

The chroniclers, all hostile to al-Aswad, give us little insight into his motivations. Presumably, he sought the personal gratifications of power, and also tried to rid Yemen of outside control. Of modest origins, he had no firm power base and was obliged to rely, during his fleeting rule in Sanaa, upon precisely those elements best able to challenge his authority: the native aristocracy, and the Persians whose rule in Yemen had been confirmed by the Prophet Muḥammad. He appointed a Ḥimyarite prince, Qays bin ‘Abd Yaghūth, to command his armed forces, and two Persians, Fīrūz al-Daylamī and Dādhawayh, to be ministers. He furthermore took the risky step of making Āzār, widow of the murdered Shahr, his wife. Soon al-Aswad confronted his three advisors with accusations of disloyalty, citing the authority of his familiar spirit. Feeling their lives endangered, the three conspired with Āzār to break into his palace in Sanaa, kill him, and reaffirm Yemen's submission to Medina's authority. Al-Aswad had held Sanaa a mere three months.

Whether al-Aswad died before or after the Prophet is a point on which traditions differ. According to one account, Muḥammad was informed from heaven that the false prophet had been killed, and when asked the identity of the slayer by his entourage named the "blessed scion of a blessed house," Fīrūz al-Daylamī. In any event Abū Bakr, who endeavored to model his conduct exactly after Muḥammad's precedents, confirmed the "Sons" in the rule of Yemen, naming Fīrūz governor, with Dādhawayh and Khishnās as assistants.

Yemeni restiveness at outside control did not disappear with al-Aswad. The Ḥimyarite Qays bin 'Abd Yaghūth was encouraged by Muḥammad's death to try to free the country of Persian and Hijazi rule. The local magnates, considering him compromised by his recent collaboration with the "Sons," rejected his appeal, save for the Zubaid chief and future commander of Muslim armies, 'Amrū bin Ma'dī Karib. Numbers of rank-and-file tribesmen, however, rallied to Qays, as did the late al-Aswad's army, who had turned highwaymen and were committing depredations along the caravan trails as far north as Taif, just south of Mecca. With these heterogeneous forces Qays and 'Amrū took Sanaa, forcing Fīrūz to flee to Khawlān, where he had a tribal alliance by marriage. The two leaders began rounding up the "Sons" and their families in preparation for deporting them to Persia. Meanwhile two Muslim armies were converging on Yemen: one freshly returned from the successful foray against Byzantine Palestine which the Prophet was planning when death overtook him; and one which had crushed a rebellion in Hadramaut. Few Yemenis had the stomach to resist the advancing forces, and the independence movement disintegrated. As their cause grew desperate, each of the two leaders sought to save his own skin by betraying the other. 'Amrū succeeded by strategem in taking Qays prisoner, and delivered him to Muhājir, commander of the army approaching from Hijaz. Muhājir arrested both and sent them to Abū Bakr for judgment.

No further obstacle of consequence blocked the incorporation of Yemen in the nascent Arab Empire. The most populous region of the peninsula, it furnished a large proportion of the manpower, and some of the distinguished commanders, of the armies which carried the Muslim conquests westward to Spain and eastward to China; it also supplied many of the colonists who settled in their wake. The Arab political center had migrated northward to Medina; fundamental decisions were now made by Hijazi, not Yemeni, Arabs, and issues were fought out in other terms than specific Yemeni interests. Over the next two centuries, as the orthodox caliphs were succeeded by the Umayyads and then the Abbasids, the imperial metropole receded progressively further, and Yemen became a backwater, governed, then misgoverned, and at length left virtually ungoverned, by the central authority of Islam.

Islam as a Political System

Firmly entrenched by the middle of the seventh century, the Islamic faith remains a major force in Yemeni society. The 1971 Constitution of the Yemen Arab Republic begins with an extended Koranic invocation, and its preamble asserts that "we Yemenis are an Arab and Muslim people."[2] As Islam makes no theoretical separation between piety and good citizenship, it is appropriate to examine its basic principles as they relate to politics.

Above all, Islam offers its followers the means of escaping damnation and the fires of hell by submitting to the will of God and by ordering their earthly life according to God's precepts. These were revealed to the Prophet and collected as the Koran, supplemented by Muḥammad's spoken interpretations, and further clarified by his practice as leader of the early Islamic community. Together, these elements provide the basis of the *sharī'a*, the Islamic law, elaborated over a period of three centuries by jurists and theologians, and assuming definitive form in the tenth century. Its rules embrace a wide range of human behavior: strictly ritual activities such as prayer, pilgrimage, and fasting; matters of family status such as marriage, divorce, and inheritance; and the Muslim's conduct as a member of the broader society. Of primary political interest is the principle that the community of Muslims constitutes an *umma*—a nation—with the individual's place in it derived from the pattern of intra- and inter-tribal relations in seventh-century Arabia.

This general view sets the community of Muslims in opposition to people of other religions, and establishes as a universal value the conversion of non-Muslims, or their subjection to the

Islamic state. In practice, communal solidarity proved to be beyond the capability of the Muslims to achieve. Islamic factions, sects, and peoples came to wage war on each other not only in the name of the true faith, but also for strictly secular objectives.

The tribal outlook of early Islam is reflected in its conception of the status of the individual. The basic demand of the citizens on their ruler was that he should provide secure conditions, permitting each to gain a livelihood for himself and his dependents, and carry out his religious duties, especially that of worship.[3] This right followed from membership in the community, not simply from the fact that he was a man. In many particulars, the duties, privileges, and identity of a Ḥāshid tribesman, say, who became a Muslim were analogous to those which defined him as a member of Ḥāshid. Islam brought him no bill of rights and guaranteed him no individual freedoms. It entitled him, however, to expect certain patterns of action by other Muslims toward him, not because this was his right as an individual, but because "God has commanded the others to act, or refrain from acting, in these ways."[4] Koranic insistence upon the brotherhood of all Muslims added religious sanction to the principle of communal solidarity. This had corollaries at the personal and at the social levels.

> In many cases this seems to have made a man *want* to be the same as his fellows and to feel that there was something wrong with him if he behaved or thought differently. To belong to the community meant so much to him—life apart from the community was unthinkable—that everything which separated him from his fellows was to be avoided.[5]

This implied the acceptance of social pressure, including official coercion, to enforce conformity. On the theoretical level, Muslim jurists accepted the notion of consensus—*ijmāʿ*—as a source of law; authority was contained in Koranic injunctions to Muḥammad to consult with the faithful in their affairs, and in his own assertion that the Muslim community would never agree upon an error.

> The "consensus" was variously interpreted, and might at one extreme be the agreement of a small body of jurists and at the other that of the whole community of Muslims. . . . In actuality, however, consensus meant the acceptance in theory of what most of the community had accepted in practice.[6]

As the perfect and final revelation of God's will regarding how men should live and order their communal affairs, the *sharī'a* is assumed to be complete and immutable. Laws are not made to suit new or special circumstances, but rather found, by diligent search in scripture and the prophetic traditons: by *ijtihād*. As truth is moreover indivisible, the welfare and salvation of the Islamic community is peculiarly dependent upon reliable knowledge of the *sharī'a* and its uniform application.

Islam thus established the norm of a single polity in which all men were equally servants of God and anxious to achieve the goal of salvation. The community agreed unanimously that God had revealed how this was to be accomplished by ordering their conduct according to detailed rules, and recognized the proper role of coercion in securing observance of these rules. In addition to its consummate concern for the spiritual well-being of members of the community, the revelation bore upon many details of the Muslims' temporal welfare and the manner in which their day-to-day social and economic relationships were to be conducted. The full content of the divine message fell within the Prophet's administrative purview as leader of the Islamic society. There was no legitimate authority save that exercised in his name and according to his wisdom as the sole recipient and authentic interpreter of God's will. In theory, thus, a polity existed with complete coincidence of values between ruler and ruled, and with a perfectly hierarchical pattern of authority. The moral worth and legitimacy of Moḥammad's successors was a function of their faithfulness to his precept and precedent.

Islam did not, in the event, fully displace the existing social and political structures and values. After considerable effort, it stamped out worship of tribal dieties, without eliminating certain customs and superstitions originally related to them; some of these persisted in Yemen well into the twentieth century. It failed to submerge tribal structures and loyalties in an all-embracing nation of Islam. In Yemen, tribal and inter-tribal law and custom remained intact in competition with the *sharīʿa*, with which they conflict on many points.[7]

The first two caliphs strove vigorously, but with only partial and temporary success, to make the ideal polity a reality. Expansion of Islam beyond the Arabian Peninsula had as yet barely begun under Abū Bakr, who was able to maintain close supervision of his commanders and officials, and to reserve to himself unquestioned authority to decide issues of particular moment or not covered by clear rules. Under ʿUmar, the task was more difficult. Vastly more complex problems resulted from the conquest of many non-Arab peoples, some with far more sophisticated cultures than that of the conquerors. The iron determination and acknowledged rectitude of the caliph enabled him to control his generals and governors, or to dismiss the recalcitrants. ʿUmar died of the effort, at the hand of an assassin. According to tradition, he was stabbed by a slave of the deposed governor of Basra, al-Mughīra bin Shuʿba, in protest against an onerous tax which the caliph refused to annul.[8] The effort of his weaker-willed successor, ʿUthmān, to maintain centralized power culminated in another assassination, schism, and civil war within the Islamic community.

While many sources of disunity were present, the focus was on the question of succession to the Prophet's temporal power. Revelation provided a clear idea of the form legitimate authority should take, but no unambiguous clue to identifying the individual who should head the hierarchy. The struggle placed in question the legitimacy of authority throughout the empire. The schism and sectarianism which ensued have never been resolved in Islam, and the consequences for the politics of Yemen are sufficiently far-reaching to require a brief statement of the political factors in the ancient dispute.

Shī'ism and Yemen

The first two caliphs had been selected, in the absence of a divinely-prescribed procedure, by consensus among a handful of the late Prophet's associates, in harmony with Arab tribal custom in selecting a chief. On his death-bed 'Umar, in an effort to provide for an orderly succession, is said to have nominated a six-man council to make the decision. Factions and candidates were numerous, and 'Uthmān was in some respects a compromise, his undistinguished personality balanced by his membership in the powerful Umayyad clan of Quraysh. He acceded at a delicate juncture. The empire's expansion was decelerating. The enormous booty from the early conquests had permitted 'Umar to institute a civil list according to which militant Arabs had claims on the state treasury. Revenues now depended mainly on the tribute from Christians and Jews, and taxes on productive lands seized; these were inadequate to pay the soldiery, meet the institutionalized demands, and cover the privileges 'Uthmān was too weak to withhold from his Umayyad relatives. By the tenth year of his rule the empire was in economic crisis and the provinces of Iraq and Egypt were in virtual revolt.

The question of the locus of leadership in Islam had meanwhile come to engage popular conscience as well as the theoreticians. On the one hand, many saw the caliph as a mere temporal leader, without authority in the matter of dogma, whose function was simply to administer the *sharī'a* and provide for civil defense. This attitude became the cornerstone of Sunnī Islam. On the other hand, many Muslims yearned for a continuation of divinely-guided leadership.[9] In statements attributed to the Prophet, they found grounds for assurance that personal impeccability and theological infallibility would in fact be preserved in his descendants; this group held the conviction that Muḥammad had actually designated 'Alī bin Abī Ṭālib as his successor. 'Alī was the son of Muḥammad's childhood guardian, Muḥammad's cousin, the husband of his daughter Fāṭima, and the first convert to Islam after Khadīja. He became the center of a faction—*shī'a*—which grew in size

and enthusiasm as dissatisfaction with the policies of ‘Umar and ‘Uthmān spread.

In 655 an armed force from Egypt marched to Medina to settle accounts with ‘Uthmān. After inconclusive negotiations, in which ‘Alī’s role was somewhat ambiguous, the caliph was besieged in his house and then murdered. ‘Alī was acclaimed caliph by one faction. He lacked the political acumen to thread his way through a complicated situation. The Umayyads, led by Mu‘āwiya, the able governor of Syria, demanded satisfaction against the late caliph’s murders, whose support ‘Alī needed. When civil war erupted, mainly in Iraq, ‘Alī’s vacillating policies produced dissension within his own camp. The defectors—Khārijites—took up arms against him. Many details of the struggle are in dispute.[10] It will suffice here to recall that ‘Alī was assassinated by a Khārijite in 661. Mu‘awiya founded the Umayyad dynasty which ruled the Arab Empire from Damascus until 749. The Abbasids, finally, assumed power in 749, again to the exclusion of the Prophet’s direct descendants.

The Shī‘a meanwhile continued to flourish underground, as separate sects formed in the entourage of one or another of ‘Alī’s descendants. He had fathered at least seventeen daughters, and fourteen sons of whom five had children who survived. The clan proliferated in the face of persecution by the imperial authorities, and dispersed to the most distant provinces of the empire, founding an aristocracy still revered in Muslim lands. Schisms arose within the Shī‘a over the true succession to the imamate, i.e., the combined spiritual and temporal leadership attributed to ‘Alī. Orthodox Shī‘ism, which ultimately prevailed in Iran, admits of twelve imams, after whom the succession is believed to have been permanently interrupted: ‘Alī himself, his sons Ḥasan and Ḥusain, then Ḥusain’s descendants in the direct male line. This main Shī‘a branch did not take permanent hold in Yemen. Two off-shoots are pertinent to our concern with Yemen. The first, the Zaidis, we shall discuss in some detail later. The second arose from disagreement as to the identity of the successor to the seventh imam, Ismā‘īl, the schismatics choosing the latter’s son Muḥammad rather than his brother, Mūsā al-Kāẓim. This “sevener” branch then ramified lux-

uriantly. Some considered Muḥammad the last imam. Those with whom we are concerned maintained that the line continued, conducted clandestine operations against the earlier Abbasid caliphs, founded the Fatimid state in North Africa, and succumbed to Saladin in the time of the Crusades.

The civil war involved the passions and interests of the entire Islamic community, and Yemenis were participants on both sides. ʻAlī, as we have seen, served as judge in Yemen on behalf of the Prophet, and again visited the area in the reign of Abū Bakr; as a result of these personal contacts, his party there became firmly established. Yemenis composed the bulk of the army of ʻAmr ibn al-ʻĀs, which conquered Egypt in 640; numbers settled there, and by Muʻāwiya's time they are said to have numbered 27,000 in Alexandria alone. A particularly zealous propagandist against the Caliph ʻUthmān was a native of Sanaa, ʻAbdullah bin Saba, a late convert from Judaism, who traveled to Iraq, Syria, and finally to Egypt in ʻAlī's cause. Some accounts credit Yemenis with instigating the Egyptian attack against ʻUthmān.

During the Muʻāwiya-ʻAlī confrontation, both appointed governors to Yemen, and sent armies to back them up. Myʻāwiya's appointee acted with such harsh cruelty that he can have won few hearts. He provided the Shīʻa with martyrs, the two small sons of ʻAlī's governor, who had fled. Their memory is still preserved in the name of a Sanaa mosque. With ʻAli's death, overt resistance came to an end and Shīʻa sentiment was forced underground. Its intensity increased after the martyrdom of ʻAlī's son Ḥusain at Kerbala in 680, during the reign of the second Umayyad caliph, Yazīd. The sectarian passion aroused by the schism is suggested by an incident in the reign of the Caliph ʻUmar bin ʻAbd al-ʻAzīz (715-717). A liberal and pious monarch, he ordered the suspension of the curse upon ʻAlī and his family which had been an officially required feature of Friday sermons throughout the empire from the accession of Muʻāwiya. When the preacher of the Sanaa mosque replaced the customary curse of ʻAlī with a Koranic quotation that "God has ordained justice and prudence," the Yemeni notable Ibn Maḥfūẓ exploded with rage, accusing the orator of abrogating the Sunna, and set off on his mule for

Syria, announcing his intention to rouse its people against such an infidel caliph. A posse of Sanaa citizens pursued him to the village of al-Manjal, west of Sanaa, where they stoned him to death, along with the mule. The spot became the scene of ritual lapidation, a custom which endured for centuries.

Yemen under the Umayyads and Early Abbasids

Mu'āwiya and his successors divided South Arabia into two provinces, with capitals at Sanaa and Janad, the latter's responsibility extending to Hadramaut. During much of the Umayyad century, rule of Yemen was entrusted to members of the al-Thaqafī clan, which produced a number of able servants of the dynasty. In addition to providing a measure of administrative continuity, this tended to spare Yemen the necessity of furnishing family fortunes to a rapid succession of favorites, or political creditors, of the imperial court, as became the custom under the Abbasids. Yemen was, however, expected to contribute to the central revenues at a rate which fluctuated with the policy of individual caliphs.

The Umayyads were condemned en bloc by their numerous enemies as secular usurpers; in practice they varied considerably in their reverence for Islamic precepts, notably in the matter of taxation. The second caliph, Yazīd (680-683), imposed upon Yemen a fixed annual contribution to the central treasury. He also authorized the imposition of a series of customs, tolls, and market dues without basis in the *sharī'a*, which gears taxes to actual production and accumulated wealth. Such fiscal exactions could obviously be oppressive in lean years.

Intermittently, the gathering of taxes was conducted with compassion and personal disinterest by the governors. It is related of 'Urwā bin Muḥammad al-Thaqafī, appointed by the caliph Sulaimān, that upon arriving in Yemen he addressed the people, pointing to the mount on which he had made the journey: "This is my riding camel; if I depart with anything more, I am a thief." It is said that he left Yemen in 721, after a tour of twenty years, carrying with him only his sword, his spear, and his Koran.[11] During his brief reign, the caliph 'Umar bin 'Abd al-'Azīz suspended the innovative and unorthodox exactions introduced by his predecessors, telling his governor,

"Rather than authorize such a practice I would prefer to see you bring me no more than a handful of millet from Yemen." His successor, however, reversed the decision and instructed his appointee to "take it from them even if they are at the end of their rope and on the point of death; pay no attention to people's condemnation, which will soon pass, and don't worry about sin."[12] The anecdote indicates the antiquity of a political issue which remains today on the Yemeni agenda, and continues to condition Yemeni attitudes toward the legitimate use of coercion.

The governor Muḥammad bin Yūsuf al-Thaqafī, appointed by 'Abd al-Malik bin Marwān, distinguished himself for his harsh and arbitrary rule. While the allegation may well be an invention of anti-Umayyad propaganda, he is said to have died just before carrying out a plan to incinerate the lepers of Sanaa, for which he had already gathered firewood.[13] This governor's oppression of the Sanaa citizens had been such that they proceeded each Monday and Friday night to cast dirt on his tomb, and the dirt is said to have burst miraculously into flame. The belief persists: a recent Yemeni historian claims to have seen the grave often aglow at midnight, from the minaret of the great mosque of Sanaa.[14]

The same governor reportedly ordered the graves of recently-deceased Ḥimyarites opened and the contents plundered, as the Ḥimyarites were accustomed to inter a man's wealth with his corpse. This information suggests not only the governor's avarice but also the persistence of pagan customs among the Ḥimyar tribe. Their chiefs remained an elite with aspirations to political power. The Umayyads made occasional efforts to appease them by appointing Ḥimyarite governors for brief periods. They revolted openly, however, during the governorship of Yūsuf bin 'Umar al-Thaqafī (725-738) under their prince 'Abbād al-Ru'ainī; the movement was harshly suppressed.[15]

Other challenges to Umayyad rule in Yemen were part of more general cleavages within Islam. Yemen gave its allegiance to the rival caliphate in Mecca of 'Abdullah bin Zubair, and received his governors over a period of a decade (ca. 683-693). The rapid succession of governors is attributable to the instability of 'Abdullah's regime, the need to accommodate a

large number of worthy but needy job-seekers, and the caliph's apprehension that a governor left too long in Yemen might set himself up as an independent monarch. Yemen was twice invaded by Khārijites: by the Ḥarūris in 690, and by the Ibāḍīs at the close of the Umayyad period. The Yemenis gave these movements little support, nor did they oppose them energetically in the Umayyad interest, or that of Zubair. Rather they permitted themselves simply to be ransomed where prudent, and waved the invaders on to their principal objective, the holy places in Hijaz. Khārijism left no lasting imprint on the quality of Islam in Yemen.

Umayyad suppression of the 'Alids' political aspirations forced them either into exile, into grudging truce with the regime, or into circumspect retirement, where the special spiritual virtues attributed to them among the people nevertheless kept their cause alive. A parallel underground movement, more secular in orientation, was conducted by a distant branch of the Prophet's clan, and maintained agents throughout the empire, including Yemen.[16] The principal Hashimite relationships may be simply diagrammed as shown in figure 2.

When the last scion of the declining Umayyad house was slain in 750 by Abū 'Abdullah al-Saffāḥ (the "Blood-Shedder"), it was popularly supposed that an 'Alid would at last succeed to the caliphate. Instead, al-Suffāḥ took the position for himself and his family, thus founding the Abbasid state, based upon Sunnī Islam and centered at Baghdad. The Shī'a regarded this as a betrayal and a new usurpation, and while the immediate threats to the new dynasty came from Khārijites and Qarmatians, 'Alī's partisans continued to build centers of political influence in various regions of the empire, and contributed to its eventual fragmentation.

No chronicle credits the Abbasids with concern for orderly, equitable government in Yemen. The province was too remote from the capital for close supervision, and the governors distinguished themselves by capricious, bigoted, and arbitrary rule and forceful suppression of movements toward local autonomy. Al-Saffāḥ named a governor for each of the five years of his rule. The three great Abbasid reigns (al-Manṣūr,

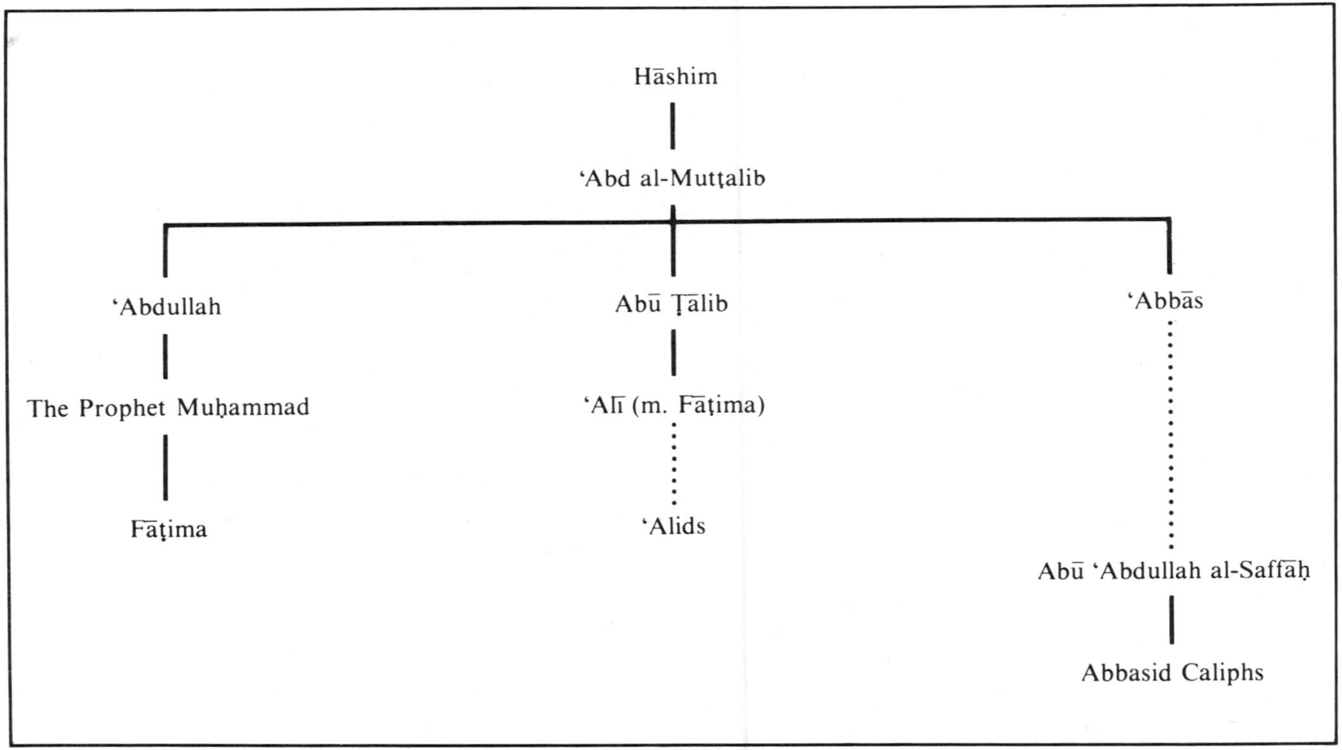
Hāshim
‘Abd al-Muttalib
‘Abdullah
Abū Ṭalib
‘Abbās
The Prophet Muḥammad
‘Alī (m. Fāṭima)
Fāṭima
‘Alids
Abū ‘Abdullah al-Saffāḥ
Abbasid Caliphs

Figure 2

754-775; al-Mahdī, 775-785; and Hārūn al-Rashīd, 786-809) saw the appointment of a total of six governors, which suggests a modicum of administrative competence and of political stability. It was, however, a period of declining loyalty to the principle of a single central authority in Islam, and of reassertion of independence by the disparate peoples of the empire. Al-Manṣūr's governor Ma'n bin Zā'ida al-Shaibānī, incongruously described by the historians as unusually generous, slaughtered two thousand people in putting down a revolt in the southern Yemeni district of Ma'āfir. From there he went to Hadramaut to crush a rebellion at the cost of fifteen thousand additional lives. (The surviving shaikh of the dissident tribe tracked Ma'n all the way to Seistan, where the governor had been transferred, and murdered him in revenge for his slain parents.) Ma'n is further credited with compelling the Yemenis to wear black, the Abbasids' symbolic color, which remains the usual color of the Yemeni peasantry.[17] The Tihama tribes rebelled in the year 800. Hārūn al-Rashīd recalled the governor, Muḥammad bin Barmak, and adjured his successor, Ḥamad al-Barbarī, to "listen for me to the voices of the Yemeni people."[18]

Governors proliferated under al-Ma'mūn, who sent at least thirteen to Yemen during his nineteen-year reign. Several were discharged when popular outcry against their tyranny was heard even in distant Baghdad; their successors were often obliged to conduct military operations against the discharged officials in order to assert their own authority. The governor Yazīd bin Jarīr waged a "racist" campaign against the Persian "Sons," who had not yet been absorbed into the population, torturing them to force them to divorce their Arab wives. A successor, Isḥāq bin al-'Abbās, strove to eradicate anything distinctively Ḥimyarite, going so far as to cut down all apricot trees of the variety then known as "Ḥimyarite." His excesses led the people of Sanaa to throw him out of the capital by force.[19]

Disorder and misrule were not, of course, peculiar to Yemen. The Abbasid state with all its far-flung and heterogeneous members was sinking into what a recent writer has aptly termed the era of the "war-lords":

> leaders who have such military force at their command that they are virtually independent. The Caliph is not strong enough to make them obey him. Some may have been provincial governors, others the leaders of a rising. . . . Though the caliph was powerless against them, they were content to be in theory his subordinates. Perhaps they felt that this strengthened them by giving their rule an appearance of legitimacy.[20]

Effective Abbasid rule in Yemen ended when Muḥammad bin ʻUbaidallah bin Ziyād, appointed in 822 by Ma'mūn to govern the Tihama, threw off all pretense of obedience to Baghdad beyond causing the Friday prayers to be said in the caliph's name, and founded the Banū Ziyād state, laying out and building the city of Zabīd as its capital. Ephemerally, the Banū Ziyād reunited nearly in its entirety the South Arabian state of the Ḥimyarites. They were unable to hold the hinterland, however, against the many separatist movements which arose. The Ḥimyarites asserted their autonomy in the central highlands, at times acknowledging a vague Ziyādī suzerainty, and invoking the Abbasid caliph in public prayers. The tribes in the north, between Nejran and Ṣaʻda, refused any outside control or interference in their mutual quarrels until they themselves called in the first Zaidi imam as umpire. In the southern and west-central mountains, the continuing development of Shīʻa sentiment provided opportunity for founding the first Fatimid regimes in Yemen. At the beginning of the tenth century, thus, Yemen was divided among four essentially independent entities.

The Islamic faith had introduced, on a quite abstract plane, the notion of the unity and brotherhood of all Muslims. The principle was soon vitiated by schisms among the Prophet's followers, and competing claims to universal leadership produced rival propaganda networks seeking, in Yemen as elsewhere, to win the loyalty of the people to one or another concept of the appropriate mode of accession to power. The idea of unity was nevertheless not devoid of meaning. The era of the "war-lords" endured for several centuries, at least until Rasūlid times. But the charismatic figures who formed virtually independent states claimed to rule in the name of one or another caliph symbolizing the unity of the faithful. The effectiveness of the claim was dependent not only upon the war-lord's military prowess and administrative skill but also upon the impact on the public of propaganda for the caliph whose name he invoked.

Nothing in Islam suggested to South Arabians that they constituted a distinct political entity within the larger Muslim community. Nevertheless, the political direction taken by Islam promoted intensification of divisions already existing, reinforcing parochial loyalties to the tribe. Astute leaders could exploit tribal consciousness and tribal rivalries for their own ends, and indeed they were obliged to do so. None succeeded for long in maintaining a stable balance among the tribes, or in fostering the sense of belonging to a distinctively Yemeni community taking precedence over kinship ties. The ancient activities which depended upon large-scale organization and common effort by large numbers of citizens had died out. Economic life had become largely local, recalling the similar deceleration of commercial exchanges in Europe of the early Middle Ages.

Legitimacy became a remarkably fragile and unstable proposition. The ruler could not assert beyond dispute his divine right to exercise power; competing doctrines were at hand to justify rival claimants. The individual citizen was not dependent upon the state for his identity, and the state did not facilitate his pursuit of a livelihood in any obvious way. Aspirants to power could, and did, win individual supporters by appealing to religious principles; such followers, when faith was inconsistent with tribal solidarity, made a risky choice. The ruler's authority inevitably impinged upon the freedom of action of the tribal chiefs, whose loyalty was intermittent and often a matter of expediency. Under determined and assertive leadership, a large cohesive tribe could, and frequently did, avoid external coercion.

Islamic ideals of universal unity did not supplant, but were simply added to, the particularistic values of the tribesmen and their shaikhs. The two sets of values remained in lasting tension. The synthesis of the consummatory and instrumental values by which the Ṣulayḥid rulers sought to satisfy their subjects' aspirations and their own has a quality which appeals to us across the intervening centuries; their eventual failure to create a viable, enduring state emphasizes the dimensions of the task they undertook.

3
The Fatimid States in Yemen

The decline of Abbasid authority in Yemen was one indication that the Islamic revolution had been at best only partial. Secular political concerns competed with those of the faith, and the conflict encouraged political fragmentation and instability.

Insofar as political values were a function of religious belief, the situation was a perplexing one for the Yemeni conscience. Moral uncertainty is suggested by the frequent defections and conversions from sect to sect which are characteristic of the era. It would be wrong to suppose that these abrupt shifts of loyalty by individuals, clans, and even entire tribes were purely a matter of expediency and opportunism. People responded readily to a persuasive proselytizer, by paying him their tithes and by joining military adventures in a religious cause. They risked reprisal by such authorities as chanced to be constituted. Leadership able to remove doubt as to the doctrinally correct manner of performance of one's religious duties had great moral force. This force depended upon the leader's continued success, however, and could easily revert to incertitude if he suffered reverses. The demonstration of unusual piety, adherence to generally acknowledged injunctions of the faith, and a reputation for authoritative theological knowledge were bases from which temporal power could be attained.

A contrast is already perceptible at this historical period

between the respective social structure of the northern and the southern Yemen highlands. North from the vicinity of Yarīm, Yemeni territory is distributed in parcels with reasonably well recognized borders, among tribes whose genealogy is firmly fixed in tradition.[1] Place names are only occasionally identical with those of the peoples resident there.[2] Tribes, as such, figure prominently in the chronicles. They engage in the time-honored business of raiding each other according to accepted rules, and fight, individually or in shifting constellations, over rule of areas embracing many tribes. In the tenth century as in the twentieth, detailed knowledge of tribal interrelationships, and accommodation to their sensibilities, were necessary elements of effective government in northern Yemen.

Below the Sumāra Pass south of Yarīm we find no large tribes, and no system of traditional genealogy. Northerners are grouped into broad confederations—Ḥāshid, Bakīl, Madḥij, Ḥimyar, Quḍā‘a—all united ultimately by a remote common ancestor, Qaḥṭān. Among the people of the southern Yemen highlands, social solidarity beyond the extended family rests mainly on common residence in a town or village. In describing the population of the area, Yemeni writers list "tribes" by their geographical locations, but adduce no interrelationships among groups and propose no genealogy for them.[3] Hence, while local challenges to central authority occur, no firm social basis exists for the formation of powerful coalitions to challenge or sustain a ruler. Yemenis of this region have acquired a reputation for relative docility, as contrasted with the "warlike" northerners.[4] The conduct of government in the south has consistently presented fewer problems than in the north.

The moving forces in Yemeni society in the ninth century were thus diverse and not cohesive. In the economic circumstances of the time the livelihood of the people was not particularly dependent upon efficient, centralized government, and attachment was strong to small social units which central control was likely to threaten. The ideal of a unified society of all Muslims retained appeal; but not only did it impinge upon local material and moral interests, it was invoked by rival aspirants to central power, each urging upon the Yemeni his exclusive right to rule. In the absence of an effective consensus, central authority tended to be fragile and weak. The region was in fact fragmented into several petty states, each enfeebled by domestic disaffection and the hostility of its neighbors.

The Fatimid Movement

The situation in Yemen was well appreciated by one branch of the 'Alids which was preparing to assume power in part of the declining Abbasid empire. This group was informed of the weaknesses of the local power structure by an efficient intelligence service, and its clandestine missionaries judged the field fertile for promotion of its cause. Yemen was considered a likely venue for the inauguration of a Fatimid state.

The Fatimids always refused to discuss their family origins, whether through proud disdain for the idea that these could be questioned, or through fear of revealing a skeleton in their closet. To protect the secrecy of their activities, the early leaders assumed so many aliases as thoroughly to confuse their contemporaries and baffle scholars even to our own day. From a document in the Fatimid archives,[5], we learn that Ja'far al-Ṣādiq, the sixth imam in the "twelver" line, appointed as his spiritual successor not Ismā'īl, as commonly supposed, but another son, 'Abdullah, who used the aliases "Ismā'īl" and "Mubārak." The latter's son Muḥammad achieved such effective cover as "Maymūn the Oculist" that doubts were raised that he really was a member of the the family. "Maymūn's" son 'Abdullah was able to dispense with an alias. In the next generation, however, Aḥmad assumed the name "Muḥammad." In turn, he named as the next imam his son Muḥammad, publicly known as "Ḥusain." In charge of operations was another son whose real name was Ḥusain, and who conducted the propaganda in such a manner as to advance his own son, Sa'īd, as potential caliph. This pretender was liberally supplied with aliases—" 'Abdullah," " 'Alī," and " 'Ubaidallah"—as well as with the title al-Mahdī. Al-Mahdī became a ruling chief of state in North Africa. When he died, the succession reverted to the line of his uncle Muḥammad ("Ḥusain"); the latter's eldest son, 'Alī, had already died, and Alī's son Muḥammad was acclaimed imam and caliph with the title al-Qā'im; he was publicly represented as al-Mahdī's son. This genealogy helps us to understand how the first Fatimids were able to operate their network under the very nose of Abbasid counterintelligence.

Yemeni enemies of the Fatimids applied to them the epithets "Ismā'īlī," "Qarmatian," and *"bāṭinī,"* terms never used in their own literature. We have seen that there is some doubt that they recognized Ismā'īl as the seventh imam, or that they were his descendants; it would be pedantic to depart from the usual classification, however, and we shall often refer to the Fatimids as Ismā'īlīs. The Fatimids shared a common origin with the Qarmatians, a populist movement with communist overtones, but the two sects early became differentiated. The Fatimid caliphate in Egypt maintained relations with the independent Qarmatian state in Bahrain, but its military establishment was much preoccupied with defending Fatimid holdings in Syria against the depredations of Qarmatians there. The adjective *bāṭinī* applies correctly to the Fatimids in that their doctrine posited a hidden interpretation of the scriptures, derived by applying the methods of the Greek and neo-Platonist philosophers; the insights thus gained were supplementary to, not a replacement for, the esoteric meaning of the Koran, to which initiates remained obligated. The occult interpretation was imparted only to an elite in the Fatimid hierarchy, and otherwise held tightly secret.

By the late ninth century the Fatimids were conducting a ramified international underground movement centered in Iraq. It was out of the question to move directly against the base of Abbasid power, and planning focused upon the provinces—successively Syria, Yemen, and the Maghreb—where conditions appeared propitious for a secessionist state. The Iraqi leaders had become expert in selecting able men for key posts. In 880 two remarkable individuals were chosen to lead the movement in Yemen, both being first converted from the "twelver" sect of Shī'ism.

'Alī bin al-Faḍl and Manṣūr al-Yaman

To head the team the choice fell upon a resident of Kūfa, Abū al-Qāsim al-Ḥasan bin Faraj bin Ḥawshab bin Zaydān, a descendant of 'Alī's brother, 'Āqil bin Abī Ṭālib. By careful cultivation, the current imam, Ḥusain bin Aḥmad, won him to service of the cause in Yemen.

Through his secret agents the imam had advance knowledge of the arrival on pilgrimage to the Shī'a shrines in Iraq of the promising young Yemeni, 'Alī bin al-Faḍl al-Jadanī al-Khanfarī al-Jaishānī. It was not difficult to direct his apparently genuine and fervent Shī'a sentiments into channels useful to the Fatimid movement in his homeland. He gave the imam an optimistic, coldly objective assessment of the prospects:

> By the Almighty, the time is ripe in Yemen, and the ground prepared for your appeal. Our cunning will work effectively against them, for I know how simple-minded they are and how little they know about the dictates of the Muḥammadan *sharī'a*.[6]

The imam instructed his new agents to concentrate on accumulating money and recruits. He asked them to oblige their followers to observe strictly the precepts of the faith in prayer, fasting, and austerity, and to play down the esoteric aspects of Fatimid doctrine, promoting instead the exoteric, less controversial fundamentals. He adjured Abū al-Qāsim to give close guidance to his younger colleague, and the latter to be obedient to his senior partner in all things.[7] The two missionaries traveled together to Ghalāfiqa, at that time the port for the Ziyādī capital, Zabīd; they arrived early in 881. They then separated, Abū al-Qāsim proceeding to Aden Lā'a, a town beside Mt. Miswar, west of Sanaa.[8] There he assumed direction of a going concern. His predecessor as chief of the Fatimid mission had recently died as a prisoner of the Yu'firid lord of Sanaa; Abū al-Qāsim took over the Fatimid chief's house and married his daughter. 'Alī bin al-Faḍl meanwhile settled in the southeast among the Yāfi' tribe. Each man set about establishing his reputation for piety and knowledge of the faith, and gathering wealth and recruits in preparation for armed action. That both were soon in a position to call publicly for rebellion against the ruling princelings speaks both for their unusual abilities and for the appeal which leadership invoking strict Islamic principles, acting in the name of the Prophet's descendants, held for many Yemenis of the time. The prospect of a share in booty from anticipated military enterprises was undoubtedly an additional stimulus to recruitment.

The Ziyādī state was firmly entrenched in the Tihama, and enjoyed loose suzerainty over a sultan at Aden, whose authority extended eastward along the coast. The Banū Ziyād, on the other hand, had no influence in the highlands. The Abbasid court continued to send governors to Sanaa. By the year 845 the Abbasid's authority was effectively disputed by Yu'fir bin 'Abd al-Raḥmān al-Ḥuwālī, a descendant of the pre-Islamic Ḥimyarite kings. He expelled the Abbasid governor, Ḥimyar ibn al-Ḥārith, in 861, and ruled an area from Sanaa south to Janad, while acknowledging Abbasid symbolic sovereignty and paying tribute to the Ziyādī state. Yu'fir's son Muḥammad, whose influence extended over Hadramaut, was formally invested with the rule of Sanaa by the Abbasid caliph al-Mu'tamid about 872. The Yu'firids were not distinguished by family solidarity. Prince Muḥammad made a two-year pilgrimage to Mecca (871-873), leaving his son Ibrāhīm as regent in Sanaa. According to some accounts, Ibrāhīm savored this taste of power, and within a few years of his father's return assassinated him. The murder of his mother, his paternal uncle, and the latter's son followed. Ibrāhīm's reign was cut short by his own death, and his son As'ad succeeded to the rule of a principality disrupted by the rivalries of his surviving relatives. These disorders afforded opportunity for another Ḥimyarite aristocrat, Ja'far al-Manākhī, to sieze control of the southern highlands, under the vague suzerainty of the sultan of Aden. The tribes of northern Yemen, around Ṣa'da and Nejran, meanwhile, prosecuted their mutual quarrels free of outside intervention.

By astute maneuvering among the local Hamdān chiefs, Abū al-Qāsim gained possession of the minor fortress of 'Abr Muḥarram on Jabal Miswar as a base for military activity. By 878 he had conquered the entire Miswar massif with its several important fortified towns, had won the title of Manṣūr—"Victor"—al-Yaman, by which he is best known, and had embarked on the systematic extension of his influence in the western highlands. Opposition was bitter, but it was local, sporadic, and finally ineffectual. A stubborn and determined

Abū al-Qāsim consistently pursued a long-range goal which fired his followers with enthusiasm: that of building a state obedient to the Prophet's descendants. Given the disarray in Sanaa, he succeeded in gaining the cooperation even of some members of the Yu'firid clan.

'Ali bin al-Faḍl meanwhile was pursuing the same objective by similar means in the south. Exploiting a dispute between Ibn 'Alī al-'Alā', Sultan of Laḥej and Abyan (Aden), and his feudatory Ja'far al-Manākhī, 'Alī combined with the latter against the sultan, agreeing to divide the spoils equally. The allies defeated and killed the sultan in 906, the enormous booty falling into 'Alī's hands.[9] This feat won for him the collaboration of the important Madhḥij group of tribes. It also placed him in position to attack his erstwhile ally on a trumped-up pretext. After a brief but hard-fought war in which Ja'far received Ziyādī assistance, 'Alī defeated and killed his adversary in the Wadi Nakhla. He then exhibited sound esthetic taste by appropriating as his own capital the town of Mudhaikhira, which Ja'far had built in a beautiful mountain setting near the present 'Udain. 'Alī next directed his military effort toward the north. He had entered Sanaa in 905, but was unable to hold the city. It submitted briefly to the first Zaidi imam, al-Hādī Yaḥyā, who interned the Yu'firids trapped there. The captives soon escaped, and under As'ad's leadership recruited a force and recaptured the capital. 'Alī returned to the attack in 911; this time he consolidated his hold, and set up a thoroughly terrified As'ad as governor there.

'Alī bin al-Faḍl's successes made his assertion of absolute independence a realistic and tempting alternative to obedience to the Fatimid imam. The Banū Ziyād, by preserving their independence from the Abbasids, offered one precedent already of long standing; 'Alī's contemporary, Sa'īd al-Jannābī, provided another when he threw off Abbasid sovereignty and founded an autonomous Qarmatian state in Bahrain in the 890s. 'Alī bluntly renounced his twenty-year allegiance to the Fatimids after his conquest of Mudhaikhira. Abū al-Qāsim found him increasingly insubordinate, but loyally supported the unsuccessful forays into the Tihama which 'Alī undertook against his advice. Abū al-Qāsim remonstrated to no avail against ‘Alī’s defection, reminding him of his oaths and of the fact that he owed his advancement solely to the imam’s sponsorship. Finally, the two warred against each other, to the great detriment of the Fatimid cause in Yemen.

‘Alī has no apologists among the chroniclers. The Zaidis, particularly, seem to have attributed to him as a “Qarmatian” the most heinous of crimes, among them approval of fornication, incestuous marriages, wine-drinking, and banning of the pilgrimage to Mecca. It seems probable that, through political motives, ‘Alī did in fact condone ancient customs repugnant to Islam but to which many of the common people remained attached.[10] Abandonment of the consummatory values represented by the Fatimid cause, on the other hand, left ‘Alī’s state without any structurally cohesive element; it simply evaporated upon his death. He was poisoned in 905 by a clever operative of mysterious antecedents, posing as a *sharīf* and accomplished surgeon, and working in collusion with the Yu‘firid Prince As‘ad. The medieval accounts differ as to whether the assassin was sent on his mission by the Fatimid headquarters, by the Abbasid chancery, or by God himself.

The sister regime had been endowed with a somewhat tougher texture by Abū al-Qāsim, who doggedly pursued the goal of building a state obedient to the Fatimids. His ability and loyalty led the imam to entrust him with supervision of a number of operations outside Yemen; he directed missions to Oman, Yamāma, Sind, and even on occasion to Egypt and the Maghreb. His was the first political entity to acknowledge Fatimid sovereignty openly, and under his rule it made substantial moral and material contributions to the cause. He did not long survive his wayward colleague, and his state fell prey to rival factions. On his deathbed he enjoined his son, Abū al-Ḥasan, and his chief assistant, ‘Abdullah bin ‘Abbās al-Shāwirī, to continue as equals in the mission’s work, while requesting the Imam al-Mahdī to name one or the other as chief. Al-Shāwirī contrived to get his application in first, and the nomination went to him. Abū al-Ḥasan traveled to Tunisia in a vain attempt to induce al-Mahdī to reverse the decision. Returning disillusioned to Yemen, he found opportunity to kill al-Shāwirī, publicly proclaimed his conversion to Sunnī Islam, and set about raising the tribes, many of which responded with alacrity, in persecution of the Ismā'īlī sect, which was soon forced back underground for a time. In 1007 a Yu'firid prince of the Ismā'īlī persuasion, 'Abdullah bin Qaḥṭān, succeeded to the rule of Sanaa, and even made a successful foray against that stronghold of Sunnism, the Ziyād state in the Tihama, now in its decline. This Ismā'īlī resurgence was of brief duration. For a century and a half no central power of consequence existed in the Yemen inland from the Tihama. Most of the local rulers invoked the Abbasid caliph in the Friday prayers; they repressed overt manifestations of Ismā'īlī sentiment, but offered no persuasive ideological alternative.

It is probable that 'Alī bin al-Faḍl's defection tipped the scales in the Fatimids' decision to found their state in North Africa rather than in Yemen.[11] Their independent entity was proclaimed in Tunisia in 910. By 972 they were emperors, firmly established in Cairo, with ample resources to keep their Yemen underground organized, manned, indoctrinated, and heartened.

The parlous situation of Yemen in this period of troubles is described by a Zaidi chronicler:

> From [1014 to 1056] ruin prevailed in Sanaa and elsewhere in the country of Yemen by reason of the prevalence of disputes, rivalries, and disunity within this single nation. Darkness fell over Yemen, its desolation became universal, and public order disappeared. Sanaa and its suburbs became as if they had burned down. Every year, even every month, some new sultan seized power; the inhabitants became so extenuated that they dispersed in all directions. The city fell into ruin. Construction declined to the point where there were only a thousand houses, whereas in the time of al-Rashīd there had been one hundred thousand. However, Sanaa recovered somewhat in the time of the Ṣulayḥids, who gathered the lords of Yemen around themselves.[12]

The Ṣulayḥids

The Yemeni chroniclers, after the recital of each year's battles and travails, were at pains to record the names and antecedents of the men learned in Islamic theology and jurisprudence who died during that year. The genealogy of these jurists, scribes, and teachers, the enumeration of the doctors from whom they had gained instruction and licenses, and the names of their prominent pupils were significant facts for the people of the time. Islam impinged upon the everyday activities of all the people. Correct ordering of one's conduct was directly pertinent to one's prospects for admission to heaven. Evidence that the magistrates who judged the citizens and counseled them were following sound doctrine was a psychologically necessary reassurance. Within a few centuries after the rise of Islam the rules were compiled into voluminous compendia of law by various schools of jurists working for the most part independently of the secular authorities. Authenticity in the interpretation and application of the codes depended greatly upon person-to-person transmissions—from the founders of the four orthodox schools of law to succeeding generations of students, in the case of Sunnī Islam, and from various imams in the case of the Shī'a.

These systems of jurisprudence represented a body of knowledge of which the general public could obviously not achieve command, and a specialized professional class, the ulama, grew up to preserve, perfect, and administer it. Recruits were from a variety of social strata. In Umayyad times we find the Persian Ghiṭrīf al-Daylamī, whose father, al-Ḍaḥḥāk, and grandfather, Fīrūz, had governed northern Yemen for the Prophet and Abū Bakr, serving as chief judge of Sanaa.[13] Learning was not despised as a pursuit unbecoming to an aristocrat, as it sometimes was in medieval Europe; princes were often scholars themselves as well as patrons of the learned. In somewhat later times, pious endowments provided facilities for less advantaged youths to gain the education necessary for admission to the profession. The structure of relations between the ulama and governments varied from time to time and place to place, and, as is typical of professions, standards of integrity and competence were flexible and adaptable, within limits. The new class, however, provided a service essential both to the citizenry and to government, whatever the latter's nature. It served, furthermore, to preserve the fundamental ideals of Islam regardless of sect, and thus to promote uniform attitudes among the people toward one set of values. A judge of exceptional repute for learning, wisdom, and integrity could acquire significant influence. In eleventh-century Yemen the ulama fostered a modicum of social integration which might not otherwise have existed in the absence of central political authority, and where local power was the object of chronic contention among petty notables.

The future founder of the second Fatimid regime in Yemen was born to such a judge: Qāḍī Muḥammad al-Ṣulayḥī, of the Ḥāshid branch of Hamdān, a member of an aristocratic family, but one which had never held autonomous power. A Sunnī of the Shāfi'ī rite, he held office in the village of Qatar, in Ḥarāz district, two days journey northwest of Sanaa. By his upright life and conduct he commanded the obedience of his kinsmen and of the community he served. Such a prominent personage was a natural target for the attention of the Fatimid underground, and in fact its chief, Sulaimān bin 'Abdullah, of the noble Zawāḥī clan of Ḥimyar, cultivated the Qāḍī's acquaintance. He observed the extraordinarily promising qualities of the judge's young son, 'Alī. Sulaimān won the boy's confidence and instructed him in the secret Ismā'īlī doctrines, at the same time encouraging his political ambitions. When 'Alī was thoroughly versed in both the overt and the occult aspects of the Ismā'īlī sect, as well as in the Sunnī system of jurisprudence, and when Sulaimān was convinced of 'Alī's devotion to the cause of the Fatimid imams, the missionary requested and received permission from the caliph al-Mustanṣir to name the youth his successor as Fatimid agent in South Arabia.

The measure of 'Alī al-Ṣulayḥī's acumen is that he saw the utility of gaining a broad following among the general public based upon high principles to which all could subscribe, rather than upon kinship or sect. For nearly fifteen consecutive years (1031-1046) he led the Yemeni pilgrimage to Mecca, northward from Sanaa to Ṭā'if and the holy cities. This function, one of great prestige and responsibility, gave him opportunity to develop his reputation and win adherents throughout Yemen.

He carefully concealed his own commitment to the Isma'īlīya from all but a trusted few. As his renown spread, the people were

> in the habit of telling him . . . that according to what had come to their knowledge, he was destined to rule over the whole of Yemen, to earn a great name, and to be the founder of a dynasty. Al-Ṣulayḥī censored and disavowed what was thus said to him, though it was a thing that had spread far and wide among the people, and was on the lips of all, both high and low.[14]

During the 1046 *ḥajj* a group of sixty men, chiefly 'Alī's fellow tribesmen of Hamdān, swore fealty to him, promising to sacrifice their lives in support of any enterprise he might undertake. He now considered himself in a position to act openly toward instituting Fatimid rule in Yemen, and obtained the permission of Caliph al-Mustanṣir to do so. Upon his return to Yemen the next year, he consulted with the chief functionaries of the network, who agreed that the moment was favorable for decisive operations. Money, equipment, and supplies were gathered secretly, and on an agreed night several hundred armed men ascended Mount Masār, the loftiest peak of Ḥarāz, and hoisted the caliph's banners. The next day the mountain was surrounded by twenty thousand tribesmen, whose threats 'Alī parried by insisting that he was not pursuing personal ambition but was acting in the interest of all by establishing justice in accord with God's revelation. The besiegers gradually dispersed, and the small army spent a month transforming the bare summit of Masār into a permanent settlement and secure fortress. Meanwhile, propaganda was intensified, and commanders of castles throughout Yemen were urged to submit to al-Ṣulayḥī.

The petty rulers in the vicinity soon combined against al-Ṣulayḥī. The current Zaidi imam, Abū al-Fatḥ al-Daylamī, allied himself with the lord of the western mountains, Ja'far bin al-'Abbās al-Shāwirī, to attack the upstart. 'Alī's forces defeated both allies decisively. These early victories enhanced the morale of his troops, won him additional recruits, and dampened the enthusiasm of the northern tribes for war against him. 'Alī moved against the Ḥaḍūr district, northwest of Sanaa, and defeated its ruler, Ibn Jahūr, after the latter unsuccessfully sought the aid of the Najāḥ, the black dynasty which had fallen hier to the Ziyād state in the Tihama.

In secure control of a substantial and contiguous portion of central Yemen, al-Ṣulayḥī won the sympathy of the common people by his justice, virtue, and impeccable conduct. He expanded his domain by negotiation with the remaining lords, resorting to force only when persuasion failed. His most powerful and irreconcilable enemy was the Najāḥ state, the stronghold of Sunnism, with which he could not prudently come to grips before consolidating his position in the center of the country. He held this opponent at bay by a combination of intrigue, threat, and tentative acceptance of Najāḥ suzerainty. Sanaa fell under his rule in 1048, after he defeated a force under its lord, Ibn Abī Ḥāshid.

The Zaidi imam succeeded in fomenting hostility between al-Ṣulayḥī and the Najāḥ, but his ability to rally the northern tribes was waning:

> [In 1048] the people desisted from their support of Imam Abū al-Fatḥ because of the obvious power of al-Ṣulayḥī, the prospering of his fortunes, and his defeat of all who resisted him. The imam was obliged to keep moving from one area to another; thus he went from Khawlān to 'Ans and then to Dhībīn out of fear of al-Ṣulayḥī. In 1052 al-Ṣulayḥī attacked him in the 'Ans country and killed him, along with no less than seventy of his followers, on the Jāḥ Plain, just east of Radā'.[15]

The imam's persistent opposition led 'Alī to make an example of him in an uncharacteristically grisly manner: the Zaidi leader's head was severed from his corpse and exhibited to public view in Sanaa. The disaster effectively eclipsed the Zaidi movement for nearly a century; an imam appeared during the years 1060-1066, but thereafter no one summoned up the courage to assert leadership of the sect until the appearance in 1137 of Aḥmad bin Sulaimān.[16]

ʻAlī al-Ṣulayḥī needed several years to consolidate his authority over the northern tribes, which were unaccustomed to any strong outside influence; a major campaign was required to subdue his own Hamdān kinsmen. He was then able to turn south and subject the Ḥimyarite princelings one by one. He overran Aden and its hinterland, but showed a realistic appreciation of the limits of his resources by keeping its rulers, the Banū Maʻn (who were already espousing the Fatimid cause), as his tributaries and allies rather than assuming direct administration of the territory. He then concentrated his energies upon subjugation of the Tihama. By the close of 1063 he had defeated the Banū Najāḥ, who fled to the island of Dahlak off the Ethiopian coast. Yemen was now unified substantially within the extent of the pre-Islamic Ḥimyarite state, under an indigenous sovereign.

Apart from the *bāṭinī* aspects of the king's religion, the medieval Arab writers find little to reproach in his conduct.[17] The procedures he used to gain power, and the manner in which he employed it, indicate that he was guided by the basic Islamic concept of the ruler's responsibilities: the unity of the community of believers and the maintenance of their material and spiritual welfare. Sunnī Muslims were virtually unmolested in the practice of their rites, and ʻAlī engaged in none of the sectarian persecution which was a common feature of government in medieval Islam. At the same time, there can be no doubt of his commitment to the Fatimid imams or of his conviction that leadership of the entire Muslim community belonged to them by right. The common base of Islam provided a set of values on which the king and his subjects could agree. Sectarian differences were nevertheless not eliminated; particularism, in the form of tribal sentiment, survived as a value system inconsistent in many ways with the aims of the monarch. The legitimacy of the early Ṣulayḥid state thus rested on a somewhat equivocal foundation.

ʻAli endeavored to assert his personal authority and ideals throughout the kingdom. The princes he had defeated in unifying the country he treated with respect and honor; but he required them to live in impotent ease under his surveillance at Sanaa, where he built numerous palaces for their accommodation. The natural leaders of insurrection were thus removed from the provinces, and the king replaced them with governors, often his own close relatives, whose administration he supervised personally and minutely, without the intermediary of a chief minister (an office which became customary in both the Abbasid and the Fatimid courts, to the detriment of royal authority). From what is told of ʻAlī's brother-in-law, Asʻad bin Shihāb, governor of the Tihama, these officials were thoroughly indoctrinated with the king's own high standards of administration. Asʻad felt deep gratitude and humility toward ʻAlī, and toward Queen Asmā', who had arranged his appointment, and "revulsion at the thought that he might lend his hand to some act of oppression toward any citizen or official." In retirement, he reflected: "I was governor for fifteen years, and to my knowledge no man has a grievance against me."[18] Under Asʻad the provincial administration had an executive and a judicial branch, headed by royal appointees; the governor was assisted and advised by a third appointee of the king. All three, Asʻad says, were "to assist me in carrying out my orders respecting the conduct of the people, their livelihood, and the probity of their mutual dealings." The civil administrator "had charge of all aspects of the provincial administration from Wadi Ḥaraḍ to near Aden. He relieved me of the burden of settling disputes among the functionaries and of collecting revenue, and I did not restrict his actions save for reasonable cause or where large sums of money were involved. The chief judge was the son of a former Abbasid governor of the Tihama; he handled affairs of canon law for me, working hard to discharge his responsibilities and to guard against infractions." Each year Asʻad sent his chief secretary and the civil administrator to Sanaa with the revenue of the province (valued at one million dinars) and for a meticulous review of its affairs with the king and his consort. "My two colleagues," he said, "never returned to me without a gift from our Lord and Lady of 50,000 dinars, which I shared with them."[19]

As al-Ṣulayḥī's rule of Yemen became secure, the Fatimid caliph al-Mustanṣir's appreciation of his abilities and services increased. The caliph placed upon him increased responsibilities, which ʻAlī accepted eagerly. Hijaz was added to the scope of his mission. The holy land's affairs were in disarray at the time. A branch of the 'Alids had established themselves in control of Hijaz, and were autonomous when no military force of either great Muslim empire was at hand to impose obedience. They auctioned off the saying of prayers in Mecca (a source of great prestige and legitimacy) between the Fatimids and Abbasid caliphs, and supplemented these bribes by waylaying and despoiling the pilgrimage caravans.[20] In 1061 a suspension of prayers for the Fatimid imam coincided with the disappearance of the ruling branch of this clan, and al-Ṣulayḥī wrote al-Mustanṣir for permission to assume personal rule of Hijaz and to reform its affairs. The caliph endorsed the proposal, stipulating that it should not result in the shedding of Muslim blood. The king accordingly made the pilgrimage that year, with an armed retinue of sufficient size to discourage resistance. Upon completing the prescribed rites, 'Alī brought forth gifts for the adornment of the shrines, and money and provisions for distribution to the populace.

> He treated the public with kindness and conducted himself with justice. He won the hearts of the people; prices declined. The pilgrimage enjoyed a security it had never known before, insomuch as people were able to perform the *'umra*[21] day or night with their possessions under reliable guard, and their persons in full safety.[22]

Before returning to Yemen the next year 'Alī appointed, in agreement with al-Mustanṣir, a member of the local 'Alid clan as governor of Hijaz. He was Abū Hāshim Muḥammad, the ancestor of the Hāshimite Sharīfs of Mecca and the twentieth-century kings of Iraq and Jordan.[23]

'Alī had felt his control of Yemen secure before undertaking his pilgrimage; as he wrote to his Ma'n feudatory in Aden:

> The government is impregnable, our power firmly established, our banners fly on all sides, our soldiers are triumphant, the swords of justice are renowned, and the settled areas, by good fortune, are well protected.[24]

During his absence, nevertheless, the regime was faced with insurrections with which his governors were unable to cope: a renewed Ethiopian invasion, a resurgence of Zaidi dissidence, and rebellions by Ḥimyarite notables in the south. The king restored his position without undue difficulty upon his return, but within two years felt called upon to undertake a new expedition abroad.

The king's organization in Mecca had disintegrated. His viceroy's authority was challenged, and mention of the Fatimid caliph in the public prayers was again suspended. ʻAlī sought al-Mustanṣir's permission to campaign anew in Hijaz, and also to appear personally before the court in Cairo. The caliph agreed to the latter proposal only reluctantly, after attempting to persuade al-Ṣulayḥī to move instead against Hadramaut, which remained beyond the king's control. Egypt itself had fallen into civil disorder. The vizir, Badr al-Jamālī, was presently to exploit the situation by usurping the caliph's power and making al-Mustanṣir and his successors mere figure-heads. Neither the caliph nor his first minister wished al-Ṣulayḥī to observe the disarray in Egypt; perhaps they feared that he might be tempted to turn the situation to his own advantage, or that his own kingdom might again rebel in his absence, or that his loyalty to the Ismāʻīlī cause might wane.

The king made elaborate plans for further construction and embellishment in the holy cities, and assembled a lavish collection of gifts to bestow upon the caliph. The king's eldest surviving son, al-Mukarram Aḥmad, already confirmed as his spiritual and temporal heir, was appointed viceroy for the period of the king's absence, and received careful instruction to pursue justice, sound conduct, and policy; to obey God in public and private; to act in accord with the *sharīʻa* and its tenets; and to stamp out deviations from it.

The Najāḥ Prince Saʻīd al-Aḥwal had meanwhile returned secretly to the Tihama from Dahlak, and was conducting an intensive subversive campaign against the Ṣulayḥid state. The king did not fully appreciate the dimensions and effectiveness of this threat. ʻAlī confidently set his pilgrimage caravan in motion in the fall of 1067. In order to ensure unencumbered passage for his own entourage, he sent his baggage train and a large force of African mercenaries in advance. Some days later he set out himself from Sanaa with a large cortège including his queen, Asmā'; the fifty princes whom he had destituted and whom it would be risky to leave behind; and numerous tribal chiefs anxious to perform the pilgrimage. The royal caravan arrived late one day near the town of al-Mahjam in the northern Tihama. During the confused moments when tents were being pitched for the night, the royal party was infiltrated and attacked by a rabble of blacks, many armed with nothing more than defoliated palm fronds tipped with nails. They were commanded by Sa'īd al-Aḥwal, who had intelligence from 'Alī's soldiers of the king's movements and vulnerability. Few of the Arabs escaped massacre. The severed heads of 'Alī and his brother 'Abdullah were impaled on spears and affixed to the howdah in which Queen Asmā' was carried captive to Zabīd. In the Najāh capital the heads were displayed beneath the window of the room in which the queen was held prisoner.

The Yemeni tribes reacted immediately to the king's disastrous fate by rebelling aganst Ṣulayḥid rule, and the new king was besieged in his capital at Sanaa. Invoking the heavenly rewards promised in scriptures to Muslims steadfast in the faith, al-Mukarram formed several armies[25] and sent them in all directions: against a newly-declared Zaidi imam supported by Hamdān tribesmen in the north; against dissident Ḥimyar tribes in the western mountains; to the northwest where, significantly, the populace besieged the loyal commander of the late king's fortress of Masār, while the noblemen remained faithful to the dynasty; to the east, where the Khawlān mounted a spirited separatist movement; and to the south, where the Banū Najāḥ took advantage of al-Mukarram's discomfiture in the north to advance into the mountains.

These operations absorbed an entire year, before al-Mukarram judged his position secure enough to undertake a commando raid against Zabīd to rescue his mother. Within another year he could mobilize sufficient force to avenge his father against the Najāḥ and restore Ṣulyahiḍ rule in the Tihama. During the next several years the kingdom reached its maximum geographic extent and the apogee of its influence abroad. The Fatimid caliphate entrusted al-Mukarram's court with the operation of its missions to the east as far as India. Hadramaut, which King 'Alī had been unable to subdue, was absorbed, while Dhofar and Hijaz were under Ṣulayḥid political suzerainty.

Al-Mukarram has been described as a dashing warrior and eloquent orator, with striking ability to arouse the Arabs to revenge and to the defense of honor. These traits served him well in preventing the break-up of the kingdom. He shared his father's noble Islamic ideals and his commitment to the cause of the Fatimid imams. Within a few years of his accession he was, unfortunately, striken with paraplegia and, probably on the advice of his doctors, gradually abandoned the direct conduct of affairs. While retiring from public view, he retained the title of *dā'ī*, or chief of the Fatimid mission, and the confidence of the caliph al-Mustanṣir, with whom he remained in close correspondence. There is thus reason to doubt that his retirement was due to lack of ability or character, or to surrender to the temptations of drinking and other sensual pleasures, as some contemporary writers alleged.[26] Al-Mukarram's sons were still infants, and the measure of the ailing king's wisdom is that, instead of delegating authority to one or another of his ambitious cousins, thereby setting the scene for rivalry and fragmentation of the realm, he entrusted rule to his wife, al-Sayyida al-Ḥurra Arwā bint Aḥmad al-Ṣulayḥī.

Among the attractive features of the Ṣulayḥid clan was that they educated their daughters to the same standards as their menfolk, instilled in them the same moral and political principles, and made them their equals in astuteness, ability, and judgment. The founder of the state consulted and at times deferred to his queen, Asmā'; their son al-Mukarram continued to rely on her counsel during the years between his father's demise and her death (1067-1074).

Arwā was born to a collateral branch of the Ṣulyaḥid family. Her father died in her infancy and, her mother being remarried to a Ḥimyarite prince, she was reared in the royal palace by Queen Asmā'. King 'Alī is reported to have had premonitions of her distinguished future: "Treat her with respect," he admonished the queen, "for God has ordained that she will be the guarantor of our descendants, preserving this regime for those of us who survive."[27] She received as thorough an academic training as was available to any of her contemporaries, and developed an uncommon critical sense. She was

> well-read and herself a fine writer. She was versed in the chronicles, poetry, and history. She knew well how to read between the lines and distinguish between the literal and the true meaning.[28]

She received from Asmā' a common sense which kept her policies well within the limits of her capabilities throughout her long reign. She was married to al-Mukarram in 1065, at the age of eighteen, a year before his accession. She received from King 'Alī as a dowry the revenue of Aden, then amounting to roughly one hundred thousand dinars. Arwā played no direct role in state affairs until Asmā's death in 1074. She assumed her husband's responsibilities reluctantly. "A woman's place is in bed," she insisted, "she is not suited for the management of affairs. Put me where I belong." Al-Mukarram was not persuaded.[29]

Queen Arwā at once tried to minimize the use of armed force in governing the Ṣulayḥid state. She sought to win the loyalties of its subjects through sound administration in the material interests of the people, and by political maneuver. The removal of the court from Sanaa to Dhū Jibla in the southern mountains symbolized the shift. Her first act was to tour her domain. On her return to Sanaa she asked her husband to assemble the people of the city and suburbs in the public square. When the populace had convened she addressed al-Mukarram:

> "Look at them! What do you see?" Wherever he looked, only the flash of swords, the glint of naked blades and spearheads met his eyes.
>
> Then she went with him to Dhū Jibla and told him to summon its people and those of its environs. When they were come, early the next day, she said, "Look, milord, at these people." On all sides his glance met only a man leading a sheep, or carrying a vessel full of oil or honey.

> She said, "Life is better among people such as these." So King Mukarram moved to Dhū Jibla.[30]

Some change in the style of rule was unavoidable. 'Alī and al-Mukarram had been, by appointment of the Fatimid caliph, commanders of their armed forces, chiefs of the civil administration, and heads of the state religion. Arwā could hardly lead soldiers into battle, inspiring them by the example of courage and prowess with sword and spear. She could, and did, conduct the business of the Fatimid missionary apparatus, but as a woman she could not hold the title of its chief *dā'ī*. She faced two sets of problems: the maintenance of civil control of the kingdom, and the overlapping question of spiritual leadership. The power structure of the state rested in part upon a coalition between the Ṣulayḥid clan of Hamdān and the Zawāḥī clan of the Ḥimyarite aristocracy. Able and ambitious individuals of both families sought to exploit the assumed weakness of a woman's rule to seize local or central power. The same presumption encouraged separatist movements of various sorts throughout the country. The Najāḥ dynasty, the symbol of Sunnī Islam, was only temporarily in eclipse; it proved too dynamic to be long denied control of the Tihama. Arwā's reign saw the slow and final disintegration of the Ṣulyaḥid state. However, the decay was gradual, and she maintained herself at the head of a Fatimid kingdom, however diminished in extent, until her death at the age of ninety-two, in 1137.

There were three areas of special interest in Arwā's reign: the question of who deserved titular representation of the Fatimid caliphs in Yemen, an issue which split the aristocracy; second, the manner in which the queen's authority was exerted; and last, the progressive territorial shrinkage of the Ṣulayḥid kingdom.

Al-Mukarram had recommended to the caliph the designation of his distant cousin, Abū Ḥimyar Saba bin Aḥmad al-Muẓaffar bin 'Alī al-Ṣulayḥī, as *dā'ī* of the Fatimid mission in Yemen. Arwā was dissatisfied with her husband's decision on two counts: it excluded her two infant sons, 'Alī and Muḥammad, from the succession; moreover, in her view, the appointment was the prerogative of the imam alone. When al-Mukarram died in 1084 she wrote to al-Mustanṣir asking him to name her son 'Alī to the spiritual and temporal leadership, under her own regency. The imam had reason to disregard the question of minority, as he himself had assumed the caliphate at the age of eight. He was furthermore wise enough regarding the affairs of Yemen to see that any choice other than the queen's son would lead to her exclusion from conduct of the kingdom's business, in which she had already proved herself an able and faithful servant of the Fatimids. Finally, her exclusion could be expected to produce dissension among various sectors of the Yemeni aristocracy, whose loyalty and solidarity were essential to the cause. He therefore named the child 'Alī as chief of the mission, directing that all correspondence between the two courts be drafted in his name. The measure nevertheless touched off a dispute and armed clashes among the noble families of Yemen. One faction, led by Saba, who considered himself wrongfully deprived of rights bequeathed him by al-Mukarram, rejected the titular leadership of a small boy; the opposing faction, supporting the queen, was led by her half-brother, 'Āmir bin Sulaimān al-Zawāḥī. The caliph al-Mustanṣir intervened personally by writing to the principal contenders urging them to obey the queen and to keep the peace in the higher interests of the true faith. The caliph's moral authority was sufficiently persuasive to put an end to the strife, and Arwā salved Saba's feelings by naming him 'Alī's deputy and protector of the kingdom. The entire question was re-opened within a few years, however, when Arwā's two small sons died in rapid succession.

We are indebted to Saba's memory for some refreshing pages of Yemeni history. Endowed with small stature ("even on horseback he didn't seem tall"[31]) but with high ambition, he saw in the new situation an opportunity to gain power by marrying the queen. A conventional proposal being rejected, he pressed his suit by force of arms, and attacked Arwā's castle at Dhū Jibla. Advised by 'Āmir that she would never consent to marriage except by order of the caliph, Saba sent an emissary to Cairo with an appeal for the issuance of such an order. Al-Mustanṣir,[32] misled by the ambassador respecting the true state of the queen's inclinations, wrote to Arwā instructing her to contract the marriage. He sent two functionaries of high rank to deliver the message and draft the marriage contract, which was to specify a dowry from the groom of one hundred thousand dinars cash and other valuables worth half that sum. After a spirited court scene with much pleading by the caliph's ambassadors and her own ministers, the queen set her name to the document.

The dowry being paid over, Saba set forth from his fortress of Ashyaḫ to claim his bride. Arriving before Dhū Jibla, he found the castle gates tightly closed, and encamped with his large retinue. Daily for a month the palace kitchens worked overtime producing such sumptuous repasts for delivery to Saba's camp that the dowry was entirely consumed. Meanwhile, the common people continued to speak of "Our Lady," while none acclaimed Saba king. Perceiving that he was cutting a sorry figure, he at length wrote secretly to the queen pleading for admission to the castle, even if only for a night, for appearances' sake. She agreed. Upon arrival he was escorted to a bedchamber where he was soon joined by a serving-girl somewhat resembling the queen. She stood before him throughout the night, while he sat without so much as glancing at her. At dawn he said his prayers and departed, after telling the girl, "Inform Our Lady that this is noble sperm which shall be placed only where it belongs." Thereafter Saba foreswore sexual intercourse, as well as the drinking of intoxicants. He was, incidentally, already married to a lady of high degree and attainments, al-Jumāna, who put the best possible face on her new situation by observing that she never had occasion to be jealous of her husband.[33]

Saba was not simply a comic of overblown ambition. Notwithstanding his humiliation at the queen's hands, he served her faithfully and effectively. From his castle of Ashyaḫ, overlooking the Tihama, he provided a bulwark against Najāḫ encroachment from the coast and against the Banū Ḫātim clan of Hamdān from the north. Sanaa was lost to the Ṣulayḫid state only after his death in 1097. Saba furthermore retained the title of *dāʿī*. The term as it had applied to Manṣūr al-Yaman and ʿAlī al-Ṣulayḫī implied the concentration in one person of all powers, spiritual and temporal, exercised in the name of the Fatimids. The title was now becoming diluted, and prominent members of several governing families bore it: Ṣulayḥids, Zawāḥis, Yāmis, Banū Ma'n, and the latter's successors in Aden, the Zuray'. This development accompanied a growing functional distinction between civil and religio-judicial affairs. Saba's responsibilities, including advice to the queen, were restricted to civil affairs, notably the defense of the realm.

Nor did Arwā herself exercise the absolute power King 'Alī had wielded. Even before al-Mukarram's death, the Fatimid court had sent a chief justice to Yemen, Lamak bin Malik, who remained in the office until his death in 1116; his son Yaḥyā succeeded him for the remainder of Arwā's reign. The judge's responsibility extended to advising the queen on the management of the Ismā'īlī missionary effort in Yemen itself and to the east in Oman, the Persian Gulf, and India. This effort she conducted officially with the title *al-ḥujja*, a rank in the Fatimid hierarchy second only to that of *dā'ī* and to that of the caliph's chief doorkeeper.

Early in the reign, thus, the pattern of authority was oriented toward decentralization, and the trend extended through the lower levels of the administration. The result was the progressive erosion of the queen's authority, the assertion of autonomy by her appointees, and the gradual loss of territory. When Ḥātim bin al-Ghāshim al-Mughlisī proclaimed himself independent sultan of Sanaa and its districts, Arwā resigned herself to the fait accompli and endeavored to strengthen what remained of the kingdom. In dealing with domestic challenges to her orders she relied upon persuasion and conciliation, even bribery, rather than force. Her efforts to recover lost territory were both few and abortive.

The employment of a chief minister was more a practical necessity for Arwā than a sign of weakness. When Saba died, she named a Ḥimyarite nobleman, al-Mufaḍḍal bin Abī al-Barakāt bin al-Walīd, commander of the army and head of administration. She relied heavily on his advice, and channeled her orders through him. His ability and loyalty did not suffice to preserve order in the kingdom, as the circumstances of his death indicate.

Upon the death in 1110 of Fātik bin Najāḥ, ruler of the Tihama, three of his relatives disputed the succession. Fātik's brother, ʻAbd al-Wāḥid, having seized Zabīd, the late ruler's son Manṣūr took asylum with Queen Arwā, and offered her one fourth of the Tihama's revenue in exchange for assistance in gaining its throne. She sent her minister, al-Mufaḍḍal, with an army to Zabīd, which surrendered after a protracted seige. Six Sunnī ulama had meanwhile taken advantage of al-Mufaḍḍal's absence to seize his fortress, Taʻkar, near the Ṣulayḥid capital. He hastened back to find the jurists in possession of the fort, supported outside its walls by a mob of twenty thousand local Sunnī citizens reinforced by six thousand Khawlān tribesmen from the north. Al-Mufaḍḍal set siege to his own castle. One day, to humiliate the minister, the intruders obliged the women of his harem to dress in their best finery and dance, with tambourines, on the battlements of the castle in view of the public. The shock was fatal to al-Mufaḍḍal, who died forthwith. Arwā now went up from Dhū Jibla, camped before Taʻkar, and entered into negotiation with the jurists. The queen recovered the fort by paying a substantial ransom and promising immunity for the rebels.[34]

Arwā appointed al-Mufaḍḍal's cousin, Asʻad bin Abī al-Futūḥ, to succeed him. Established in Taʻizz and Jabal Ṣabr, he served well for a decade. His murder in 1120, by his own retainers, marks a stage in the decline of the Ṣulayḥid state. The queen now saw no Yemeni prince either able or willing to impose her will on the increasingly self-assertive aristocracy, and appealed to Cairo to provide her with a chief minister. The ability of the Fatimid establishment to select able personnel persisted even in the decline of the caliphate, as indicated by its choice of al-Muwaffaq ʻAlī bin Ibrāhīm Ibn Najīb al-Dawla.

The new minister briefed himself cleverly for his new duties. He interrupted his journey to Yemen by stopping at Dahlak, where he had arranged to meet with an experienced Fatimid agent in Yemen, Muḥammad bin Abī ʻArab. Muḥammad

> revealed to him all the secrets of Yemen: the situation of all its people, their names, their qualities, their nicknames, their dates of birth, and the birthmarks, warts, and scars

> from wounds or burns concealed beneath their clothing. Then when Ibn Najīb al-Dawla spoke of these obscure matters he was believed to be possessed of second sight.[35]

He worked energetically and with some success to reassert the queen's authority. The Khawlān adventurers who had been carpetbagging in the very capital were driven back north, and lords of castles within the realm were obliged to respect orders from the court. The methods used did not spare the sensitivities of the aristocracy (no effective ones could have), and the popularity the minister won among the common people by providing security and lowering prices in the markets was vitiated by the opposition of the notables. The latter exploited the dynastic quarrel then raging among the Fatimids to denounce Ibn Najīb al-Dawla falsely to the incumbent caliph, al-Āmir, as a partisan of the pretender, Nizār. Convinced by trumped-up evidence, al-Āmir's court recalled the minister and had him executed.[36] Arwā was well aware of his innocence, but had insufficient strength to defy both the caliph and her own court. She sent an ambassador, with a lavish gift, to al-Āmir to intercede for Ibn Najīb al-Dawla; the captain of the ship on which the envoy sailed from Aden was bribed by the Yemeni nobles to throw him, and the queen's gift, overboard in the Bāb al-Mandab.

Arwā's remaining eight years are twilight. On principles of legitimacy, she opposed the accession of al-Ḥāfiẓ in 1130 to the Fatimid caliphate. His reign was engineered by the vizirs to the exclusion of al-Āmir's son al-Ṭayyib, whom Arwā considered the rightful heir. This stand deprived her of moral and material support from Cairo and estranged her definitively from the Banū Zuray' in Aden, who had long since ceased paying the tribute to which her dowry entitled her, and who gave their allegiance to al-Ḥāfiẓ. Little is recorded of Arwā's last minister, her late husband's cousin 'Alī bin 'Abdullah bin Muḥammad al-Ṣulayḥī. Manṣūr, the son of al-Mufaḍḍal, loyally held for the queen all the fortresses and towns controlled by his father at his death in 1110. After the queen died, in 1137, Manṣūr kept the territory in the Ṣulayḥid name until discouraged by advancing age. In 1152 he sold, for the sum of one hundred thousand dinars, twenty-eight castles and towns, including Dhū Jibla and the formidable castle of Ta'kar, to the lord of Aden, Muḥammad bin Saba bin Abī Sa'ūd al-Zuray'ī. He also divorced his young wife, who then married Sultan Muḥammad. A Ṣulayḥid princess, her name was Arwā.

The disintegration of the Ṣulayḥid state was inevitable from the first because of the dissonance between the goals of the monarchs and those of many of their subjects. The motivation of the royal family is quite clear. Devout Muslims, they sought to provide good government according to the tenets of Islam. In order to govern well, one must first be in a position to govern, and they sought control over all Yemeni territory. They were firmly attached to the cause of the Fatimid imams. This implied no derogation from sound rule; despite the carping of their detractors, the Fatimids consistently urged upon the Ṣulayḥids the most beneficent principles of government. On the other hand, the Fatimid connection implied a subtle effort to convert the people to Ismā'īlism. Those who remained unconverted, and they were the great majority, were reminded weekly, when the Fatimid caliph was invoked in the Friday prayers, that their rulers were heretics.

It is a striking fact that the Arabs of the Tihama did not welcome and support the rule of Arab princes descended from Qaḥṭān in preference to foreign blacks whom we know to have been often oppressive. We have noted the concern of 'Alī's governor there for the just treatment of his subjects. Mukarram successfully restrained his army from looting Arab property when he reconquered the Tihama in 1069. The coastal Arabs nevertheless interposed no opposition to the return of the Najāḥ from Ethiopia. A bizarre situation developed during the years 1069-1084 while they were reconsolidating their regime. Prince Saba, who occupied a line of forts in the western mountains overlooking the Tihama, conducted a desultory war with Jayyāsh, the Najāḥ Sultan:

> In cool weather the Arabs mobilized and descended into the Tihama. Jayyāsh was obliged to evacuate the territory, but did not go far away. Saba proceeded to collect the canonic taxes, but without injustice or oppression of any

> citizen; he required his officials to deduct from their exactions what Jayyāsh had collected during the summer and fall. At the end of the winter and spring the Arabs moved back to the mountains and Jayyāsh resumed control, sometimes after fighting, sometimes not. When Jayyāsh re-entered Zabīd, copies of the Koran were distributed to the people, prayers were said in his name, jurists appeared openly in public, and the ulama were everywhere to be seen. Jayyāsh also required his functionaries to take account of the taxes which Saba had collected during the winter and spring.[37]

At length Jayyāsh drew Saba and his forces into an ambush near Zabīd and inflicted a punishing defeat on them; thereafter, the highland Arabs did not return to the Tihama.

In Upper Yemen a different outlook operated to the detriment of the Ṣulayḥids. The latter were of Hamdān. They did not, however, play up tribal solidarity in asserting their legitimacy; their appeal was to all the people as Muslims. The Banū Ḥātim, who led Sanaa out of the Ṣulayḥid state, were also Hamdānīs and faithful to the Ismāʿīlī cult. This they preached with fair consistency during their rule at Sanaa, despite the fact that it was under heavy local attack not only from Sunnī ulama but also from the Zaidi Shīʿa. Here, the sentiment which could stir the people to rebellion was the attachment to local autonomy and distaste for remote, centralized control.

In speaking of the ancient states, we referred to the coincidence of political and economic fragmentation. This was not a unique phenomenon. A comparable decentralization occurred in late Merovingian France. A student of the period sees a necessary relation between the two:

> Any regime based on a landed aristocracy, especially at a time when material life is essentially local, tends irresistably to render political life itself local. . . . One eats the products of one's own domain, spins the wool of one's own sheep, fashions on the spot clothing, shoes and the—quite primitive—tools with which the land is cultivated.[38]

Without overburdening the analogy, we may suggest a further parallel. Out of a western Europe thus fragmented, Charlemagne built an imposing political structure based on consummatory values kept alive by the Church of Rome. His empire nevertheless remained economically weak and disunited; it collapsed within a generation, and his grandsons squabbled and warred over the fragments. The Ṣulayḫids, too, revived an ancient empire by their talents, basing their work on lofty political and religious principle. The latter, however, did not coincide with the aspirations of many of their subjects. Nor do the Ṣulayḫids seem to have had a clear concept of Yemen as an economic unit to be strengthened and articulated. A notion of this sort emerges, if dimly, with the Ayyūbids and Rasūlids whose regimes we shall later consider. It was, and remained for a millennium, alien to the ideology of the Zaidi imamate which arose in Yemen almost simultaneously with the Fatimid movement.

4
The Zaidi Imamate

The Zaidi imamate, introduced into Yemen at the close of the ninth century A.D., asserted for over a thousand years an exclusive claim to authority by divine right. Its doctrine, which remained constant throughout these centuries, formed a central element of Yemeni politics well past the middle of the twentieth century. In a work published in 1951 by order of the reigning imam, the historian al-Jarāfī states the "establishment" view that the Zaidi regime represents fulfillment of an early Islamic prophesy that "authority will remain with Quraysh so long as even two of them survive."[1] The state was founded, he asserts, by the efforts of the Yemeni people themselves, and continues to draw strength from their tribes, notably Hamdān, with its Ḥāshid and Bakīl components. The truth of the prophecy is demonstrated by the fact that, whereas states more populous and prosperous rose and fell, the Hāshimite imams in Yemen remained, cleaving to the dictates of the true faith, merciful yet zealous in commanding good and forbidding evil.[2]

This interpretation of the Zaidi state's legitimacy conceals a conflict. The link between the authority of the Prophet's descendants, sanctioned by divine will, and the role of the tribes is of fundamental importance, but is imperfect. The imamate was instituted by action of the tribes, and remained throughout its history dependent upon them. From the first, on the other hand, the tribes acted from secular motives arising out of the age-old structure of their society, not from the religious precepts which the imams sought to make binding upon them. Tension between the two value sets persisted to the very end of the Zaidi era.

The Tribes of Northern Yemen

The Hamdān Arabs who entered, or perhaps re-entered, Yemen from the north were in place in antiquity, and were already divided into the major branches, Ḥāshid and Bakīl. The early Islamic genealogists explained that the Ḥāshid lived on the west side of a north-south line between Nejran and Sanaa; the Bakīl lived to the east. The tribes did not in fact divide themselves strictly according to such a neat blueprint. Generally speaking, the Ḥāshid tribes live in a narrow north-south region between Sanaa and Nejran, almost completely ringed by Bakīl areas. The two territories overlap, and one may find a pocket of Ḥāshid well within Bakīl territory or vice versa. We find enclaves throughout the Hamdān areas peopled by tribes who claim Ḥimyarite descent. Two branches of Ḥāshid, furthermore, preserve the ancient patronymic: Hamdān bin Zaid, who live just south of Nejran, and Hamdān al-Yaman, who live just north of Sanaa. In the northwest we find Khawlān al-Shām, a Bakīl tribe, and in the Jawf, east of Sanaa, Khawlān al-Ṭiyāl. The Khawlān al-Ṭiyāl are often classified as Bakīl but are considered by some genealogists as Ḥimyarites of the Quḍā'a branch and so look upon themselves.[3] The chroniclers do not always define their terms precisely, and the reader must often rely upon the context to judge whether, in speaking of "Hamdān," for example, a writer is referring to the global community descended from the patriarch Hamdān, or to one or another of the Ḥāshid sections retaining the ancestral name. Finally, while the villages and smaller towns of Upper Yemen may or may not be homogeneous in population, the inhabitants of the larger urban centers typically include members of various tribes.

At the close of the ninth century, the tribes of Upper Yemen were unaccustomed to stable, central authority. We have seen that governors under the Abbasid caliph Ma'mūn sometimes had difficulty maintaining themselves in the capital, Sanaa;

their deposed predecessors often found asylum with one or another tribe, and gathered partisans to assist their challenge to the imperial writ. Under the same caliph, a clan of 'Alids, descended from Ḥasan bin 'Alī bin Abī Ṭalib, achieved control of Hijaz and named one of their number, Ibrāhīm, to govern Yemen; while endeavoring to assert authority in Upper Yemen, Ibrāhīm demonstrated his right to his nickname al-Jazzār—the Butcher—by demolishing the city of Ṣa'da in 815, as well as the al-Khāneq Dam at Rahbān.[4] This association with Hijaz was fleeting. The Ḥimyarite Yu'firids presently established themselves in Sanaa; they had quite enough to do to maintain their influence in the capital and its immediate surroundings without seeking control of the far north, which was left to its own devices.

We are ill informed concerning the relations within and among the far northern tribes during this anarchic period. No doubt some customary code existed, as we find some centuries later, designed to control the loss of life and property attendant upon raids and disputes. However, no evidence exists which would permit us to study the reasons for the code's failure to function. We do know that by 893 chaos in the town of Ṣa'da reached the point where its people felt the need of outside help in regulating their affairs;

> The region . . . was in a state of decline as a result of protracted tribal quarrels. The disastrous consequences of these quarrels had moreover been aggravated, it is related, by a drought and bad harvest. It appears that the population lived overwhelmed by the existing situation, and was disposed to place itself under the aegis of a leader who would maintain himself above parties. Certainly they could properly expect salvation from a descendant of the Prophet among all others.[5]

In that year representatives of two principal clans in Ṣa'da appealed to Yaḥyā bin Ḥusain bin Qāsim al-Rassī, a highly regarded member of the 'Alid clan mentioned above. They asked him to come from his home near Medina to supervise their affairs, promising their submission to all his commands.

Those involved were the Fuṭaimī clan of Khawlān, and the 'Ukail of Rabī'a, a tribe of 'Adnānī (i.e., non-Yemeni) origin. The first imam thus came to Yemen at the request of some people in one troubled town, not, as Jarāfī suggests, on the initiative of the Yemeni people.

Zaidism—Origin and Political Doctrines

The Shī'a sect thus obscurely introduced into Yemen takes its name from Zaid, son of 'Alī Zain al-'Ābdīn, the fourth Shī'ite imam. Zaid's brother, Muḥammad al-Bāqer, to whom the "twelver" spiritual succession passed, lived a respected, scholarly, retired life in Medina, punctuated by family quarrels over money and the working of thirty-one miracles.[6] Zaid, by contrast, was an activist in the cause of undermining Umayyad authority seeking power for the 'Alids. Disregarding a warning of Muḥammad al-Bāqer regarding the unreliability of the people of Kūfa, Zaid went to that Iraqi city and soon became the ringleader of a conspiracy embracing Kūfa, Mosul, and the countryside in between. There large numbers of people swore allegiance to him as imam. When revolt was declared openly in 740, the Umayyad governor in Baghdad was well aware of the plot and prepared to deal with it. As the imam had foreseen, most of the Kūfans defected; Zaid was killed with a handful of loyal supporters, and his corpse, minus head, was nailed to a pillory.

The movement nevertheless remained alive. Zaid's son, Yaḥyā, escaped with a band of partisans to Khorasan, already a hotbed of 'Alid sentiment. Pursued by Umayyad agents, he met death in battle; his remains were disposed of according to the precedent set in his father's case, Yaḥyā's head being sent all the way to Medina for public exhibition. Memory of these martyrs persisted in Central Asia where, a century later, the 'Alid Ḥasan bin Zaid founded a Zaidi state on the southern shore of the Caspian Sea. This state survived, with an occasional hiatus, into the twelfth century. Other Zaidis took refuge in Hijaz, and a few in Yemen. In Medina, the Ḥasanid Qāsim al-Rassī (d. 864) aspired to political leadership without notable success. His fame as the progenitor of the great majority of Yemen's imams rests upon his work as a theological and legal scholar;

some of his works are still regarded as authoritative.

The imam Zaid himself acquired a reputation as theoretician only after his death. The anecdotes in which he is portrayed as a profound religious savant may well be posthumous legend, and the treatises attributed to him may be by other hands.[7] He emerges in the annals of al-Ṭabarī as "not lacking a certain intelligence, without, however, distinguishing himself in the practice of the sacred sciences."[8] Dispersed in various places of asylum, the scholars among the survivors of Zaid's overthrow laid the legal and theological foundations of the sect. The group soon divided into a half-dozen branches, whose contrasting views on theological questions are not relevant here. Zaidism as a whole preserved a stable political orientation: an attitude toward the succession to the Prophet's temporal and spiritual authority inspired from Zaid's beliefs and actions; a spirit of militance directed toward avenging the slaying of Zaid and his son; and the aspiration to restore power to its rightful possessors, the descendants of 'Alī and Fāṭima. The resulting doctrinal school might be described as "pragmatic Shī'ism"; minor ritual prescriptions aside, it differs from Sunnī Islam chiefly in its insistence upon the institution of the imamate.

Its practical bent is reflected in its rejection of the idea of a "hidden" imam, expected to reappear with the prophets on the eve of Judgment Day. Rejected also is the notion of an occult exegesis of the Koran and the Traditions accessible to only a few, and its corollary, the systematic dissimulation practiced by the Ismā'īliya and some other Shī'a. When Ṣūfī—mystical—schools and secret brotherhoods later appeared, the Zaidis condemned them, and suppressed them where they were in a position to do so. Flexible and eclectic in law and theology, Zaidi doctrine was receptive to opinions from all competent sources, including the Sunnī schools, on condition that their validity be confirmed by critical examination. Zaidism regarded the refinement of interpretation of the sources of law as an ongoing process; the door to this progressive development of jurisprudence by scholarly endeavor—*ijtihād*—was not closed, as it was in Sunnī Islam, which became largely frozen in a tenth-century mold.

Zaidism did not endorse the orthodox Shī'a claim that the Prophet had nominated 'Alī to be his successor, and that Abū Bakr and 'Umar were hence usurpers deserving the most violent condemnation. In the Zaidi view, 'Alī was entitled to the succession because his unique personal qualities made him the man best qualified to succeed Muḥammad. These qualities, in Zaidi theory, are inherited by the descendants of 'Alī and Fāṭima, although not in uniform degree.[9] Among them, the choice in any generation is on the basis of demonstrated talent in learning, piety, martial temperament, etc. To the founder, Zaid, is attributed the declaration:

> The imam whom Muslims must obey is the one among us, the Prophet's family, who draws his sword, who invokes his Lord's Book and His Prophet's Tradition, who forms his judgments according to them, and whose conduct is known to conform to them. It is not permissible to withhold recognition from him. But a lackey who sits in his house, lolling behind his curtain, submitting meekly to unjust government, neither commanding the right nor forbidding the evil: he is no imam.[10]

This concept of the legitimate leader remained stable through the centuries. A twentieth-century Arab-American traveler interpreted the attitude of Yemeni Zaidis thus:

> "Maybe you want an imam forever present everywhere but never seen anywhere, but we want nothing of the sort. We want to see the imam before our eyes even if in a single place and at a single moment in time." In my opinion their view was inspired simply by the idea of a sword asserting their beliefs. They said, "After Ḥasan and Ḥusain the imamate belongs by law to their descendants. Any of them who fights conspicuously in the cause of his faith, and who is learned and pious: he is the expected imam."[11]

The qualifications for the imamate were codified as follows: he must be adult; male; free (i.e., not a slave); adept in the interpretation of the sources of law (*mujtahid*); of proved descent from 'Alī and Fāṭima; just, generous, and God-fearing; of sound mind; courageous in war; sound of body and limb; able as politician and administrator; and a distinguished warrior.

Zaid's Iraqi adherents pledged allegiance to him in these terms:

> We appeal to you in the name of God's Book and the Traditions to combat those who commit injustice, to defend the oppressed, to requite the disinherited, to distribute the state's booty equitably among those who have a right to it, to restore property wrongfully taken away, and to relieve from time to time the troops on active duty.[12]

The emphasis on social justice in this formula reflects the topical preoccupations of Iraqi citizens of the time and their grievances, temporal and spiritual, against their Umayyad rulers. Allegiance, in this historical context, is due to one who insists that justice is to be achieved by strict application of Koranic and Traditional injunctions. These rules are to be vindicated by armed force against adversaries who are themselves Muslims. The Zaidis were soon to regard themselves as the only true Muslims, and to look upon their enmity with other Islamic sects as the prosecution of holy war—*jihād*. Thus, strangely, a sect liberal and accommodating in theology and jurisprudence became intransigent and aggressive on the level of politics.

This Zaidi conception of the proper locus of authority and mode of its application was exemplified by the words and deeds of Yaḥyā, al-Hādī ilā al-Haqq al-Mubīn (Guide to the Manifest Right), the sect's first imam in Yemen.

al-Hādī's Concept of Government

Yaḥyā was born at Medina in 854, one year before the death of his illustrious grandfather, Qāsim al-Rassī, and grew up in the household of his father, Ḥusain. We have few details of his life before his appearance in Yemen at the age of 35; his biographers later filled the vacuum with appropriate anecdote and celestial signs. There is no reason to doubt that he was endowed with an unusually quick intellect and a vigorous physique, or that he gained the respect of his family and entourage at an early age for the profundity of his learning in the sacred sciences, his piety, and the austerity of his personal life. The authors of his invitation to Yemen probably did not foresee the ultimate implications of their appeal. By contrast, Yaḥyā himself had closely examined his conscience concerning his right to rule, the goals he was to pursue, the nature of his obligations toward his subjects, and their duties toward him.

Yaḥyā was convinced that God had endowed him uniquely with the attributes of the imamate, and that failure to use them for divine purposes would be sinful. He said:

> I swear to God, if I knew there were at this moment someone better qualified than I for this task, or if I were aware of some son of the Prophet whose aspirations were of greater excellence than mine, I would join him wherever he might be, or fight under his orders. But I know no one of that sort.[13]

The assertion of authority was his clear duty:

> By the one God and the right of Muḥammad, I did not seek power. I did not march forth of my own volition, but simply because I was obliged to; I had no valid motive for staying home. I should like to have been free to remain at ease . . . but I was faced with the choice between marching forward or making myself guilty of disbelieving God's revelation to Muḥammad.[14]

Since the imams are invested with authority by God, men owe them obedience

> because they are born in the line of the Prophet, because of their knowledge of God, their piety, their knowledge of what is permissible and prohibited in the eyes of God, and the needs of men in practice of their religion, because of what they take by right and give by duty without coveting

> worldly goods, forgoing the temptations of this transitory life; because they are prepared to draw their sword openly and raise their banners for the love of God; because they enter the lists against the enemies of God, publish their appeal for men to turn toward Him, are animated with passion in his cause, put into practice the scriptures and the Tradition, establish law and justice. Further, because they see clearly through the obscurity of certain parts of God's revelation, a gift given only to him whom God invests with power and to whom He entrusts the imamate, for it is he to whom He accords wisdom and endows with special excellence. Finally, it is by virtue of their courage in battle, their stubborn perseverance in adversity, and their unbounded generosity.[15]

From this argument flows the principle that any man or group of recalcitrants to the imam's authority is infidel and an appropriate object of holy war.

Upon his arrival in Yemen, Yaḥyā spelled out the reciprocal obligations between himself and his subjects in a proclamation:

> In order that we and you together may ordain the right, and that we and you, the people, together may forbid evil, fighting for the sake of the former and forsaking the latter, I lay upon myself in your presence the obligation of governing according to God's Book and the Traditions of His Prophet. I undertake the obligation of giving you precedence over myself in the relationship which God has established between you and me, giving you preferment, taking no advantage for myself, giving you the first portion of any wealth, and placing myself personally in the forefront of any encounter with our common enemy. In return, I lay upon you two obligations: that you heed the admonitions of God Almighty and my own, in private and in public, and that you obey my command in all your affairs insofar as I remain obedient to God in my dealings with you. Should I depart from obedience to Almightly God, however, I shall have no claim on your obedience; should I alter or distort the Book of God, I have no rights over you.[16]

On the practical, administrative plane, we have a document in Yaḥyā's hand instructing his agents in outlying districts on the performance of their functions.[17] The imam is anxious that his regime project an elevated moral image. Upon arriving at the town to which he is assigned, the official is to make his entry in peace and dignity, invoking the name of God. He is forbidden to commandeer quarters, but must rent a house at a fair price for his residence. He may not demand or accept gifts for his personal use; any gratuity tendered must be deposited in the state treasury. He is to ensure that the people say their prayers properly; for those insufficiently familiar with the Koran, he must provide instruction as thorough as they are able to absorb, in the elements of the faith, the virtue of *jihād* and of those who lead it, and the obedience to Muḥammad's descendants which God requires of men.

Yaḥyā provides meticulous guidance on tax-collection, which fulfulls a scriptural obligation, while seeking to prevent abuses or arbitrary exactions. The minimum taxable harvest is carefully specified, as are the equivalents between Yemeni measures and those of Iraq (with which most of his appointees, being immigrants, were more familiar). Two different types of grain, e.g., wheat and barley, are not to be added together to make up a taxable total. The canonical tax rates of ten percent and five percent respectively, are to be applied to crops grown on land watered by rain or flowing streams, and land irrigated from wells or impoundments. Due diligence is to be applied to ascertaining the ownership of land; if a man is part-owner of a number of plots, his share of all the harvests is to be assembled in one place for assessment.

The revenue in kind or in money is reserved for God's purposes. The official may draw upon it for his own subsistence and that of his staff, and for the care of wayfarers fatigued by their travels. He is closely circumscribed in disposing of the one-fourth of the revenue destined for relief of the poor. He is to draw up a register of all the poor and needy in his jurisdiction, distinguishing carefully between those who are utterly destitute and those who, while needy, have at least some source of livelihood. He is then to write to the imam informing him of the numbers in each category; Yaḥyā will provide instruction for distribution, according to the current state of the general treasury and the feasibility of assisting the merely needy as well as the destitute.

The imam's preoccupation with rigorous collection of the *zakāt* was due both to a concern for the discharge of Islamic duties and to the collective interest of the community in prosecuting the *jihād.* Far from benefiting personally from Yemeni revenues, he held that consumption of any part of the state revenue was canonically prohibited to descendants of the Prophet; he went so far as to refuse to dry himself or to hide his head from the sun with a cloth belonging to the public treasury.[18] His own modest requirements were satisfied by the income from his property in Hijaz. He assured his biographer-to-be,

> If I were faced with the choice of eating bread and meat belonging to the tithe on my own authority without having bought it with my own money, or of eating carrion to preserve my life and avoid starvation, I would eat the carrion rather than the bread and meat of the tithe, for God has permitted the eating of carrion in case of dire necessity, but not such a use of the tithe.[19]

On the other hand, his policy concerning the use of the treasury for state purposes was flexible, often departing from rigorous observance of the canonical categories of its allocation. He was permanently at war, whether to battle heretical neighbors or to restore fractious subjects to obedience. While he regularly ordered the destruction of capital property—vines, date-palms, buildings, etc.—as a war measure, he required his soldiers to respect private property and upbraided them severely when they violated this injunction. The troops, of which he was in constant need, could thus be sustained only from the public funds, often to the detriment of the claims of the poor. Challenged on this point

> the imam replied that he had disposed of the tithes after the example of the Prophet, as the necessity of the

> moment demanded. When Islam and the Muslims were able to do without it, where the need for these tithes was limited, he had apportioned them according to their categories as far as they would reach; but he did not hesitate to devote these revenues—the only ones the country yielded—in the interest of the community, for the equipment and subsistence of troops, for thanks to them territorial integrity and order were maintained, and with order prosperity was safeguarded. Prosperity, furthermore, must necessarily result in advantage to the poor and less well-off.[20]

Yaḥyā's political values were thus typically consummatory, firmly oriented toward spiritual salvation and obedience to the will of God. His vision was of a community in which a divinely designated leader would ensure the prospering of the true faith and the spiritual welfare of his subjects. He made sure, by force if necessary, that they fulfilled to the letter the ritual requirements of Islam; gave of their wealth for the common good in proportions prescribed by holy writ; accepted without question the leadership of the Prophet's son; and followed him into battle for the single purpose of promoting Islam. In terms of administration, the realization of such a vision required a staff of representatives of the imam impinging closely upon the conduct of the citizen, overseeing his property, and applying the imam's decisions down to the measuring out of a ration of grain to a poor man.

It is clear from the reaction of the Yemenis who had invited him in that this is not what they had had in mind. They had sought a benevolent, prestigious, nonpartisan mediator for their intertribal quarrels. They were now called upon as individuals to adhere rigidly to an austere code of behavior, to give systematically of their wealth, and to go to war with no prospect of a share in booty. These Yemenis were already Muslims; the practical burdens of religion had nevertheless rested lightly on them heretofore. The early years of the Zaidi imamate were absorbed in the effort to nurture among the people new values consonant with those of the ruler.

The Early Zaidi Regime

If the representations of his Ṣa'da petitioners led Yaḥyā to expect that the Yemenis would readily adapt to the sort of regime he contemplated, he was soon disillusioned. He enlisted a small band of supporters in Hijaz and traveled to Yemen, arriving in Ṣa'da in 893 with fifty men. In anticipation of his coming, the opposing factions in the town had already patched up their differences. Their leaders renewed their oaths of allegiance to him and he sent agents into the surrounding country to consolidate his rule. He himself moved as far as the village of Sharafa, southeast of Ṣa'da. We have few details of this first sojurn in Yemen. It is clear, however, that Yaḥyā soon observed that the people were not in fact obeying his commands, nor living in peace with one another as they had sworn to do; he returned abruptly to Hijaz.

During the next four years the social situation in Upper Yemen again deteriorated. Tribal feuds intensified to the previous level; drought conditions returned—as God's punishment, according to some, for the people's disobedience. At length the Ṣa'da community leaders persuaded Yaḥyā to mount another attempt at putting their affairs in order; he returned in 896, this time to remain permanently. No sooner had he settled in Ṣa'da and installed his agents in the countryside than he received an appeal from certain inhabitants of Nejran to mediate their disputes, with assurances of their submission to his authority. The population in the chain of villages in the Wadi Nijran and the surrounding area was still more heterogeneous than at Ṣa'da. It included the Banū al-Ḥārith tribe of the Madhḥij group, and various Hamdān elements, both Bakīl and Ḥāshid. The people were further divided between Muslims and those still adhering to Christianity and Judaism, the latter representing a propertied and wealthy segment of the community. Yaḥyā set forth from Ṣa'da with an escort of Khawlān; as he approached Nejran, representatives of the Hamdān clans came out to meet him and to pledge allegiance to him. The Ḥārith leaders soon came in submission, and the imam spent a few months arranging a balance among the various hostile factions, dispensing justice, effecting the restoration of property wrongfully seized, and appointing officials in the outlying districts. He concluded a reasonably magnanimous concordat with the non-Muslim communities, confirming them in possession of their real estate (which he had initially contemplated expropriating for the Muslims) and imposing a slightly heavier tribute (*jizya*) upon them than the *zakāt* to which the Muslims were subject.[21]

The imam then turned his attention southward from Ṣa'da, where his growing reputation for just rule earned him the nominal submission of numerous clans. The governor of Sanaa, Abū al-'Atāhiya, an appointee of the Yu'firid sovereigns, entered into correspondence with the imam, offering to turn the city over to him.

Al-Hādī's fourteen-year reign, thus propitiously launched, was one of constant warfare to restore discipline over rebellious and sinful subjects, to halt renewed intertribal hostilities, and to extend Zaidi influence southward. Both the peace imposed by the imam and the oaths of loyalty and obedience sworn to him proved remarkably fragile and in constant need of renewal. The Ṣa'da truce of 895 incorporated the Awlād Shākir group of Bakīl tribes, including Dhū Muḥammad and Dhū Ḥusain in the Jabal Baraṭ region southeast of Ṣa'da. Nonetheless, al-Hādī was opposed by force when he visited the area later in the year, and was obliged to lead a military campaign to reinstate his governor, who had been evicted.[22] The Nejran peace was shattered later in the same year. Thereafter, revolts by the Banū al-Ḥārith occurred frequently; six outbreaks requiring the imam's presence are recorded during the decade 898-908.[23] Rebellions took place around Ṣa'da in 899 and 902 among Khawlān and the Wā'ila branch of Shākir, the very tribes whose representatives had twice prevailed upon al-Hādī to order their affairs.

In the south, the objective most anxiously sought was control of Sanaa. After two years of negotiation, Abū al-'Atāhiya, one of the few Yemeni notables to be converted wholeheartedly to Zaidism, arranged the imam's entry into the capital in 900. He held the city only a few months; the Banū Ṭuraif, Abū al-'Atāhiya's kinsmen, took advantage of the imam's absence in Jabal Miswar to provoke a revolt, expel al-Hādī's governor, and reinstate their Yu'firid suzerains. The arrival of reinforcements the next year from far-off Tabaristan enabled the imam to renew operations against Sanaa, which he took by force after sharp fighting with the Ṭuraif and other allies of the Yu'firids. His financial resources were now depleted. The people of Sanaa refused his appeal for a loan to pay his troops; he abandoned the city and withdrew to Ṣa'da. (News of his retreat arrived in Baghdad just in time to forestall the dispatch of an army which the Abbasid court had mustered at Yu'firid request to drive al-Hādī from Yemen.)

The Ismā'īlī 'Alī bin al-Faḍl seized Sanaa for the first time in 905. When 'Alī proceeded to the Tihama, the city revolted against his governor and invited al-Hādī back. Al-Hādī was soon, however, obliged to evacuate the capital upon the approach of a large Ismā'īlī force. Al-Hādī's final presence in Sanaa, in 909, was equally brief, and ended for the same reason.

While accepting force as an instrument of policy, al-Hādī envisaged its use only outside a community made cohesive by common submission to God's commands and those of His designated leader, in the interest of the true faith. He failed to achieve such ideal solidarity within his own territories, and to maintain authority was forced to tactics not much different from those of his war-lord rivals. In 897, the second year of his rule, he had to contend with a band of Wādi'a tribesmen in Wadi Nejran, who had waylaid and plundered a convoy carrying to Ṣa'da the local accumulation of tithes. Al-Hādī proceeded to Shawkān, in the upper reaches of the Wadi, where the leader of the band, Ḥubaish, lived and owned

> many date palms, vineyards, and houses. The imam had members of [Ḥubaish's] own clan exhort him to submit and to return the stolen goods. As he refused, al-Hādī had his palm-trees and vines cut down and one of his houses destroyed. Ḥubaish and his thieving companions fled. But God's justice, which al-Hādī had invoked against him, overtook him. One night as he was preparing to attack the imam's forces, he was stricken ill. He died two days later, and his son soon after him.[24]

Such indiscipline and impiety so disheartened al-Hādī that toward the end of that year he determined once more to abandon Yemen. However, some of the notables were so conciliatory, imploring him to remain and apologizing profusely for the deeds of the miscreants, that he agreed to stay, on condition that all the stolen property be restored.[25]

Given al-Hādī's strict adherence to canonical precepts in raising revenue, his resources were inevitably slender. The people avoided paying their tithes wherever they could do so with impunity; that is, wherever the imam's officials were not at hand to persuade or compel. His appointees were, moreover, not uniformly worthy of his trust. 'Abd al-'Azīz bin Marwān, his governor in Jabal Baraṭ, is said to have made off with accumulated taxes of five thousand dinars.[26] Perhaps al-Hādī's success in secular terms might have been greater had he resorted to pillage as a means of swelling state revenue, as his contemporary, 'Alī bin al-Faḍl, did. The latter, however, abandoned the principal moral source of his authority, loyalty to the Fatimids, and his career left no permanent mark on Yemeni politics.

A millennium has not obliterated al-Hādī's imprint. Certainly he did not see the fruits which grew from the seeds he planted. The changes he instituted were at once less sweeping than those he strived to effect, and qualitatively different. In the simplest terms, he sought to replace tribal values, and their material satisfactions, with the consummatory values of Islam. His general objective was similar to that of the primitive Islamic missionaries of three centuries before, with the addition of the imamate concept. He made only a minor dent in the tribal anarchy of the time; but he accustomed tribal chiefs to the idea that a Zaidi imam was a judicious mediator when their quarrels produced intolerable chaos. His preaching did not persuade the Upper Yemenis to order their lives strictly according to the requirements of their souls' salvation and to abandon the gratifications of raiding, fornication, theft, drunkenness, and brigandage; but the citizens learned to expect Zaidi officials to concern themselves with morality, as their indigenous leaders often did not. Accustomed to the notion that power belongs to one able to seize it by force, the Yemeni people could in time accept the Zaidi refinement that the seizure should be by an ʻAlid and in the name of the faith.

Al-Hādī created no self-sustaining administrative structure. His teachings might have disappeared with him but for the fact that one part of his entourage remained in Yemen as the nucleus of a future aristocracy. Al-Hādī was accompanied by a brother, a first cousin, and his own sons, all of whom left progeny in Yemen; other ʻAlids, closely or remotely related to al-Hādī, followed in succeeding generations. These "sayyids" dispersed and settled in the countryside and towns, but preserved a distinct identity through their patrilineal descent. In the early centuries of Zaidism in Yemen, they served in a sense as the Upper Yemeni conscience, keeping the founder's principles and moral standards present in the minds of the people through long periods of adversity. Respected, as in other Muslim lands, for the *baraka*—charisma—associated with their descent from the Prophet, they often served a practical function in the honored role of peacemaker in private and tribal disputes. They contributed decisively to the gradual development of Zaidi political attitudes among the turbulent tribesmen, to such effect that the major Hamdān groups, Ḥāshid and Bakīl, were to become known as the "two wings" of the imamate, and to contribute the lion's share of its military strength against external foes, regardless of the tribes' restiveness under its discipline.

The Setting of the Ayyūbid Conquest

Several centuries were to elapse before Zaidism became a decisive political force in Yemen. The founder's role was played on a narrow stage embracing Nejran and Ṣaʻda, extending south only occasionally to Sanaa and the Jawf, and never to the coastal plain. Al-Hādī's entry into Yemen coincided with the rise of Ismāʻīlism, and on the broad Yemeni political scene the decisive contest was between Sunnism, symbolized by the Abbasid state, and the Shīʻism embodied in the Fatimid movement, both credible claimants to universal legitimacy within Islam. The Fatimids made two lasting conversions. The mountaineers southwest of Sanaa were won to their cause by Manṣūr al-Yaman and recruited again by ʻAlī al-Ṣulayḥī; they remained attached to the sect and are still known as Banū Ismā'īl. The Yām tribe, a section of Hamdān widely dispersed to the east of the Sarāt, also embraced Ismā'īlism, and provided Yemen with two notable dynasties, the Banū Zuray' and the Ḥātim sultans of Hamdān.

The Zuray'ids were installed in Aden by the Ṣulyaḥid king al-Mukarram Aḥmad. Upon the death of his father the Banū Ma'n, the Ṣulayḥids' vassals in Aden, declared themselves independent and terminated payment of the tribute which was Queen Arwā's dowry. In 1081, as soon as his authority was consolidated, al-Mukarram advanced against the rebels, deposed them, and installed as co-rulers 'Abbās and Mas'ūd, sons of the Yām chief al-Karam al-Jushamī. 'Abbās' son Zuray', from whom the dynasty derives its name, endeavored to assert sole authority. The century-long rule of the family is marked by incessant quarrels and rivalries among its members. The costs of these internecine wars were defrayed by the substantial income from the international trade at Aden and the inland distribution of imported goods. A rough idea of the principality's prosperity is gained from the wealth reportedly left by Bilāl bin Jarīr, a vizir who died about 1151, after governing Aden for a dozen years on behalf of the Zuray'id prince Saba' bin Abī Sa'ūd. Jarīr's estate included 650,000 Maliki dinars, plus 300,000 dinars in Egyptian coin; several camel-loads of silverplate; warehouses full of clothing, perfumes, and other costly merchandise; arms; and horse-trappings, fine textiles, and other luxury articles from North Africa, Egypt, Iraq, Oman, Kirman, and China.[27] Representation of the Fatimid court, which passed to the Zuray'ids upon Queen Arwā's death, lent the dynasty some prestige even in the decline of the Ismā'īlī movement, and much of the Ṣulayḥids' territory was absorbed in this Southern Yemeni statelet.

In the central highlands, politics during the tenth, much of the eleventh, and the first three quarters of the twelfth centuries was a matter of confused intertribal rivalry and warfare, with the customary shifting of coalitions and breaches of sworn loyalty. Magnates included the Ḍaḥḥāk clan, chiefs of Ḥāshid with intermittent influence throughout Hamdān, and the Da''ām shaikhs of Arḥab. They shifted allegiance opportunistically among the rival Islamic sects, with little stability of religious conviction. The last Yu'firids abandoned Sunnism, embraced Ismā'īlism, and were appointed missionaries—*du'āt*—by the Fatimid court: a conversion which failed to prevent their extinction as a dynasty by 'Alī al-Ṣulayḥī. When the Ṣulayḥid grip on the north loosened with the death of the Dā'ī Saba in 1099, control of Sanaa and much of the north passed into the hands of the Ḥātim sultans of Hamdān, chiefs of Yām. Loyal at first to Ismā'īlism, they warred with the Sunnīs in the Tihama and with Zaidi imams based in Ṣa'da. As the Fatimid caliphate declined, this commitment weakened; the last of the line, King 'Alī bin Ḥātim bin Aḥmad, acknowledged the suzerainty of the Zaidi imam Aḥmad bin Sulaimān.

The Zaidi community was no less troubled by conflicting ambitions and challenges to constituted authority than its neighbors. Al-Hādī's eldest son, al-Murtaḍa Muḥammad, was acclaimed imam upon the founder's death in 911. He had little stomach for the endless task of imposing discipline and moral conduct on the turbulent tribesmen; within a year he recalled his agents from the districts and retired to a life of contemplation and scholarship. Of tougher stuff, his brother, al-Nāṣir Aḥmad, spent two decades punishing wickedness, and raiding heretic territory as far as Aden. Even before his death in 943, his three sons quarreled bitterly among themselves. Two of them, al-Manṣūr Yaḥyā and Qāsim al-Mukhtār, claimed the imamate. The ensuing struggle lasted a generation, with the tribes ranging themselves on one side or the other in kaleidoscopic patterns. The Zaidi capital, Ṣa'da, was utterly destroyed and depopulated, to be rebuilt on a new site. The career of al-Manṣūr's son Yūsuf was long (977-1012) and dolorous, as suggested by the title he took: al-Dā'ī—the Claimant. He warred continuously with various Ḥāshid combinations led by the Ḍaḥḥāk shaikhs; with Khawlān; and with the Persian Abnā', who still comprised a distinct element of the population of Sanaa and its environs. His trials encouraged other 'Alids to challenge al-Hādī's direct line for the imamate. Two descendants of the founder's uncle, Muḥammad bin al-Qāsim al-Rassī, (the two "'Iyānī" imams, 977-1012) claimed the dignity for a time. Yemeni Zaidism was so weakened by these divisions that gaps began to appear in the succession when no sayyid had the courage to assert his claim. In 1046 an ʻAlid from the Zaidi state of Daylam in Persia, Abū al-Fatḥ al-Daylamī, appeared in Yemen and proclaimed himself imam. His arrival coincided, unfortunately for the Zaidi cause, with the rise of ʻAlī al-Ṣulayḥī, who, as we have seen, defeated and killed Abū al-Fatḥ in a pitched battle in the Jāḥ. Zaidism was forced underground by the Ṣulyaḥids and the first Hamdān sultans. It revived in the year of Queen Arwā's death (1137) in the person of al-Mutawakkil Aḥmad bin Sulaimān, a sixth-generation descendant of al-Hādī, and a man of genuine stature. His operations against wine-bibbers and fornicators extended over a surprisingly broad area, southward beyond Dhamār. His relations with the Ḥātim sultans in Sanaa alternated between inconclusive war and wary truce. In 1153 he planned an invasion of Aden, which aborted when the Sultan Ḥātim bin Aḥmad, solicitous for his Zurayʻ cousins, bought off the Madhḥij tribesmen the imam had recruited for the expedition.

Imam Aḥmad's intervention in the Tihama hastened the extinction of the Najāḥ state, whose last sovereigns had allowed their power to slip into the hands of incompetent ministers and scheming women. The situation afforded an opportunity for an ambitious Ḥimyarite of the Ruʻainī clan, who had become wealthy through the beneficence of the queen mother, to make a bid for power. He fortified himself in the mountains adjoining the northern Tihama, enlisted a force of the local Khawlān, and led repeated raids onto the coastal plain. Finally he laid protracted siege to the capital, Zabīd, beginning in 1157. The townsfolk appealed in desperation to the Zaidi imam, who assembled a force and entered the city. The reigning Najāḥ prince, Fātik bin Muḥammad bin Fātik, was notorious as a passive sodomist and a masturbator. The outraged imam ordered him executed, and withdrew to the mountains after a stay of one week, leaving Zabīd at the mercy of the insurgents. The Ḥimyarite ʻAlī bin Mahdī took the city in 1159, thus consolidating his control of the Tihama.

This successful warlord was also a megalomaniac who aped the conduct of the Prophet Muḥammad in various superficial ways. He survived his victory at Zabīd by only a few months, but the momentum he generated carried his two sons, who fought between themselves for the succession, on plundering raids inland. It is said that they captured the treasuries of twenty-five Yemeni princes and occupied their castles. Aden resisted, and was besieged in 1172. The Banū Zurayʿ appealed for succor to their Ḥātim kinsmen in Sanaa. The latter formed an alliance with the Hamdān and Madhḥij tribes, and went on to lift the siege and inflict several defeats on the Mahdist forces. The coalition disintegrated, however, before the allies could advance into the Tihama and extinguish the Mahdist regime.

From the foregoing brief account, it may be seen that in one sense there was a Yemeni polity during these troubled centuries. At no time did the values and objectives of would-be rulers and of the population at large agree. Tribes, dynasties, and religious leaders nevertheless acted frequently, if intermittently, over most of Yemen's territory (see figure 3, p. 100) for political ends. The ad hoc, evanescent coalitions formed are characteristic of a segmental pattern of authority, and thus of weakness of the political system as a whole. Some dynasties—the Ṣulayḥids, the Zurayʿids, the Najāḥ—succeeded in assembling substantial material resources, and were wealthy by the standards of the time; but they failed in the essential task of mobilizing the human energies needed to build and defend a viable Yemeni state. The consequent debility made Yemen an attractive target for foreign ambitions, and the country was in fact to become a family colony of the Ayyūbids.

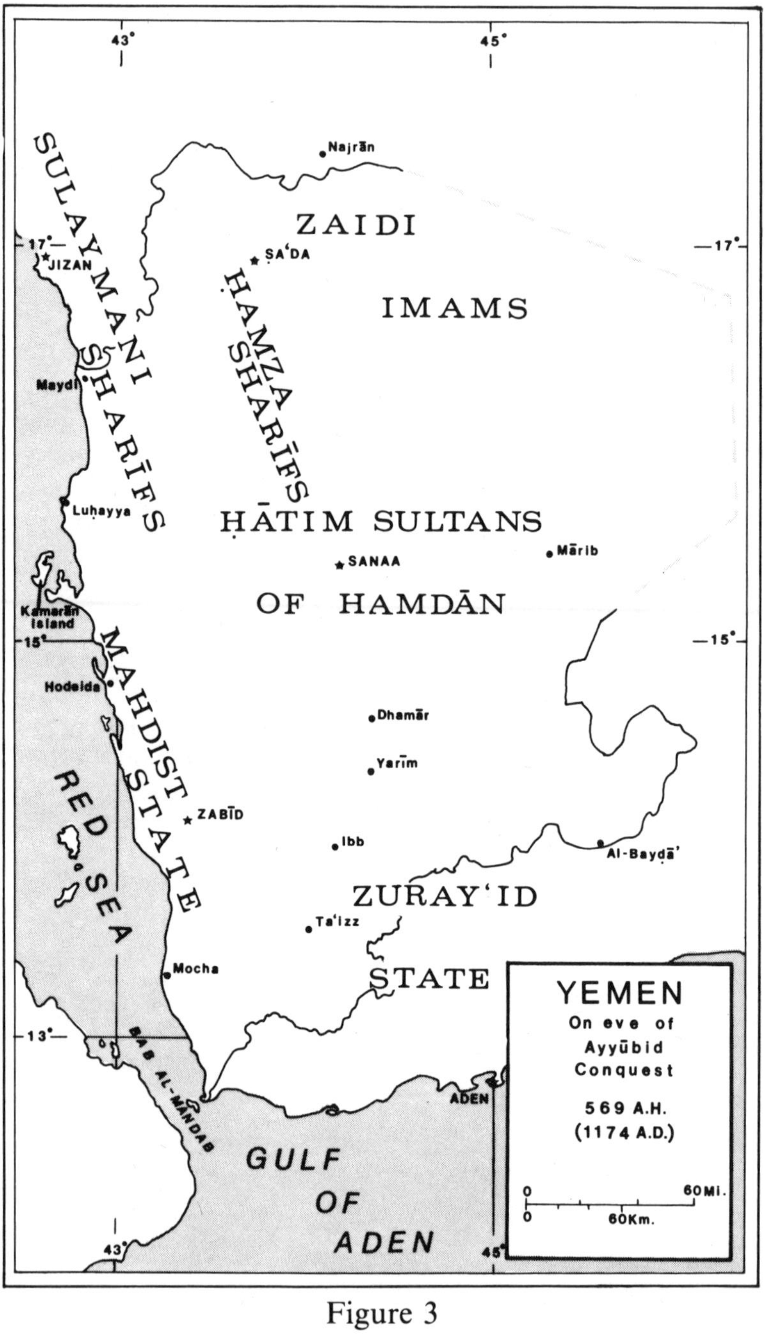
43°
45°
17°
15°
13°
Najrān
ZAIDI
IMAMS
SA'DA
JIZAN
SULAYMANI SHARĪFS
ḤAMZA SHARĪFS
Maydi
Luḥayya
ḤĀTIM SULTANS OF HAMDĀN
SANAA
Mārib
Kamarān Island
MAHDIST STATE
Hodeida
Dhamār
Yarīm
RED SEA
ZABĪD
Ibb
Al-Bayḍā'
ZURAY'ID STATE
Ta'izz
Mocha
BAB AL-MANDAB
ADEN
GULF OF ADEN
YEMEN
On eve of Ayyūbid Conquest
569 A.H. (1174 A.D.)
0
60 MI.
0
60 Km.

Figure 3

5
The Rasūlid State

The Ayyūbid Occupation

As power was transferred from the last Ayyūbid ruler of Yemen to the first Rasūlid sovereign by a subtle transition, without political upheaval, it is of interest to examine briefly the circumstances of this colonization of Yemen. The energetic and talented Ayyūbid clan, by origin Kurds from Azerbaijan, had entered the service of Nūr al-Dīn Maḥmūd al-Zanjī, sultan of Aleppo, in his wars for the defense of Syria against the Crusaders. Disorder in the decaying Fatimid state invited outside intervention in Egypt, possession of which was disputed between the Crusaders and the Syrians, acting in the name of the Abbasid caliph. After a five-year conflict, Nūr al-Dīn's Ayyūbid general, Asad al-Dīn Shīrkūh, prevailed over the Franks, and in 1169 was installed as vizir by the powerless Fatimid caliph, al-'Āḍid. Shīrkūh soon died, and his position passed to his nephew Ṣalāḥ al-Dīn bin Ayyūb (Saladin). In 1171, when al-'Āḍid was on the point of death, Saladin proclaimed the end of the schismatic caliphate and returned Egypt to Sunnism and allegiance to the Abbasids.

The conquest of Egypt had been an Ayyūbid family accomplishment. It was conducted under Nūr al-Dīn's authority, however. Saladin and his brothers feared that their suzerain might divest them of Egypt so as to reserve its revenues for himself. They therefore cast about for some domain which they might rule in undisputed independence. Saladin's brother Tūrānshāh, whose Egyptian fiefs were inadequate to sustain his lavish tastes, made a reconnaissance into Nubia, but found that land unpromising.[1] His attention then turned toward Yemen. The jurist 'Umāra al-Yamanī wrote his history for the specific purpose of encouraging Tūrānshāh to undertake the conquest of Yemen; the rhymed climax of this work emphasizes the abundant wealth of the country and the debility of the existing government there.[2]

The Mahdist regime in the Yemeni Tihama ended mention of the Abbasid caliph in the Friday prayers. This omission aroused concern in Baghdad, and the caliph appealed to his vassals in Syria to restore his nominal authority in Yemen. Nūr al-Dīn was preoccupied by operations against the Crusaders, so the mission devolved upon Saladin, who was only too glad of a sanctioned opportunity to pursue an already existing aim. He fitted out Tūrānshāh with an army, which arrived in Yemen in 1173 and had little difficulty in subduing the disunited territory. Tūrānshāh added another title to his name[3] and ordered it coupled with that of the caliph in the prayers. He reported his success through proper channels: to his elder brother, to Nūr al-Dīn, and finally to the caliph, from whom he sought and received confirmation of the legitimacy of his rule in Yemen. Three generations of princes held the territory during the period 1173-1229: al-Mu'aẓẓam Tūrānshāh; al-Mu'izz Tughtakīn, another brother of Saladin; Tughtakīn's two sons, al-Mu'izz Ismā'īl and al-Nāṣir Ayyūb; and al-Mas'ūd Yūsuf, a youthful grandson of Saladin.

Thirst for wealth and power was clearly the salient motive in the Ayyūbid invasion. We may doubt that Saladin and Tūrānshāh would have undertaken the operation simply to restore the symbol of Islamic orthodoxy and unity. The rulers jealously kept the country's revenues for themselves, and repeatedly took action to exclude even their own close relatives from influence there.[4]

Tūrānshāh's sojourn was brief. He did not enjoy life in Yemen, and sought the broader stage of Egypt and Syria for his ambitions. He died in 1197, and the Mameluke governors he had left in Yemen took the opportunity to act independently within their provinces and to war among themselves. The current Zaidi imam took advantage of the situation to make territorial gains in the north. Seeing the country in danger of slipping from his grasp, Saladin sent Tughtakīn to reassert control. Tughtakīn understood in some measure that if the cow is to be milked not only must her horns be held but she must also be fed. He improved the facilities of Aden's port in order to foster a revival of trade. Seventy or eighty ships called annually at the port of his time, and annual revenue averaging 600,000 dinars was delivered to the treasury in a fortress in Ta'izz.[5] The figure compares favorably with the 500,000 which Queen Arwā at first received from Aden. (As a matter of perspective, we may note that in the year 1254 the revenue of the important Egyptian port of Damietta was estimated at 30,000 dinars.[6]) Tughtakīn was, at the same time, determined to maximize his revenues, and tried to appropriate to the state all Yemeni agricultural land, as the Ayyūbids had done in Egypt:

> He felt a compulsion to acquire Yemeni land wherever it might be located. He summoned appraisers and ordered them to evaluate it. He wanted it all to belong to the royal household: whoever desired to cultivate any part of it had to apply to the royal chancery and rent whatever land he wished to till. This caused extreme hardship for the people of Yemen. A group of respected Yemenis assembled in a mosque, where they stayed three days, fasting during the day and keeping vigil all night. At dawn on the fourth day one of them emerged, crying aloud "O Sultan of Heaven, take away from the Muslims the evil of the sultan of the earth."[7]

Providentially, Tughtakīn died at this very moment, perhaps of poison.

The Ayyūbids did not bother to advance consummatory values as a legitimizing basis for their rule.[8] Aside from a common adherence to Sunnī Islam and the acknowledgment of Abbasid suzerainty, few political values were shared between the Yemeni public and these intrusive kings beyond the common interest in economic prosperity. Legitimacy was thus maintained at the crudest level by preponderant force. The Ayyūbids could not, obviously, expect to recruit loyal troops among the Yemenis themselves; they depended upon medieval Islam's device of servile military forces. In the generation after Saladin, the Mamelukes had become household armies of individual Ayyūbid princes, each contingent maintaining a separate identity through endogamous marriage, with advancement in rank determined by proved merit. Slaves only in a limited sense, the soldiers had to be paid to fight. They were often an effective weapon in the hands of the princes, but, as they developed consciousness of their own potential power, they became a dangerous one, requiring careful manipulation. They extinguished the Ayyūbid state in Egypt and Syria when dynastic quarrels paralyzed defense against the Mongols, and ruled Egypt thereafter until the Ottoman conquest in the sixteenth century. In Yemen, under the Ayyūbids and their Rasūlid successors, they often acted as political arbiters at critical junctures. The megalomaniac al-Mu'izz Ismā'īl was assassinated not by the Yemenis whom he had tyrannized, but by his own Mamelukes.

Three distinctive features of the Ayyūbid regime in Yemen passed to the house of Rasūl along with political power. The first was an interest in personal and exclusive possession of wealth and authority, overriding ties of family solidarity and other worldly aspirations. The second was a rudimentary appreciation of the role of organized, on-going administration in maximizing state revenues, a concept absent in the Zaidi imamate discussed in the preceding chapter. The last was the reliance upon servile forces, or Mameluke armies, a source either of state power or of turmoil according to specific historical circumstances.

Both the early imamate and the Ayyūbid-Rasūlid systems contrast strangely with what we may glimpse of an independent regime in Hadramaut, a territory which the Ayyūbids occupied only briefly but which was absorbed by their successors. In the year 1216, its former sultan, 'Abdullah bin Rashīd bin Abī Qaḥṭān al-Ḥimyarī, died.

> He was a just and celebrated prince, possessing knowledge of the *ḥadīth*, frequenting people of knowledge and austerity. His sleep was undisturbed during the years of reign, and his era was the best which Hadramaut had known. He was accustomed to say, "There are three features of my country on which I pride myself among sultans: there is no land-tax; there are no thieves; and there are no indigent persons." He renounced rule toward the end of his life, and inclined toward submission.[9] Criticized for his abdication, he replied, "I can find no just man to succeed me."[10]

The aims Sultan 'Abdullah was thus gratified at achieving would, we may suppose, have been incomprehensible to Saladin's sons. His values might have appeared downright impious in the eyes of an imam, in whose view the payment of taxes and the giving of alms were religious duties. Lest an idyllic impression be left of Hadrami society at this time, we should note that in his retirement the sultan "went out to make peace between two tribes, and was murdered by treachery."[11]

The Rasūlids and Their Accession

According to the genealogists, the remote ancestors of this dynasty were of the Azd tribe and were therefore descendants of Qaḥṭān. Displaced by the collapse of the Mārib Dam they moved north, stopping in the Tihama and Hijaz. One clan attained to the rule of Syria as the Ghassānids, and allied itself with Byzantium. The last monarch of this line became a Muslim but, subjected to an affront by an 'Adnānī Muslim, reverted to Christianity and moved to Constantinople. His children, Muslims again, drifted to Central Asia and lived among the Turkmen without, however, losing their family identity. In the twelfth century one of them, Muḥammad bin Hārūn, migrated westward to Baghdad, entered the caliph's service, and distinguished himself as a diplomat, earning the sobriquet of Rasūl—messenger—by which his descendants are known. He later moved with his sons to Syria and Egypt in the employ of the Ayyūbids. The family's position and talent were such that the Ayyūbids regarded the group as potential rivals. The Ayyūbids considered placing the Rasūlids in charge of Yemen (yet to be conquered), but ultimately eliminated them from the Egyptian and Syrian scene by including them in Tūrānshāh's expedition in the south.

Five Rasūlids figured in the Ayyūbid conquest: 'Alī Shams al-Dīn, son of Muḥammad the Messenger; and his four young sons, entitled Badr al-Dīn, Nūr al-Dīn, Fakhr al-Dīn and Sharaf al-Dīn. All five served in responsible posts under successive Ayyūbid sultans. The circumstances of the transfer of authority in Yemen are mystifying unless seen in the context of events in the north. Upon Saladin's death in 1192, his brothers and sons warred among themselves for the throne and for undisputed possession of fragments of the empire he had erected in Syria, Iraq, and Egypt. Two sons reigned precariously for a total of eight years. Then a third son, al-Kāmil Muḥammad, took possession of Egypt, but was unable to hold it in the face of the superior forces of Saladin's brother, al-'Ādil Abū Bakr, who had seized the Asian territories. Al-Kāmil was obliged to submit to his uncle's suzerainty. Such was the situation in 1215 when, in Yemen, Tughtakīn's second son, al-Nāṣir Ayyūb, died of poison administered by the Kurdish commander of the Mamelukes. The late king's mother sent for a distant relative, a great-grandson of Saladin's brother Shāhanshāh Nūr al-Dīn, to assume rule. Al-Kāmil, however, had aspirations for his own branch of the clan, and fitted out his adolescent son al-Mas'ūd Yūsuf with a strong force. With the advice and help of the Rasūl brothers, Mas'ūd succeeded in capturing his rival and sent him in chains to Egypt.

Mas'ūd appointed the Rasūlid Nūr al-Dīn 'Umar his atabeg, an office which covered command of the troops as well as counsel to the young prince. Friendship between the two grew close during the fourteen years of Mas'ūd's reign in Yemen. Al-Kāmil succeeded to the Ayyūbid throne upon al-'Ādil's death in 1218, and some years later summoned Mas'ūd to govern Syria on his behalf.

Mas'ūd's departure was marked by a thorough looting of

Yemen, and by the contingent transfer of power to his atabeg. He caused an announcement to be broadcast in the port towns inviting those merchants who wished to travel to Egypt to accompany his suite. They assembled, with their merchandise, in Aden, where he offered to buy it all, exempting them from payment of the usual tithe. They took the bait, and received in payment drafts upon the revenues of various districts in Yemen. In the quaint words of al-Khazrajī's nineteenth-century translator,

> they cried out, "Alas! Ruin!" But he took no notice of them, and the greater part of them never received one tittle therefrom.[12]

Seventy ships were not enough to load the spoils of this transaction:

> Among the rest were 1000 eunuchs, 500 cases of gorgeous stuffs and clothing, 300 loads of aloes wood yet fresh and of the finest ambergris, 400 slave girls, of gems, pearls and precious stones an untold store, 70,000 pieces of Chinese brocade wrought with gold, and of works of art what cannot be limited as to number.[13]

Mas'ūd addressed Nūr al-Dīn thus:

> Should I die, thou art more worthy of the principality of Yemen than my brothers; for thou hast served me, and I have recognized in thee loyalty and devotion. And if I live, thou art as thou hast been; beware, then, that you leave not any one of my kin to enter Yemen even though my son, Malik Kāmil[14] should come unto thee folded up in a letter.[15]

Nūr al-Dīn expressed fear that his own three brothers would contest the power thus placed in his hands. Mas'ūd undertook to deal with this problem by seizing the three Rasūlids and sending them as captives to Egypt.

The contingency for which Mas'ūd had made provision soon occurred. He died in Mecca before completing his journey to

Egypt. Nūr al-Dīn played his cards cautiously. He sent a handsome gift to Sultan al-Kāmil with assurances that Yemen was ruled on behalf of the Ayyūbids. Within a couple of years, perceiving that his suzerains were too preoccupied with their internecine quarrels and their struggle with the Crusaders to intervene, Nūr al-Dīn proclaimed himself sultan of Yemen with the title al-Manṣūr. He asserted his independence by striking coins in his own name; by causing prayers to be said in his name in the mosques; and by eliciting formal authentication of his rule from the Abbasid caliph. Shortly he was contending on equal terms with the Ayyūbids for control of the Islamic shrines at Mecca.

The Rasūlid State

As the accompanying genealogical chart (figure 4) indicates, the house of Rasūl ruled over the greater portion of Yemeni territory for well over two centuries. Theirs was thus the most durable Sunnī regime which South Arabia has known in the Islamic era. It may well have been the most prosperous also; it was certainly richer than twentieth-century Yemen. In part this affluence was due to a revival of trade. As the Abbasid caliphate declined and Iraq fell into disorder, the node of the east-west trade shifted back from the Persian Gulf to the Red Sea. Aden and lesser South Arabian ports once again became key entrepôts for commerce; Yemeni merchants were stationed in the important cities of Egypt, and many Egyptian traders conducted affairs in Yemen. Agriculture also prospered. Exactions of the Rasūlid regime upon the country's peasants were severe; but the demands were systematic, usually predictable, and just flexible enough to avoid crossing the point of diminishing returns.

Fortuitously, the Rasūlid state was not the object of imperial ambitions on the part of other major powers of its time. The last Ayyūbids and the early Mameluke sultans were too absorbed with the Crusades to look south beyond the holy cities of the Hijaz. The Baghdad caliphate was destroyed in 1258 by Hulagu, and defense against his successors in command of the Mongol hordes continued to absorb Egyptian and Levantine energies. The Ottoman state, founded in 1297,

THE RASŪLID SULTANS

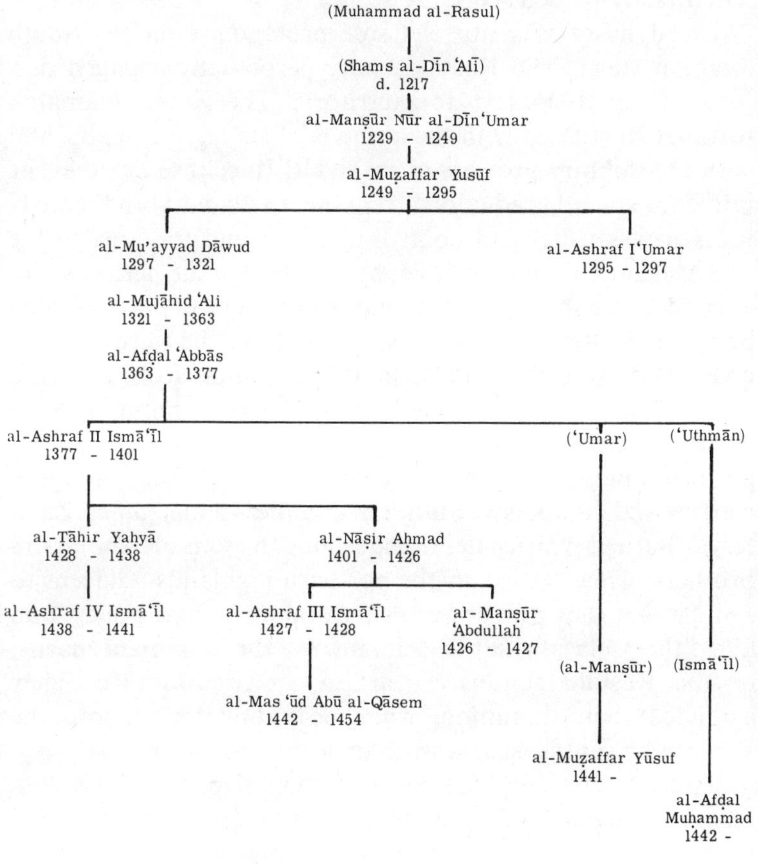

NOTES:

1. Names in parentheses are of individuals who did not reign.
2. Several Rasūlid princes contended for the throne during the decade beginning 1442.

Figure 4

required two centuries to consolidate Anatolia, reduce Byzantium, and recruit the strength to expand southward to Egypt and the peninsula. By the time Portuguese navigators presented a challenge in the Red Sea and Indian Ocean which neither the Mamelukes nor the Ottomans could ignore, the Rasūlids had already passed from the scene.

The dynasty was not the sole protagonist on the South Arabian stage. The Rasūlids were perpetually engaged in a three-cornered contest for territory. The Zaidi imamate's fortunes fluctuated with the abilities of successive imams and with the military prowess of its rivals. In eclipse at times, its influence spread gradually during the Rasūlid era. In the early years it was usually in control of Ṣa'da and the area to the southeast, including the Jawf; by the close of the period it had expanded due south, and the imams were typically in control of Sanaa and Dhamār, raiding south to Ibb. The third party in contention were the Ḥamza sharīfs, a spin-off from Zaidism. Descendants of Qāsim al-Rassī and early immigrants to Yemen in al-Hādī's wake, the Ḥamza clan produced a distinguished imam, al-Manṣūr 'Abdullah (d. 1217), a doughty warrior and compulsive author of countless pious tomes. Zaidi fervor burned with a paler flame among the sons of 'Abdullah's brothers. They settled in the northern highlands adjacent to Asir, where they pursued a secular, opportunistic policy, and allied themselves with the Zaidi imams, the Sulaimānī sharīfs, or the Rasūlid sultans, according to circumstance. They extended their dominion, when occasion offered, into the Tihama or southeast toward Sanaa.

Three factors combine to give a characteristically violent flavor to Rasūlid annals: the constant pressure from their rivals to the north; the unremitting effort to impose obedience upon restive tribes in the Tihama and the foothills; and recurrent struggles among the Rasūlids themselves for a monopoly of power.

The family disharmony we noted among the Ayyūbids was intensified among Rasūl's descendants. The founder devised a means of removing his brothers from Yemen. His nephew, Asad al-Dīn Muḥammad bin Ḥasan, remained in the sensitive post of governor of Sanaa. Asad al-Dīn's loyalties were remarkably fickle; he was occasionally in league with the Zaidi imam against al-Manṣūr's authority, and was imprisoned more than once in the sultan's Ta'izz fortress. The sultan's leniency in pardoning and reinstating him was his own undoing. Disturbed by reports that the sultan intended to divest him of his command in favor of the sultan's own grandson, Asad al-Dīn incited al-Manṣūr's Mamelukes to assassinate him, which they did in 1251.[16]

Al-Manṣūr had already created a murky situation respecting his succession. His weakness for a young wife, Bint Ḥawza, led him to advance her two sons, Mufaḍḍal and Fā'iz, over his eldest son, Muẓaffar, and he had required the Mamelukes (who now numbered about a thousand) to swear allegiance to Mufaḍḍal as his heir. This oath notwithstanding, the Mamelukes elected to acknowledge as sultan the late king's nephew, Fakhr al-Dīn Abū Bakr bin Ḥasan bin 'Alī, Asad al-Dīn's brother. However, Muẓaffar's daughter, al-Dār al-Shamsī,[17] and his mother, contrived the escape of Tāj al-Dīn, a eunuch devoted to Muẓaffar, from the Zabīd prison where Bint Ḥawza had had him confined. The two ladies provided him money, with which he was able to raise a force of irregulars and neutralize the Zabīd garrison. Muẓaffar, who had been governor of al-Mahjam, in the northern Tihama, meanwhile advanced on Zabīd, recruiting troops among the tribes along the way. Fakhr al-Dīn moved from his fief at Fashāl[18] to intercept him; his Mamelukes deserted him. Taken prisoner, he soon escaped and made his way to his brother Asad al-Dīn at Sanaa. Maẓaffar soon consolidated his hold over the Tihama and Lower Yemen, then moved northward.

Asad al-Dīn was at this time hard pressed by the Zaidi imam, who had seized Sanaa and besieged the adjacent fort, Barāsh, which Asad al-Dīn still held. Asad found it expedient to join forces with the imam against Muẓaffar, who was advancing with a strong army. No sooner had the sultan occupied Sanaa than he received news of the arrival in Yemen of his two uncles, Abū Bakr and Asad al-Dīn's father, Ḥasan, who had been released from their confinement in Egypt. Concluding a hasty truce with the imam, the sultan hastened to meet these kinsmen, whom he promptly arrested and incarcerated for life.

Following his father's precedent, Muẓaffar pardoned Asad al-Dīn and restored him to command in the north. The prince's treasonable resources were not yet exhausted; after a further betrayal in 1260, he surrendered himself to Muẓaffar, who reunited him with his father and uncle in their enforced retirement.

This experiment in shared power during the first two reigns produced results as unsatisfactory as it had among the Ayyūbids in the north; it was not repeated by the Rasūlids. Although later sultans avoided placing any relative except their own sons in sensitive positions, they frequently had to assert their succession by force of arms. Al-Ashraf I, to whom Muẓaffar turned over power before his death, was challenged by his brother al-Mu'ayyad; the latter was captured and imprisoned, but was released by the Mamelukes and enthroned following al-Ashraf's early demise. Al-Mujāhid was involved in a protracted, bitter struggle for the throne with his cousin, al-Ẓāhir. Al-Ashraf II was overthrown by the troop commanders in favor of his uncle, al-Ṭāhir. Finally, the dynasty foundered after two concluding decades of strife among several Rasūlid princes.

Correlative to the concentration of power was the consistent Rasūlid endeavor to maximize capabilities by extracting as much revenue as practicable from their domain. In the territories firmly under the sultan's control, the gathering of revenue—a principal object of public administration of the period—was conducted systematically by a body of functionaries which had many of the attributes of a bureaucracy: the requirement of specialized training; a complex code of regulations; the opportunity for social mobility; and a well-developed sense of prerogative. As we have seen, the rules applied by the Zaidi imam al-Hādī's officials were simple, and derived solely from the Koran and *ḥadīth*; under the imam's close guidance, a fairly rudimentary knowledge sufficed for their interpretation and application. Rasūlid officials had a much more complex tax system to administer. While the core of the rules had roots in the *sharī'a*, many other regulations were introduced for the sake of uniformity and increasing revenue. In the field of agriculture, for example, the unit of length for the measurement of land areas was standardized for the first time, eliminating previous abuses.[19] The terms of tenant-landowner agreements became a matter of legislation.[20] Tax rates, rather than immutable, became a function of policy. We even find a land reclamation project undertaken on the sultan's initiative:

> Now the district called Nūrī was an extensive waste lying between Ḥays and Zabīd . . . so he built therein a mosque, placing therein two imams. And he made it a condition that whoever should settle there should be treated considerately in respect of his sown crops. So people settled there . . . until there had sprung up a nice village, from which the people derived a great benefit.[21]

Concern for the peasant's welfare is a recurring theme in the chronicles. Al-Mujāhid introduced the system of averaging production of a peasant's land over several years as a basis of taxation (rather than simply using the historical maximum), and ordered the deduction from the taxable produce of the proportion of grain to be sown as seed.[22] Al-Ashraf II abolished an oppressive tax on cotton introduced by a deputy tax-collector in the days of the sultan's predecessor.

Assessments on commercial traffic through the ports were second only to taxes on the produce of the land as a revenue source, and the state developed minutely detailed regulations for customs administration. Modern scholars have described a manuscript of the early fifteenth century which amounts to a complete customs classification and tariff.[23] The sophistication of the customs regime to which the document applied is suggested by the fact that, as one example, the category "textiles and articles of clothing" lists eighty-one carefully distinguished items. Ibn al-Mujāwir describes in detail the efficient methods of the Aden customs inspectors in preventing smuggling.[24]

Special training, obviously, was requisite to the staffing of such an administration, and education in the fundamentals was provided, for the most part, in institutions established as pious endowments by the sultan, members of his family, or other well-to-do persons. Such a school might be staffed with an imam and one or more instructors, the whole supported, supposedly in perpetuity, by agricultural land donated in mortmain (*waqf*) and administered by the state. The first Rasūlid, al-Manṣūr, founded six such schools, and one of his eunuchs established a number of others.[25] Al-Manṣūr's successors (and their womenfolk) followed the precedent, and according to a survey conducted in 1391, the number of "colleges" and mosques, where instruction in the traditional Islamic learning was also conducted, reached 230 in Zabīd, the winter capital, alone. Whether obtained in such endowed schools or from tutors in the homes of the wealthy, the learning acquired was prerequisite to service in the civil administration as well as in the court system.

Such endowments normally provided for the subsistence and education of a specified number of orphans or other poor children. This implies that education and employment in public service provided an avenue to upward mobility for the less privileged strata of Yemeni society. Within the bureaucracy, mobility was lateral as well. As indicated by the content of the biographical dictionaries pertaining to the period[26] and the obituaries interspersed in the chronicles, a judge or administrator might serve in up to a half-dozen posts throughout Lower Yemen during his career.

Jurisdictional rivalries occurred among the branches of the Rasūlid administration. Sultan al-Mu'ayyad was persuaded by an official in his chancery to transfer the handling of trust estates (*awqāf*) from the judicial system, where responsibility for them had previously lain, to the exchequer.[27] A later sultan was obliged to intervene in a dispute between the governor of Zabīd and the chief judge of that province over jurisdiction in a civil case:

> The judge . . . wrote to the Sultan and complained of the governor in respect of his encroachment on the jurisdiction of the sacred canon law. The Sultan gave command to someone on the instant to go to the governor and turn him out of his house, making him go to the house of the sacred canon-law judge as an act of equity to the judge and as a mark of respect to the judge and to the august law.

> The judge required the governor to appear before the Sultan. . . . When they arrived with him at the gate of the palace the Sultan drew nigh and reproached him, loading him with very violent vituperation. And had it not been that the Sultan had an affection towards him for his good contact toward the people, he would not have escaped.[28]

It should surprise no student of bureaucracies that Rasūlid civil servants at times thwarted the sultan's purposes, and took measures which raised for him knotty problems of policy. On one occasion al-Ashraf I ordered his minister to effect a reduction of tax assessments against the peasants following a severe locust infestation,

> but the wezir continued to press them . . . (and) did not give effect to any indulgence toward them as the Sultan had commanded. So they complained to the Sultan a second time, who then wrote to him: "O such-a-one, withdraw thy hand from them, and disperse them not against us, for it would be hard for us to collect them together again."[29]

It would be interesting to have fuller details on the inertia of the bureaucrats in one Tihama district in which al-Ashraf II ordered a tax reduction to encourage the local people to defend themselves against incursions of predatory tribes. "But the tax-collectors did not consent to this," says the historian laconically, "as they had to consider another matter also."[30] The same monarch had the unenviable job of deciding the standard measure according to which the grain produced by Tihama peasants was calculated for taxation. Fixed at 240 dirhams early in the Rasūlid era, it was increased by 80 dirhams by a predecessor of al-Mujāhid and remained there until late in that monarch's reign.[31] In 1360, another 40 dirhams was added by the Zabīd controller of excise on is own initiative.

> Later on the controllers of exise in Zabīd made a plaything of it, and they would increase its size in an unascertainable manner. When the question became a scandal in the reign

> of Sultan Malik Afḍal, and when Malik Ashraf began to reign, then the Sultan . . . took the matter into his consideration, and it was ascertained that this state of things was detrimental to the subjects and of no benefit to the exchequer. So . . . the Sultan . . . commanded that the capacity should be established permanently at four hundred dirhams saying: "Were we to abolish the whole of the scandalous augmentations at once, this would itself be manifestly a scandalous thing; therefore will we abolish them little by little."[32]

A dearth of grain then intervening, however, the sultan altered his decision in the interest of the consuming public by fixing the measure at 500 dirhams.

> This increase became permanent, and thereby all the cultivators were made to suffer loss, while everybody else besides them were gainers.[33]

Sultan al-Afḍal intervened against bureaucratic freewheeling in the customs. One year he broke precedent by wintering in Aden rather than Zabīd. While there, he occupied himself by "dealing out measures of justice such as are not usual. He gave robes of honour to the ship captains, and abolished many things recently introduced by the collectors of taxes. So the merchants departed recounting his praises and his abundant gifts in all quarters by land and by sea."[34]

The only theoretical limitations upon the sultan's authority were those divinely imposed. He appointed the high officials, and had the unquestioned right to remove or punish a functionary with whom he was displeased. At the middle and lower levels, appointments were made by the chief minister or the chief justice (the two offices were at times combined) and by the senior provincial officials. The Rasūlid pattern of authority was thus in principle hierarchical, but in practice had many pyramidal features through the discretion often left to the bureaucracy. We should not be misled by historical reference to the granting of "fiefs" by the sultan to favored individuals, usually his sons. Such appointments were not hereditary, were held during the sultan's pleasure, and did not involve the delegation of civil administration, which continued to be the function of the sultan's officials. Such grants entitled the recipient to the official revenues of the area, usually in exchange for defense duties in the border regions. The Rasūlid state was not feudal in the medieval European sense, nor even in the way that the Ayyūbid state in Egypt and Syria was. (We should except from this statement the province of Dhofar, conquered in 1279 in retaliation for the local ruler's interference with international shipping. The area was left largely to its own devices thereafter, under the rule of a collateral branch of the Rasūlid dynasty.) We do not read of tribal or aristocratic leaders having prominent state functions, as they did under the later Ṣulayḥids and in the adjacent Zaidi and Ḥamza regimes. Only in the final decades of Rasūlid rule did the relaxation of central authority afford an opportunity for the Ṭāhirids, protégés of the Rasūlids, to usurp their place.

If power and wealth were the Rasūlid monarchs' salient values, they nevertheless had less instrumental ones, shared with their subjects. The tax burden they laid upon the Yemenis was a heavy one, and we may assume that the peasants and merchants derived no satisfaction simply from meeting the exactions of the sultan's fiscal agents. Had no goals save economic ones been pursued, force alone would likely have been inadequate to sustain the regime as a prosperous, viable state commanding international prestige. They were under constant pressure from hostile neighbors, over a period comparable in duration with, say, that of the Bourbons in France. One is led to the conclusion that, in a number of respects, the attitudes and conduct of the Rasūlids corresponded with the values and aspirations of much of the population they governed.

The dynasty was accepted by the Yemenis as of aristocratic and indigenous origin. An incident related by Khazrajī suggests a certain feeling of Qaḥṭānī solidarity against the Zaidi aristocracy, who were of course 'Adnānīs. In 1252, when the unreliable governor of Sanaa, Prince Asad al-Dīn, defected from Sultan al-Muẓaffar, he joined forces with the Zaidi imam and advanced against the sultan's army commanded by the eunuch Tāj al-Dīn. However, when Asad al-Dīn

> saw the multiplicity of the Imam's troops and their repeated arrivals in his support, there came upon him the old Arabian zeal and the warmth of the pristine Ya'rubian blood-relationship, and he cautioned the eunuch Tāj al-Dīn, recommending him to go back, and saying to him: "Verily, if thou return with those forces safe and numerous, our lord the Sultan will come up and no one will be able to stand before him.[35]

The implication of the passage is that the governor's second betrayal was prompted by his unwillingness, as a Qaḥṭānī, to permit Qaḥṭānī forces to suffer an overwhelming defeat at the hands of the Adnānī imam.

As men of their time, the Rasūlids were conscientious and devout Muslims, and Sunnīs from the first. We have seen how the legitimacy of the Ṣulayḥids, despite their benevolent motives, was compromised in the eyes of the majority of Yemenis by their obedience to an anti-caliph. The Rasūl family came to Yemen from Egypt, where the Ḥanafī school of Sunnī jurisprudence was already dominant, but they soon embraced the Shāfi'ī rite to which most Southern Arabians subscribed. A tradition, complete with chain of transmission, gives the conversion a supernatural aura:

> Says Janadī in his history: "My teacher Aḥmad bin 'Alī al-Ḥarāzī informed me, basing himself on what he had been taught by the Imam 'Abdullah Muḥammad bin Ibrāhīm al-'Aṣalī, teacher of *ḥadīth* at Zabīd, and one of the instructors of Manṣūr, saying: 'The Sultan Nūr al-Dīn Manṣūr informed me, in these very words, that he was of the Ḥanafī school of orthodoxy, but that he saw the Prophet in a dream, who said to him "O 'Umar, thou hast passed over to the Shāfi'ī school of orthodoxy." So he rose in the morning and began to examine Shāfi'ī books, becoming confident in their way of reasoning.' "[36]

The Rasūlids strove to project an image of rule in accord

with established Islamic moral principle. In 1295 Sultan al-Muẓaffar, shortly before his death, transferred power to his son, al-Ashraf I; he had the act proclaimed to the public in terms strikingly faithful to the Islamic political theory we examined in chapter 4:

> He is our esteemed son, our luminous meteor, our provision laid up according to our desire, our aider through whom we hope for the prosperity of the dominions and people, wishing for him from God forgiveness and salvation in the resurrection. We have enjoined unto him some of the means of repelling the attacks of enemies and the protection of subjects, the beacons also of gentleness and consideration. . . . We have prescribed unto him that he prove himself to you clement and merciful, munificent and generous, so long as you obey him. . . . But whoso shall show himself perverse, forsake obedience and rebel, verily he shall abase him, even though the whole world cleave unto him by the tie of blood-relationship.[37]

Reflecting the orthodox Muslim respect for the community consensus, the proclamation was issued by the council of notables of the realm, not as the sovereign's personal act. The Rasūlids sought at least the appearance of public support for major decisions. The opinion of high state officials, it is recorded, was unanimous as to the accession of al-Ashraf II upon his father's death.[38] Another case in point is the manner in which Sultan al-Mu'ayyad dealt with the case of Judge Jalāl al-Dīn Muḥammad in 1317. Although the judge had "experience that had drawn milk from all the teats of fortune,"[39] he made a faulty medical prognosis concerning an illness from which the Sultan was suffering. Assuming the malady terminal, he committed the lèse-majesté of writing to al-Mu'ayyad's nephew (not his son, the heir-designate) urging him to claim the throne, and furthermore wrote to officials in the chief towns in his support. The sultan recovered, put down his nephew's rebellion, and arrested the judge, whom he chained up in the castle at Ta'izz. The decision, however,

> took place in a council held by the Sultan with a large number of the jurists of the highlands and of the low countries of the seacoast, unanimity being secured in the decision.[40]

There is a final element in the propriety of Rasūlid rule as seen by their subjects. The expectations of the general run of the people were modest, and when these were frustrated the blame was attributed either to divine providence or to the maleficence of isolated individual officials rather than to the political regime per se. We have referred to a number of occasions on which the sultans responded favorably and effectively to public grievances. While the chroniclers leave us less well informed about public opinion than we might desire, it is plausible to infer that the people considered their rights, as they saw them, secured as well under Rasūlid government as under any alternative of which they could realistically conceive.

This was a workable political configuration which, for over a century, furnished the monarch the resources needed for effective pursuit of aims approved by the generality of the people. Coercion was used intensively, but usually for ends regarded as legitimate by both sovereign and subject throughout the reigns of Manṣūr, Muẓaffar, Ashraf I, and Mu'ayyad. Among the later Rasūlids we find them unwilling or unable to select high officials devoted to carrying out their policies; nor did they monitor officials' performance closely. They entrusted authority to men who sought objectives consonant neither with those of the sultan nor with those of the common people. The result was lasting political change reflected in a decrease of the sovereign's ability to pursue his aims effectively. The phenomenon was exhibited most strikingly in the decline of the Tihama's agricultural productivity and the transformation of its social structure. This took place as a long transition of which the lines became clearly marked during the reign of Sultan al-Mujāhid (1321-1363).

Except along the intermittent streams descending from the Sarāt, present-day agricultural development in the Yemeni coastal plain is a process of reclaiming virgin desert. An effort of imagination is required to visualize the Tihama as an intensively cultivated, populous region which sustained the strong Ziyād and Najāḥ states for three centuries and netted 'Ali al-Ṣulayḥī an annual million dinars in revenue. Then, as now, the wadi banks were the most closely settled districts. In the intervening areas transhumant tribes followed the traditional way of life, herding livestock and presenting a chronic threat to the security of the sedentary population and its wealth. So long as the settled areas enjoyed a reasonably equitable rule, the people had the incentive both to produce revenues and to defend themselves against incursions by the nomads. Misrule by the Rasūlid sultans' agents began as early as the reign of al-Mu'ayyad; gradually the state ceased to feed the cow, and became unable even to hold her horns.

During his brief reign (1295-1297) al-Ashraf I inherited a situation where exactions by tax collectors on the date-growers in Wadi Zabīd exceeded the productive capacity of the trees. No man who owned a date palm could find a wife; none would marry a woman who had one; marriage contracts commonly stipulated that neither party was so "unfortunate" as to possess date trees. Al-Ashraf had the problem investigated, and corrected it by ordering that the tree count be made by pious jurists.[41] The more general problem of bureaucratic rapacity remained. Under al-Mu'ayyad (1297-1321) disaffection spread among the large Ma'āziba tribe (later to be known as the Zarānīq), some of whom were settled along Wadi Zabīd. As early as 1300 the sultan authorized a punitive expedition during which a number of tribesmen were killed, hostages taken, and many date palms cut down, thus destroying a capital asset. In 1337, when Sultan al-Mujāhid arrived in the Tihama for his winter sojourn, he found that a great many cultivators in Wadi Zabīd had abandoned their lands and taken to the desert and foothills. He invited their leaders to present their grievances. They explained,

> Our lord the Sultan, we are faced with demands for produce of all kinds on behalf of the royal chancery in the planting season as well as in the harvest season when there

> is plenty and prices are low. But they assess us by last year's prices when food was scarce and prices highest. And they don't keep to one standard measure, but use many measures. What they require of us is grain we have already planted or its value at the time of greatest scarcity. That is why we went on strike and ran away.[42]

The sultan declared, "This is obviously unjust, and you are not to be blamed for running away." Again, however, reform measures provided only temporary relief.

Al-Khazrajī, writing while these and similar events were of recent memory, dates the ruin of the Tihama to the year 1353, and ascribes it to the malevolence of a deputy governor at Fashāl, Qāḍī Shihāb al-Dīn Aḥmad bin Qabīb.[43] For reasons only partly clear, this jurist nursed a venomous hatred toward the Ashā'ir tribe, settled on the banks both of Wadi Zabīd and Wadi Rima'.[44] He encouraged the provincial governor to try to extort a large sum of money from Aḥmad bin 'Umar bin 'Abdullah, shaikh of the Ashā'ir. The latter retreated to al-Mukhairīf, the tribal capital, where the governor presently pursued him with a military force, vowing to cut off his head. After a futile attempt to make peace through an intermediary, Shaikh Aḥmad arranged to have the governor assassinated. Qāḍī Shihāb al-Dīn prevailed upon the sultan to send a large punitive expedition the following year, and incited the Qurshiyūn, a neighboring tribe, to attack the Ashā'ir. These operations resulted in the permanent depopulation of eight villages along Wadi Rima'; in a desperate decision, Shaikh Aḥmad told his people, "We lack sufficient strength to fight against the sultan. You must leave this country." The Ashā'ir dispersed far up Wadi Rima' and into the neighboring wastelands.

The more numerous Ma'āziba had meanwhile become desert Arabs, well supplied with horses, and constantly preying upon the sown lands. Displacement of the Ashā'ir gave them free access to both wadis, and their raids on the productive areas gradually devastated the land and put to flight much of the sedentary population. The Ma'āziba were furthermore able to put together broad tribal coalitions to prosecute their traditional feud with the Ashā'ir and to oppose the forces sent against them by the government. In 1356, as merchants were driving Yemen's annual crop of horses toward Aden for export to India, the Ma'āziba intercepted them at Fashāl and captured the entire herd. Both Fashāl and al-Kadrā'[45] were sacked and razed the next year. Wadi Sahām as well as Wadi Rima' passed beyond government control. Communications were severed with the north Tihama capital, al-Mahjam. Zabīd itself was for a time virtually under siege.

The Rasūlids frequently faced insurrection among certain highland tribes also, notably in the Ibb and Ḥujariya districts. These agriculturists, however, lacked the ability to form the large alliances required for a serious, extended challenge to the central authority.

Decline manifested itself in other directions. The Rasūlids abandoned the effort to contest control of Upper Yemen, and contented themselves with defending the south against Zaidi pressure. They retrenched similarly with regard to affairs of Hijaz, over which they had long disputed with the Mameluke sultans of Egypt. The last notable Rasūlid expedition to Mecca, undertaken by al-Mujāhid in 1350, was so ill-fated that the sultan himself was captured by the Mameluke forces, and interned in Egypt for more than a year.[46] The last Rasūlid sultans, finally, departed from the hierarchical pattern of authority which had been a major factor in the polity's viability. The most momentous departure was the appointment of successive members of the Ṭāhir clan to govern Aden, the crucial base of Rasūlid trade revenue. The ascendency of this family was marked by the fact that a son of Sultan al-Nāṣir (d. 1423) married a daughter of the clan and assumed her family name as his title: al-Ṭāhir Yaḥyā. Al-Ṭāhir, a younger son, was not in the direct line of succession, but came to the throne when Ṭāhirid and other magnates deposed the incumbent, al-Ashraf III, by force in 1429. Thereafter, by contrast with previous successions, where disputes were fought out strictly among Rasūlids, other magnates engaged in, and soon arbitrated, the contests. A rebellion by the Rasūlids' Mamelukes at Zabīd deprived the last claimant of the resources required to assert his authority, and provided the Ṭāhirids with an opportunity to usurp the entire Rasūlid patrimony.

The Rasūlid Political Legacy

Rasūlid rule in Lower Yemen set the society on paths which remain important in present-day Yemeni political dynamics. Above all, the dichotomy between Upper and Lower Yemen was consolidated during their era. Differences in social structure between the two regions predate Rasūlid rule by many centuries. Regimes both before and after the rise of Islam had nevertheless dealt with the territory as a political unit, with varying degrees of success. The Rasūlids were not militant proselytizers by temperament, and chose to maximize their secular satisfactions within the productive areas they could handily govern, rather than to dissipate their energies in an apocalyptic struggle for control of territory which had little to offer in the way of potential revenue. For two centuries the two regions coexisted in a state of mutual hostility, under sharply contrasting styles of leadership.

In the south religious sectarianism waned as a political issue for which numbers of men would sacrifice their wealth and lives. Most adapted comfortably to Rasūlid rule within the framework of Sunnī Islam to which the great majority adhered. Reassured by the return to orthodoxy after a succession of schismatic rulers, they sought from the political system the two basic satisfactions we previously identified in the Islamic concept of government: the pursuit of an adequate livelihood and fulfillment of their religious obligations. We have referred to incidents showing the common interest of ruler and subjects in the health of the country's agriculture and trade, and to the effective, if intermittent, dialogue between the two on economic matters. Prosperity depends upon orderly, centralized administration, and by providing such a service, the Rasūlids, in their best days, fostered among the people some notion of the role of their political system in the satisfaction of their needs.

In the north, consummatory considerations remained overwhelming for the Zaidi imams, and for some other elements of the population. The area was isolated from international trade routes, and had little surplus production to export through organized channels. The rulers looked upon production as a "given," not as something to be created and nurtured; they took the canonical proportion of what there was, when and where they had the means to exact it. Their resources were concentrated upon enforcing Zaidi norms of conduct, and propagating their version of the faith both in Upper Yemen and in the adjacent areas where Sunnism was predominant. They effectively eliminated other Islamic sects from the north, except in the Ismā'īlī enclaves which still survive. Most people became attached to a rather simplified set of Zaidi principles: the legitimacy of an imam's authority transcended that of local leaders in matters of religion; the imam had the right to threaten or to use force in collecting the canonical tithes; and the people were willing to fight, as members of their tribes, under an imam's command against non-Zaidis. The imamate was nevertheless irrelevant, and sometimes inimical, to the principles of tribal solidarity and entrenched custom, which continued to govern many aspects of life. A serious handicap for the imamate was the doctrinal ambiguity regarding the transfer of power from one imam to the next.

The Rasūlids had their successional difficulties; but for nearly two centuries their throne passed regularly from father to son over eight generations, with a single minor aberration;[47] the average reign lasted a full quarter-century. No such regularity obtained in the Zaidi state. The imam's claim to authority depended peculiarly upon his personal qualities; each was, in effect, obliged to create his own political structure, which disappeared at his death. Between 1222 and 1436, at least twenty individuals, representing ten distinct 'Alid clans, laid claim to the office. Of these families, seven were descendants of Qāsim al-Rassī, but only three were descended from his grandson al-Hādī. Two clans were non-Rassid progeny of Zaid bin Ḥasan bin 'Alī, and one was descended not from Ḥasan but from the Shī'a martyr Ḥusain. While there were periods when no sayyid found the courage to announce his candidacy, in the three years after 1330 there were three rival imams, and in 1436 no less than four claimants. Only twice did the succession pass from father to son. Authority had to be asserted by force, which in practical terms meant armed action by the tribes. In this way tribal feuds and rivalries became entangled with the succession to the imamate, and contributed to the survival of a tribalism which other aspects of Zaidism might have been expected to discourage and weaken.

The Rasūlid era thus saw the consolidation of what might be considered two political systems in Yemen, with differing concepts of legitimate authority and contrasting expectations from those in power. Succeeding regimes, both intrusive and indigenous, have faced this situation in different ways; none has been able to ignore it, including the contemporary Yemeni Republic.

6
The Sharaf al-Dīn and Qāsimī Dynasties

The four centuries following the Rasūlid era began and ended with foreign occupation of Southern Arabia. In the intervening period the Zaidi imamate reached its broadest territorial extent, ruling for the first time all the territory of the present-day Yemen Arab Republic, often Asir, and occasionally Aden and its hinterland. Free of external challenge, it had the opportunity to demonstrate its strengths and weaknesses as a political system. Wide fluctuations occurred in the pattern of authority, and in the regime's vigor and capabilities. These changes, however, reflected a reordering of priorities within a constant set of political values. No significant alteration of the Yemeni social structure occurred, nor any modification of the social elements participating in political activity. Not until the twentieth century did new political aspirations and new social components arise as a basis for fundamental political change.

These occupations differed in kind from the colonization by European powers of many "third world" countries, introducing revolutionary technologies, novel social and political roles, and fundamentally new values. Certainly the Mamelukes and Turks were not Arabs, and had an appreciable technological advantage over the indigenous people. All were nonetheless members of a single Islamic society, and shared some political values and aspirations.

The series of conquests began with the invasion of Southern

Arabia by the Circassian Mamelukes in 1516. Their role was taken over by the Ottoman Turks, who occupied the coastal regions in 1539, moved into the highlands in 1547, and were finally expelled in 1635. Yemen was then left to its own devices until the nineteenth century when, curiously, a series of international events far to the north culminated again in an Egyptian invasion followed by Turkish occupation of the Tihama in 1848. The Porte extended its rule into the High Yemen beginning in 1872, and retained a foothold there until the Turks were obliged to withdraw in 1919, following their defeat in World War I.

The Circassian Invasion

The Mamelukes who overthrew the last Ayyūbids and succeeded to the rule of Egypt and Syria were for the most part Turkmen. They are known also as the Maritime Mamelukes, as their barracks were situated on the island of Rawḍa in the Nile at Cairo. The later Turkmen sultans became alarmed at the boisterous disunity prevailing among the commanders of their own military community, and sought to keep the army in check by forming a new servile force. Circassian youths from the Caucasus were purchased for the purpose; they became known as the *burj*—"tower"—Mamelukes, for their quarters in the famous castle on the Muqaṭṭam Hills above Cairo. They seized the sultanate from their masters in 1382.

Like their Ayyūbid and Turkmen predecessors, the Circassian sultans were vitally interested in the international trade through the Indian Ocean and the Red Sea, and maintained close trade relations with Yemen. At the same time they were competitors of the South Arabians, whom they endeavored to eliminate as middlemen by encouraging the shipment of merchandise from India and other sources direct to Jidda and other Red Sea ports under their control. To foster healthy trade, Cairo maintained close diplomatic relations with the South Arabian rulers, and also with the potentates of Calicut, Gujerat, and other principalities in southern India. The Mameluke sultan Qānṣūh al-Ghūrī was consequently both well informed and quite alarmed at the intrusion of the Portuguese, who, after Vasco da Gama's second expedition to the Indian

Ocean in 1502, established their base at Goa and set about seizing the eastern trade for themselves. Qānṣūh al-Ghūrī was thus disposed toward positive action when the ruler of Gujerat, Maḥmūd II Shāh, appealed for military help against the invaders, and when a parallel request arrived from the Ṭāhirid sultan in Yemen.[1]

As the Portuguese consolidated their position in East Africa and India, they realized the strategic importance of inhibiting Muslim maritime traffic into the Persian Gulf and the Red Sea. They attacked Hormuz unsuccessfully in 1507, but assumed effective control in 1515, thus commanding access to the Gulf. The celebrated Albuquerque seized the island of Socotra in 1507, thinking that shipping to and from the Red Sea could be inhibited from there. The Portuguese soon discovered, however, that the real key was the port of Aden; their efforts to gain possession of it extended over several decades, but were in the end frustrated.

Portuguese inroads into the eastern maritime trade had broad international repercussions. The Portuguese entry was disastrous to Venice and the Mameluke state, and sharply curtailed the revenues of the Ṭāhirid regime. Aden's sheltered harbor, well suited for defense against attack by sea, became the principal haven and base for such Muslim shipping as managed to evade Portuguese raiders. The volume of Muslim trade nevertheless dwindled, and its revenue became inadequate to support the ambitions of Sultan al-Ẓāfir II 'Āmir bin 'Abd al-Wahhāb (1489-1517), who had embarked on a program of expansion northward at the expense of the Zaidi state, itself resurgent under a vigorous imam, al-Mutawakkil Yaḥyā Sharaf al-Dīn (1507-1558).

A Mameluke fleet under command of Ḥusain al-Kurdī sailed from Suez in November 1505. It spent some months fortifying Jidda, so as to protect the Islamic holy places, then sailed for India, staging at Aden, where Sultan 'Āmir provided it ample provisions. It dispersed a flotilla of infidel galleons in one minor naval engagement off the Malabar coast, but sustained a discouraging defeat at Diu on February 2, 1509. Portuguese attacks had meanwhile occurred against Aden and several Red Sea ports. When the Mameluke force withdrew, it stopped at

Kamaran Island off the Yemeni coast, a spot only recently abandoned by an ill-fated Portuguese garrison, and began construction of fortifications there before returning to Egypt.

As Portuguese incursions into the Red Sea continued, and as appeals for help were renewed by the Gujerat sultan, Qānṣūh al-Ghūrī planned a second naval expedition, with substantial support from the Ottoman sultan, Bayazīd II (1481-1512). Several years in preparation, the new force was placed under the joint command of Ḥusain al-Kurdī and the leader of a contingent of Ottoman volunteers, Salmān al-Rūmī.[2] Leaving Suez in mid-1515, the expedition concentrated its attention upon the security of the Red Sea. After completing the fortification of Jidda, it sailed south to Kamaran and set about perfecting the island's defenses. Ḥusain al-Kurdī called upon the Ṭāhirid court for the necessary equipment and supplies. Sultan 'Āmir, who had successfully defended Aden against Portuguese attack, was less disposed than before to give of his diminishing resources, and likely regarded the Mameluke force as a potential threat to his own independence.

In a passage faithfully cribbed by later Arab historians, Ibn al-Dayba' (d. 1537) piously attributes the collapse of the Ṭāhirid state to Sultan 'Āmir's seizure in 1508 of half the income of the *awqāf* in the Zabīd area for the benefit of the hard-pressed royal treasury, over the protest of the custodians.

> King al-Ẓāfir (God Almighty have mercy on him) was exceptionally devout and pious. He grew up in obedience to God, and no childish passions were attributed to him. He was devoted to reading and citing God's word. He gave many alms, and left fine monuments: mosques, schools, charitable institutions, and hospitals. He fought many praiseworthy battles. He had no blameworthy trait save for his interference with the *awqāf* against the will of the jurists. In my view, that was the reason for the extinction of his regime and the loss of all he possessed.[3]

The more proximate cause of 'Āmir's misfortunes was his negative response to the Egyptian appeal. He was at first inclined to give Ḥusain what he required. His minister, however, insisted that a positive reply would merely encourage an endless series of demands for further aid.

> A counsel of greed is always persuasive. Miserliness and tight-fistedness are deeply rooted in men's character, and their advice always seems sound.[4]

Thus swayed by his minister's argument, 'Āmir refused support, and forbade his governors in the Tihama to provide supplies to the Mameluke force. Infuriated, Ḥusain resolved to avenge the affront. He found a source of supply at Zaila', on the opposite shore of the Red Sea, and willing allies in Yemen itself. 'Āmir had extended his conquests northward beyond Sanaa, and upon the Circassians' arrival at Kamaran, Imam Sharaf al-Dīn had proposed to them common action against the Ṭāhirids. At Jizan, the Sulaimānī sharīf of the time, 'Izz al-Dīn bin Aḥmad bin Duraib, had been forced into a tributary status under the Ṭāhirid sultan, and was only too willing to act against his suzerain. Finally, an independent warlord at the port of Luḥaya, the jurist Abū Bakr bin Maqbūl, offered guide and reconnaissance services. Ḥusain thus had a formidable coalition with which to attack the sultan. His decisive advantage was his possession of muskets and artillery, weapons never before used in Yemen. 'Āmir and his kinsmen fought valiantly in a series of battles, but his troops were repeatedly terrorized and put to flight by these revolutionary arms. The Mamelukes pursued the sultan into the central highlands, demolished his remaining forces, killed him, and took possession of Sanaa. Of the recently vigorous Ṭāhirid state there remained only Aden, which held out against Egyptian attack by both land and sea under the leadership of a young Ṭāhirid prince, 'Āmir bin Dāwud, and a few scattered forts in the interior. The naval contingent of the expeditionary force meanwhile withdrew to Jidda under command of Salmān al-Rūmī. The ground force set up a semi-independent regime centered on Zabīd, tributary to the Mameluke sultan, subsisting by pillaging the local people, and absorbed in the jealousies and rivalries of its several commanders.

The world in the north had meanwhile been turned upside

down. In 1512 Bayazīd was deposed by his son, Selīm I the Grim, whose voracious appetite for his neighbors' territory was immediately manifest. Qānṣūh's only possible ally against the Ottomans, the Safavid Shah Ismā'īl of Persia, sustained a disastrous defeat in the valley of Chaldiran in 1514. The Mameluke army was destroyed two years later at Marj Dābiq, near Aleppo, in a decisive battle in which Qānṣūh himself was slain. His successor, Tūmānbay, lacked strength to stem the Turkish advance, and Selīm's forces overran Egypt in 1517.

The collapse of the Ṭāhirid regime eliminated the motive for Zaidi collaboration with the Circassians, but not the latter's hunger for Zaidi territory. Hostilities soon erupted, and news of the Turkish conquest of Egypt arrived as the Mamelukes were besieging Imam Sharaf al-Dīn in the fortress of Thulā, northwest of Sanaa. With no prospect of reinforcement, and justly fearing attack by the people of Sanaa and the highland tribes, the force sought to withdraw to the Tihama. Plundered and decimated along the way, the column joined the main force at Zabīd. Their numbers were presently augmented by members of Salmān al-Rūmī's force, which had remained at Jidda awaiting the outcome of the Mameluke-Ottoman struggle, passing the time plundering the residents of the holy land. Unable to hold any broad expanse of Yemeni territory, the Circassians formed a perimeter around Zabīd, which they succeeded in defending against attack by Zaidis, Ṭāhirids, and Arab tribesmen for twenty-two years. Prayers were, as a precaution, offered in the name of the Ottoman sultan as well as the local commanders.[5]

The Turkish Occupation

Ottoman policy gave the Mamelukes this respite. Selīm I, and his son Sulaimān the Magnificent, who succeeded him in 1520, claimed to have inherited the Islamic caliphate and thus sovereignty over the entire Arabian Peninsula. They were much occupied with consolidating their Syrian and Egyptian conquests, and with the perennial struggle against the Christian powers in the Mediterranean basin. From the Mamelukes, however, they assumed direct responsibility for action against the Portuguese in the Indian Ocean and adjacent seas. Their efforts were at first concentrated on the African coast and on defense of the Red Sea littoral. While they took pains to ensure the safety of Hijaz and the holy cities, they countenanced minor operations by Egyptian freebooters farther south along the coast. It was not until 1538 that a major Ottoman expedition was directed toward Southern Arabia and the Portuguese presence in the Indian Ocean.

In that year the Porte entrusted to its governor of Egypt, Sulaimān Pasha al-Khādim, command of a large fleet, which had been under construction for seven years at Suez, and was destined for India. A slave of the late Selīm I, Sulaimān was crafty, craven, cruel, and treacherous. On the outward voyage the fleet called at Kamaran. While there, Sulaimān Pasha received an appeal for help from Prince 'Āmir bin Dāwud, beleaguered in Aden, against the Zaidi imam. Pretending to oblige, Sulaimān sailed to Aden. Prince 'Āmir's spoon proved too short for him to sup safely with the Turkish devil. The pasha sent troops ashore, who seized 'Āmir and his chief advisors, rowed them to the anchored ships, and hanged them from the yardarms. Leaving a garrison in the port, Sulaimān proceeded to India, where he made himself cordially hated by the local rulers and carefully avoided coming within reach of the Portuguese. Returning westward within a few months, he stopped at Mocha, lured from Zabīd the current Circassian commander, Aḥmad al-Nākhōda and slaughtered him along with two hundred Mamelukes. The Ottoman forces seized Zabīd, and enlisted those Circassians whose lives they spared. Thus began a direct Turkish rule in Yemen which was to last ninety years. At first confined to the southern Tihama, the Turks were offered an opportunity to expand into the highlands by calamitous dissension within the family ruling the Zaidi state. The Porte relied mainly upon Egypt to furnish the military personnel for the subjugation of South Arabia, and the burden was an onerous one. In 1547, even before the largest campaigns were mounted, the Egyptian accountant-general told a friend,

> We have seen no foundry like Yemen for our soldiers. Each time we have sent an expeditionary force there, it has

> melted away like salt dissolved in water. Rarely does one come back. We reviewed the registers in the Egyptian chancery from the days of Ibrāhīm Pasha up to the present,[6] and found that during this period 80,000 soldiers were sent from Egypt to Yemen; those now remaining in Yemen amount to less than 7,000.[7]

By mid-century Imam Sharaf al-Dīn was old and full of years, but was not to be vouchsafed the tranquility his exertions deserved. He had been continually at war with enemies both domestic and foreign: rival imams allied with the Ḥamza sharīfs, who had now settled in Nejran, Ṣa'da, and the Jawf; Ismā'īlīs in the northeast and in Harāz; perennially fractious tribes, such as the Khawlān; the Ṭāhirids; and, latterly, the Circassians. As his vitality ebbed, Sharaf al-Dīn entrusted increasing responsibility to several of his many sons. Of these the eldest, Muṭahhar, was the most vigorous, ambitious, and astute. In 1518, at the age of sixteen, he had taken Dhamār and Radā' for his father. But he was lame and misshapen, and had not troubled himself to become expert in theology and religious law; thus he was not qualified for the imamate. Sharaf al-Dīn designated as his successor another son, 'Alī. The allegation that 'Alī was a drunkard[8] is probably simply Turkish propaganda, and the suggestion that he defected from Zaidism to Sunnism and engaged in treasonable correspondence with the Turks[9] is not firmly substantiated. Clearly, though, he lacked his brothers' martial spirit; overshadowed by the charismatic Muṭahhar, he never pressed his claim to the imamate, or sought to lead ambitious military enterprises. Only Shams al-Dīn approached Muṭahhar in vigor and martial qualities, and he and Muṭahhar were often at serious odds. The imam allotted to Shams al-Dīn general responsibility for the south, to Muṭahhar the central and western highlands. Another able son, 'Izz al-Dīn, occupied the less conspicuous but equally taxing role of defending the north against Mu'ayyad pretenders backed by the Ḥamza and Sulaimānī sharīfs.

In 1545 pilgrims returning from Medina to the village of Jarāf, the imam's seat, fell ill with plague; the imam desired to move temporarily to Fadda, in Wadi Ḍahr, not far from

Sanaa. The locality was in al-Muṭahhar's hands, and he obliged the imam by removing his own family and effects to Ṭayba, not far away. Shams al-Dīn had meanwhile asked his father to build several houses for him on Jabal Murthid, overlooking the wadi, and the imam undertook the construction at considerable expense. These moves led Muṭahhar to suspect that his father and brother were seeking to restrict his activities and influence. Sycophantic retainers of both brothers contributed to the growth of mutual suspicion and rancor. Shams al-Dīn resolved to seize and imprison his brother, and conspired to capture him during prayers at a mosque Muṭahhar had built in Wadi Ḍahr. Forewarned by a younger brother, Muṭahhar summoned soldiers from Ṭayba, and the plot was aborted. The incident rapidly became public knowledge. Strenuous efforts by the ulama to reconcile the brothers were unavailing. Muṭahhar moved to the family fortress of Thulā, and began plundering the surrounding countryside. The imam, now back at Jarāf, and Shams al-Dīn assembled such troops as they could, and sent them against Muṭahhar. The latter, learning that Jarāf was left undefended, sent a force to capture the imam. The troops decided to pillage the town's market along the way. This delay permitted the imam to enlist the aid of the governor of Ḥarāz, who fortuitously appeared with five hundred men; to summon reinforcements from Sanaa; and to repulse Muṭahhar's army.

Muṭahhar now sent messages to tribal leaders throughout the country urging them to withdraw their allegiance from Imam Sharaf al-Dīn. At once, the people began to ignore the orders of the imam's officials, and to withhold their taxes. Muṭahhar furthermore wrote to Uwais Pasha, commander of the Ottoman troops at Zabīd, inviting him to attack the imam's territory.

Uwais responded by advancing on Ta'izz. The governor there, Jurist Yaḥyā al-Nuṣairi, resisted courageously, to such effect that the Turks were on the point of withdrawing to the Tihama. Meanwhile, however, not far to the north, Marjān al-Zabīdī, commander of the fortress of Ta'kar on behalf of Shams al-Dīn, had so tyrannized the people in the countryside around Jibla that they revolted and expelled him from the castle. Nuṣairi's forces, except for a small contingent from the north, were from Jibla. Upon learning of the developments at Ta'kar these troops deserted and joined the Turks, who entered Ta'izz without further opposition. Nuṣairi fled up Jabal Ṣabr with his Upper Yemenis, and under cover of night escaped northward, where they placed themselves at the disposition not of Shams al-Dīn, but of Muṭahhar.

The fall of Ta'izz brought home to the imam and Shams al-Dīn the enormity of the mistake they had made in antagonizing Muṭahhar, and they desperately sought a reconciliation. His terms were sweeping—de facto control of the entire realm—and he had the power to impose them. Leaving a few castles in the hands of his father and brothers, he entered Sanaa in state and asserted his sovereignty by minting coins in his own name.

Meanwhile the Turks extended their control over Lower Yemen and advanced steadily northward. In 1548 they besieged and captured Sanaa, with much destruction of property and loss of life. Uwais Pasha was assassinated by a faction of his own troops; his successor in command of the Ottoman forces, Uzdumur Pasha, moved against Muṭahhar, who led the Zaidi resistance from the fortress of Thulā.

The original Ottoman objective in South Arabia had been the protection of the area against Portuguese encroachment, not direct rule of the hinterland. However, Sulaimān Pasha al-Khādim, during his India expedition, had tried to enhance his reputation at Istanbul by falsely asserting that Imam Sharaf al-Dīn had formally submitted to Ottoman sovereignty. Resistance to Ottoman authority by Zaidi leaders was thenceforth regarded at the Porte as rebellion, and as intolerable. Distraction of the Turkish forces in the Yemeni highlands afforded opportunity for tribal leaders in the vicinity of Aden to seize the port from its Turkish garrison, and to enter into negotiations with the Portuguese for mutual cooperation. The Porte thus had two compelling motives for urgently dispatching reinforcements to Yemen. Portuguese vessels arriving to occupy Aden in March 1548 found the Ottomans already back in control, and withdrew without a fight. Inland, Muṭahhar conducted a spirited and successful seven-month defense of Thulā, a feat which greatly impressed the Yemeni public. He was nevertheless politically isolated. The Ḥamza sharīfs and his own brother Shams al-Dīn were won over by Uzdumur's diplomacy to the Ottoman cause, while 'Izz al-Dīn, preoccupied in the north, refused effective aid. Disunity among the Zaidi leaders permitted the Turks to advance as far as Ṣa'da. At length a truce was concluded between Muṭahhar and Uzdumur by which the former accepted the symbols of Ottoman sovereignty—the coinage, and mention of the sultan's name in public prayer—while retaining direct rule of the territory remaining in his hands. Muṭahhar agreed to the stationing of a small Turkish garrison in Ṣa'da as witness to the Porte's sway over all Yemen. The agreement was reached early in 1543.

The story of the ensuing decades is a tangled and dolorous one of Turkish oppression and localized revolt in all parts of Yemen. Ottoman governors followed one another in rapid succession. Few had any notion of orderly, equitable administration, and all were preoccupied with maximizing revenue, both to enhance their reputation at the Porte and to make their personal fortunes. One particularly disastrous method was the progressive debasement of the coinage. The standard unit was the Ottoman sultan's gold dinar, of which the weight at this period was one *dirham* and two *qīrāṭ*. (The *qīrāṭ* was one-sixteenth of a *dirham*, or 0.195 gram; the gold dinar thus weighed 3.4 grams.) The dinar was subdivided into *'uthmānīs*, a coin of which the value varied from one Ottoman province to another. At this time, the dinar was worth sixty *'uthmānīs* minted in Istanbul, and eighty of those struck in Egypt. The avarice of the governors in Yemen led to an increase in the copper content of the nominally silver coin to the point where, in 1561, the dinar was worth one thousand Yemeni *'uthmānīs*. Maḥmūd Pasha, who arrived as governor in that year, falsely blamed the Yemeni director of the mint for the depreciation; he executed him, confiscated his property, and then further debased the *'uthmānī* by half.

The Porte promulgated a universal wage schedule for Ottoman troops expressed in *'uthmānīs*, but did not account for the difference between the coin's values in the various provinces. Soldiers were paid from ten to one hundred *'uthmānīs* per day, according to rank, from which they were expected to purchase their own subsistence. A *sanjaq*—a high-ranking officer—drawing one hundred *'uthmānīs* a day, thus received in standard terms only one dinar and a half per month, not enough to pay for the coffee he drank, let alone his other wants and necessities. Many destitute soldiers sold their uniforms and arms, deserted, dispersed into the countryside, or joined dissident Yemeni magnates like Maṭahhar. Above all, they despoiled and robbed the citizens, while the governors paid no notice.[10]

So lacking were most of the Porte's governors in political sense that they made no effort to cultivate the loyalty of the Ismā'īlīs who, as objects of Zaidi persecution, had rendered important service in the Ottoman conquest; nor did they recognize Shāfi'ī elements who had been of similar help and who willingly acknowledged both the spiritual and the temporal authority of the Ottoman sultan. Misrule thus induced a potential unity among Yemenis. Dissatisfaction increased when, on the recommendation of Maḥmūd Pasha, the Porte divided Yemen into two provinces—*beklerbekiyas*—without taking so much trouble as to delimit their boundaries precisely. This ensured dissension between the respective governors, and also redoubled the exactions from the local population. Raḍwān Pasha, governor at Sanaa, at once attempted to establish direct administration (and taxation) of the Ismā'īlī districts, and also of Sharaf al-Dīn family estates, in violation of the fragile truce with Muṭahhar. The latter cleverly exploited the situation by offering submission to Murād Pasha, governor at Zabīd, denouncing Raḍwān's unjust rule. He meanwhile fomented disaffection with Turkish rule throughout the land. Through astute propaganda and maneuvering, he forged a remarkably comprehensive coalition against the occupation, embracing the Ḥamza sharīfs and the Ismā'īlīs who had theretofore served the Ottomans, the Mu'ayyad rivals of the Sharaf al-Dīn clan, and the key leaders of both Zaidi and Shāfi'ī tribes. Celestial signs completed the stage setting for a country wide revolt under Muṭahhar's leadership.[11] Garrisons scattered throughout Yemen were attacked and overwhelmed, and within two years (1565-1567) the Ottoman presence was extinguished save for a toehold at the city of Zabīd. Agents of the Sharaf al-Dīn prince took the place of Turkish district officials.

Now headed by a new sultan of less than sublime character, the Porte was not prepared to accept the loss of Yemen to a schismatic ruler scarcely more acceptable than the infidel Christians. Selīm II the Sot felt it his duty to maintain intact his heritage from Sulaimān the Magnificent. More particularly, he feared that Aden, where large quantities of artillery and firearms had been stocked, could not be defended adequately by the Arabs, who were as yet inexpert in the use of these weapons. The possibility that Muṭahhar might lose Aden to the infidels opened up the prospect of a Christian attack against Jidda and the holy cities: an intolerable insult to the entire community of Islam. A major effort was thus imperative to recover Yemen, and the sultan ordered Muṣṭafā Pasha al-Lālā, governor of Egypt, to organize an expeditionary force.

Muṣṭafā Pasha had little more stomach for the task than the Egyptian *fallāḥīn* he tried, desultorily, to recruit. Hoping either to avoid a military campaign or to ensure an easy victory, he wrote to Muṭahhar through the intermediary of the sharīf of Mecca, beseeching him to submit to the sultan's authority in order to spare Muslim blood and treasure; the gambit won him merely a defiant reply. Muṣṭafā's vacillation ensured the success of intrigues by an able and ambitious rival, who shortly replaced him in the rule of Egypt and in command of the Yemen expedition. Sinān Pasha's soldierly ability and political acumen were to be amply proved in South Arabia and in Tunisia. His mobilization spared only Egyptians who were decrepit, lame, or ailing. His forces set out from Suez by land and sea in January 1569, securing Hijaz, Asir, and the Yemeni Tihama as they moved southward. The capture of Ta'izz permitted a combined naval and land attack on Aden; it was occupied, leaving Sinān free to move against Muṭahhar's power base in the north. The national consensus Muṭahhar had formed had been cemented only by common opposition to the Turks. During his two-year independent rule, the great aristocratic clans resumed pursuit of their private, secular interests. The pattern, recurrent in Yemeni history, of oppression by Zaidi northerners in the Sunnī south, reasserted itself, and numerous Shāfi'ī collaborators helped to ease the way for Sinān's advance. Dhamār made no show of resistance, and Muṭahhar humanely evacuated Sanaa to spare it the horrors of certain siege and sacking.

The Zaidi north thus sank back into the woeful disarray which the pathetic efforts of Imam Sharaf al-Dīn had been insufficient to prevent. In 1552 his eyesight failed and he moved into retirement at Ẓafīr, the fortress of Ḥajja. Realizing that his own sons were little more than warlords, he wrote to the Mu'ayyad clan of sayyids at Ṣa'da urging them to raise up a godly and vigorous man among them as imam. They demurred at first, protesting that they would acknowledge the octogenarian Sharaf al-Dīn's authority through his lifetime, despite his blindness. As the old man persisted, they put forward 'Alī bin 'Izz al-Dīn, who sought recognition under the title al-Hādī. The unlucky claimant was refused allegiance by many of his own kinsmen; the local Ḥamza sharīfs made war on him; and the patriarch's moral suasion failed to gain al-Hādī the support of any Sharaf al-Dīn prince. Consummatory values were thus in virtually total eclipse within the Zaidi community; authority within it lapsed into a segmental pattern, and it lost the capability of mobilizing resources to pursue any common objective.

A modern traveler fortunate enough to reach Thulā will be entranced by the aspect of the town; its multistoried houses are uniformly built of a glowing, tawny stone, expertly worked, with a surprising virtuosity in the artistic treatment of the windows. He will readily appreciate the strategic position of the fortress, constructed on a rock pinnacle high above the town, commanding both the relatively level expanse of land extending southeast to Sanaa, and also the broad, richly cultivated Bawn Plain which must be crossed by traffic between Sanaa and Ṣa'da. Thulā shares a vast mountain massif with Kawkabān, an equally powerful fortress, and al-Ṭawīla, commanding a major route westward from the capital. Muṭahhar and his forces retreated to this strong defensive complex, he himself taking Thulā as his headquarters, while Kawkabān was under the command of his nephew, Prince Muḥammad bin Shams al-Dīn.[12] There they were strongly besieged by the Ottoman forces, Sinān concentrating his principal effort on the capture of Kawkabān. Muṭahhar mounted a fresh propaganda program, calling for *jihād* against the Turks and reminding Yemenis of what they had suffered at Turkish hands: seizure of their possessions, violation of their women, and enslavement of their children. Public response was sufficient to enable Muṭahhar to sustain a valiant resistance for eight months. His nephew's resolution, however, was gradually eroded by the protracted strain. Prince Muḥammad submitted to Sinān (although Muṭahhar managed to prevent the surrender of Kawkabān), and set about persuading his uncle to do the same. In late 1570 Muṭahhar accepted a truce with the Ottomans, under terms analogous to those agreed upon two decades before with Uzdumur Pasha. The next year Sinān Pasha left Yemen, bequeathing its administration to a procession of lesser men. In 1572, a star brighter than the planet Venus appeared in the path of Ursa Minor,[13] and Muṭahhar died.

The next quarter-century witnessed the utter disintegration of the Upper Yemen polity, which might have preserved a measure of solidarity under Ottoman suzerainty. Muṭahhar left five sons who, together with Muḥammad bin Shams al-Dīn warred incessantly among themselves, each seeking to seize the maximum possible territory, and allying himself when opportune with the Ottoman governor. The people wearied of the constant turmoil, and many tribes abandoned any allegiance or obedience not imposed by force. The collapse of indigenous authority and common purpose made it possible for the Turks to move against the Sharaf al-Dīn princes and other magnates one by one, and to extend direct rule over their lands. A single credible claimant to the imamate arose, al-Ḥasan bin 'Alī, who took the ironically undescriptive title al-Nāṣir: the Victorious. His followers were attacked by the Ḥamza sharīfs, by Muṭahhar's sons, and by his own cousins of the Mu'ayyad clan; in 1585 he was betrayed into the hands of the Turks. A single glimmer of elevated political purpose was exhibited by a Mu'ayyad aristocrat, Aḥmad bin Ḥusain. Beginning in 1571, he recruited tribesmen, forced the boisterous Ḥamza clan to remove from Ṣa'da to the Jawf, neutralized the imam, and established an autonomous regime, under Ottoman suzerainty, in an area extending from Nejran south to Khaiwān. His rule endured eighteen years. "He followed the best of policies, causing justice to reign and reviving schools of learning. Students from the entire country flocked there, until there came to be eighty centers of learning."[14] By 1585 the imam and all leading members of the Sharaf al-Dīn family were prisoners of the Ottoman governor, who sent them in a body to Istanbul, where they lived out their remaining years interned by the Porte. Yemen was left relatively tranquil despite a Turkish occupation which was both rapacious and arbitrary. The rulers' exactions were at least predictable, and they maintained the modicum of public order which permitted agricultural production and trade to survive.

The Qāsimī Dynasty

Imam Sharaf al-Dīn succeeded briefly in asserting control of all Southern Arabia except the cities of Zabīd and Aden, and his son Muṭahhar ruled even Aden for a time. Their military successes resulted from the aspiration, shared between them and their subjects, to repel successive invasions by Ṭāhirids, Circassians, and Ottoman Turks. Their political constructions disintegrated as rapidly as they had been created. The work of the first Qāsimī imams was somewhat more durable, but it too eventually deteriorated into near anarchy.

Zaidi political thinking assumes that once men have sworn allegiance to an imam they can be expected to fulfill of their own will the obligations of the faith in matters of taxation, the ordering of civil affairs, and the *jihād*. There should be no necessity for a formal, specialized administrative apparatus to enforce duties which all acknowledge. Imam Sharaf al-Dīn sent agents into his various districts; they were, however, ad hoc personal representatives, not professional administrators. The loose authority pattern was manifest in the frequent roadblocks against which Sharaf al-Dīn inveighed and which occasioned many of his punitive expeditions. The question was not always one of banditry; the tribes reserved the right of sanctioning passage through their territory not simply as a matter of local autonomy, but also as a way of accounting for the security of travelers, a task clearly beyond the capability of the imam's own personnel.

The locus of legitimate authority and the major purposes of its use were defined largely in terms of the *jihād.* A polity resting on such a foundation was peculiarly unstable. Rarely did the doctrinal list of qualifications designate without ambiguity one individual as the true imam to whom all owed obedience. As the sayyid aristocracy grew in size, the number of plausible claimants rose, and military prowess was as likely to be demonstrated within the community itself as against an external enemy. While *jihād* was capable of uniting the community behind a vigorous imam for finite objectives, when these were achieved the consensus was lost. Some sort of political change became inevitable. In the event, the rulers regularly adopted secular objectives, instrumental chiefly for themselves and their close kinsmen, and the polity lost the values which brought community cohesion.

At the turn of the seventeenth century a certain innovative imagination was required to conceive that the fragmented Yemeni society, garrisoned by a large foreign force well armed and trained, could be inspired to a common, sustained effort toward any single goal. The stature of the first imams of the new dynasty is measured by the fact that they formulated the objective of expelling the Turks from South Arabia; established it among the people as a salient aspiration; pursued it doggedly through many vicissitudes; and asserted the propriety of their leadership by benevolent civil administration based upon unassailable moral and religious principle.

Like the Sharaf al-Dīns, the Qāsimīs (see figure 5) were direct descendants of the first imam, al-Hādī Yaḥyā, through his great-grandson Yūsuf al-Dā'ī, the tenth-century claimant whose star refused to rise. The Sharaf al-Dīns had produced a half-dozen imams over the centuries. The Qāsimīs, though respected for their pedigree, had lived more obscurely. Aristocrats but not magnates, they had not been participants in the multilateral struggle for secular power, and were thus "available" for a leadership transcending selfish material interests.

Thus when Qāsim bin Muḥammad proclaimed himself imam in 1598 with the title al-Manṣūr Billāh—Victorious by the Grace of God—coupling his appeal for obedience with the

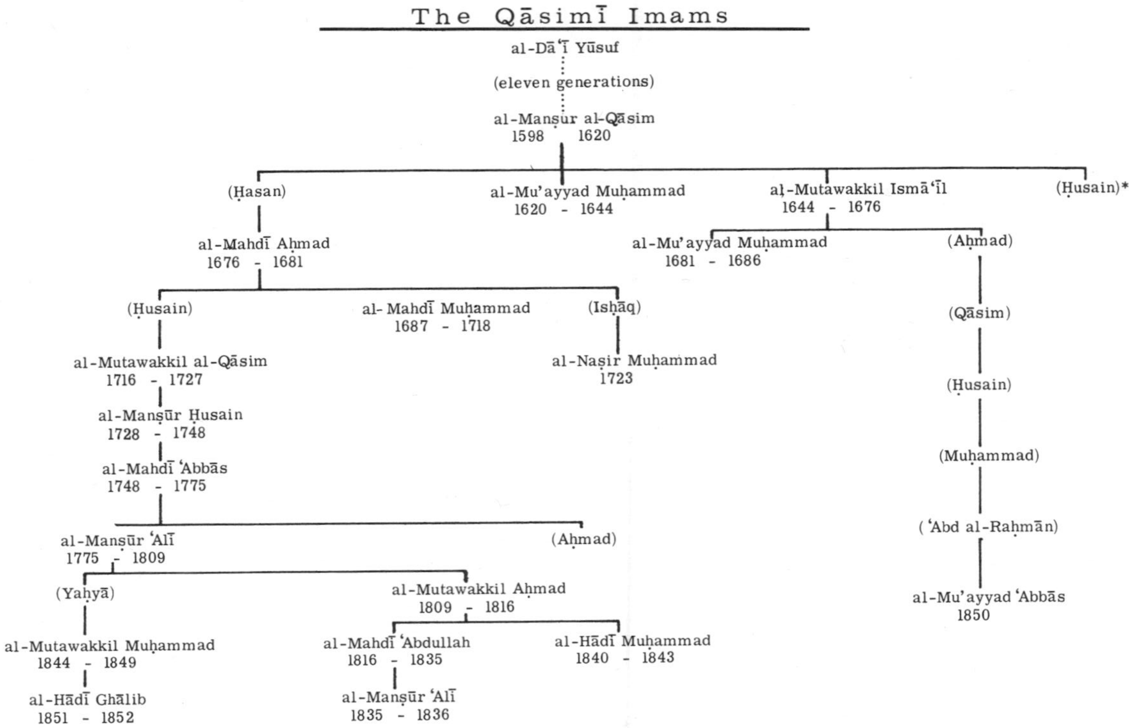

* Ancestor of Ḥamīd al-Dīn imams: al-Manṣūr Muḥammad bin Yaḥyā (1890 - 1904), al-Mutawakkil Yaḥyā (1904 - 1948), al-Nāṣir Aḥmad (1948 - 1962), al-Manṣūr Muḥammad al-Badr (1962 - 1970).

Figure 5

exhortation to attack the Turkish garrisons, his claim was broadly credible. Within a year, a spectacular series of local successes placed many of the mountain fortresses in his hands, and revolts occurred in areas as remote as Yāfiʻ. The Turks reacted vigorously after recovering their balance. Nevertheless the imam was able to seize and hold a slice of territory in the northern mountains which served as a base for the accumulation of resources and the conduct of propaganda operations over the next two decades of inconclusive, modest-scale warfare. On the initiative of the Ottoman governor Jaʻfar Pasha, who arrived in 1607, a truce was concluded confirming the imam in possession of the territories he already controlled. Peace was preserved until 1613, when Ibrāhīm Pasha, who came with a fresh military force to replace Jaʻfar, was waylaid and killed near Dhamār on his way to the capital. Jaʻfar returned to Sanaa and undertook concerted operations against the imam, which ended in a painful Turkish defeat at Athla. The reinstated truce, confirming an expanded Zaidi enclave, was respected by al-Mu'ayyad Muḥammad, Qāsim's son, who became imam upon his father's death in 1620.

The concern of the early Qāsimīs that their rule should be flexible as well as firm is suggested by their handling of the north. In 1622 the people of the Ṣaʻda country defected and withheld their taxes. The imam mobilized a force against them under his brother Saif al-Islām al-Ḥasan, who soon put down the revolt. Ḥasan introduced a program of administrative reform which won the confidence and esteem of the masses. The imam appointed him governor of the area. His reputation for just rule spread, and soon he was able to enlarge its sphere peacefully, by incorporating areas to the west which had never come under any central authority. It is important to note the precedent here established of substantial delegation of the imam's authority to a close relative, a practice which had contributed to the weakening of the Sharaf al-Dīn imamate.

By 1626 al-Mu'ayyad was ready to resume the initiative against the Turks. Astutely, he chose as the occasion an issue to arouse Yemeni public sentiment: the arbitrary murder, by servants of the governor, Ḥaidar Pasha, of a respected jurist whose only offense had been the collection of *zakāt* for the imam's account voluntarily offered by the people of Sanaa. The imam conducted, and publicized widely, a fruitless correspondence with Ḥaidar demanding that the murderers be brought to trial. Having clearly demonstrated that justice was not forthcoming from the Turks, the imam had solid national support for a military campaign. At the end of two years he held all the Ottoman forces besieged in Sanaa, Zabīd, and Mocha. His prestige was such that two ranking Turkish military commanders defected and joined his service. Ḥaidar Pasha was obliged to petition for a truce, under cover of which he evacuated his forces at Sanaa to Zabīd. In violation of the truce terms, he then appealed to the Porte for reinforcements, and a new Turco-Egyptian army arrived. In 1635 the augmented Ottoman force was defeated in an attempt to advance from its Zabīd perimeter to Ta'izz, and surrendered. The imam provided enough camels to transport the survivors to Hijaz. Under agreed terms, those Turkish soldiers who so wished were given the opportunity to remain in Yemen, in the imam's service; many did so. The Ottoman state, enfeebled by its interminable wars with the Christian powers and a resurgent Persia, by rebellion in Syria, by insubordination of the Janissaries, and by harem intrigue, made no further effort to reassert control of Yemen until the nineteenth century.

The now independent Zaidi state extended its influence by the conquest of Baiḍā and Yāfi' in 1654, and established a loose suzerainty as far east as Dhofar in 1658. This was the high-water mark; thenceforth retrenchment was the trend. The Yāfi' tribes threw out their Zaidi governor in 1681, and successive efforts to restore the imam's rule were defeated. Laḥej and Aden asserted local autonomy in 1728, and achieved full independence three years later. The areas to the east, which were to form the British protectorate of Aden in the late nineteenth century, gradually followed this lead. In the first years of the nineteenth century, the Tihama slipped from the imamate's grasp into the hands first of the Wahhabis from Nejd, then of the Sulaimān sharīfs of Asir; the area was then ruled successively by Egypt, the sharīfs of Mecca, the Turks, and the Idrīsids before its recovery by the Zaidis after World War II.

Thus the Zaidi imamate in the seventeenth century once

again had achieved a salient Yemeni national goal, but offered no on-going values of a quality to preserve the unity momentarily created. The imamate agan became simply a lucrative prize by which individual appetites could be gratified with minimal responsibility toward other segments of the society.

The competition among Qāsim's numerous descendants was lively. As early as 1644 rival claims were advanced by two brothers of al-Mu'ayyad Muḥammad, who died in that year. The elder, Aḥmad, was the first to place his bid, but his younger brother Ismā'īl soon elicited the oaths of the ulama in his entourage and of other members of the royal family. A serious dispute was averted when Aḥmad acknowledged his brother's superior attainments in learning and political wisdom, and abandoned his own claim. Aḥmad received the governorship of Ṣa'da and the north as a sop, and other Qāsimī princes were named to administer key areas. Ismā'īl's succession, in 1676, was sharply disputed. A second Aḥmad, son of Ismā'īl's brother Ḥasan, was opposed by al-Qāsim, son of al-Mu'ayyad Muḥammad, who held the fortress of Shahāra; Aḥmad was obliged to mobilize an army and besiege the stronghold to force his cousin to obedience. At the end of Aḥmad's five-year reign his son Muḥammad faced counterclaims by relatives in Radā' in the east; Shahāra in the northwest; Ṣa'da in the north; and Manṣūra in Lower Yemen. The diplomacy of the ulama succeeded in eliminating the rival claims without bloodshed. The next succession, in 1686, saw no fewer than seven contenders in widely separated sections of the country, and was decided by force of arms. The many-titled victor, Muḥammad,[15] had a long reign with a certain external prestige. (In 1701-1702 he received embassies with sumptuous gifts from the Shah 'Abbās and from the Ottoman governor of Mecca.) His rule, however, was punctuated by revolts and challenges of various kinsmen, and ended in a decade of violent strife among many Qāsimī princes.

The subsequent history of the dynasty follows the pattern outlined by these incidents. That the imamate survived at all during these turbulent centuries and remained in the hands of the Qāsimīs, who were only one of many eligible 'Alid clans, is explained by the prevailing mode of authority, and by the respective political roles of the imams, the ulama, and the major northern tribes.

With consummatory values relegated to a secondary position in the society, an ambitious sayyid needed material resources in order to lay claim to the imamate. The Qāsimī manner of rule tended to concentrate wealth, and thus the ability to assemble military strength, in the hands of the dynasty; however, wealth was dispersed among its members. Administrative decentralization was imposed by circumstances. Without an organized civil service, and without means of rapid communication through the rugged Yemeni terrain, the imam's personal and continuous reach was quite limited. From the outset the imam entrusted to near relatives the rule of such areas as could be subjected to close administration without undue military effort, and which at the same time were sufficiently productive to sustain a princely establishment. The central highlands between Sanaa and Yarīm might accommodate one or two such provinces; other such areas were the northwestern highlands around Shahāra; the Ḥajja area; Ṣa'da and the north; Lower Yemen; and the Ḥāshid area centered on Khamir. The southern Tihama was now too poor to serve, while large areas to the east and northeast, the home of major Bakīl and Khawlān tribes, simply were not amenable to continuous control by outsiders. The holders of such administrative fiefs came to regard them as personal possessions by right, rather than as a trust to be managed in the imam's interest. Their situation gave them the financial and manpower resources necessary to press a claim to the imamate, whether against an incumbent or when the office fell vacant. A sequence of events in 1676, the last year of al-Mutawakkil Ismā'īl's reign, suggests the dynamics of these relationships:

> A dispute arose between the governor of Ṣa'da, Prince 'Alī bin Aḥmad bin al-Qāsim, the Prince Ḥasan, son of the Imam al-Mutawakkil. The reason for this was that the imam had sent his son Ḥasan to Ṣa'da, ordering him to reside there. Thus Prince 'Alī bin Aḥmad thenceforth had no power to command or forbid in the Ṣa'da country, which he had governed as had his father before him. He

> prepared for war, rallying the people on whom he could rely from the Ṣahār, Al 'Āmmār, and other tribes, reminding them of his good conduct, of their hardships at the hands of the imam's son Ḥasan, and of the imam's declining health by reason of strange maladies.[16] He claimed to be imam, and took the title al-Manṣūr Billāh. The Imam al-Mutawakkil 'alā Allāh ordered his nephew Ṣafā al-Islām Aḥmad bin al-Ḥasan to advance against the lord of Ṣa'da. He ordered all districts to contribute to equipping this army. Aḥmad bin al-Ḥasan went forth from al-Ghurās into the neighboring districts to recruit soldiers. While he was making his preparations, he received word of the death of the Imam al-Mutawakkil.[17]

Prince Aḥmad now claimed the succession, with the title al-Mahdī.

> A group of people, learned and of good character, swore allegiance to him. He was opposed by al-Qāsim bin al-Mu'ayyad Billāh Muḥammad, who rose at Shahāra and entitled himself al-Manṣūr Billāh. Al-Mahdī assembled an army against him and besieged him in Shahāra; al-Qāsim's claim collapsed with his surrender.[18]

The new imam, al-Mahdī, now proceeded to Ṣa'da, where he was warmly welcomed by Prince 'Alī (who pressed his own claim no further), and by the local tribesmen, who promised him their loyalty.

We may infer from this account that an essential element was missing in the lord of Ṣa'da's bid for the imamate: the support of some appreciable group of recognized ulama. The body of licensed jurists and theologians played a morally independent role in the selection of the imam, and to some degree in monitoring his acts.

The Ulama and the Tribes

Recruited both from the sayyid aristocracy and from among learned commoners, the ulama served as the conscience of the Zaidi polity, and provided a sort of continuity of which the imamate itself was incapable. Their function as peacemakers and censors was in no way institutionalized; it was performed ad hoc, according to the circumstances. Their role in the succession to the imamate was similarly unstructured. They were, of course, dispersed throughout the country as judges, teachers, civil officials, or simply scholars, and there was no question of assembling them in formal conclave to form a consensus. When the imamate fell vacant, action to provide a replacement could be instituted in two or more places, either by the initiative of a claimant who sought the adherence of the ulama in the vicinity, or by the initiative of the local ulama themselves, who might urge a qualified sayyid to claim the office. The ulama continued to play a part in contests among rival claimants by mediating, or by throwing their support to the best-qualified candidate. The right of the ulama to censure the sovereign's conduct was an accepted principle, though at times it was risky for the practitioner. When he refused to recognize this right, the imam al-Mahdī 'Abdullah in 1831 precipitated a challenge to his throne from outside the Qāsimī clan, in the person of Sayyid Aḥmad bin 'Alī al-Sirājī, who claimed the imamate with the title al-Hādī.

> A large body of learned men rallied round him, and certain of the tribes responded to his appeal. The reason for the assertion of his claim was the obvious disorder of al-Mahdī's conduct and his execution of the learned Shaikh Muḥammad Ṣālih al-Samāwī after the latter had criticized his government and condemned certain of his acts. The tribesmen who had concentrated around Sanaa dispersed after money was sent out to their chiefs, and the ulama returned to Sanaa.[19]

The incident emphasizes the two indispensable elements supporting the authority of the imamate: the moral suasion of the ulama and the military power of the tribes. The imam and other influential princes were able to maintain modest permanent slave and mercenary forces. Where issues of broad import were involved, these permanent forces were often inadequate to enforce a decision. The preponderance of military strength was in the hands of the great northern tribes, where it remains today.

The turbulence of Yemeni politics in the Qāsimī era was intensified by a contradiction. Although the imamate was dependent upon the brute strength of the tribes, it was unable either to make them the instrument of a strong central government, or to prevent them from pursuing aims irrelevant, or hostile, to those of the Zaidi regime. The frequent primacy of tribal tradition and values over the public order the imams sought to enforce is emphasized by the fact that punishment by the imam for disobedience was taken by the tribes as calling for revenge. A case in point is provided by events of 1725-1726 involving Arḥab, a Bakīl tribe centered at ʻAmrān, on the principal route between Sanaa and Ṣaʻda and thus in a sensitive geographic location:

> In the year 1138 (1725 A.D.), men of the Dhībīn section of Arḥab committed many acts of aggression, robbery and pillage on the roads. There happened to a be a group of them in Sanaa, and they agreed among themselves to produce a riot in the city and to loot its *sūq* on Friday, 7 Shawwāl of that year. After the imam had completed Friday prayers and reviewed the troops in the palace square, the Arḥab men fired their rifles at the palace gate. The imam ordered an attack upon them, while the troops fired at their backs. The imam ordered the city streets and avenues patrolled, and the doors to the houses shut. The fighting continued until evening, some of the dastardly rebels being killed or captured, while others fell from off the city walls.[20]

The matter did not end there; the following year

> Arḥab tribesmen invited Ḥāshid and Bakīl to join them in taking revenge and in wiping out the dishonor they had sustained. The tribes responded. ʻAlī bin Qāsim al-Aḥmar, Paramount Shaikh of Ḥāshid,[21] and Nāṣir bin Juzailān, Paramount Shaikh of Bakīl, proceeded to ʻAmrān, where they met with al-Ḥusain, the imam's son, whom they persuaded to join them. Arḥab descended on

> al-Rawḍa, where they looted and spread disorder, while others advanced to the west of Sanaa. The imam mobilized his army against them and moved to Bāb al-Manjal, west of Sanaa, with his soldiers to fight them. Then the learned sayyid al-Badr Muḥammad bin Ismā'īl al-Amīr acted as intermediary to arrange a truce.[22]

It is indicative of the tribes' unstable allegiances that Prince Ḥusain's disloyal attempt on this occasion to ingratiate himself with Ḥāshid and Bakīl availed him little. His father died a few months after the truce, and these tribes unsuccessfully supported his cousin, Muḥammad bin Isḥāq, against Ḥusain's claim to the succession. As imam, Ḥusain was nevertheless able to enlist Ḥāshid and Bakīl in a fruitless effort in 1731-1732 to put down a rebellion in Yāfi'; it is safe to assume that the prospect of loot was the deciding factor.[23]

The military capability of one tribe was often enlisted in support of the imam's effort to discipline another. Tribal loyalty could not, however, be commanded at will by the imam. In 1816, for example, having resolved to recover the Tihama from the Wahhābis, the imam al-Mahdī 'Abdullah summoned the fighting men of Dhū Ghailān to Sanaa and ordered them to undertake the expedition. When they declined, he had their senior shaikh seized and executed. This act was looked upon by the tribe as a disgrace which had to be avenged; the following year they ferociously sacked the Sanaa quarter Bīr al-'Azab.

The tribes seldom moved against the person of the imam, although this was not entirely unknown. The imam al-Nāṣir 'Abdullah was waylaid and assassinated in 1840 in the Wadi Ḍahr by Yām and Hamdān tribesmen. The Qāsimī princes enlisted a force of Khawlān and Arḥab to punish Hamdān. We are here given a glimpse of the complex relations among the warlike tribes; the imams had to know these relationships intimately and use them effectively in order to maintain any discipline over the tribes. The offenders in the case mentioned above were not neighbors. Hamdān, in this context, refers to the Ḥāshid tribe located immediately to the north of Sanaa. The Yām were far from home. Their tribal area was to the east of Nejran along the present Saudi border; they were of Ḥāshid descent, Ismā'īlīs by sect. The punitive force could not, obviously, come from Ḥāshid. There was, at the same time, a security advantage in composing the army of several tribes. Furthermore, if the punishment were not itself to generate a new series of feuds, members of the force should not be immediate nieghbors of Hamdān. The choice of Arḥab, a Bakīl tribe to the north, with two tribes intervening between its territory and Hamdān, and of Khawlān, well to the southeast of Sanaa, appears to have been a logical and carefully-weighed one. A full exposition of Yemeni tribal dynamics is not essential to the point. Clearly the imamate, to maintain itself and its control over productive areas with populations amenable to close administration, was obliged to deal with tribes largely in terms of their own traditional standards of behavior. Defiant acts by the tribes were not illegitimate applications of force in the eyes of the tribesmen, who held values differing from those of Zaidism. The Qāsimī state did not hold a monopoly of legitimate coercion.

Depredations by the northern tribes in Lower Yemen were a recurring phenomenon dating, as we have noted, at least to the Ṣulayḥid era, when Khawlān tribesmen despoiled the population between Ta'izz and Ibb. During the Qāsimī period the most frequent authors of such forays were Dhū Ghailān, of the Jabal Baraṭ region in the northeast.[24] This tribe had played an indispensable role in the establishment of the Qāsimī dynasty, but this fact by no means signified a willingness to accept Qāsimī discipline. The imam al-Mahdī 'Abbās (1748-1775) mounted a formal expedition to expel Dhū Ghailān from Lower Yemen. The local populace naturally looked to the imam to ensure security for their daily lives. Several years later the same imam sent a force under command of his son to intercept the tribesmen on their way south:

> They overtook them at the locality of al-Madāra, near Jahrān, and inflicted exemplary punishment upon them. Some of the leaders were killed, others taken prisoner. The heads of about sixty of their slain chiefs were cut off, with which the troops returned to Sanaa, arriving after

> Friday prayers. This was a victory for the faith and a deterrent for rebels and perpetrators of outrage.[25]

Dhū Ghailān were not permanently deterred. In 1835 they were settled in a number of forts they had seized in Lower Yemen; al-Nāṣir 'Abdullah himself led an unsuccessful campaign to dislodge them in that year. We may assume that the sovereign's failure contributed to the southerners' receptivity to a millennarian movement which appeared at this time under the leadership of a *ṣūfī* (mystic), Sa'īd bin Ṣālih Yāsīn al-'Ansī. From a well-fortified headquarters near Ibb, Sa'īd published a claim to be the "awaited *mahdī*," and managed to collect a sufficient following to evict the northern tribesmen. His claims, and his striking of coins—of pure silver—in his own name represented an intolerable challenge to the imam, who captured and executed him in 1841.[26]

We are fortunate to have a description of the Qāsimī state when its decline was well under way, as seen by the first Europeans to visit Yemen out of scholarly curiosity rather than commercial interest. King Frederick V of Denmark, seeking to enhance the luster of his reign, sponsored an expedition of scientific discovery to the East which sojourned in Yemen December 1762–August 1763. Its senior members succumbed to disease, but a German survivor, Carsten Niebuhr, survived to write a description of the situation in Southern Arabia remarkable more for the insights he managed to derive from his cautious, reluctant informants than for its occasional misapprehensions.[27] His visit coincided with a moment of respite between periods of turbulence. The reigning imam, al-Mahdī 'Abbās, had recently mastered a determined rebellion in Ḥujariya, and was not yet confronted with the revolt of his own sons. The prevailing fragmentation reminded Niebuhr of the countless German baronies of his time, the conflicting interests among which were "naturally fatal to trade and industry."[28] Several of the territories beyond the borders of present-day Yemen had been ruled by the third Qāsimī imam, al-Mutawakkil Ismā'īl (1644-1676), but were now under independent sovereigns: Aden and its hinterland; Yāfi'; Nejran and its environs; and Asir. Within Yemen proper, Niebuhr was given to understand that several principalities were governed in full sovereignty by sayyid families: the Saḥān region centered on Ṣaʻda (presumably by the Mu'ayyad clan); the eastern Jawf; the Mārib area; the Lower Khawlān, where the al-Kibsī family were also traditional leaders of the Yemeni *ḥajj* caravan; and Kawkabān, where (Sharaf al-Dīn) sayyids were believed to be beyond Qāsimī authority. Certain tribal areas are construed as similarly independent under their shaikhs, including Khawlān al-Shām (west of Ṣaʻda); the Nahm tribal domain; and the entire territory of Ḥāshid and Bekīl. Curiously, the latter is taken to be outside the imam's domain and a threat to it, but also an important source of military manpower.

> The Imam of Sanaa, and the Sharīf of Mecca, entertain each several regiments of those highlanders and pay them better than their other troops. They must have officers of their own nation; and the shaikhs usually both raise the regiments and nominate the officers. For this reason, the Imam fears to quarrel with the confederates. When they go to war with the sovereign of Sanaa, their countrymen in his service desert and join them.[29]

The imam's territory thus was construed to be confined to the Tihama and the highlands southward from the Hamdān tribe just north of the capital. Even within this domain, fifty or more enclaves were governed by independent shaikhs, which we may probably take to mean that there were no resident officials of the imam, and that taxes were collected and disbursed locally. The central revenues derived from land and poll taxes, duties on merchandise, and a twenty-five percent ad valorem export tax on coffee; they had declined from an estimated 830,000 crowns monthly in the reign of al-Mahdī Muḥammad (1687-1718) to perhaps 500,000 at the time of Niebuhr's visit, as a result of the loss of territory and the grant of lucrative fiefs to members of the ruling family.[30] Niebuhr, while recognizing the weakness of the Yemeni polity he observed, considered that its constitution, "as ancient as society itself," would "probably last while the country endures in which nature has established it."[31]

The Second Ottoman Occupation

Niebuhr could not know that a militant Islamic revival movement already asserting control of Nejd would presently produce shock waves of international amplitude. By the turn of the nineteenth century, proselytes for the unitarian doctrines of Muḥammad bin 'Abd al-Wahhāb, seconded by the political acumen and military vigor of the House of Saud, had penetrated much of the Arabian Peninsula and won sympathizers in the Zaidi capital itself. The Sulaimānī sharīf Ḥamūd in Asir, who resisted the reform movement, was deposed by its converts in 1804 and moved southward into the Yemeni Tihama. The aged Zaidi imam, al-Manṣūr 'Alī, whose nine sons were already bickering over his succession in his very presence, had no means of countering this usurpation.

When, a few years later, the Wahhabis seized Hijaz and the holy cities, Muḥammad 'Alī of Egypt loyally took on the task of reconquering them for his suzerain, the Ottoman sultan. Egyptian forces, moreover, occupied Asir. Muḥammad 'Alī, who soon aspired to possess Yemen's coffee trade, instructed his commander in Arabia, Aḥmad Pasha Yakan, to secure Yemen's ports. The Greek revolt then supervened and Muḥammad 'Alī was called upon by the Porte to suppress it. He therefore negotiated an agreement with Iman al-Mutawakkil Aḥmad (1809-1816) whereby the imam's sovereignty over the Tihama was recognized, against payment—in coffee—of a substantial annual tribute to the sultan, through the Egyptian governor in Jidda. This understanding was of limited profit to the imam, since Sharīf Ḥamūd remained in actual possession of the Tihama. By 1832 Muḥammad 'Alī had broken with his suzerain and had instituted military operations against Ottoman territory in the Levant. A commander of his Albanian irregulars in Jidda, Turkī Bilmāz, conceived the notion of revolt against his sovereign and of becoming governor of Hijaz on behalf of the Porte; it obliged by issuing him the relevant commission. Muḥammad 'Alī promptly sent Aḥmad Pasha back to the Peninsula with a large force. At their approach Turkī hastily loaded his followers onto ships seized in Jidda harbor and sailed to the Yemen coast, where he took the ports of Hodeida and Mocha. Pursued by the Egyptians, the Albanians escaped to India aboard a British vessel. The Egyptians instituted an occupation of the Tihama which endured five years (1835-1840). A three-cornered dispute among Qāsimī claimants to the imamate afforded opportunity for expansion inland to Ta'izz and 'Udain. When pressure by the European powers forced Muḥammad 'Alī to reduce his military establishment, the Yemen garrison was withdrawn, and rule of the Tihama was turned over to the Sulaimānī sharīf Ḥusain bin 'Alī bin Ḥaidar, who had been in Egyptian employ.

Egyptian operations in Arabia had disturbed the British, who judged that preponderant influnce of a single strong power in the Red Sea as well as the Persian Gulf represented an unacceptable threat to their communications with India. A reconnaissance mission by Captain S. B. Haines in 1835 confirmed the suitability of Aden as a coaling station near the entrance to the Red Sea. The following year he took occasion of the plunder of a distressed British ship in the vicinity to elicit an agreement from the 'Abdalī sultan for British possession of the port. The act was repudiated by the sultan's relatives, and Aden was seized by force in 1839. Henceforth, British efforts to ensure a stable hinterland for this foothold on the Peninsula by cultivating relations with the rulers of the inland principalities constituted a challenge to both the Yemeni state and the Ottoman government.

A momentous consequence of the Asir sharīfs' conquest of the Tihama was the loss to the Zaidi imamate of a key source of revenue. The disruption prevailing in the highlands had already resulted in a decline in its productivity. The Egyptians established a monopoly of the coffee trade during their occupation, and Muḥammad 'Alī, well aware that the volume of coffee had diminished, made inquiries of his commander, Ibrāhīm Pasha Yakan. The latter laid the blame on misrule by the imams who, by depriving the warlike tribes of their "customary rights," had encouraged them to harass the owners of coffee plantations, who had therefore lost the incentive to plant and maintain their groves:

> If we conquered Sanaa, as is our fondest hope, stayed the hands of those who are disrupting public order, and

> conciliated the coffee tree owners by merciful Khedivial rule, coffee trees would be planted with great assiduity, and the crop would increase year by year until it reached its former level.[32]

The British occupation of Aden, and its development as a modern, efficient port, had similarly grave consequences. It became more profitable to transport Yemeni coffee to Aden, particularly by smuggling, than to take it to the inefficient and deteriorating Red Sea ports for export. Efforts by authorities in Yemen to prevent this diversion simply encouraged cultivators to abandon coffee and plant instead the narcotic shrub *qāt*, which had been introduced into Yemen from Ethiopia in the year 1543, simultaneously with the coffee plant.[33]

Notwithstanding their absorption in family quarrels and tribal insubordination, the Zaidi imams did not resign themselves passively to the loss of the coastal plain. In 1847 Imam al-Mutawakkil Muḥammad bin Yaḥyā demanded from Sharīf Ḥusain the surrender of certain port towns. The sharīf demurred, hostilities began, and the imam invaded the Tihama. At the town of Quṭay‘, the imam's force defeated the sharīf, who was taken prisoner. The undisciplined Zaidi tribesmen thoroughly looted the stocks of the local merchants. The sharīf's Isma‘īlī allies of the Yām tribe came to his rescue, defeating the imam's troops and releasing his prisoner. Meanwhile the despoiled merchants of Quṭay‘ had complained to the Porte. The latter ordered the commander of Turkish forces in Hijaz, Tawfīq Pasha, and the sharīf of Mecca, Muḥammad bin ‘Awn, to establish Ottoman order in the Tihama; this was accomplished by a joint expedition in 1848. The imam, hard pressed by rivals to the throne, traveled to Hodeida to enlist the Turk's support in asserting his authority. They responded to his appeal and ascended to Sanaa, whose fortress the imam turned over to them. The citizenry at once rebelled against this coalition. They seized the imam, whom they presently put to death, and besieged the Turkish troops so stringently that they were only too glad to retreat to the Tihama under a safe-conduct supervised by a new imam.[34]

Upper Yemen relapsed into near chaos. Claims to the imamate by members of various sayyid clans proliferated, none receiving more than local and intermittent support. A member of the Wazīr family, al-Manṣūr Muḥammad bin ʻAlī, led a fruitless campaign to dislodge Arḥab tribesmen who had occupied Ḥaima; he then retired to his ancestral estates at Sirr, adjudicating such disputes as were voluntarily brought before him. Dhū Ghailān resumed their plunder of Lower Yemen. The Makārima, Ismāʻīlīs who had migrated from Nejran to the Ḥarāz area a century before, began a militant expansion, occupied part of Ḥaima, and threatened the capital. The people of Sanaa, finding no imam capable of ensuring order, chose successive commoners to direct their municipal affairs. At length, in 1872, despairing of a return to public security and of any curb on the tribal lawlessness which had destroyed commerce and communications, the Sanaa notables sent a delegation to the Turkish commander in Hodeida, who had just put down a rebellion in Asir, inviting him to occupy Upper Yemen. The Ottoman forces responded promptly, and began the thankless dual task of introducing order and security in the more productive regions of the interior, and of establishing a rational bureaucratic administration.

Standards of Ottoman imperial rule had improved somewhat during the centuries intervening between the two occupations of Yemen. The regime took some modest steps toward introducing modern education, improving communications, and creating conditions in which the people could pursue their livelihood. On the other hand, Turkish administration was often harsh and arbitrary, and tax exactions burdensome. For the Shāfiʻī majority the abuse of coercion prevented the development of shared purposes which might in time have endowed the occupation with legitimacy. This was never possible in the north, where the tribes remained opposed to direct rule, and where conscientious Zaidis could not conceive of legitimate government under other than ʻAlid auspices, let alone government conducted by secular rules only remotely rooted in Islam. Above all, the regime was foreign, and opposition to it was a principle on which most sectors of

Yemeni society could unite. Ottoman rule was opposed by violence from the first. A new line of Qāsimī imams, the Ḥamīd al-Dīn, became after 1879 credible leaders of a national liberation movement. The ability of the imamate to mobilize wealth and manpower was dramatically enhanced.

The Ḥamīd al-Dīn Compromise with the Turks

The magnitude of the Turkish effort to suppress the revolt fluctuated with the broad policies and capabilities of the Porte. The struggle endured for forty years, with a loss of life estimated at a half-million on either side.[35] It was punctuated by attempts by the Porte to reach some settlement with the imamate without encouraging dissident movements elsewhere in the empire. Negotiations, ultimately successful, took place with the imam al-Mutawakkil Yaḥyā, who succeeded his father, al-Manṣūr Muḥammad, in 1904. They give us a detailed conception of the imam's view of legitimate government, and shed light on his later conduct as a fully independent monarch.

During his first year as imam, Yaḥyā led the tribes in an intensive series of guerrilla attacks on Ottoman military garrisons. The campaign completed the demoralization of the occupying forces, whose pay was badly in arrears and whose terms of enlistment had in many cases long since expired. The Porte opened discussions with the imam, who set forth a list of conditions on the basis of which he was prepared to make peace. He stated:

> Relying on God's aid, I have agreed to conditions for peace between myself and the agent of the Sultan of Islam . . . so as to extinguish the flames of war which have been ignited, to replace chaos and enmity with friendship, to save the country from anxiety, to spare bloodshed, to end suffering in this region, to ensure security, to establish indissoluble ties of brotherhood among the Faithful, and to eliminate tyranny from among them.[36]

Judicial process, Yaḥyā demanded, was to be conducted according to the *sharī'a*. The appointment and removal of judges and magistrates was to be the province of the imam, and also the punishment of traitors and bribe-takers. Civil officials were to be paid sufficient salaries that they should not be forced to accept bribes. The administration of *awqāf* was to be in the imam's hands, in the interest of promoting education. Muslim and Jewish criminals were to be punished as provided by the canon law. Taxes on agricultural produce and livestock were to be assessed at the rates set by the *sharī'a*, and collected by the local shaikhs under the supervision of Ottoman officials; any such official who exacted more than the canonical rate could be removed or fined by the imam. The latter was to have no role in the collecting of taxes and duties imposed by the Ottoman regime. Certain impoverished tribes whose land had been devastated during the recent disturbances were to be exempt from taxation for a period of ten years. Either side was to be obligated to extradite traitors. A general amnesty was to be promulgated by the Turks. No Christian or Jew was to be placed in authority over Muslims. The Porte, finally, was to be responsible for defense of the area against attack by foreign powers. Anticipating dissatisfaction among Yemeni merchants serving as sutlers to the Turkish forces, whose business would decline with the reduction of the garrison upon the conclusion of peace, the imam specified that the terms be embodied in a *firmān* of the Ottoman sultan.[37]

These stipulations reflect an obvious concern for the conduct of public affairs in strict harmony with religious precept. Secular accretions introduced by the Turks were to be minimized, and the integrity of administration was to be ensured by the imam's close supervision. The contemplated relationship with the Turks is interesting. The imam clearly sees the general community of Muslims as a single entity, whatever his insistence upon his own authority over the Zaidi sect. He tacitly recognizes a sort of Ottoman sovereignty by acknowledging the Porte's responsibility for national defense. On the other hand, while deferring to the sultan, he avoids giving him the title of caliph, to which Abdül Ḥamīd II currently attached great political importance. In Zaidi doctrine, of course, that office was reserved to the descendants of 'Alī and Fāṭima, and could not conceivably be held by a Turk.

The Ottoman government, faced with aspirations toward local autonomy by various ethnic components of the empire, decided that the proposed arrangements would set a precedent dangerous to the integrity of its domain, and rejected them out of hand. The war resumed, and other approaches were explored toward a peaceful accommodation. The Porte organized a visit to Yemen by ten prominent ulama of Mecca in October 1907. These divines failed to win Yaḥyā's submission, but received from him a letter which gives us further insight into his concept of his right to authority over the people of Yemen.[38]

God, the imam asserts, has provided the Muslims with the soundest of religions by which to order their affairs, and sent them the most perfect of prophets to demonstrate how the faith is to be put into practice. The period of the Prophet's earthly presence was the most perfect of eras in human history; any manifestations of heresy or injustice were immediately eradicated. After Muḥammad, however, corruption steadily grew under self-seeking rulers who, until the rise of the Ottoman sultans, became incapable of defending Islam against hostile unbelievers.

Since the third century A.H., the imam continues, Yemen has been ruled in whole or in part by an unbroken line of the Prophet's divinely favored descendants. They have been in constant struggle against rivals, a struggle which could be sustained only because of the Yemeni people's desire to be ruled by their sayyids, whom they know to be motivated solely by the determination to command the right and forbid evil, and their consequent acceptance of the duty to fight for their imams.

Yaḥyā states that the conduct of Ottoman officials since their occupation of Yemen has steadily deteriorated. Their open debauchery is offensive to Yemeni moral principles, and their greed leads them not only to the imposition of non-canonical taxes but even to outright confiscation of the citizens' property. Public indignation inspired Yaḥyā's father, al-Manṣūr Muḥammad, to lead them in the struggle against Turkish corruption. He himself assumed the leadership not for love of power, prestige, or wealth, but simply to ensure the establishment of justice and upright conduct; to revive religious education (which he declares the Turks had abolished); to instruct the people in the duties of the faith; and to reinstate the authority of the *sharīʻa*. The imam complains bitterly of the duplicity of the Ottoman governors, who had flagrantly violated truce terms. He claims that they turned the sultan against him by slanderously denouncing him as a heretic or even infidel, and by suborning Yemeni citizens into abetting this campaign of defamation against himself and Zaidism. He and the Yemeni people, in opposing Ottoman officialdom, are merely exercising the right, confirmed to them by scripture, to defend themselves, their possessions, their daughters, and their sons.

The basic thesis asserted by the imam is common to a number of revivalist and modernizing movements in the Islam of his time,[39] although he states it from his Zaidi point of view. Social injustice and the weakness of the Muslim community vis-à-vis the Christian powers are consequences of departure from, and accretions to, the *sharīʻa* and the *sunna*. Yaḥyā and the Yemeni people share the aspiration to restore the purity and strength of primitive Islam. There is furthermore a shared conviction that this can be achieved only under the leadership of the Prophet's descendants, with their unique ability to discern right from wrong within the dictates of the faith.

In 1911, hard pressed by war in the Balkans, by the Italian seizure of Libya, and by more than usually costly defeats by the Yemeni rebels, the Ottomans concluded peace with the imam, in the Treaty of Da"ān.[40] This curious arrangement applied specifically to the Yemeni highlands roughly along a line from ʻUmrān and Ḥajja southward to, and including, Taʻizz. By implication, a free hand is acknowledged to the imam in the northern areas already under his control, while direct Ottoman administration of the Tihama is uncontested. The imam's objective of establishing the supremacy of canon law is achieved to the extent that he is empowered to appoint judges in the Zaidi areas; to establish a court of appeals; to direct the administration of the *awqāf*; and to make representations to the Ottoman governor concerning abuse of authority by Turkish officials, or their collection of taxes in a manner detrimental to the *sharīʻa*.

The imam is not expressly given the right to collect the

canonical tithes in the region where authority is shared; the point is made subtly, however, by a provision that Yemenis of the Zaidi sect have the "right" to present "gifts" to the imam, either directly or through their local shaikhs. That the harvest from such gifts is expected to be substantial is reflected in the provision that the imam is to pay over to the Ottoman government one tenth of his revenues. The imam accommodates himself to Turkish determination to preserve the outward forms of the Porte's sovereignty, and the appearance of an administration centralized in Istanbul. The imam's judicial appointments, as well as decisions of the courts, are subject to review and confirmation by the shaikh al-Islām in the Ottoman capital. As a further concession, the imam agreed to forgo for a period of ten years the taking of hostages from Sanaa, Ḥarāz, or ʻAmrān, a device of control without basis in the canon law. The treaty furnished a workable basis for coexistence during the remaining years of Ottoman occupation, which ended in 1919, not through Yemeni action but by Turkey's defeat in World War I.

Although the Da"ān compromise relieved the Yemeni people of the trials of war, it potentially weakened the Yemeni polity. Resistance to Ottoman rule had been a salient aspiration of the Ḥamīd al-Dīn imams, shared by much of the population irrespective of sect. The treaty signified the abandonment of this unifying principle, in contrast to the continuing resistance to Turkish authority of the Idrīsid regime in neighboring Asir. It suggested that the imam was resigned to the status of leader of the Zaidi community, rather than of a Yemeni nation. The country was now divided constitutionally along sectarian lines into three distinct regions, two of which were governed primarily by the Sunnī Ottomans and the Zaidi imam, respectively. The third, the most populous and productive, was subjected to an incoherent authority structure which called into question the legitimacy of both regimes, and resulted inevitably in a duplication of exactions from the people. Subsequent politics in Yemen revolve around the creation or discovery of shared values and aspirations by Yemenis of all sects, callings, and orientations which would render legitimate in their eyes the authority of their rulers.

The second Ottoman occupation had other impacts of political significance. The period coincided with the Turkish movement toward administrative modernization and westernization, and the formation of new concepts of the functions of government. The Porte's officials in Yemen were preoccupied simply with staying there, and the new norms were ignored or regularly violated. The Turks did nevertheless built some hospitals in the tranquil areas of the country, and a few schools designed to provide training in nonreligious subjects. The idea that these were proper functions of the state survived the occupation, at least in part. Imam Yaḥyā's independent regime kept the hospitals open, no matter how badly they were staffed and managed. The mechanical trades school in Sanaa, on the other hand, was converted to a jail. Turkish efforts to develop Yemen's communications facilities by building a railway from the coast to the capital, and to exploit its supposed mineral resources, were abortive. These enterprises would have instituted diversification of Yemeni society by the creation of new economic and administrative roles; in the event, this development was postponed for a few decades. Of immediate practical political importance was the telegraph network bequeathed to the country by the Turks; taken over and expanded by Imam Yaḥyā, it served as a source of revenue, but more particularly as a means of asserting his will throughout the country and of keeping himself informed of events such as had been available to none of his predecessors.

The most significant Ottoman legacy was in the military field. The imams had traditionally kept a small body of armed retainers; servile or mercenary forces, they in no way constituted a professional standing army. For operations of any considerable scope they were supplemented or replaced by citizens and tribesmen mustered or hired for a limited period and a specific objective. They were led in battle by the imam himself, his relatives, members of the sayyid aristocracy, and even by scholars and judges: people, that is, who concurrently occupied other important social and political roles. Imam Yaḥyā took over from the Ottomans the idea of a professional army and militia under the command of a corps of officers whose status and role were fully differentiated. He employed the services of a number of Turks who chose to remain in Yemen, rather than be repatriated after World War I. They organized and trained the new forces, and administered a military academy to produce future commissioned officers. The new element thus established within Yemeni society quite predictably developed interests and orientations distinct from those of other social segments and became an important agent of lasting change in Yemeni politics.

7
The Mutawakkilite Kingdom

When the Da"ān Treaty was signed, Yemen had few attributes of a single, viable polity. During the Ottoman-Zaidi condominium and later during the independent monarchy, Imam Yaḥyā performed the notable feat of constructing a unified state. One inveterate conspirator against his rule, and that of his son, Imam Aḥmad, says:

> It is an acknowledged fact that by his action he succeeded in unifying the greater part of Yemen under his absolute authority. This was an enormous accomplishment, for at the end of the Turkish war Yemen ran the risk of fragmentation through the rise of no less than a hundred amirates, shaikhdoms, and sultanates. Nothing had survived its chaotic tribulations save the appeal of Zaidism and its content of revolutionary spirit.[1]

Yaḥyā created a regime which endured for four decades. It gave the superficial impression of a static, medieval society in which efficient, if arbitrary, rule by an absolute, theocratic king ensured a remarkable degree of stability and set immovable obstacles in the path of social and political change. Upon close examination, however, we find that significant evolution was in fact in progress during these two reigns. In this chapter it is proposed to study how change came about. We shall examine the structure of Yemeni society at the outset of the Mutawakkilite era, and the expectations various groups placed on the political system; the values of the ruling imams, with particular attention to the shifting emphasis among their objectives; the growing dissonance between the aims of the rulers and the demands of their subjects, aggravated by an increasing complexity in the society's changing political values; and finally, as a result of these processes, the loss by the Ḥamīd al-Dīn imamate of the legitimacy on which its survival depended.

The Yemeni Political Outlook

Commonly, broad generalizations concerning entire societies lead to a long series of qualifications and exceptions. While of dubious usefulness in themselves, such sweeping statements may at least serve as points of reference for further study. We are often told that the Yemeni citizen of this period was typically a partisan tribesman, a bigoted religious fanatic, a xenophobe, and such a quarrelsome and intense individualist that only a draconian regime such as that of the Zaidi imam could subject him to a modicum of discipline.

On the eve of his 1922 tour of the Arab kingdoms, the Arab-American Amīn al-Rīḥānī asked a Yemeni whom he met by chance in New York to tell him about his country.[2] The Yemeni replied,

> Our country has a good climate and water, but the people are always fighting. . . . We have fought the Turks, the tribes, and the Idrīsī; and we are always fighting each other. [The imam] rules only a small part of Yemen. We Yemenis submit to no one permanently. We love freedom and will fight for it. We would cut the throat of our nearest relative to be independent. We tell the imam, "We don't want this man as governor," then we set up one of us as shaikh and tell him, "You are our ruler; you are our imam." If the imam's governor refuses to give up his position: We'll slit his throat.[3]

Asked whether foreigners could live in Yemen or visit there, the Yemeni replied in the negative. If a foreigner nevertheless arrived, "We'd slit his throat."[4]

As representative of the outlook of the aristocrats, al-Rīḥānī quotes Sayyid 'Abdullah al-Wazīr:[5]

> Through the virtue of the imam this country of ours is a land of right, justice, faith, honesty, and loyalty. You will find perfect, equitable government among us in Yemen. There is no wine, no prostitution, no fornication, no murder, no theft, no discrimination, no bribery, and no strikes. All this is because we preserve our faith, acting in accord with the Book of God, striving in the way of God Almighty. . . . We practice what we preach. Others preach but do not practice, or else they preach the good and practice evil. The Arabs are despicable liars. They prefer the foreigner's money to *jihād* for the cause of God. We fought the Turks again and again. We waged holy war against the treacherous non-believers in the Tihama. And we shall fight anyone who tries to filch an inch of our territory or deprive us of the least of our rights.[6]

A sayyid of more modest station who escorted Rīḥanī from Dhamār to Sanaa expressed a contrasting view of his countrymen:

> You complained of how cramped and depressing our houses are, with their low ceilings and narrow windows. If you traveled in Asir you would find the houses still smaller and darker. Do you know why? The people of Yemen and Asir are still savages. None of them trusts or relies on his brother. They live in constant fear and anxiety. . . . They are like wild beasts, afraid of anyone who comes near them. In Yemen, as you have seen for yourself, everyone goes armed. They all fight, and they fight over trifling matters. . . . If there is a dispute between two families in this village for instance, everyone will get mixed up in it

> and divide themselves into two factions, one supporting either disputant. The flames of war break out, and when they are extinguished, people ask each other, "What was the fight about between so-and-so and so-and-so?" They fight first, then they investigate. That's the way we act in Yemen. We even fight within our own families. Brother fights brother, the son his father. If that is how we treat each other, how will we behave toward foreigners?"[7]

We could easily multiply quotations in this vein, often accompanied by explanations in terms of environmental determinism. Yemenis are mountaineers, it is alleged, and the difficulties of communication in broken terrain encourage the growth of individualism, bigotry, and xenophobia. The persuasiveness of the argument is somewhat impaired when we are told that Arabs of the flat desert, because of the physical environment in which they live, become imbued with the same love of freedom, xenophobia, and religious intolerance. Whatever the source of these frequently-noted traits, it is sufficient here to recall the central position which Islam had occupied in the public and private life of the country for more than a millennium, and to suggest that the Yemenis' recent contacts with foreigners, whether Turks, Italians, British, or fellow Arabs, had given few Yemenis reason to expect advantage from close association with them.

The Kingdom's Social Structure

The domain of Imam Yaḥyā received its definitive boundaries (the eastern border, of course, remains undemarcated) with the settlement following the 1934 war with Saudi Arabia. It contained a population divided sharply along sectarian lines as a consequence of the historical events we have traced. Agriculture was the preponderant base of the economy, between eighty and eighty-five percent of the people deriving their livelihood directly from the land. The ruling elites were mainly townsfolk; the role of rural and tribal leaders in government beyond their local communities was intermittent, becoming of moment only in times of crisis. The rural population was furthermore heterogeneous, and several patterns of relationship between the people and the imams' regime may be distinguished. For this purpose we will discuss successively the closely-settled highlands extending from 'Amrān to the South Yemen border; the coastal plain; the tribal region forming a broad arc to the north and east of the high mountains, extending to the open desert; and the urban communities.

The Central Highlands

The first of these regions accommodates Yemen's densest populations and produces the majority of the country's grain, coffee, *qāt*, fruit, and vegetables. The area of individual cultivated fields is sharply restricted by the broken terrain; terraces, built in antiquity and carefully maintained, are necessary to conserve both topsoil and moisture. Agricultural techniques are simple, though effective, and technological dependence on the outside is minimal. The ancient caravan routes skirted the area to east and west, and while some attention was devoted to the construction of roads by the Ṣulayḥid queen Arwā (for economic reasons) and by the Turks (for military purposes), no major effort was undertaken until late in the reign of Imam Aḥmad to develop efficient communications facilities. "As it is," wrote a member of the British-Turkish boundary commission during the Ottoman presence,

> farm produce and requisites must be carried by hand, or in absurdly small loads on donkeys, which have to be half carried themselves up some of the mountain tracks. When the husbandman has got his produce to a caravan-route, he is faced with exhorbitant transport, unless he is a camel-owner himself, and then there is a question of fodder and maintenance. To crown it all, the caravan routes themselves are beset by marauders, toward the coast, where his best market is. . . . Finding his market remote and uncertain, he confines himself to meeting local requirements. This means under-production, which brings its own penalty, for any marked scarcity of rain in the agricultural district entails a general famine, as the people are living from hand to mouth. Centuries of strife,

> past taxation and present commercial depression have all tended to establish this procedure.[8]

Like most generalizations, the foregoing needs some qualification. It ignores a number of internal trade patterns of great antiquity and importance. The present writer observed one of these in operation in the early 1960s, by which herdsmen in the semi-desert region of Marīb mined salt locally and transported it by camel caravan for sale in Sanaa, Dhamār, Yarīm, and occasionally even Ibb, using the proceeds to purchase bread-grains, not raised in their own country.

The significant point is that the Yemeni highlanders had few economic demands to make on the central political system. They held government responsible for the security of trade routes, but not for their maintenance and improvement. They looked to central authority to restrain incursions by outside predatory tribesmen, but local order was a function of tribal tradition or of mediation by local ulama. They accepted the principle that the ruler had the right to gather the canonical tithes, and tolerated, if unwillingly, collection of market taxes, circulation dues, fees for official acts, etc., some dating at least from Ayyūbid times, others introduced by the Turks.

The people to the north of Yarīm had long since been converted to Zaidism, and thus accepted the notion of a combined political and spiritual leadership. As cosectarians of the imam they enjoyed a preferred status in the eyes of the regime over the Shāfi'īs to the south; this distinction was expressed in many ways, of which the margin of discretion left to Zaidi local headmen in assessing the *zakāt* was merely the most obvious. Other factors accentuated the distinction. Kinship ties embraced larger groups than in the south; there were many tribes of substantial size known for their descent rather than their geographic location, such as Hamdān, the two Ḥaima tribes, Banū al-Ḥārith, and others. Larger coalitions than in the south could be organized for representations to the central government. Communication was facilitated by the fact that this area furnished both civilian and military personnel to the imam's administration, and these men preserved their tribal identity undiluted. Finally the capital was itself situated in the northern highlands. The population consequently had ready access to the ruler's attention and adjudication, an advantage not enjoyed by the southerners during Imam Yaḥyā's reign. (Imam Aḥmad took the southern city of Ta'izz as his seat.)

The Sunnīs of the southern mountains recognized the legitimacy of some central authority, but conceived it as secular, guidance in spiritual and civil-status matters remaining the province of the Shāfi'ī ulama. This partial acknowledgment of the imams' authority naturally influenced their attitude toward the Shāfi'īs. They did not seek to eradicate Sunnism; Shāfi'īs remained judicable in courts applying their own system of law, and Sunnī religious instruction was available to their children. On the other hand, Shāfi'īs were not recruited for responsible positions in the public administration, nor promoted even to the middle ranks of the armed services. A pattern was instituted in which authority over Shāfi'īs was exercised by Zaidis. The latter came to regard their higher status as normal and right. Ascriptive inferiority was understandably a source of resentment for the Shāfi'īs, although it took nearly two decades for them to place blame for their grievances on the political institution of the imamate and to decide that it was within their power to effect a change.

Social isolation in the south was not a particular handicap under the Turks, who were also Sunnīs. By contrast, the Shāfi'īs were seldom able to mobilize effective mediatory pressures upon the Zaidi imams. While the rulers' policies aggravated economic stagnation and social backwardness throughout the country, their different treatment of the northern and the southern highlands produced the contrast noted by an American diplomat who toured Yemen in 1945: whereas the condition of the common people around Sanaa was "poor," it was "appalling" in some of the southern areas.[9]

The Tihama

By contrast with the highlands, over which sovereignty was transferred without contest from the Turks to Imam Yaḥyā, the coastal plain had to be conquered by the Zaidis. Except for the decayed port of Mocha, the imams had no foothold on the

Red Sea coast for more than a century. The population was solidly Sunnī. The political outlook of the people of the port towns, notably Hodeida, was directly related to the security and prosperity of their trade with the outside world. The rural population, which had little stake in international trade except as an object of loot, principally sought freedom from any external authority. At the end of World War I, Britain undertook on behalf of the Allies to supervise the surrender of Ottoman forces in Yemen. Those at Hodeida resisted for a time, and Britain sent warships and troops to bombard and seize the port. The occupation continued while the British weighed various alternative dispositions of Hodeida, and we are given reliable insights into political attitudes in the central Tihama at this time through the reports of British officials who conducted a sort of opinion poll. Not surprisingly, the views of the rural and of the urban population differed sharply.

The inland population consisted in the main of warlike tribes of ‘Akk descent, jealous of their autonomy. They had been a thorn in the Turkish flesh through their depredations against caravans moving goods between the ports and the mountains; Ottoman officials kept the problem within tolerable bounds by paying subsidies to the more important shaikhs. The largest of these tribes was the Zarānīq, in the area between Hodeida and Zabīd. A smaller tribe, the Quḥra, occupied a strategic position astride the trail from Hodeida through Bājil to Sanaa.

In August 1919 the Quḥra captured and held for three months a British mission destined for Sanaa, headed by Col. H. F. Jacob. Although Jacob's purpose in the Zaidi capital was simply to sound out Imam Yaḥyā's views, the Quḥra became convinced that he purposed to negotiate the turnover of Hodeida and its hinterland to the imam.[10] Their shaikhs were at the time engaged in discussions with both the imam and Sayyid ‘Alī al-Idrīsī, ruler of Asir, most probably with the intention of avoiding submission to either. The Jacob party were released on two conditions: that they return to Aden without proceeding to the Zaidi capital; and that Imam Yaḥyā should have no control over them or their country.[11] The tribe's outlook was expressed by one of their shaikhs:

> Who is the imam? We are Quḫra, tribal people. God gave us freedom, and we are numerous. We have more grain than we need. Our houses are secure. We get our *qāt* from Jabal Rīma by a special arrangement. We want nothing more.[12]

Like the Quḫra, the Zarānīq sought to perserve their autonomy by a combination of intrigue and force of arms:

> In the era of the Turks the Zarānīq were, as they remain, arrogant rebels. They accepted pensions from the government, but nevertheless cut the telegraph lines, despoiled caravan traffic by land and dhows at sea. Their shaikhs are not lacking in political acumen and duplicity. They always play two or three roles on the Tihama stage, and lean in the end in the direction where there is the most money and arms. One of their shaikhs negotiated with the English, undertaking to support them against the Turks in exchange for arms and ammunition. Then he accepted an offer of employment by the Ottoman governor of Yemen, and became *qā'imaqām* of Zabīd. They supported the Quḫra tribe in their capture of the English mission at Bājil, then helped those seeking to procure their release. Not surprisingly, some Zarānīq are leaning toward the side of Imam Yaḥyā today, and others toward the Idrīsī Sayyid.[13]

The tribe was thus not monolithic; it was in fact divided into two principal branches, north and south. On the border between the two, inland from the coast, lay the town of Bait al-Faqīh, of which the inhabitants were fired with the same fierce individualism as the surrounding tribesmen:

> Bait al-Faqīh . . . is free, independent and absolutely sovereign. It recognizes no imam, no foreigner nor any Zarnūq as its master. Moreover, it is itself divided into five sections, or wards, each with a population not exceeding one thousand.[14] Each ward is a free and independent city, ruled in the name of God and its thousand souls, freely

> and independently, by a shaikh who has no relationship with his colleagues, and concedes them no authority within his own jurisdiction.[15]

The people of Hodeida, on the other hand, had other preoccupations. Of relatively cosmopolitan composition, the community was a mercantile one, without unifying kinship ties but possessing a common interest in the freedom and security of commerce through their port. With one hand the British permitted their wartime ally, the Idrīsī Sayyid, to move a battalion of soldiers to the vicinity of Hodeida. With the other they conducted a survey of views among leaders of opinion in the city regarding their future. The results were disconcerting.

The British contemplated three alternatives: rule by Imam Yaḥyā; rule by the Idrīsid state of Asir; or their own continued presence. The poll placed the Hodeida merchants in an unenviable position. They had no love for the British, infidels whose warships had destroyed much property and many lives, and who refused compensation for the damage. Nor did they desire to be governed by the imam. The latter had shown himself willing to sacrifice their interests during the 1905 negotiations, and his anti-Sunnī policy was already apparent inland. On the other hand, they might lay themselves open to reprisals if they openly expressed repugnance for his rule. As for the Idrīsī, his troops were already at hand and in a position either to enforce his will or to stir up the Tihama tribes against the defenseless port.[16] Furthermore, if he became their ruler, he could hardly be expected to promote the prosperity of Hodeida to the detriment of his own port of Jizan.

Rejecting the British alternatives, the Hodeida consensus openly favored the restoration of rule by the Turks, under whom the merchants had conducted their business in freedom and security. Failing this, they wished to be ruled by the Egyptian government. Neither proposition was realistic from the standpoint of the British, who left their options open by simply withdrawing, leaving a local notable in charge under their patronage.[17] He was soon overthrown by the Idrīsī, who continued to receive British arms and funds. After a few years of Idrīsī misrule,[18] Imam Yaḥyā seized the port of Hodeida in March 1925. The population submitted without overt opposition.

The Tihama tribes, notably the Zarānīq, were not so easily subdued. They endeavored to continue their independent and predatory way of life, their acts of murder and robbery becoming an intolerable challenge to the imam's authority. In 1928, after a series of minor punitive expeditions, an army reported to have numbered a thousand men was dispersed among the Zarānīq villages.[19] In a remarkably coordinated action the tribesmen slaughtered the soldiers to the last man one night as they slept. The imam gave Crown Prince Aḥmad, then governor of Ḥajja, the job of reducing the tribes to obedience. This he did in a two-year campaign of the utmost savagery and efficiency.[20]

After Sayyid 'Ali al-Idrīsī's death in 1922, his succession was disputed among relatives of less ability. Prince Aḥmad at Ḥajja was conveniently situated to infiltrate the coastal plain. By the alternate use of military force and diplomacy, he extended the Zaidi state's control by 1926 approximately to the present border with Saudi Arabia. In that year Aḥmad accompanied shaikhs of Wā'iẓāt, 'Abs, Qays, Khāmisīn, Banū Marwān, and smaller north Tihama tribes to Sanaa, where they pledged loyalty to the imam.[21] Affairs of the area, relatively unproductive economically, were left mainly in the hands of traditional leaders; the region thenceforth raised no serious problems for the Mutawakkilite government.

The Northern and Eastern Tribes

The particularistic and warlike predilections of the tribes north and east of the capital remained undiminished when Yemen became independent. The Turks compromised the theoretically exclusive jurisdiction of Imam Yaḥyā over these largely Zaidi communities by allotting subsidies to their key shaikhs. Like his predecessors, the Imam had been unable to introduce consecutive administration among them or fully to replace customary law with the *sharī'a*. Intermittent campaigns over a period of fourteen years were required to impose the imam's authority. (These operations precipitated the 1934 war with Saudi Arabia.) Few years in the history of the kingdom passed without some sort of tribal challenge to it. The tribesmen's priority of values has been described thus:

> A man, for example, of the Arḥab tribe does not consider himself a citizen of a Yemen which extends from the Gulf of Aden on the south to the Hijaz country on the north, and similarly east and west. On the contrary, he is above all an Arḥabī, and will fight any non-Arḥabī in defense of the Arḥab system of government and customs. For Arḥabism he will sacrifice connections of nationality and ties of religion. Only after this is he a Yemeni and a Muslim. Yemeni patriotism and Islam do not concern him to the extent that solidarity of the tribe in which he was raised does. The same may be said of all Yemeni tribes.[22]

The weakness of national and Zaidi loyalty among the tribes was apparent from the first years of the regime. Arriving in Sanaa in 1922, Amīn al-Rīḥanī was kept incommunicado for a time because of Imam Yaḥyā's absence. The imam was attending to an outbreak of disaffection among tribes near Shahāra, his ancestral seat:

> [The imam] was absent in the north upon our arrival, settling dissidence among the Ḥāshid and 'Iyāl Ṣarīḥ which had gotten out of hand. We had been told along the way that some of the chiefs of those tribes were in negotiations with the Idrīsī Sayyid with a view to joining him and assisting him to defeat the Zaidis.[23]

While the imams were not thereafter troubled by such treasonable movements against the kingdom's territorial integrity, they were never able to supplant the tribal law codes. One feature of such codes bore on the right of women to inherit property; according to tribal custom they were either entirely excluded, or received a much smaller portion of the estate than the *sharī'a* prescribes. In 1925 the imam mounted an expedition against Ḥāshid to enforce the canon law on this point. As late as the summer of 1962, this writer's legation received circumstantial reports of resistance by the Duhma tribes to the regime's efforts to nullify their traditional law.

Imam Yaḥyā devoted an extraordinary share of his time to

the personal dispensing of justice in his daily *majlis*, to which the lowliest of his subjects had access. There is no reason to doubt that he considered these labors his duty as a Muslim ruler. At the same time, there was certainly an element of calculation in this effort. It was one effective means of creating links between himself and the people, and facilitating the maintenance of a hierarchical authority pattern. These links short-circuited the moral position of the ulama who had helped him to gain the imamate, as well as the authority and functions of the tribal shaikhs. Imam Aḥmad, in a less direct way, assiduously cultivated such personal contact with key tribes, making it possible for him to turn the tables on those who attempted to force his abdication in 1954.[24]

Tribal standards of honor, with the related concept of revenge, also persisted. ʻAlī al-Qardaʻī, shaikh of the Murād tribe, was executed in 1948 for the murder of Imam Yaḥyā, and the shaikh's son, Muḥsin, was imprisoned at Ḥajja. Released in February 1962, Muḥsin returned to his people bearing his father's blood-stained garments. He so inflamed the tribesmen that they proclaimed themselves in revolt against the Ḥamīd al-Dīn; a party of them proceeded to Sanaa and attempted to set fire to Imam Yaḥyā's tomb. Crown Prince al-Badr called upon the tribes in the vicinity of the capital for help in suppressing the revolt; few responded.

The Urban Communities

Except for the tribal shaikhs, Yemenis with pretensions or aspirations to leadership were residents of the cities and towns. The most prominent segment of the urban population was the hereditary sayyid aristocracy, of which the royal family was a part. The particular insight in matters of the faith ascribed to the sayyids by reason of their descent from the Prophet set them above the lay population; as the imamate was in some respects theocratic, it was natural that the sayyids should be a primary source of recruitment for high government office. Their economic status covered a wide range. Some, notably those who had imams in their ancestry or who occupied positions (governorships or judgeships) in which wealth could be accumulated, were among the most prosperous Yemenis;

they were often absentee owners of large tracts of agricultural land. Many were less prosperous, however, and lived modestly as teachers, traders, or minor government functionaries. They were a privileged class, and their status gave them a stake in the existing political order, reinforcing a usually quite genuine religious conviction.

Among Zaidi commoners, wealth and position were a matter of inheritance, or of achievement through service to the ruler. Through learning and ability, a number of qāḍī families achieved influence and wealth comparable to that of the great sayyid clans. We may cite the al-'Amrī family; Qāḍī 'Abdullah served as Yaḥyā's prime minister throughout his independent reign, and his son Muḥammad was one of Imam Aḥmad's most skilled and trusted diplomats; Qāḍī Muḥammad 'Abdullah al-Shāmī[25] for many years conducted Yemen's delicate dealings with the Aden Protectorate while serving as governor at al-Baiḍā'; Qāḍī Aḥmad al-Siyāghī accumulated large holdings of land as governor at Ibb. These and other such families unquestionably belonged to the governing elite. Less able or less fortunate Zaidis had perhaps a less vital material stake in the imamate, but they nevertheless enjoyed preferment over Sunnīs.

The Zaidi ulama were drawn both from the aristocracy and from educated commoners. The high status associated with the role of jurist, and the opportunity it often provided for material gain, attached the ulama firmly to the traditional order, if not necessarily to the person of the reigning imam. Their outlook included a certain obscurantism, although the following indictment by a progressive sayyid is rather exaggerated:

> [They look] upon life as awake whereas it is asleep, in motion when it is frozen, morning when it is dark. Between these people and the forces of progress and uplift lie barriers built of fairy tales, error, fanaticism, and stultification. Anything not contained within the narrow confines of their books is atheism, delusion, and sedition. All mankind's aspirations toward the benefits of civilization are forbidden, being the work of unbelievers. To seek

> wisdom elsewhere than in the books of our precursors and ancestors is error and outrage. Well-being, peace, and Islam consist in leaving things as they are, without thought for the future, following blindly the ways of our forefathers.[26]

Although their reactionary views correspond in many aspects with those of Imam Yaḥyā, the ulama had not abandoned their role as the conscience of the ruler and censor of his acts when these violated the canon law. Toward the end of Yaḥyā's reign the Sanaa ulama submitted to him a petition for reform of certain abuses of which the public was complaining. They counseled the imam:

1. to trust to the conscience of the citizens to pay their taxes, rather than permitting them to be despoiled by the military under the guise of tax collection;
2. to eliminate taxes not authorized by the *sharī'a*, and to forbid the inflicting of corporal punishments exceeding those prescribed by the scriptures;
3. to lift the death sentence against political exiles, and to adopt a conciliatory attitude toward them;
4. to prohibit public officials and royal princes from engaging in trade, in unequal competition with the public;
5. to release and rehabilitate political prisoners; and
6. to raise the salaries of public officials, so that they should not be forced by penury into extortion and bribe-taking.[27]

Some of these recommendations are reminiscent of demands which Yaḥyā himself had made of the Turks. His preoccupations were now of a different order, however, and the petition remained a dead letter.

At the outset of the Mutawakkilite era, Yemen's intelligentsia was coextensive with the ulama. Admission to its ranks was by license,[28] according to carefully maintained standards of accomplishment in the traditional disciplines of language, law, and theology. The required instruction was available only from established scholars whose tutoring lasted over a number of years; no formal, endowed schools offered more than rudimentary training. For both social and economic reasons, thus, higher learning tended to be reserved for those already well-to-do, and did not often serve as a channel of upward mobility for gifted and ambitious members of the less privileged classes. While the ulama and the imamate were mutually dependent and mutually supporting, the ulama's allegiance, in terms of consummatory values, was to the institution rather than to a particular imam or sayyid clan. The distinction is necessary in explaining the ambiguous or openly disloyal attitude of many ulama during some of the regime's crises.

The Shāfi'ī sect, of course, had its ulama, recruited and trained along similar lines. While rejecting the concept of the imamate, the Sunnī divines accepted the imam's temporal authority in theory, and since the appointment and removal of judges was the imam's prerogative, a sort of loyalty existed based upon practical interest. Both Yaḥyā and Aḥmad respected the integrity of the Shāfi'ī courts, and imposed some limits on the exploitation of Sunnīs by Zaidis. Nevertheless, sectarian spirit was strong, and hatred of Zaidism among the Shāfi'ī ulama survived the 1962 revolution.[29]

Excluded from responsible government posts, the Sunnī urban population, aside from the ulama, were chiefly tradesmen—merchants, small traders, and craftsmen. A guild-like organization existed within the traditional trades—builders, carpenters, smiths, tailors, etc.—and provided a reasonably effective mediation between the workers and officialdom. Skills were typically passed from father to son, and little movement occurred into or out of these occupations. The merchants were the Shāfi'ī urban elite. It was a disaffected one, since the regime denied them free conduct of trade and social status, while exploiting their talents and specialized knowledge.

Industrial labor, in the modern sense, appeared only toward the close of Aḥmad's reign. There were unskilled wage-earners: stevedores in the port towns and tanners, oil-pressers, potters, spinners, and weavers, and others, particularly in the Tihama. These laborers were not totally dependent upon wages for their livelihood. They were also peasants, and their social and political ties and orientations remained those of their villages. The largest industrial establishments in Yaḥyā's time were two state enterprises in Sanaa, in which technical operations were directed by European technicians. One diversified installation produced ammunition, castings, and machined parts for steam engines and pumps; wheels and iron rims for military wagons; and furniture. The other plant was a partially mechanized textile mill producing cloth for military uniforms, and a variety of other materials from gray sheeting to fancy draperies. The labor force included several hundred orphans who were wards of the state. The imam established a school where they were given the rudiments of literacy and instruction in the faith. As workers in the imam's factories they received, in 1945, a monthly wage of M.T.[30] \$6.00 or \$7.00, plus a ration of grain; wages were somewhat less in the textile mill.[31]

The inventory of Yemeni society would not be complete without mention of several groups marginal to the Yemeni polity. The great majority of a Jewish community of perhaps fifty thousand migrated to Israel following the first Palestine war. (Reliable estimates indicate that between 1,400 and 1,700 remained in 1971.) Their status, including certain disabilities, privileges, and a special tax regime, had been defined by agreement with the first Zaidi imam and survived a millennium; the Jewish community made no demands upon the political system beyond the observance of this concordat. The Ismā'īlī community, of comparable size, lived a communal life in isolation in the Jabal Ḥarāz massif. Finally, a depressed class of uncertain origin called the *akhdām*—"servants"—who performed the most arduous and menial tasks of the society, played a negligible role.

Yemen thus had a certain social diversity despite a relative ethnic homogeneity. The population was mostly distributed between two religious sects with contrasting conceptions of legitimate authority. It was socially divided between large tribes in the east, north, and west, where large coalitions could be formed for common action; and other tribes in the central and southern highlands, where coordinated activity could be achieved only by a village or a few villages. The urban population, which included all those pretending to influence on a national scale, was set off from the rural areas, which were the country's sole source of wealth. The aristocracy was set distinctly apart from the rest of the population by birth. Membership in social class was by ascription: a Yemeni was born a sayyid, a Shāfiʿī, a peasant, a craftsman, an Arḥabī, etc., and that was his life-long identity.

There was a notably restricted range of roles, most of which were monopolized by the elite. A Sanaa sayyid might well be a Zaidi by religion, an aristocrat by birth, a scholar, a poet, a merchant, a theologian, a government official, a royal advisor, an occasional military commander, and by politics a sympathizer, opponent, or rival of the sovereign. A workman in the imam's foundry was that, a Zaidi, and little more.

Certain social roles were missing. The learned professions were absent: no doctors, scientists, or legal advocates. As politics and religion were not distinct, there were no politicians, and no political parties. Civic duties were few, and were at the same time religious obligations or simply commands backed by force. Mass communication was in its infancy; the few newspapers were government ventures, which appeared irregularly, and had tiny circulation; there was no radio broadcasting until well into Imam Aḥmad's reign. The low volume of internal commercial exchange, together with the primitive state of travel facilities, offered few opportunities for the exchange of ideas and information among regions of the country. Communication was largely vertical: the transmission of the imam's will downward through his officials to the people, and the raising of petitions from subject to sovereign, directly or through his appointees.

Many of these characteristics are those ascribed to "traditional" societies in various typological systems: notably the adherence to received, time-honored values; the distribution of social roles by attribution; and the low degree of social mobility. A traditional society is not necessarily a uniform, stable, or peaceful one. Received values do not always form a harmonious and consistent pattern; hostility among social groups may itself be established by tradition, as indeed it was between the two major sects in Yemen. Strife in itself is not an index of social or political change, nor does the transfer of power by violence from person to person necessarily indicate a break from tradition. Social change occurs when new values are acquired, moving men to the pursuit of new goals supplementing or replacing inherited ones; it usually accompanies new social and economic roles within the society, or a significant redistribution of existing roles. Political change takes place when groups express new aspirations through the political system, and seek to satisfy them through the use of legitimate coercion; it may also occur when the rulers themselves pursue goals departing from the traditional scheme of values. In a heterogeneous society, with two or more contrasting sets of values, a basis for the legitimacy of authority must be found which is compatible with these values. If a regime of a particular configuration is to survive, the values of each politically significant element in the society must be at least partially consistent with the values and aims of the ruler.

The Ḥamīd al-Dīn Imams

The ostensible values which Imam Yaḥyā sought to promote in concluding the Da"ān Treaty were religious ones. As an independent sovereign he continued to reflect Zaidi goals. These were soon supplemented by additional objectives not derived from the faith, which in fact conflicted with Zaidism in some respects, but which were nevertheless compatible with traditional Yemeni values. Yaḥyā bequeathed these attitudes intact to his son and successor, and it is thus possible to treat the Mutawakkilite era as a single historical polity. The salient aspirations which seem to have moved the two imams were the preservation of a Yemeni society in which behavior was governed by the principles of the faith; the continued primacy of their own dynasty; and the maintenance of control over the material resources of the society sufficient to attain the first two objectives.

There is no reason to question that both monarchs felt deep responsibility for the salvation of their subjects' souls, or that they aimed to conduct the kingdom's affairs according to the pattern laid down by the *sharī'a*. That much is conceded even by the regime's most vitriolic critics:

> Without doubt [Imam Aḥmad] believed profoundly that he was responsible before God for keeping his people on the straight road of the *sunna*, and feared that the people would be corrupted by foreigners, and by contemporary arts and techniques.[32]

This outlook was translated into the policy of keeping Yemen isolated from the external world insofar as practicable; keeping at a minimum the movement of foreigners into the country (and drastically restricting the activities of those who were admitted); discouraging the travel of Yemenis abroad (and trying to monitor their attitudes and activities at a distance); channeling education along traditional lines; and avoiding contractual relationships with foreign agencies, whether governments or private enterprise.

The reluctance and infrequency with which the imams permitted outsiders, whether Westerners or Arabs, to enter Yemen scarcely needs documentation. Once there, visitors' movements and activities were subject to the closest surveillance. Amīn al-Rīḥānī was kept for a week under house arrest pending clarification of his credentials from King Ḥusain of Hijaz. (He describes the experience in a chapter entitled "The Imprisoned Guest.")[33] Returning from his visit in 1945, the American consul at Aden reported,

> Notwithstanding the privilege we had in visiting this fascinating country, we had a distinct feeling that we had escaped from oppression when we had passed through the barrier gate at the Yemen border. When the barren rock of Aden was finally visible above the desert sands no landmark had ever seemed more friendly and welcome.[34]

This atmosphere persisted through Aḥmad's reign. In August 1960 the imam ordered the discontinuance of public film showings which the Soviet, Chinese, and American legations had been conducting, and forbade Yemenis to attend private showings by foreigners. He was reported alarmed and confused by the activities and way of life of many foreigners in the country, and his apprehensions were exacerbated by the numerous, and often tendentious, reports he received from his informers throughout the land. Aḥmad simultaneously issued a decree appointing committees to police the morals of his subjects in the larger cities.

Concern for the people's spiritual health had implications for the education of Yemeni youth, implications which were evident soon after independence. Rīḥānī asked a Yemeni schoolboy what he would do if he had some extra money. The boy replied,

> Sir, I like schools. In the time of the Turks there were schools in which geography and mathematics were taught. They gave us books, slates, paper, ink, pencils, notebooks, and chalk—everything, and all free. Sir, I am sad. We have no schools today and no teacher except the *faqīh*. The *faqīh* is stupid. He doesn't like to teach but takes eight riyals a month anyway. In the mosque he goes to sleep with the book in his hand. Paper, ink and books went away with the Turks. If I had extra money I'd open a school, fire the *faqīh*, bring books, tablets, paper, slates, and chalk, and pass them out to the children free.[35]

A few schools separate from the mosques were opened over the following decades. In 1945 Consul Clark was given a tour of those at Sanaa. The director of education stated that there were fifty thousand students in the country, including eight thousand in Sanaa. The range of subjects taught was said to include writing, reading, the Koran, bookkeeping, geography, and mathematics, including algebra.

> We had no way of determining the quality of the instruction. Books were little in evidence, and other materials included maps such as might have been used in colonial American schools. . . . The teachers were especially interesting to us. A few spoke English, but the remainder appeared to me to be a fanatical group of ascetic Moslems, and I wondered what qualifications they had for their positions. I asked Abdul to observe closely what the pupils

> in the Geography class said when they were asked to point out dominating features on an ancient map of North America. A sample of the misinformation the children must be absorbing was given by one pupil who said that the North American continent had two million inhabitants.[36]

Although allowance must be made for the polemical context, Ibrāhīm al-Wazīr's assertion appears substantially accurate that

> the four so-called secondary schools in Sanaa, Hodeida and Ta'izz do not have even a primary curriculum. Their graduates have to make all this up when they enter Egyptian schools. The Imam (Aḥmad) sent a group of princes to secondary school in Egypt, but they had to have special tutors to catch them up on what Egyptian pupils learn in kindergarten and primary.[37]

Pitifully low as the standards of these secular schools were, they were a continual source of concern to the imams. Shortly before his death, Yaḥyā ordered the Sanaa secondary school to prohibit youths from reading printed books, on the principle that, being modern, they contained corrupting ideas and might incite dissension.[38]

It was not possible to prevent Yemeni youths from going abroad to study, though the imams made the effort. Numbers of Yemenis reached Aden, hoping to proceed to other Arab countries for study, only to be thwarted by the impossibility of obtaining visas without the acquiescence of the imam's officials. "Many of these youths returned to their country, where the jails welcomed them with open arms."[39] In 1947 under pressure from other Arab governments and from the Muslim Brotherhood, Imam Yaḥyā sent forty students to Lebanon.

> Soon they were transferred to Egypt, where they were joined by a substantial number who had gone abroad on their own, so that they numbered more than one hundred. The Yemeni Government has been uneasy about them, and has tried to break up the project by cutting off the

> students' monthly allowances or by refusing to sponsor youths who went abroad on their own. This led to pressure by other Arab countries and periodic occupation of the Yemeni Legation in Cairo.[40] The Government occasionally succeeded in forcing the return of a student, in which case he was usually jailed.[41]

Imam Yaḥyā's suspicion of foreign influence as subversive to Zaidism was reinforced by the conviction that ties with foreigners would inevitably jeopardize Yemeni independence. His experience with outsiders was not such as to breed confidence. He reached accommodation with the Turks only after years of warfare. He viewed his Idrīsī neighbor as an usurper of Yemeni territory who was subsidized and supported politically by Britain and Italy. The Italians had brought hardship to his people by blockading the Yemeni coast during the Turco-Italian War of 1911-1912. The British exercised influence in a large region which, on tenuous historical grounds, he considered Yemeni; they had shelled and occupied Yemeni ports, and maintained contact with restive Tihama tribes. Saudi Arabia had replaced the Idrīsīs in occupation of Asir. It is not surprising that the imams were cautious in their dealings with outsiders; that they made contractual arrangements only reluctantly with other governments or foreign businessmen; and that they left unexecuted a succession of agreements into which they had felt constrained to enter. Yaḥyā expressed himself frankly on the subject to a Syrian visitor in the 1920s:

> He greatly fears concluding any agreement with foreigners because such an agreement would one day provide an excuse for foreigners to interfere in the affairs of Yemen. . . . "Don't you know, my son," he said, "that the colonization of India, China, and other weak oriental countries came about because the governments of those countries gave foreigners concessions for the extraction of salt, petroleum and other resources? I would rather that my people and I remain poor and eat straw than let foreigners in, or give them concessions, no matter what advantage or wealth might result from their presence.[42]

Similar attitudes were often attributed to Imam Aḥmad.

Maintaining the purity of the faith by keeping Yemen in isolation, however, became incompatible with another aspiration rooted in Zaidism. We have previously emphasized the centrality of the *jihād* in the Zaidi faith. The title which both imams assumed, Commander of the Faithful, symbolized the theoretical permanence of the state of war between the Zaidi community and nonbelievers. In policy terms, the imams asserted a claim to all territory which the imamate had held at any time in the past: at a minimum, all of Southern Arabia north to Hijaz and east to Dhofar. As it became specifically territorial, the objective lost its direct relation to the faith, and became indistinguishable from any dynastic or national aim. In his encounters with the Turks, and later with the British, Yaḥyā learned that in order to assert the *jihād* in the face of modernized armies, tribal hosts armed with antiquated rifles were simply inadequate. As early as 1922, he negotiated with a French commercial mission for the supply of modern arms;[43] a foreign technician was already operating a workshop producing small-arms ammunition and shells for the artillery left by the Turks.[44] Gradually the imams formed links with other countries chiefly for the procurement of sophisticated weaponry.[45] Yemeni personnel then had to learn to use this equipment, and in 1936 a group of Yemeni cadets was sent to the Baghdad Military Academy for study.

The significance of this training mission has been emphasized by writers of all shades of opinion; its members participated in successive conspiracies against the imams, and the survivors played a prominent role in the republican regime after the 1962 revolution. Explanation of the cadets' role has tended to be in terms of introspective imagination[46] rather than of what there was in Iraq for the Yemeni cadets to observe. Soon after their arrival the Bakr Ṣidqī coup occurred, the first military seizure of power in an Arab country. The new government claimed to have won King Ghāzī's sympathy through the efforts of "the people" under the army's leadership.[47] The popular-front cabinet formed as a consequence was a disappointment to civilian reformers; the reins of power remained obviously in the hands of Ṣidqī as chief of staff. When the latter was assassinated the following year, it was other army officers, not civilians, who organized a new government. The Yemeni trainees were thus thoroughly exposed to the spectacle of officers seizing and wielding political power.

Presumably, the possible impact of these events upon future officers of his army alarmed Imam Yaḥyā; he withdrew the mission well before the completion of the scheduled training, and arranged instead for an Iraqi mission to instruct his cadets in Yemen itself. This team of instructors returned to Iraq after the agreed tour, except for Lt. Col. Jamāl Jamīl, who feared prosecution for his part in the Ṣidqī coup, and obtained the imam's permission to stay on in Yemen as an artillery instructor. He was among those executed in 1948 for his prominent part in the murder of Imam Yaḥyā.

The common interest with certain other Arab states in opposing the British presence in the Middle East led the imams into several alliances. Iraqi military assistance followed upon a treaty of friendship signed in 1931. There followed the Treaty of Arab Brotherhood and Alliance (1936, with Iraq and Saudi Arabia); the Arab League Pact (1945); the Jidda Pact (1956, with Egypt and Saudi Arabia); and in 1958 the United Arab States' arrangement with the United Arab Republic. These ties generated pressures on the imams to liberalize various activities in the diplomatic, cultural, economic, and military fields, pressures which they were unable to resist totally. By 1948 there were Egyptian instructors in Sanaa schools, and several Yemeni diplomatic missions had been opened abroad. Beginning in 1954, a new generation of Yemeni army officers received Egyptian training, both in Yemen and in Egypt. Without exception, these contacts provided the Yemenis involved with opportunity for invidious contrast between economic, social, and political conditions in the developing Arab countries and those in their homeland. The imams were well aware of this; they did what they could to secure the required skills and the desired support while preserving their subjects' devotion to the Zaidi system. These two objectives, although ultimately rooted in concern for the faith, were incompatible, and their simultaneous pursuit contributed to the eccentricity and incoherence of the imams' policies.

The ambition of both monarchs to ensure the continuation of the imamate in their own family, through transmission to the eldest son, was a departure from pure Zaidi theory; it had repercussions on their relationship with the ulama and with the aristocracy. Yaḥyā's father, al-Manṣūr Muḥammad, had never been without rivals for the throne, and he himself was not the sole candidate in 1904. It is recounted that the leading notables met at Shahāra to decide the succession:

> Imam Yaḥyā closed the door of the room in which those were assembled who were to elect a new imam after the death of al-Manṣūr, and left Nāṣir Mabkhūt al-Aḥmar to guard the door. When this guard heard them exchange views on whether to elect Imam Yaḥyā or to choose another, he burst in upon the meeting and threatened them with death, declaring, "None shall be imam save Sīdī Yaḥyā."[48]

While Yaḥyā himself thus gained the imamate by the traditional process, he was determined to decide his own succession. As early as 1927, he proclaimed his son crown prince, apparently not only to aggrandize the Ḥamīd al-Dīn family but also to forestall the instability which would accompany contention among the great sayyid families. The measure went counter to the aspirations of several aristocratic houses which had produced imams during the nineteenth century. It further deprived the ulama and other notables of their function in the choice. Finally, it intensified hostility between Aḥmad and several of his numerous brothers, some of whom were also plausible contenders with popular support. The decline of the sentiment within the aristocracy that Yaḥyā had a clear right to rule contributed to the 1948 coup.

Imam Aḥmad followed Yaḥyā's precedent. His son Muḥammad al-Badr's qualifications were challenged in various quarters. His competence in canon law was disputed; a slight limp raised a question of his soundness of limb; his style of life did not set the expected example of piety and asceticism; and in early manhood he embraced vague secular notions concerning the aims and processes of government which, however liberal and laudable in themselves, were not those of the faith. Although well aware of these reservations, and frequently at odds himself with Badr's opinions and acts, Aḥmad handed over power to Badr increasingly as his own energies waned, and at last formally designated him his heir. The act had the same consequences as Yaḥyā's: the rise of factionalism within the royal family, the dissatisfaction of the conservative ulama, and the alienation of ambitious sayyids.

There is a close parallel between the course of the Qāsimī imamate after the expulsion of the Turks in the seventeenth century and that of the Mutawakkilite Kingdom. *Jihād* was no longer the salient value, the rulers pursued ends instrumental primarily for themselves, by means which changed the authority pattern from hierarchical to pyramidal. In the later phase of both eras, political capability was peculiarly dependent upon the concentration of wealth, which was necessary to secure and maintain influence over people. The Ḥamīd al-Dīn worked vigorously both to ensure the maximum share of material resources for the national treasury, and to accumulate private fortunes. While reliable historical data on the Yemeni economy are lacking, there is some reason to believe that large areas of the country have suffered a long-term, progressive desiccation, and that its productive capacity has declined. Whether demographic pressure on the available resources increased during the past century is simply not known. The dynasty has been the object of an extraordinarily virulent propaganda campaign, in which it has regularly been accused of despoiling the people through motives of greed and lust for autocratic power. Many of the imputed attitudes and acts are surely pure invention. Even unbiased observers from outside judged the situation by standards alien to Yemen. The most that can be said with much confidence is that the Ḥamīd al-Dīn, in order to maintain a preponderant position, had to command resources greater than those of their domestic enemies, and that they perceived no necessity for devoting public revenues to economic development: a concept (as explained in Chapter 4), foreign to Zaidi political thought. Thus, as we have noted, Imam Yaḥyā resisted pressures to abolish non-canonical taxes. While he was persuaded to bring in a few agricultural technicians, he ignored their reports and took no action on their recommendations.[49]

As his sons reached maturity, Yaḥyā appointed them to provincial governorships and other offices where there was opportunity to accumulate personal wealth. Prior to the mid-1930's, only Aḥmad, the eldest, had held high office; the senior appointees were drawn from prominent families such as the Wazīrs, who held two governorships at the time of Rīḥānī's visit in 1922. By 1945 the most lucrative provinces were governed by Ḥamīd al-Dīn princes: the crown prince in Ta'izz; Ḥasan at Ibb; and 'Abdullah at Hodeida. Aḥmad's comportment was described to Clark by an Italian doctor long resident in Ta'izz:

> Aḥmad does not have the restraining influence of his father or the close competition of his brothers, and therefore has been able to override all officials and influential people in the Southern Province. He has gathered almost absolute control of the whole economy of the Province into his own hands. As a result the people are being gouged to a greater degree than in High Yemen.
>
> Aḥmad's heavy taxation of trade through Ta'izz was illustrated by the example of six automobiles which were being driven from Aden to Saudi Arabia via Hodeida. He levied an arbitrary tax of 1,000 M.T. dollars per car, which would very nearly equal the cost price of the vehicles in the United States. Any goods imported into this area are lodged in Aḥmad's own warehouses, and he personally distributes them to the merchants. Only that afternoon Dr. Toffolon had seen the Prince standing in a shop hawking some new goods like any vendor. . . .
>
> Aḥmad has done little to promote the health or education of the people in his Province. When Dr. Toffolon once warned him that a typhus epidemic then raging would result in many hundreds of deaths if the Prince did not obtain a large quantity of medical supplies at once, Aḥmad instead took over a large plot of land for a cemetery.[50]

Prince 'Abdullah's use of his position at Hodeida, according to the British political officer of that city, had made him

> so heartily disliked that his oppressive economic regime has been good propaganda for Aḥmad. 'Abdullah controls the export of most commodities from Hodeida and reportedly makes a huge profit out of the trade.[51]

Such activities set a pervasive pattern for the whole administrative establishment. In the south, taxes in the countryside were gathered with the help of Zaidi troops, whose abuses were restrained only when they became so flagrant as to come to the imam's attention.

While land tenure under the Ḥamīd al-Dīn has not been adequately investigated, it seems probable that abuses were common. Areas where the terrain was adapted to extensive cultivation were coveted by actual or aspiring landowners who used official pressure, manipulation of tax assessments, and usury to force the sale of small holdings. In the central highlands, where land could be tilled only in small, terraced plots, the process of inheritance probably led to some fragmentation. Whether for smallholders, tenant farmers, or sharecroppers, tax exactions were severe enough to deter production.[52] Taxes and other debts forced numbers of peasants off the land. As no alternative means of livelihood was available within the country, these peasants emigrated to Aden, Saudi Arabia, Great Britain, Africa, the Far East, and even America.

The exodus was not only from the land. Considerable numbers left to study abroad, with or without government blessing. Others became political refugees, at first in Aden, later principally in Egypt. The business community contributed to the exodus; they left to escape Aḥmad's attempts, before and after he became imam, either to monopolize the country's trade (as he did in pharmaceuticals) or to make sure of a cut as sleeping partner in large commerical transactions.

No informed estimate puts the number of expatriates at less than one million, or between one fifth and one forth of the population. The emigrants were mostly young males; those who had families usually left them behind. The largest single concentration went to Saudi Arabia after the discovery of oil, where they comprised the backbone of that country's unskilled and semi-skilled labor force. In Aden they provided the port's manpower, and formed an important segment of the business community, and a significant proportion of the politically active population, including school teachers and trades union organizers.

The imams endeavored to retain both ideological and fiscal control over the emigrants. Ibrāhīm al-Wazīr writes,

> A Yemeni exile told me, under oath, that the tax imposed on any Yemeni who goes to sea is 50%, for a factory worker 45%, etc., in addition to the many customs duties and taxes on the emigrant's family, so that only a trifling amount remains in his hands. Many emigrants have complained to the Imam . . . over the oppressiveness of these taxes. He replied that he had found them in his father's ledgers, and it was impossible to change them in any circumstances.[53]

It goes without saying that the effort to tax the expatriates had very little success.

The imams were occasionally able to persuade the British in Aden to place restraints on the emigrants' agitation against their regime. Six political refugees, including the future Free Yemeni leaders, and two high officials of the future republic, Aḥmad Muḥammad Nu'mān and Muḥammad Maḥmūd al-Zubairī, wrote to the American Consul in Aden in November 1944 requesting political asylum as a consequence of this cooperation.[54] The imams employed informants and agents provocateurs among the emigrants to discover and report on their political attitudes, and allegedly used their families as hostages:

> A Yemeni emigrant in London . . . wrote a moderate newspaper article about the lack of reform in his country and also wrote a letter to the Imam in those terms. The Imam—Defender of the Faith and Commander of the

> Faithful—immediately responded to this just petition by sending 180 soldiers to the emigrant's home with orders to teach his family a harsh lesson. They beat the women and tore off their veils, revealing what God has forbidden to show, and plundered the house they lived in. Our friend expected a reply from the Imam. He received a reply, indeed, not from the Victorious Imam, but from his own stricken family, his relatives and friends begging him to show mercy to his family by remaining absolutely obedient to the Imam.[55]

No tactics available to the imams could, of course, have prevented the emigrants from becoming attached to the secular, liberal ideas which prevailed in many of the countries in which they lived, worked, and often became prosperous. From there, it was a short step to the conviction that injustice and poverty in their homeland were due to ancient, theocratic principles of government and to the rulers who applied them. Some formed the notion that they could promote change through their own efforts. Financed by wealthy Yemeni businessmen, expatriates and those still resident in the country organized themselves as the Free Yemenis in Aden at the end of World War II, and began a campaign of propaganda and subversion against Imam Yaḥyā's regime. Their activities so disturbed the imam that in April 1946 he sent Crown Prince Aḥmad to Aden in an effort to silence their attacks. Aḥmad made vague promises of liberalization, but the Free Yemenis were soon convinced that the imam's only intention was to temporize and to eliminate opposition. The talks came to nothing, and the dissident movement gained a dramatic increase in prestige when, the following November, Yaḥyā's ninth son, Prince Ibrāhīm, moved to Aden and joined the dissidents.[56]

Ibrāhīm's defection symbolized the spread within the country of political ideas alternative to those of the Zaidi imamate, a process to which returning emigrants and other travelers abroad contributed. By this time there were Yemenis who had completed their working careers abroad and had retired to their homeland. Their new orientations, discretely disseminated in the towns and the southern highlands, encouraged the focusing of dissatisfaction upon the existing political system. It was only toward the end of Imam Aḥmad's reign, however, that there were repatriates who were disaffected from the regime, and felt they could change it to their own advantage by their own combined efforts. These repatriated citizens were of two types: Yemenis who had been forced from African and Asian countries by nationalist economic pressures; and laborers, attracted home by opportunities of employment on the development projects now being undertaken in Yemen, who had acquired abroad, along with their skills, the idea of group action in defense of common economic and political interests. The new values took hold most readily, of course, among young Yemenis. Prince Ibrāhīm's break with his father's regime was an early indication of a "generation gap" which became rapidly more pronounced.

The inconsistencies in the aspirations of the imams emerge clearly from the foregoing discussion. They were committed to autocratic rule for the spiritual welfare of their subjects, and thus to isolating them from corrupting foreign influences. They were also committed to holy war, interpreted as the recovery of territory historically ruled, however briefly, by their predecessors. But to prosecute the *jihād* they required modern arms, technical training, and the political support of Britain's other adversaries. These objectives compromised the aim of isolation. Furthermore, the *jihād* set many Yemenis against their cosectarians; the British-protected sultanates in South Yemen which the Zaidi regime sought to annex were solidly Shāfi'ī.[57] The dynastic ambitions of the Ḥamīd al-Dīn were incompatible with the Zaidi doctrine of succession and thus repugnant both to the ulama, on consummatory grounds, and to the aristocracy, whose status and role were thereby impaired. Insistence on primogeniture excluded the principle of selection by merit even within the royal family, and produced intradynastic rivalries. Cupidity, finally, lead to further derogation of the *sharī'a* in matters of taxation; to usurpation by the royal family of the roles of the business and landowning communities; and to the disregard of one primary function of an Islamic ruler, that of ensuring conditions in which the citizen may provide for his family and accomplish in security the ritual requirements of the faith. Seen in this way, it is a mixed collection of goals the Ḥamīd al-Dīn imams pursued for over half a century. Small wonder that Yemen became the object of derision and embarrassment to her sister Arab states, as well of exasperation to other countries which sought to conduct relations with the kingdom according to conventional forms.

The Decline of the Regime's Legitimacy

Although the imams pursued a uniform set of aims throughout the period, the emphasis shifted over time. Broadly speaking, Yaḥyā's preoccupation up to 1919 was with the assertion of his authority; from that date until 1934 and the treaties with his two neighbors, he was concerned with the policy of *jihād*; and from then until his death, he worried about ensuring his dynasty's future. Aḥmad's reign opened with a four-year period when the assertion of his authority was paramount; then followed a campaign of *jihād* against the British; his policy during his final four years fluctuated between the preservation of his own autocratic rule and the ensuring of his son's succession. In terms of shared values between the imams and major segments of the society, a fair consensus existed in support of the *jihād*. Consolidation of Ḥamīd al-Dīn power was a matter at best of indifference to the Shāfiʿīs. It commanded Zaidi support insofar as it implied preservation of the Zaidi political system, as distinct from the preeminent status of the Ḥamīd al-Dīn. Material aggrandizement of the royal house was not a goal legitimized by any important social segment, and was detrimental to the interests of most.

In principle, a hierarchical pattern of authority was suited to the Zaidi imamate because of the qualities of wisdom and justice attributed to the monarch, and of his preponderant role in decision-making and leadership. The theory holds in an ideal society where a limited set of consummatory values and a single concept of legitimate authority are universally held. Such a society had never existed in reality. Many Yemenis had always been motivated by secular concerns, and attached to ways of ordering their collective affairs differing from those of Zaidism. In consequence, a substantial degree of force had always been needed for the system to operate effectively. It had worked best when an energetic imam exerted his will in support of aims clearly imposed by the faith, notably in periods of intense *jihād*. It tended to disintegrate when the range of goals pursued by the imam broadened, and also when he began to delegate authority. These were not systemic changes. The distribution of social roles remained stable, and historical events, however dramatic, reflected a shifting emphasis among a constant set of values.

The traditional fluctuation in authority patterns continued under the Ḥamīd al-Dīn. During his years of *jihād*, Yaḥyā gathered the reins of government into his own hands with a thoroughness which provided material for numerous picturesque accounts. With the decline of his vigor and increasing concern to provide for his sons, authority was decentralized. Ḥamıd al-Dīn princes monopolized wealth-producing positions of power to the point where the imam was no longer able to assert his will without challenge. The crown prince defied his father's orders to appear in Sanaa for instruction, and ignored the imam's remonstrances regarding his harsh rule in Ta'izz.[58] The combination of pyramidal authority and the weakness of the regime's hold on the aristocracy led to the Wazīr coup of 1948, which will be discussed in the following chapter.

After crushing the rebellion, Aḥmad restored the rigidly centralized pattern of authority. This brought him into conflict with his brothers. Prince Ismā'īl was arrested for conspiracy against the imam in 1950. Five years later, Prince 'Abdullah conspired in a military revolt and declared himself imam. Ḥasan worked so effectively to gain personal following among the tribes that Aḥmad exiled him to the U.N. in 1955. Until 1955, challenges to the ruler, although associated with secular reform movements, generally took place within the Zaidi political system. Their objective was to replace one imam with another, and to revise the emphasis among existing goals and policies. Thereafter, social and political change made the Ḥamīd al-Dīn imamate as we have described it no longer viable as a Yemeni political system. The question now became whether the ruling family and elite could adapt to these changes, or whether new political forms would be introduced by force.

The inability of the existing system to adapt to the new requirements was palpable to those who, like this writer, observed it at first hand during the final years of Imam Aḥmad's reign. Goals pursued were inconsistent; policies were consequently chaotic and often self-defeating. Role assignment became increasingly irrational. Authority became so dispersed as to render impossible effective prosecution of any policy.

Throughout the era, the imams sought to extract for the royal treasury and a privileged few maximum revenues from national production. The aristocracy's moral leadership declined markedly, and the faith of much of the population in the political system's ability to ensure the community's welfare, spiritual or material, weakened. Tax policy discouraged productive effort, and profits shrank. Meanwhile the venality of the imam's servants was such that probably less than half the taxes paid found their way to the treasury. The imam reacted against particularly outrageous abuses;[59] not all came to his attention, however, and corruption, bribery, and extortion extended even into the *sharī'a* courts.

The bulk of Yemen's commerce above the retail level was in the hands of Shāfi'ī merchants who were under the dual disadvantages of their social inferiority by reason of sect, and of the imam's acquisitiveness. Post-revolutionary Yemeni writers have exaggerated the extent to which the imam's business partner, Shaikh 'Alī Muḥammad al-Jabalī, succeeded in monopolizing Yemen's foreign trade and internal transport services.[60] That his was a favored position is unquestionable, as reflected in the fact that, alone among the country's businessmen, he felt sufficiently secure to invest capital in industrial enterprise (cotton ginning). There were other prosperous merchants but, lacking security for their investment, they employed their resources and knowledge in ways tending to contract the economy. Their principal concern was to extract the maximum profit from each transaction, avoid taxation, and send the proceeds to Aden or another haven where their money would be safe from requisition. Business ethics failed to develop. Merchants charged what the traffic would bear, inflated brokerage fees, and supplied substandard or worthless merchandise, particularly when dealing with the government.

Although the position of the merchants was precarious, they had expertise indispensable to the government in its dealings abroad. There was no monetary system. None of the imam's officials had the knowledge required, for example, to arrange the overhaul of one of the imam's aircraft, or to order supplies for the government hospitals. For such services the imam was dependent upon the merchants, who took such advantage as they could. The imam's problem was dramatized to me in 1961, when I was instructed to urge his government to pay its back dues to the U.N., about $38,000, lest it lose its vote in the General Assembly. I made the appropriate representation to the deputy foreign minister. After conferring with the imam, he informed me that the latter's sole means of paying the obligation was to buy dollars from the Ta'izz merchants with silver riyals, and that they would certainly fleece him on the transaction. He therefore enquired whether I could sell him a U.S. Treasury check for the purpose. As the legation's need for riyals (to meet the monthly AID payroll) was substantial, I sought and obtained permission to do so. An exchange rate was agreed upon without haggling, and shortly a palace jeep arrived at the legation groaning under the weight of about one and one-half tons of Maria Theresa thalers sewn into burlap bags of one thousand. The coins had to be counted one by one, which required an afternoon's work by the whole staff. The sum was exact, to the riyal, and the check was duly issued.

Such anecdotes emphasize not so much the backwardness of Yemen as the disinclination of the imam to utilize the modern skills available in governing the country. This ineptitude became increasingly apparent as subsantial development projects were undertaken by foreign countries. The imams had in the first instance entered into relations with foreign powers to obtain arms and political leverage against British influence to the south. Capital projects were agreed to belatedly for various non-economic reasons. The improvement of the port of Hodeida would reduce Yemen's dependence on the British port of Aden; highways and municipal water systems would counteract British-sponsored development across the border which could be expected to reduce Yemen's political attraction for the people of the protectorates.

It is by no means clear that the imam looked upon such activity as a means of enhancing the prosperity of the country as a whole, or as anything more than a temporary increase in the existing proceeds, to be divided up according to the traditional standards. American officials involved remember painfully the imam's appointment to the position of director of public works in Ta'izz Province a man who had responsibility for coordination of the construction of a major road which the U.S. had undertaken to build. He was a sayyid whose only qualification was a marital connection with the royal family. The indifference of this official to the progress of the work, and the inability of the U.S. officials to arrange the bribes which might have won his cooperation, gravely compromised and delayed the project. Lest it be thought that attitudes toward the United States were at the root of the problem, we may mention a strike in November 1960 among workers employed on the Soviet port-construction project at Hodeida. The stoppage occurred when the governor of Hodeida Province, whom the imam had designated minister of public works, withheld his endorsement on checks deposited by the Russians for the workers' wages. He apparently intended to secure a cut for himself. Work resumed only upon direct royal order specifying payment of twelve days' arrears in wages.

The senior-generation aristocrats saw a need for economic progress, but were at the same time aware that it required administrative and technical skills which they could not pretend to offer. Progress was thus contrary to the interests of the privileged, and they worked to obstruct it. In November 1960 the director general of the "ministry of economics," then the only holder of a western-type doctoral degree in Yemen,[61] confided to an American diplomat,

> I am trying to help develop an economic development program for Yemen, but of course it is useless at present to do anything but go through the motions. The imam and his advisors know how to pat you on the back, encourage you to write reports, and then pigeon-hole them forever. I

> have with me some recommendations for customs reforms. You know what will be done with them: nothing. We play games now and wait for a better day.[62]

Nor were the sayyids able to coordinate action to assure that the system would safeguard their own interests. An experienced Yemeni diplomat[63] described the atmosphere of the royal court in August 1960:

> The in-fighting among government officials around the imam is unbelievable. No one's position or reputation is safe, and a rise in someone's effectiveness with the imam is a signal for the others to begin every sort of intrigue against him. There is no concern whatsoever among these people for the damage they do to the interests of the country and the imam. Their only motivations are jealousy and money. These intrigues are fatally confusing to the mind of the imam who, trusting no one, rules and lives by playing one official off against another. Even the younger, better-educated Yemenis, while they bitterly castigate the imam and everything he stands for, join the older Yemenis in predicting bloody chaos at the death of the imam.[64]

In such circumstances, coordination of policy was out of the question. As one example, when AID began work on the Mocha-Ta'izz road, Imam Aḥmad insisted that the wages paid Yemeni labor be kept to a minimum. A rational pay scale was agreed upon, based on living costs and such indications as could be discovered of prevailing wages. Not long afterward a young member of the royal family with high political ambitions of his own, Prince Ḥasan bin 'Alī, was appointed minister of public works. In the hope of promoting his own popularity he made anguished and urgent appeals for substantial, gratuitous wage increases across the board, leaving U.S. officials in an invidious position between two conflicting Yemeni policies.

Incoherence increased with the imam's declining energy and his delegation of authority to the crown prince. The latter, installed at Sanaa, embarked in 1962 on an attempt to introduce some order and system into the Yemeni government. He appointed a committee of progressive officials to draft a code of regulations for the conduct of public officials, and to delimit the functions of each ministry. His instructions to the committee emphasized integrity and honesty in the behavior of officials[65] and reflected a determination to avoid past mistakes where the imams had announced measures of administrative modernization and reform, for purely cosmetic reasons, and incurred public opprobrium when they failed to follow through.[66] Imam Aḥmad, in Ta'izz, remained totally indifferent to this reform movement, and father and son worked increasingly at cross-purposes. The country came to have, in effect, two governments. The imam refused Badr's request for removal of the foreign ministry to Sanaa from Ta'izz. (Badr held the title of foreign minister.) The Sanaa Court of Appeals served as court of final resort for the north, cases no longer being appealed to the Supreme Court at Ta'izz.

Disintegration of the authority pattern was a symptom of decline of the regime's legitimacy among the peasants, from whom its resources were mainly derived; among the bourgeoisie upon whom it depended for technical functions but whom it excluded from a voice in policy; and among the sayyid aristocracy, reduced from a position of moral leadership to the status of petitioners for material largesse. Finally, Imam Aḥmad fatally weakened the moral basis of his rule in the eyes of the Zaidi tribes, which were its ultimate mainstay.

The events leading to Aḥmad's alienation from the tribes must be summarized briefly.[67] In April 1959 the imam traveled to Italy for medical treatment, leaving Badr as regent. The latter attempted to use the opportunity to institute a program of reform. In the absence of the imam's strong hand, he was soon faced with mutiny among the regular armed forces. He appealed to the Ḥāshid tribes for support, which was forthcoming only on payment of a substantial subsidy. In August the imam returned to Yemen, and at once sought to retrieve the money thus lost to the treasury. The tribes resisted. The imam invited the paramount shaikh of Ḥāshid, Ḥusain bin Nāṣir al-Aḥmar, and his son Ḥamīd, to meet with him to discuss the resulting tense situation, under a safe-conduct delivered by al-

Badr. A heated argument took place during which the imam impetuously ordered both guests siezed and sent to Ḥajja, where they were decapitated. This breach of faith, and of tribal custom, alienated many Yemeni tribes. Major military campaigns were necessary to put down the ensuing rebellions in the north and east. Imam Aḥmad was discredited beyond redemption among the Ḥāshid tribes.

Political Change under the Ḥamīd al-Dīn

The outlook of many Yemenis became secularized during the Mutawakkilite era. Harlan Clark, some of whose observations in 1945 we have cited, returned to Yemen in 1964 to take charge of the American Embassy. The most striking change he found was the degree to which pious formulas had disappeared from the discourse of Yemenis of all stations, and to which material concerns had superseded religious ones.[68] The point can be clearly illustrated. In 1922 Rīḥānī's schoolboy, though saddened by the closure of the Turks' schools and contemptuous of his Koran instructor, nevertheless asserted,

> The Imam knows more than we do. If he ways "war," we'll go to war. We will all fight for the Imam. He is the best-informed of all on God's Book and the *sunna*, and on the duties of Muslims. God has commanded us to fight the *jihād*.[69]

By August 1962, secondary school students in Yemen's three largest cities were on strike, and engaging in demonstrations in which they bore President Nasser's picture and chanted slogans against Imam Aḥmad.

In 1960, assessing the political attitudes of the people of Sanaa, American diplomats found that they,

> while proud in the belief that their area is the heart of Yemen, are highly sensitive to their backwardness, and are united in the eager desire to catch up with the rest of the world. Even the lowest and most ignorant classes are no longer willing to accept present conditions as inevitable, while the middle class feels that Sanaa is a commercial

> backwater. Members of the royal family, including the Crown Prince, and the religious sayyids feel deserted by the Imam, and fearful of the consequences of popular discontent resulting from the lack of progress under their leadership. In addition to their traditional distrust of the Shāfiʿīs of Lower Yemen whom they have long subjected to their control, these highland Zaidis have become jealous of the southerners who, with better communications and commerce with the outside world, and apparently favored by the Imam and the West, have in recent years progressed more than they.[70]

Or, summarized succinctly by another observer,

> the popular feeling in Sanaa is that "the Imam and his gang are not interested in progress, and are sitting in Sukhna[71] waiting out his time while we starve. The blacks of Africa are obtaining freedom, constitutions and economic progress, and are already far ahead of us.[72]

These views indicate a conviction, which certainly would not have been found two generations earlier, that the wealth of Yemen was not a fixed quantity, or one which rose or fell according to divine will, but one which could, and should, be increased through actions of the rulers. The concept of freedom, similarly, had been redefined in secular terms; constitutions had replaced membership in kinship and sectarian groups in defining aspirations toward freedom.

This revision of values was the result of many factors operating over an extended period. The new norms were in the main of foreign origin, and reached Yemenis through a variety of channels which the imams were unable to obstruct effectively. As early as 1938, one observer remarked,

> even Imam Yaḥyā could not resist innovations forever, and during our stay he not only withdrew his opposition to the use of wireless sets, but even listened to one of his sons, Saif al-Islām Ḥusain, speaking in Arabic from London, soon after the British Arabic programme was

> inaugurated. It was noted with amusement in European circles that, the royal permission once given, the existence of many wireless sets belonging to Arab residents suddenly became known in Sanaa, far more swiftly than the sets could possibly have been transported thither.[73]

After the deposition of King Farūq in August 1952, Imam Aḥmad ordered the confiscation of all radio sets in public places, to prevent contamination of his subjects' minds, and to the end of his reign it was risky for a Yemeni to listen openly to the Voice of the Arabs (although the imam did so regularly). The battle with the transistor was a losing one; most urban Yemenis and many in the countryside followed closely Radio Cairo's intermittent campaigns against the Zaidi regime, and became familiar with the concept of government responsibility for the alleviation of ignorance, poverty, and disease. After the mid-1950s young Yemenis returned in significant numbers after study abroad; they were not often given posts of a responsibility commensurate with their competence; disaffected, they typically found their way into the jails or into the function in which they could most effectively propagate new values, the teaching of Yemeni youth. Meanwhile, foreigners arrived in growing numbers as advisors, technicians, and personnel working on economic assistance projects. Even when these outsiders did not deliberately propound values hostile to those of the imamate, their very presence implied the desirability of the assignment of status according to competence and achievement, rather than to accident of birth. The imam's government publicly committed itself to promoting national prosperity and modernization through its own action, in such agreements as the United Arab States Charter,[74] and in authoritative statements such as the crown prince's instruction to the reform committee previously mentioned.

By mid-1962 Yemenis could see at first hand some of the results of economic development undertaken by government action, through the conclusion of foreign aid agreements. A new port at Hodeida increased the country's foreign trade capabilities, and road construction had already appreciably improved internal distribution facilities. Business had been stimulated, particularly in Lower Yemen, where the U.S. AID mission employed one thousand Yemenis on a $65,000 monthly payroll, and made local purchases valued at $55,000 per month. A housing boom was in progress, and the personal expenditures of expatriate personnel fed additional sums into the local economy. The confidence of businessmen in the future of the Yemeni economy had revived to the point where, although distrustful of the government, they had invested capital in the first Yemeni corporations: mixed public and private ventures in the fields of electric power and petroleum products distribution. Perhaps not unnaturally, perceiving these benefits, the general attitude among the Yemenis affected was not gratification at their rulers' efforts at development but, rather, dissatisfaction that they were not doing more.

The economic revival encouraged the return of some hundreds of young Yemenis who had gone abroad to earn their living. This migration had important implications for the country's social structure. This was not the first outward migration in Yemeni history, but it differed from previous ones in that the migrants did not regard their movement as a permanent exile. Depending on the motive of their departure, they expected to return when their economic needs were fulfilled; or when new political circumstances made repatriation safe and congenial; or both. Thus the Yemeni expatriates remained a potential, and in some respects an actual, part of Yemeni society. Those whose families remained behind retained their ascriptive social niche. Others, whose families accompanied them abroad or who were born outside Yemen, would have no such precise identity to resume. They would, primarily, be Yemeni citizens, secondly Zaidi or Shāfi'ī sectarians, and finally members of an economic group according to their achievement.

The emigrants had moved into a wide variety of new environments, and were exposed to many different political systems and ideologies. The great majority did not participate in political activities directed at their homeland, whether through lack of motivation or through unwillingness to jeopardize their status in the host countries. In Aden and later in Cairo, however, large numbers became politically active.

By far the largest segment of the Aden labor force was Yemeni, and people such as Muḥsin al-'Ainī, Muḥammad 'Alī al-Aswadī, and 'Abdullah al-Asnag took a leading part in the organization and management of trade unions there. As in other Arab countries, the purview of unions was conceived to go beyond collective representation of workers' interests vis-à-vis employers; it embraced the structure and policies of governments. Thus the unions' activities overlapped the Free Yemeni organization in both function and personnel. Together, the two movements were of significant innovating effect in the Yemeni polity. They insistently urged upon the parts of the Yemeni public they could reach new values, in addition to those which were already becoming salient through the contradictions of the imamate. These included aspirations to Arab unity, anti-colonialism, and various attitudes associated with Nasserist Arab Socialism, Ba'thism, and other ideological currents whose sponsors sought to annex the Free Yemeni movement. Whatever their ideological coloration, members of the movement believed that any legitimate authority in Yemen must promote the values they had embraced; they were confident that their own efforts could contribute to bringing such authority into being. In principle, dedication to the new value patterns submerged differences along the traditional social and religious lines: in principle only, because frictions, particularly the Zaidi-Shāfi'ī conflict, continued to assert themselves in rivalry for leadership of the movement. In July 1960 the Free Yemenis in Aden split on such lines so violently that the colony police felt obliged to intervene to restore order.

As we have seen, the beginning of full differentiation of the army officers' role dates from the attendance of Yemeni cadets at the Iraqi Military Academy in the 1930s. Before that, senior military command had been exercised by individuals who served the imam in other capacities as well. They were always Zaidis, and usually sayyids, whose high status was independent of their military position. The cadets of 1936, except for one sayyid, were Zaidis of quite modest station. ('Abdullah al-Sallāl was the son of a blacksmith, a despised occupation.) Imam Yaḥyā appears to have calculated that his generosity in opening to them opportunity in the army would ensure their gratitude and loyalty. However, a commission in the imam's army did not confer respected social standing, and indeed the military was somewhat looked down upon, though acknowledged as a necessary institution. The cadets returning from Iraq had seen the example of army officers as final arbiters of power, within the framework of the monarchy. Their subsequent individual histories show how ardently they aspired to a comparable role and status. The next generation of Yemeni officers were trained by Egyptians, both in Yemen and in Egypt, after the Nasser revolution. They became passionately attached, as their record shows, to the goal of replacing monarchical forms with republican, and to the direct exercise of power by the army as custodian of the interests of the people. The officer corps was becoming a new class. Its members held widely varying values, but none of these coincided with those of the existing regime. This orientation was, it should be emphasized, confined to the officers. The enlisted personnel in the regular forces served for life; however, they came mostly from the northern tribes, and retained their tribal ties and values undiluted.

Thus, despite the apparent control of the imamate, significant changes took place within the Yemeni polity. Traditional values had been abandoned or downgraded, and a long list of new ones adopted, satisfaction of which was considered the duty of those in authority. The concepts which had previously defined the imamate as legitimate vis-à-vis the respective segments of Yemeni society had lost their compelling power. More and more Yemenis, belonging to traditional as well as to newly formed social components, came to believe that their own efforts could force the political system to provide gratification of the newly acquired aspirations.

These changes did not permeate the society uniformly, and one major segment remained generally committed to a set of traditional values coincident in part with those of Zaidism. Imam Aḥmad's betrayal of the Ḥāshid chiefs had destroyed his personal legitimacy in the eyes of many of the large northern tribes and seriously compromised his dynasty. Nevertheless, many of the tribesmen remained attached to the imamate itself as the legitimate form of authority beyond the tribe. This circumstance made possible a persistent effort at counter-revolution after the 1962 coup, and lies at the origin of the Yemen civil war.

8
Revolution, Civil War, and Intervention

The al-Wazīr Coup (1948)

There are qualitative differences between the unsuccessful coups of 1948 and 1955, and that of 1962 which led, by way of the ensuing civil war, to the extinction of the Zaidi imamate. The authors of the first two events sought to effect changes in the personnel ruling Yemen, and to revise priorities among received political values, without destroying the bases of the existing political order. By contrast, the leaders of the 1962 revolt were revolutionaries, in that they aspired to a significant reorganization of Yemeni society, to the assertion of aims innovative in Yemeni politics, and to a permanent shift in the locus of legitimate authority.

It is fashionable among Yemeni writers to describe as popular revolution the attempt of 'Abdullah bin Aḥmad al-Wazīr to depose the Ḥamīd al-Dīn dynasty and to occupy the throne himself.[1] The term "revolution" has acquired, among many Arabs, connotations of prestige and honor which it lacked before the extinction of the Egyptian, Iraqi, and Libyan monarchies, and before the intensive indoctrination of the Arab peoples in the desirability of sweeping social and political change. The 1948 movement in Yemen had a certain amount of popular participation; it fell short, however, of the status of a "revolution of the whole people" that has been claimed for it.[2]

The idea of a coup certainly did not originate with ʻAbdullah al-Wazīr. His motives were well within the Zaidi scheme of values. Generally acknowledged to possess the qualifications of an imam, he had served Yaḥyā in high military and administrative functions, and had married his daughter, before being shunted aside in favor of the imam's sons. He remained a daily attendant at the monarch's court, and was among those who promised to support the succession of Crown Prince Aḥmad. Nevertheless, ambitious and discontent, he was available for cooptation by opponents of the regime united in hostility to the Ḥamīd al-Dīn family but otherwise seeking diverse aims. These ranged from simply a return to orthodox Zaidi principles regarding the succession, to the total destruction of the theocratic Zaidi political system.

Maintenance of the hierarchical pattern of authority which Imam Yaḥyā had constructed during the first decade of his independent reign required two conditions: the assignment to high administrative positions of persons willing to act unquestioningly as emanations of the ruler; and the constant flow to him of reliable information on attitudes and events throughout the domain. Some of the dynasty's opponents seem to have understood these requirements, and to have made disruption of the governing apparatus, and distortion of the information reaching the imam and his immediate advisors, their objectives when they first combined for common action against the regime.

Hay'at al-Niḍāl—"the Combat Association"—was the first of two secret organizations created within Yemen toward these ends. It was founded in 1935 by Sayyid Aḥmad bin Aḥmad al-Muṭāʻ, a descendant of ʻAbbās bin ʻAlī bin Abī Ṭālib (ʻAlī's son by Umm al-Banīn bint Ḥizām, not by the Prophet's daughter Fāṭima), and therefore not of the highest aristocracy. With this background, it is not surprising that he was uncommitted to the restriction of leadership in Islam to the Fatimid line, and thus to the Zaidi imamate. As a youth he read widely among Islamic reformists and modernists, such as the Egyptian Qāsim Amīn. As an officer in the 1934 war with Saudi Arabia, he observed at first hand the maladministration of the Yemeni army; its weakness and lack of discipline; and its addiction to loot and plunder. His outspoken criticism prompted the imam's minister, 'Abdullah al-'Amrī, to relieve him from military duties and to appoint him an editor of *al-Īmān*, which served as Yemen's official gazette. He decided to work against the reactionary Ḥamīd al-Dīn regime, and formed a clandestine association with a few like-minded friends in Sanaa. As a journalist, he had plausible reason for some travel in the country, and was able to establish a few branches of the *Hay'a* in Ta'izz, Ibb, Dhamār, and Ṣa'da.[3]

Muṭā' and his fellow-conspirators appear to have perceived the sources of the regime's strength and the points at which it was vulnerable. They soon discovered moreover that the imam's own inclinations could be turned against him:

> The unity of the governing structure was the stumbling block in the path of opposition to Imam Yaḥyā's regime. Al-Muṭā' and his colleagues succeeded in moving the stone to one side of the road, and continued to chip away at it until it fell apart into pebbles.[4]

Specifically, the *Hay'a* proposed to infiltrate its sympathizers into government positions, or to recruit persons already there; to undermine the position of 'Abdullah al-'Amrī and the imam's trust in him; and to weaken the regime to such an extent that Imam Yaḥyā's own authority would collapse and that Crown Prince Aḥmad would be precluded from the succession. The program appealed to a broad spectrum of opinion, both progressive and traditional. The list of Muṭā''s contacts[5] includes shaikhs of Ḥāshid and Bakīl as well as of several Shāfi'ī tribes; members of the qāḍī-class *noblesse de robe*; sayyid aristocrats; and urban youngsters with such modern education as was accessible to Yemenis at the time. Imam Yaḥyā's advancement of his sons played into the hands of this opposition. His removal from governorships of the Wazīr amirs, 'Abdullah and 'Alī, to make way for Ḥamīd al-Dīn princes, encouraged disaffection within the high aristocracy. The younger princes who served in advisory capacities at court reduced al-'Amrī's functions as well as the scope of his information, and introduced confusion into the counsel reaching the imam. The *Hay'a* played cleverly on the mutual suspicions and jealousies of the crown prince and his brothers, and within a decade the solidarity of the royal family was thoroughly compromised. The *Hay'a* succeeded in concealing its existence as an organized and subversive group, although Muṭā' himself was imprisoned for a time in 1936.

After 1944 dissidence broadened and intensified. The Free Yemeni Party formed in Aden began agitation against the imam, the crown prince, and even the institution of the imamate. It acquired a printing press, and its broadsides were regularly smuggled into Yemen and distributed in the principal towns. In the same year a second secret organization was formed at Ibb, *Jam'iyat al-Iṣlāḥ*—"the Reform Society"—under the leadership of Qāḍī 'Abd al-Raḥmān al-Iryānī and members of the prominent Akwa' family of qāḍīs. Their immediate purpose was to undermine the positions of Prince Ḥasan, the provincial governor, and of his deputy, Qāḍī Aḥmad al-Siyāghī, and, more remotely, to establish a republican regime in Yemen. The *Jam'iya* made liaison with the *Hay'a* and with the Free Yemenis, whose tracts it helped distribute. Through its efforts, Ḥasan's standing with his father was so compromised that the imam recalled him to Sanaa, and then transferred him to Ḥajja.

The disruptive program succeeded so well that, on the eve of the 1946 *ḥajj*, Prince Ḥusain, the imam's most pious and scholarly son, had entered into an agreement with the Wazīr amirs, Amīr 'Alī bin Ḥamūd Sharaf al-Dīn, and Prince Ḥasan, Ḥusain's full brother, to oppose the succession of Crown Prince Aḥmad, and to support 'Abdullah al-Wazīr for the imamate upon Yaḥyā's death.[6] 'Abdullah had helped negotiate the Treaty of Taif ending the 1934 Yemen–Saudi Arabia war, and had formed and retained friendly ties with King Ibn Saud. He sent a message to the king, in the care of members of the *Hay'a* who were making the pilgrimage, enquiring whether the king would object to his candidacy as imam in opposition to Prince Aḥmad. The king replied that he would interpose no objection to action against Aḥmad, provided the objective was to restore government in Yemen strictly according to the sharī'a; that meanwhile 'Abdullah would be welcome to take asylum in Saudi Arabia if occasion arose; but that on no account should action be taken against Imam Yaḥyā, to whom the king was bound by treaty and oath.[7] (In transmitting the reply to 'Abdullah, the *Hay'a* representatives omitted the king's prohibition against attacking Yaḥyā.)

During the *ḥajj*, the *Hay'a* also conferred with Imam Ḥasan al-Bannā, leader of the militant Muslim Brothers, who agreed to assist in the campaign against the Ḥamīd al-Dīn regime. The Brotherhood press in Cairo at once began attacking Imam Yaḥyā, and al-Bannā furthermore sent a skilled revolutionary propagandist to Yemen: Fuḍail al-Warṭilānī, an Algerian posing as a merchant. On his way to Sanaa he conferred in Aden with the Free Yemenis, whose morale was at an unrealistically high peak with the recent defection of Prince Ibrāhīm. Warṭilānī also sojourned at Ta'izz, where he gained the good will of the crown prince; Aḥmad was pleased with his eloquence and scintillating conversation, and appeared to sympathize with his reformist ideas.

In the meantime, Aḥmad was preparing his own future with subtlety and astuteness. His conventional portrait as simply a bloodthirsty tyrant is pure caricature. Shamāḥī, who was his intimate crony in his last years, suggests his many-faceted personality while still heir-designate:

> The Crown Prince was liberal, open-handed, generous, easily excitable, murderous, a shedder of blood, fond of jokes, laughing readily at humor, delighting in praise, easily moved by poetry (by contrast with his father). At the same time, he was learned, a poet and orator, a fomentor of war, a natural leader in battle, whether in the field or at headquarters. On occasion, he mingled with the people, learned about their problems, and ordered their affairs. He dashed about furiously hither and yon. He organized literary and pleasure parties among his friends, then might disappear, go into seclusion, and withdraw himself, sometimes pondering the affairs of his government, sometimes enjoying simple pleasures and fun-making with his family and servants.[8]

Aḥmad established his own countrywide network of informants and loyal supporters, and worked with clever calculation to smoke out his potential opponents. He invited such malcontents as Aḥmad Nu'mān, Muḥammad al-Zubairī, Sayyid Aḥmad Muḥammad al-Shāmī, and Sayyid Zaid al-Mawshakī to Ta'izz. He encouraged them to express their views, solicited their advice, and permitted them to assume he shared their vision of the future. They were thus alarmed and shocked when, in the spring of 1944, he suddenly exclaimed in a large gathering, "I hope to God I don't die before drenching this sword of mine in the blood of modernists." Nu'mān and Zubairī at once fled to Aden.[9]

Aḥmad's attitude toward Warṯilānī's agitation followed this pattern. The Algerian joined with leaders of the two clandestine networks, and with the Iraqi-trained, but unemployed,[10] army officers and their Iraqi mentor, Jamāl Jamīl. Together they engaged in an intensive campaign for revolutionary ideas in the schools, the mosques, and less public forums. This activity naturally worried the imam, who several times was inclined to deport Warṯilānī, but was dissuaded by the crown prince and by a trusted foreign affairs advisor, Sayyid Ḥusain al-Kibsī, a secret collaborator of the *Hay'a*.

By the end of 1947, Sanaa, Ibb, and Ta'izz were in such a pitch of revolutionary fervor that the leaders of the internal opposition anticipated early and drastic reprisals by the imam and his chief minister. They realized that their ultimate goal of extinguishing the imamate was still well beyond reach. The movement was as yet confined to a few cities, and the work of indoctrinating and persuading the northern tribes, upon which the success of any operation depended, had not even begun. The rebels had the choice either of going into exile, or of exploiting the situation for some lesser objective which the tribes would not oppose. After hasty consultation, they decided to move simultaneously against the imam and the crown prince, and to install 'Abdullah al-Wazīr as imam, under constitutional arrangements which would ensure that he could not assume autocratic power. A constitution—*al-Mithāq al-Muqaddas*, or "Sacred Pact"—was drafted in these premises, including a list of fifty-odd individuals who would occupy high posts in the future government. The document was sent to Aden to be printed on the Free Yemeni press and published upon notification of the imam's death.

Narratives of the events leading to the coup disagree as to how, early in January 1948, the Free Yemenis in Aden received a false report of the imam's death and, as agreed, published the Sacred Pact and the composition of the new "government." According to the usual account, a Free Yemeni (nowhere identified) bungled an attempt to assassinate the imam in his palace; the conspirators, believing momentarily that he had succeeded, sent word to Aden. Shamāḥī[11] says that Crown Prince Aḥmad received intelligence of the pact from his agents among the Free Yemenis, and deliberately exposed the plot by informing the governor of Hodeida that the imam had died in suspicious circumstances, asking him to inform the Aden government through its commercial representatives in Hodeida. Upon receipt of the report, the British authorities at once expressed condolences to Prince Ibrāhīm, and the news thus reached the Free Yemenis with an official and authoritative aura.

Messages of congratulation to 'Abdullah al-Wazīr, the new imam, and the text of the pact, soon arrived over the Sanaa telegraph. The imam intercepted these and, when the unsuspecting 'Abdullah arrived as usual at Yaḥyā's daily *majlis*, confronted him with them. 'Abdullah stoutly disavowed any knowledge of the plot, and wrote an extended denial which the imam had printed in the same issue of *al-Īmān* as his own order summoning Crown Prince Aḥmad to Sanaa. Meanwhile, Yaḥyā began assembling a dossier on the basis of which to arrest 'Abdullah as soon as Aḥmad arrived. The latter was singularly dilatory in complying. Shamāḥī suggests that Aḥmad had no desire to be trapped in Sanaa by the coup he anticipated. He hoped the coup would clear the board of his father and rival brothers, whereupon he would have little trouble in mobilizing enough force outside the capital to assert his own succession.

The conspirators felt that, to save their own skins, they had to move against the imam before Aḥmad could reach Sanaa and establish control there. They urgently agreed upon a plan to assassinate first Yaḥyā in Sanaa, and then Aḥmad in Taʿizz immediately afterward. The imam was brutally gunned down on February 17, during a motor excursion outside the capital.[12] Through a farcical lack of coordination among the conspirators, Prince Ḥusain learned of his father's assassination before the coup's leaders did, and was able to send the crown prince a coded telegram informing him of the deed. Aḥmad was thereby able to take measures to prevent the news from reaching those designated to kill him, and to organize a convoy in which he traveled by way of the Tihama to Ḥajja, where the local tribes were loyal to the Ḥamīd al-Dīn. He published his own claim to the imamate along the way, and made sure of the support of notables in the localities through which he passed.

ʿAbdullah al-Wazīr's moral position was compromised from the first. Only fear for his own life persuaded him to agree to the murder of Imam Yaḥyā, his father-in-law. He had publicly pledged allegiance to Aḥmad as Yaḥyā's successor, and his assumption of the imamate violated his sworn oath. He was, apparently, only partly in the confidence of the internal conspirators and the Free Yemenis, and was immediately confronted with agitators demanding fundamental political change, in addition to the inevitable hordes of opportunists seeking public office. On the first day of the coup he confirmed his reputation for military prowess by gallantly leading an assault on Ghamdān, the Sanaa fort manned by troops loyal to the Ḥamīd al-Dīn. Thereafter, a curious paralysis of will set in, and he devoted little attention to mobilizing military forces against the tribesmen rapidly recruited by Aḥmad and his brothers Ḥasan and ʿAbbās.

It became rapidly apparent that, once Imam Yaḥyā was removed, no common goals united the conspirators. The liberal reforms announced, including a legislative assembly, freedom of speech, and a prospective constitution, alarmed conservatives. Established, older notables resented the appointment of young men to high office. Zaidis were indignant at the naming of Shāfiʿīs to responsible posts and pressed, at times successfully, for their removal. Free Yemenis who were to assume posts in the provinces went to Sanaa instead, or were rounded up by local officials or tribesmen and sent off to the Ḥajja prisons. Those in Sanaa quarreled among themselves. Al-Wazīr's authority was never, in fact, asserted beyond the immediate environs of the capital. Most local officials in the provinces remained passive, awaiting the outcome of events, and finally al-Wazīr was reduced to broadcasting increasingly frantic threats to the population, and increasingly desperate pleas for help to the Arab League.[13]

As previously noted, peparations for the coup were made only in a few urban centers. Al-Wazīr's coconspirators attributed to him, and he himself apparently believed he possessed strong support among the northern tribes. Such influence as he may have had eroded as soon as the manner of Yaḥyā's death became known. The principle of punishment or compensation for acts of violence, particularly murder, is well established in the customary law of the Yemeni tribes. The tribesmen clearly felt a deep revulsion at the assassination of an aged man so feeble that he could not walk unassisted, and their attitude toward al-Wazīr grew hostile as days passed and he failed to identify and punish the murderers. The pretender sent weapons and money, usually the most persuasive of arguments, to the Arḥab; this tribe, however, refused the subsidy, asserting, "We must first know who were the murderers of Imam Yaḥyā."[14] The Wazīr "government" sent regular Yemeni forces on two expeditions, one to occupy the strategic town of Shibām-Kawkabān, the other to secure the road to Lower Yemen. Both operations were commanded by his relatives, and both failed miserably in their encounters with tribal irregulars. The commander of the first enterprise, Sayyid Muḥammad bin 'Alī al-Wazīr, fled to Sanaa after an unsuccessful engagement, and his troops deserted to Prince Aḥmad at Ḥajja. The personnel of the effort toward the south were defeated and plundered by Ānis tribesmen.

The authors of the coup had counted on the Arab League and its member states to confirm the legitimacy of the new regime, and to provide material aid against a possible Ḥāmid al-Dīn challenge. The Arab republics, Lebanon and Syria, initially inclined toward the apparently reformist Wazīr government. Most Arab states, however, were then under monarchical regimes. Kings do not generally approve of regicide, and Farūq of Egypt was furthermore disturbed that the Muslim Brotherhood was implicated in the Yemeni conspiracy. The king of Saudi Arabia had a different, and compelling, reason to disapprove, since he believed that ʻAbdullah al-Wazīr had broken faith by ignoring his stricture against attacking Imam Yaḥyā. Ibn Saud submerged his old resentment against Aḥmad, and lent both moral and material support to his campaign for the throne. He delayed a high-level Arab League delegation which was to conduct an on-the-spot investigation in Yemen, and even imprisoned Muḥammad al-Zubairī, whom al-Wazīr had sent as a special emissary to plead for the Saudi sovereign's help.

Paralyzed by the absence of popular support, and hopelessly divided as to its objectives, the Wazīr coup collapsed. Sanaa was surrounded by tribesmen mobilized by Ḥasan and ʻAbbās, brothers of Crown Prince Aḥmad, and the city was taken after a three-day siege on March 13, twenty-four days after the coup. The tribes exercised their age-old right to sack the city, without interference from the new imam.

The story of the Wazīr coup is an interesting study in political power. The "seizure" of power is a misleading metaphor; power is not an implement passed from hand to hand intact, and with constant efficacy. If power denotes the ability of those who claim authority to elicit certain patterns of action by large numbers of people, it consists of relationships created specifically for the society and rulers concerned. The creative process is one of establishing bases of legitimacy agreed between those aspiring to rule and some or all of the groups composing the society. If agreement is comprehensive, there may be no need for actual coercion. The irreducible minimum is agreement between the ruler and a body of armed men willing and able to impose his will by force. There is no doubt that Imam Yaḥyā held a respectable measure of power, based partly upon naked coercion, but more importantly upon several abstract definitions of his legitimacy which were accepted by significant groups among his subjects. These relationships disappeared with him; al-Wazīr could not simply appropriate them. The administrators in the provinces were

Imam Yaḥyā's officials, not those of the Zaidi, or even of the Ḥamīd al-Dīn, imamate. By failing to move against Yaḥyā's assassins, the usurper failed to satisfy expectations of the proper conduct of a ruler, expectations based both upon religion and tribal custom. His announced goals placed in question the foundation of Zaidism, and thus alienated many ulama whose moral support was essential to the construction of a viable legitimacy. Finally, al-Wazīr himself, along with many ulama, tribal leaders, and other notables, was bound by oath to recognize Prince Aḥmad as the next imam. To be sure, many such pledges were given under duress and probably with tongue in cheek. Nevertheless the moral force of a sworn oath in Yemeni society was potent; it remained so in 1962, when the revolutionary leaders went to ludicrous lengths in insisting that Imam Muhammad al-Badr, to whom the country's religious and tribal leaders had pledged fealty, had perished in the bombardment of his palace.

Nor could Crown Prince Aḥmad simply step into his late father's shoes. He had to vindicate his own legitimacy. With respect to the tribes his advantages over al-Wazīr were overwhelming. Aside from the moral force of the oaths already sworn to him, his campaign had the honorable objective of avenging murder. He had practical assets as well. The Sanaa treasury available to al-Wazīr was, by his own scruple, left virtually intact,[15] whereas Aḥmad was amply supplied with funds from hoards in the provinces. Recognition of the justice of his cause by Ibn Saud brought him accretions of money and arms. He was thus able to move the tribes against his rival by the combination, indispensable throughout the imamate's history, of moral suasion and material reward. With this help, the coup was crushed and its leaders executed or imprisoned, less than a month after its inception. Aḥmad rapidly consolidated his position as successor to the imamate.

The 1955 Coup Attempt

Unlike the 1948 event, the abortive coup of 1955 against Imam Aḥmad was not preceded by advance planning of broad social and geographical scope. Again, alternate accounts of the incident conflict in important details. In particular there is disagreement concerning the extent of prior understanding between Lt. Col. Aḥmad Yaḥyā al-Thalāya, inspector general of the army, and Prince ʻAbdullah, the imam's brother and foreign minister, to depose the already aging and ailing monarch.[16] It is clear that al-Thalāya disagreed with the imam concerning the handling of an affray between soldiers and the villagers of Ḥawbān, near the capital at Taʻizz; he took the occasion to besiege the imam in his palace and to extort a letter of abdication in favor of ʻAbdullah, who promptly proclaimed himself imam. Some of the ulama and notables gave him their allegiance, while others hesitated to violate their sworn loyalty to Aḥmad. ʻAbdullah named his brother, ʻAbbās, who was then in Sanaa, prime minister, and called for obedience of the officials in the provinces. The claimant and al-Thalāya, anxious to avoid al-Wazīr's error of seven years before, did not move against the person of the imam. The consequent uncertainty gave time for Aḥmad to regain the loyalty of the army enlisted men besieging his palace, and to lead them in successful battle against the rebels. His son Muḥammad al-Badr had meanwhile hastened from his sojourn at Hodeida, assembled a tribal force in the north, and was advancing on Taʻizz. Within five days Aḥmad was firmly back on his throne, and the leaders of the effort were summarily executed.

The parallels between the two events suggest that rather little had changed in the intervening years. There was no mass participation worthy of the name in either operation, and no effort to rally popular support beyond demanding the obedience of the citizenry. In both cases the army failed to act as a unit. The enlisted men responded to their traditional loyalties rather than to the orders of their officers. In 1955 it was personnel of the regular army who seized and imprisoned the premier-designate, Prince ʻAbbās. Subordinate officials on both occasions, personal appointees of the imam, passively awaited developments, without acting either to thwart the coup or to promote its success. Like al-Wazīr, Prince ʻAbdullah spoke of reformist policies and of introducing changes in the government structure; these were, however, to take place within the framework of the Zaidi imamate.

Neither event may thus be categorized as an attempt at

revolution. It was simply proposed to transfer authority from its holders to others equally qualified to wield it according to the traditional standards. By contrast, the revolt of 1962 sought specifically to dislodge the entire ruling class from its position of authority. Its architects disagreed on many values and policies; they nevertheless were united on the principle that power did not legitimately belong by ascription to the sayyid aristocracy. The implication of this is that large numbers of Yemenis had abandoned the consummatory pattern of values by which the legitimacy of their government had been defined and agreed upon between themselves and their rulers for centuries. Yemenis were now sufficiently motivated by new, if not uniform, values to combine in numbers sufficient to destroy the old institutions by force. The course of change was not pervasive. It left the large Zaidi tribes of the north little affected. Agreement on new goals was far from complete among the leaders of the new order. The resulting incoherence led to the Yemeni civil war, to strife within each of two competing Yemeni regimes, and to foreign intervention on both sides.

The 1962 Revolution

The authors of the revolution comprised a loose coalition among several segments of the urban population: army officers, Shāfiʿī merchants, young intellectuals, industrial laborers and expatriate dissidents. They were solidly united in opposition to Imam Aḥmad's regime. Beyond that, their aspirations were diverse, and in many respects mutually incompatible.

After 1955 Imam Aḥmad, in addition to instituting economic development with outside aid, endeavored in his erratic way to modernize his armed forces. Associating himself with President Nasser and King Saud in the Arab Solidarity Pact, he sent numbers of young officers to Egypt for training, and invited Egyptian military instructors to work in Yemen. These associations had their impact upon the young officers' consciousness of their proper social status, and upon their ideological orientation. Their mentors were now Egypt's governing elite, who were entitled in their own eyes to authority because they embodied, as military leaders, the interests, aspirations, and unity of the Egyptian people. The contrast between the status of the Egyptian officers and their own was galling to their Yemeni pupils. Some of the older, Iraqi-trained officers were willing to work toward enhanced personal prestige, Yemeni modernization and development, and administrative rationalization, within the framework of the monarchy. Not so the younger generation, who were won to the goal of replacing the imamate with republican forms. There unanimity ended, however. Egyptian influence did not induce ideological uniformity even among the junior officers:

> It is difficult to pinpoint the ideological currents represented by the military. We find among them some who were simply reformers, and some revolutionary (with Marxist leanings), passing through Ba'thists, Nasserists, and Muslim Brothers. . . . The only common denominator was the overthrow of the imamate regime, the introduction of contemporary methods into the country's public services, and raising the people's standards of living.[17]

Students of revolution have pointed out that when a regime responds to discontent, whether political or economic, by introducing reforms, and then retreats or even slackens the pace of reform, revolutionary disturbances become likely.[18] The sequence is well illustrated in the case of the Yemeni officer corps. The military's association with Egypt (as well as with the U.S.S.R. in the field of aviation) certainly represented a reform which enhanced its professional competence and self-esteem. The process was given special impetus during al-Badr's regency in 1959. Not only were Egyptian instructors and advisors recruited in sharply increased numbers, but substantial increases in salary were granted to all Yemeni military ranks. These measures were summarily reversed by Imam Aḥmad upon his return. Dissident activity promptly intensified among the officers, as indicated by the distribution of anti-regime leaflets in the name of "Free Yemeni Officers," and by a succession of attempts to assassinate the imam. In December 1961, moreover, Ahmad provoked the dissolution of the United Arab States, the loose confederation formed in 1958 between the United Arab Republic (U.A.R.) and Yemen, by publishing his sensational poem denouncing Nasser's socialist policies as against Islam. Shortly thereafter, elaborate preparations for his overthrow were put in train, in the form of several distinct, but overlapping conspiracies.

The Shāfi'ī merchants were an important element in the planning, contributing funds and arranging the smuggling and stockpiling of arms and ammunition. They had previously financed Free Yemeni propaganda, but had not actively engaged in anti-regime operations within the country. Their collaboration at precisely this time is easily explained. As we have seen, the economy of Lower Yemen had received a substantial boost through foreign aid and the formation of new corporations. In profiting by this revival, the merchants had begun to invest capital in the country itself, rather than following the traditional practice of sending their earnings to foreign havens. The status of these investments was precarious under an arbitrary political regime in which the investors were third-class citizens deprived of an effective voice in decisions. The determination to protect recently gained advantages is a stimulant to revolutionary action, and the merchants had ample motive both as capitalists and as Shāfi'īs. Their important role in the plotting was acknowledged by the inclusion of two Ta'izz merchants in the first republican cabinet ('Abd al-Ghanī Muṭahhar and 'Alī Muḥammad Sa'īd) and in the naming of another, 'Abd al-Qāwī Ḥamīm, to the Revolutionary Council.

The merchants were united in the aspiration to equal social status, the freedom of trade, and the security of capital. In contrast, the intellectuals who were brought into the conspiracy as popular organizers and future administrators were quite diverse in outlook. The older generation of dissidents, educated along traditional lines (such as Aḥmad Muḥammad Nu'mān, Qāḍī 'Abd al-Raḥmān al-Iryānī, and Qāḍī Muḥammad Maḥmūd al-Zubairī), were reformers who had become convinced that reform was impossible to achieve under Imam Aḥmad's rule. The younger intelligentsia, trained abroad in Western-type institutions and numbering only a few score, were an object of distrust and even persecution by the imam.

Coming from various levels of society, but most frequently from the petit bourgeoisie, they were agreed in opposing the imamate, but otherwise had various ideological orientations One of their number writes,

> Comparison between conditions in Yemen and those in other countries necessarily imposed itself upon the intellectuals, perhaps more intensely than upon others. This sharpened their perception of the necessity for structural change, and thus of removing the chief obstacle, represented by the imamate regime, in the path of such change. The intellectuals all hoped for sweeping social transformations, motivated by their social background and by their status as intellectuals aware of the role they were called upon to play (and which each of them defined according to his own philosophical and political concepts).[19]

The personnel involved in the conspiracy thus covered quite comprehensively those elements of the population which had already benefited materially or in prestige from the expanded contacts between Yemen and the external environment, or from the nascent economic development. As none of these groups had an effective voice in the decisions of the regime, their positions were insecure, and in some cases threatened. For a significant number of Yemenis, thus, the policies and actions of the rulers themselves had fostered the growth of new values and aspirations, and the rejection of traditional concepts of authority. These politically changed Yemenis had gained modest advantages and aspired to much more. Between 1955 and 1962 they became convinced that their progress could be protected, and further advances made, only if the monarchy were done away with; they moreover became convinced that by their own effort they could bring this about. These were, and generally are, the necessary and sufficient conditions for revolution.

The narrow and preponderantly urban scope of the movement must nevertheless be emphasized. Dissatisfaction was certainly widespread throughout the countryside of Middle and Lower Yemen. Aspirations there, however, were focused on the traditional aims of livelihood and security. The peasants did not imagine that they had power to destroy the existing political system, or to improve their situation by challenging the authority of the imam's officials.

The collaboration of certain northern tribal shaikhs was solicited by the army conspirators during the eventful week between the death of Imam Aḥmad (who confounded his enemies by succumbing to emphysema) and the execution of the coup of September 26, 1962. The initiative was taken when the new imam, Muḥammad al-Badr, acquiesced in the return to Yemen from his post at the U.N. of his uncle, Prince Ḥasan, whose popularity among the tribes and ulama could be expected to contribute to the consolidation of the new reign. The Free Officers made contact with certain shaikhs among the many assembled in Sanaa to pledge their loyalty to the new sovereign. Those who were disposed to cooperate drew up a petition to al-Badr, obviously reflecting the view of the officers rather than their own, demanding the discharge of ministers who had "exploited the people," the release of political internees, and an end to bribery and corruption in the governing apparatus. The collusion between officers and shaikhs was discovered by the Sanaa provincial governor, whose report to al-Badr was intercepted by the conspirators. This, together with Prince Ḥasan's anticipated arrival, encouraged the plotters to proceed with their operation, originally aimed at Imam Aḥmad, instead of giving al-Badr an opportunity to carry through his announced reforms.[20] The hasty alliance between the rebels and the shaikhs was fragile; it embraced only a limited number of tribes, although some sections of Ḥāshid, whose paramount shaikhs were hostile to the royal family, became and remained supporters of the new regime. Generally, the tribes remained attached to their traditional values: the desire for arms and money; the preservation of their local autonomy; and reverence for the imam to whom they had given their oath. The persistence of the old outlook made possible the organization by Imam al-Badr and his relatives of a serious and protracted attempt at counterrevolution. It obliged the republican leaders to call in outside support to maintain themselves, and thus turned the Yemeni civil war into a struggle between two of the several value systems then competing for supremacy in the Arab world at large.

The fact that the revolution was neither a mass movement nor homogeneous in its objectives once the monarchy was overthrown placed limitations on its capabilities. Its leaders appreciated the necessity for mobilizing mass support. They set about creating it by organizing demonstrations, holding rallies at which senior officials explained the purposes of the new regime. They formed a "People's Conference," which was to serve as the single political organization, and enlisted a new national guard. Under the circumstances, this was uphill work which could not quickly yield power centralized in the hands of the Sanaa leaders. Four months after the coup, this writer appraised the situation thus:

> The immediate meaning of the revolution to most Yemenis was release from the ancient restraints on individual freedom. It was assumed that no one would need to take orders from anyone; everyone would be happy and prosperous. This has been manifested in the collapse of discipline among Yemeni employees of AID, strikes, and harassment of Americans and their domestic servants. There is no professional civil service to cushion the effect of anarchic tendencies. The new officials and the army are inexperienced in administration, and avoid unpleasant measures for fear of making themselves unpopular or of losing their positions. Each one is convinced that he understands the spirit, policies and intent of the revolution, and applies his own ideas without reference to higher authority. The top leadership is preoccupied with the military situation, and is probably not even aware of this chaotic situation. Development of a civil service with a sense of responsibility and public service will take years. Fortunately, as much of the population lives quietly isolated on the land, administrative shortcomings have less impact than they would in a more advanced society.[21]

The new regime thus began with the fairly general sympathy of the urban population, but with little discipline over it. This population was soon augmented by hundreds of expatriates returning from Aden and further afield to support and run the revolution, and to exploit the new opportunities which would presumably arise. The leaders did not head a disciplined, reliable armed force. The officers who executed the coup were quite aware that their innovative ideas were not widely shared among the common soldiers; they themselves carried out the bombardment of al-Badr's palace. They furthermore took the precaution of stationing tanks at the Sanaa barracks to neutralize the enlisted men who could be expected to fight for the imam; in fact a night-long battle did take place between the rebels and loyal troops. The officers' position was precarious from the first; it became dangerous when Prince Ḥasan proclaimed himself imam and persuaded King Saud to assist him with arms and funds, and later when al-Badr, who had unexpectedly survived, appeared publicly in the north and began rallying Zaidi tribesmen in preparation for the attempt to reestablish himself on the throne.

The conspirators, fearing intervention from Saudi Arabia, from the British-sponsored South Arabian Federation, or both, had prepared for the contingency by informing the U.A.R. of their plans, and by obtaining assurances of Egyptian support to ensure the consolidation of a republican regime in Yemen. The new leaders felt the need of such help almost immediately, and the first U.A.R. ship, the *Star of Sudan*, entered the port of Hodeida in the first week of October, bearing arms and several thousand troops.[22]

U.A.R. political operatives had enthusiastically encouraged the conspiracy, for reasons only marginally concerned with Yemen itself. President Nasser's persistent effort to exert discipline over the foreign policies of all the Arab states, in Egypt's own interest, had failed dismally. He had publicly undertaken to destroy the surviving Arab monarchies. Syria had renounced union with Egypt and joined Iraq in repudiating Cairo's lead of the Arab left wing. Nasser was on polite terms within the Arab world with only the new nation of Algeria. He sorely needed some external success to restore his damaged prestige. Yemen appeared to offer an opportunity to reassert leadership; strike a blow at monarchy and reaction;

and mold a new Yemeni society in the Egyptian image, all at negligible effort or cost. This judgment was reached through wishful thinking, and corresponded to no Yemeni reality.

The regime to which the U.A.R. thus committed its prestige had singularly slim resources with which to survive or pursue any national objective. The Egyptians were obliged to supply the armed force needed to preserve the republican government within an area which fluctuated widely in extent. The military confrontation soon became one between Egyptians and royalist-led tribesmen.[23] The U.A.R. presence furthermore constituted from the outset a close tutelage of the Yemeni regime in its policies and actions. Both the fact and style of the U.A.R. intervention had an effect upon the development of political attitudes and attitudes within the republican zone.

On the royalist side there was also tutelage: by the Saudis, upon whom the Ḥamīd al-Dīn princes were dependent for money, arms, and a territorial base of operations. Yemen, in effect, again had two regimes, under the respective sponsorship of rivals for influence in the Arab world at large. Not until well after U.A.R.-Saudi rivalry was submerged at the Khartoum Conference of August-September 1967 did the Yemenis become free to devise a unified government according to their own lights. Meanwhile, values and aspirations had not remained static on either side.

The Yemen Arab Republic

An immediate and decisive result of the revolution was the extinction of the ascriptive claim to authority by the sayyid aristocracy. Those members of the royal family who did not manage to escape abroad were executed, as were a few dozen high officials of the old regime. It appears, however, that they were done away with less because of their noble descent than because of their participation in oppression under Imam Aḥmad.[24] Members of some great sayyid families around whom a counterrevolutionary movement might have formed were imprisoned as a precautionary measure, or kept under close surveillance.[25] With a single exception, sayyids were excluded from the high councils of the new regime.[26] The discrimination was not pressed to the point of persecution, and sayyids were admitted to middle and lower levels in the civil service as it began to take shape. Few sayyids had university degrees. Some, however, had had secondary or technical training abroad in institutions such as the U.N.-sponsored School of Public Administration at Alexandria. Such young sayyids, many of whom were basically sympathetic to the aims of the revolution, were given positions commensurate with their qualifications. Thus the new regime instituted the major innovation of assigning roles by achievement rather than by ascription. The leveling process was exhibited in one less formal but not less significant way: from the first day of the revolution, any Yemeni citizen, regardless of class or sect, was henceforth referred to in the press, radio, and official statements as "sayyid."

The difference in status between the Zaidi and Shāfiʿī sects proved more tenacious than the privileges of the aristocracy. The revolutionary leaders announced that all sectarian distinctions were now erased, along with those of birth and race. Certainly religious doctrine was no longer a political issue. Nevertheless a feeling of identification, mutual solidarity, and opposition to others persisted among the Zaidis of Upper Yemen, and among the Shāfiʿīs of the south and the Tihama. The Zaidis were not prepared to abandon the preferred position to which they had been accustomed over many centuries. The Shāfiʿī merchants and intellectuals had played an equal and indispensable role in producing the revolution. They were at a disadvantage, however, in asserting their claim to an equal voice in its councils. With rare exceptions, they were not leaders of populous tribes; they could not enforce their views, as could certain Zaidis affiliated with important northern tribes, by threatening disaffection in wide areas of the country. As a legacy from the old regime, the Shāfiʿī position in the officer corps was extremely weak, both as to number and rank.

The contest went on at many levels, including the military. Among the first priorities of the new regime was the thorough reorganization of the regular army. A national guard was formed to ensure security until this process was completed. The Shāfiʿī leaders encouraged their constituents to enlist in the guard units; they did so in such numbers that the Y.A.R. broadcast an appeal to young Yemenis in Aden to remain where they were for the present, as no more recruits were needed. The old units of the army, manned chiefly by Zaidi tribesmen, were sometimes reluctant to surrender their responsibilities to the national guard. In January 1963 the "old" army unit garrisoning the fortress al-Qāhira in Ta'izz refused to obey an order to surrender the post to the guardsmen. A shooting affray was avoided only by the intervention of a detachment of Egyptian troops.

The struggle between Zaidis and Shāfi'īs was waged at the highest level of the government. The first Y.A.R. cabinet was exactly balanced between the two sects. By late January 1963, less than three months later, the Shāfi'īs were in a minority of one third, holding the less sensitive portfolios. The cabinet was polarized into factions, with the Zaidis regularly imposing their will upon the Shāfi'īs. The latter's efforts to redress the balance by securing a key ministry, such as interior or defense, were unavailing. Resentment began to develop in the south, where the suspicion spread that the Zaidis were determined to continue running the country as they saw fit. A Shāfi'ī member of the cabinet, on behalf of his colleagues, including Vice President al-Baiḍānī, entered secretly into contact with British officials seeking U.K. support for, or acquiescence in, the establishment of a separate Shāfi'ī state in Lower Yemen, with close economic ties to South Yemen.

U.A.R. intervention and control polarized competing sets of values within the Y.A.R. and inhibited the dialogue which might have produced unity. The earliest attempt at a formula to unify the country had been made by the first-generation Free Yemenis. The group was led by Aḥmad Muḥammad Nu'mān, an al-Azhar-educated head of a shaikhly family with a large personal following among the Shāfi'īs; Qāḍī Muḥammad Maḥmūd al-Zubairī, a Zaidi with considerable influence among the northern tribes; and 'Abd al-Raḥmān al-Iryānī, a widely respected Zaidi jurist. The former two stated their political convictions in a manifesto published in Cairo in 1956 under the title "The People's Demands."[27] Without specifically calling for the overthrow of the Yemeni monarchy, the manifesto proposes a transitional government whose duty will be to form a constituent assembly to draft a constitution. Meanwhile, the assembly is to ensure Yemen's independence, freedom, and unity, while cleansing the country of tyranny, bribery, embezzlement, and corruption. The army, whose role is confined to the national defense, is to be "soundly" organized; its food, quarters, and uniforms are to be improved, and the officers' situation enhanced so that they will not be tempted to accept bribes. The authors are preoccupied with guarantees of the full range of civil liberties; equal rights for all Yemenis irrespective of sect, place of birth, tribe, or economic, social, and political status; secure possession of life and property; freedom of movement both within Yemen and abroad; freedom of thought, expression, and association; freedom of the press; free and equal access to the courts for the redress of grievances; freedom from detention or punishment without due process of law. Commerce is to be free, with no granting of monopolies. Education is the right of all citizens, and it is the government's duty to provide it. Public employment is to be on the basis of technical competence and education, under equitable regulations. A long list of social security measures is proposed. Payment of the *zakāt* is to be left to the people's conscience, and is no longer to be assessed and collected by force; no other taxes are to be levied except by freely elected representatives of the people.

The most insistent emphasis is on the principle of administrative decentralization. The centralized rule of the imams is responsible, Nu'mān and Zubairī assert, for the sectarianism and hatred then dividing Yemeni society. Given the conditions of the country, the only suitable regime is one which strictly limits the scope of authority of the national government, and reserves the utmost freedom of action to provincial and local councils. Free Yemeni aspirations at this time are thus essentially reformist and liberal. Their stress is on the restriction of authority, rather than on its use to bring about economic or social change, or to pursue ideological ends not directly related to the material welfare of the individual citizen.

This general outlook had strong appeal to many Yemenis, as was shown by the pervasive atmosphere of release from constraint observed on the morrow of the coup. During the civil war the goal of unity was translated into that of national reconciliation, through negotiated compromise with the royalists; many worked toward termination of the Egyptian occupation and the recovery of Yemen's independence of action. Zubairī pursued these ends in founding his "Party of God"; Nu'mān, prime minister in mid-1965, convened the tribal conference at Khamir which adopted resolutions along these general premises; and the broadly based coalition which became known as the "Third Force" had a similar orientation.

Until the Egyptian withdrawal in 1967, the most insistently pressed value pattern was the combination of pan-Arabism and étatism which may be summed up as Nasserism. The basic goal in this outlook is unity among all Arabs, who are held to form a single nation. Unity is posited as historical and contemporary fact. Its practical manifestation, however, is impeded by the hostility of Western imperialism in alliance with traitorous Arab reactionaries, Zionists, and other enemies. The armies of the Arab states, the faithful repository of the people's aspirations, are entitled to a role in leadership. Unity cannot be achieved until a revolution of "national liberation" has been accomplished in each Arab state, consolidating an "Arab Socialist" regime. The state's role in the economy is to take precedence over private enterprise; government supervision and intervention are to be extended to all phases of collective activity. Large incomes are to be reduced by taxation, and only a limited role is reserved for "nationalist," as distinct from "exploitative," capital. Industrialization is to be a cardinal economic and social objective.

This set of mainly consummatory aspirations, arising from Egypt's own national experience, contrasts sharply with the instrumental program of Nu'mān and Zubairī. It appealed quite unequally to the various factions within the new Yemeni republic which claimed a voice in its public affairs. These factions, some speaking for substantial numbers of Yemenis, others representing tiny groups of individuals, may be listed along an ideological spectrum. Moving from right to left, they include:

—the Zaidi tribes, both those such as the Khawlān, which drifted in and out of the republican orbit during the civil war, and those which consistently supported the Y.A.R. against the royalists, such as some Ḥāshid tribes.[28]
— The moderate reformers—Nu'mān, Zubairī, Iryānī, etc.—with considerable influence in the urban centers as well as in the countryside.
— The large Shāfi'ī merchants, aspiring to an effective voice in government decisions, in the interest of the security and freedom of commercial activity.
— Nasserists, whether by conviction or by opportunism during the Egyptian presence; prominent in, but not confined to, the Yemeni officer corps.[29]
— Ba'thists, quite few in number, represented among both younger officers and civilian intellectuals.
— Communists; represented among Soviet-trained armed forces personnel, civilians educated in the U.S.S.R., Eastern Europe, or Western countries;[30] also among detribalized repatriates.
— National Liberation Front (N.L.F.); the radical revolutionary movement which succeeded to British rule in South Yemen and established the People's Democratic Republic of Yemen; considerable influence among laborers returning from Yemen, and some adherents also in the armed forces.

In its situation as an Egyptian puppet, 'Abdullah al-Sallāl's government had no choice but to endorse the full Nasserist ideology, and to urge it upon the Yemeni republic. Its content, except in one important respect, was either irrelevant or repugnant to most of the politically significant segments of the society, and Sallāl utterly failed to establish its legitimacy even among the army officers. Centralism was anathema to the tribes and to the merchants, as Nu'mān and Zubairī realized. Collectivism, especially where it threatened private property, appealed only to the minuscule proletariat and those whose kinship ties had been erased. Many Yemenis, having seen the army restrict their liberties and seize their property as taxes for centuries, could hardly regard the military as custodian of their interests and aspirations. Arab unity was a revered symbol across the whole spectrum of beliefs. The solidarity of all Muslims was a traditional item of faith (save among communists and the N.L.F.); however, it was not a goal to be pursued through the Yemeni political system. Antiimperialism and anti-Westernism also had deep roots in the value system. The Ḥamīd al-Dīn imams had deliberately promoted xenophobia, and used their subjects' suspicion and fear of Western influence to further their own objectives. As crown prince, al-Badr had assiduously courted the socialist countries, while holding strictly aloof from representatives of Western powers. Within three years after the revolution, the Egyptians found, to their indignation, that the persisting xenophobia had come to be focused on their own presence. It was felt that the Egyptians prevented the pursuit by successive Yemeni leaders of the moderate, purely Yemeni goals which might have made possible a workable compromise with the royalists. The latter, meanwhile, were undergoing their own political transition.

The Yemeni Royalists

The royalists withstood for five years the onslaught of U.A.R. forces numbering up to eighty-five thousand.[31] The Egyptians were well equipped with armor and transport, in total command of the air, and sufficiently determined upon victory to employ poison gas regularly as a means of terrorizing and demoralizing civil populations. The royalist effort obliged the Egyptians to barricade themselves for two years within a perimeter encompassing less than half of Yemen's territory. The royalist regime thus had very considerable strengths. The medal had its reverse, however. The royalists should have found no difficulty in crushing the republic after the U.A.R. withdrawal. In the event, they proved unequal to the task of overrunning the capital. Their regime had grave weaknesses which may be attributed to the decline of the imamate. Their strengths may be ascribed to the power of the large Zaidi tribes rather than to the royalist government per se. In addition to a fluctuating number of tribes, the royalist polity comprised the ruling family; a group of supporters, mainly sayyids, who followed them into exile in Saudi Arabia; and a handful of Zaidi commoners with tribal connections. The Saudis, furthermore, cannot be excluded from the analysis, since as the major source of Ḥamīd al-Dīn capabilities, they had very substantial control over royalist policies and actions.

The grave necessity of cooperation against the republic imposed a modicum of unity upon the royal family. However, they remained deeply divided, as the Qāsimī dynasty had been throughout the several centuries of its history. Three distinct factions within the family competed for eventual possession of the throne.

The figure of Imam Muḥammad al-Badr emerges as a forlorn and solitary one, betrayed and deserted successively by all those in whom, during the sixteen years of his public life, he placed trust. Not devoid of personal courage, he nevertheless lacked the martial élan of a traditional Zaidi imam, and neglected to cultivate a reputation for knowledge of the law, piety, and asceticism. In early youth he developed vague aspirations toward reform and modernization in Yemen. Deeply impressed by post-revolution Egyptian propaganda and the charisma of the Egyptian president, he assiduously cultivated Nasser's friendship. He emulated Nasser in embracing neutralism and in seeking economic and military assistance from the U.S.S.R. and the People's Republic of China, while avoiding involvement with the West. He had the conviction, naive in the Yemeni circumstances, that by responding to the people's aspirations and befriending them, he could win their personal and political loyalty;[32] thus, he secured from his father the release from prison and rehabilitation of two architects of the 1962 coup, 'Abdullah al-Sallāl, and 'Abd al-Raḥmān al-Baiḍānī (the latter was even given positions of trust).

We have seen how al-Badr's well-meant but fumbling attempts at reform during his 1959 regency produced little but disorder. In 1962, upon his accession, he was no more able to steer a coordinated, decisive course. The announcement of his intended reforms having alarmed the ulama, he assured the public that he would follow his father's "sound course." The innocent phrase was at once seized upon by his opponents as evidence that he intended to preserve arbitrary rule. During the early weeks after the coup, as al-Badr was making his escape to the Saudi border, his erstwhile Egyptian and communist friends were assiduously welcoming and assisting the new regime. Henceforth his only reliance was upon the Saudis, upon those Zaidis who respected their oaths of loyalty to him, and upon his own family, no member of which had wanted him to accede to the thone.

Prince Ḥasan, al-Badr's uncle, then Yemeni ambassador to the U.N., upon receiving the false news of his nephew's death, announced his own claim to the imamate, and set off to restore the throne. He went to Riyad, where he persuaded King Saud to back him with money and arms. Ḥasan had long been on public record as considering Badr unfit for the imamate, because of his secular views and his unedifying personal life. Ḥasan had cultivated chiefs of the Zaidi tribes, both at a distance and at first hand during the rare visits Imam Aḥmad permitted him to make to the countryside.[33] His piety and traditional learning appealed to the conservative ulama. Ḥasan was thus an acknowledged and formidable rival to Badr, as well as an immediate threat to the republican regime. It has been suggested that his residence abroad had placed him in agreement with the younger princes on the desirability of reform and modernization in Yemen.[34] However this may be, he was the focus of a faction within the Ḥamīd al-Dīn clan which aspired to see him installed as imam upon the crushing of the Sallāl rebellion. His partisans were led by his own able and vigorous sons, Ḥasan and 'Abdullah.

A third faction emerged during the civil war as the military and political abilities of Prince Muḥammad bin Ḥusain were demonstrated. He became the "strong man" of the royalist camp somewhat as Ḥasan al-'Amrī did on the republican side. His aspirations to the imamate itself were widely assumed, if never openly avowed. Meanwhile, his efforts to extend his personal influence within Badr's regime, and to restrict the imam's authority, were abetted by his five brothers and certain other princes of his generation.

While Imam al-Badr thus had no loyal support within the dynasty, he was the indispensible symbol of the legitimacy of the royalist regime. His fleeting reign at Sanaa had earned him the fealty oaths of many tribal chiefs, ulama, and notables, as well as the recognition of much of the international community. Saudi Arabia, Iran, and for a time Jordan continued to acknowledge him as sovereign of Yemen after the revolution. Any rival would have faced the difficult, probably impossible, task of creating a new legitimacy in the eyes of the people of Yemen and of the world at large. Pending the outcome of the civil war, the princes acted, however provisionally, in the name of al-Badr.

With few exceptions, the imam's young cousins, of whom the active ones numbered some fifteen, had been educated abroad—in Cairo, Europe, or the American University at Beirut. They were generally liberal in outlook, and sought modernization and economic development without, however, envisaging abdication of power by their family. Their ideas contrasted with the conservatism of the older aristocrats, tribal leaders, and ulama who remained in the imam's service. Liberal views were also held by a number of well-educated young sayyids, whose number increased substantially during the civil war through scholarships and other assistance provided by the Saudi government.

The movement toward revision and modernization of the imamate from within, which al-Badr had symbolized, encouraged, and led during the last years of his father's reign, accelerated after the revolution. There were reasons of practical necessity as well as of conviction. If any significant proportion of the Shāfiʿī community were to be reconciled to restoration of the Hamīd al-Dīn monarchy, it would have to be under conditions in which they were assured of equal status with Zaidis, and of an effective voice in national affairs. This implied that the discretion of the imam must be effectively curbed. Badr's proposed reforms of September 1962 were inadequate; they envisaged merely a consultative council, of which half the members would be the monarch's appointees. Two years later, the royalists published in Aden a draft constitution introducing the principle of popular elections to a true legislature, and limitations on the discretion of the sovereign. In the context of the royalist-republican meeting at

Erkowit in November 1964, Foreign Minister Aḥmad al-Shāmī spoke of a projected constitution which would make a future imam a mere figurehead with religious and ceremonial functions, while real authority would be vested in a legislature elected by universal suffrage. The intraroyalist debate developed into a contest between al-Badr, who fought to retain authority in his own hands, and his cousins, who sought to gain possession of it. The issue was decided at a conference among the princes and notables at Taif in August 1966.[35] Decision-making power was now lodged in an imamate council. This was nominally chaired by the imam, but effective authority lay with its deputy-president, Prince Muḥammad bin Ḥusain. Ḥasan's faction was accommodated by retaining the elderly prince as prime minister, and giving him the additional honorific title of the imam's deputy general.

These liberalizing innovations helped stop the cleavages within the royal family, but did nothing to enhance the position of the young royalists, mainly sayyids, who considered themselves the cadre of an administrative structure which in fact did not exist. The royal princes simply worked through the tribal shaikhs, as their predecessors had always done, leaving the aspiring administrators with no meaningful function. The resulting incoherence hampered the counterrevolutionary effort. In the spring of 1968, the Saudi government issued an ultimatum to the royalists telling them to establish their regime on Yemeni soil where it belonged, and to submerge their internal differences in the interests of a serious attempt to capture Sanaa. Preparations for a conference at 'Amāra to organize the move were the occasion for a confrontation between the royal family and a group of some thirty-five young, well-educated royalist officials. The officials made their further cooperation dependent upon reform of the arbitrary rule of the princes, and demanded authority commensurate with the positions they nominally held. The crisis was papered over. It marked change, nevertheless, within the aristocracy itself, of its definition of legitimate authority. The demands of the malcontents reflected a decline of religious principle as the basis for proper government; a growing attachment to modern, rational administrative procedures; and a significant weakening of the traditional sayyid attitude that they were entitled to special privilege and command solely by reason of their noble birth.

The decline of the traditional concept of the imamate among the personnel of the royalist government weakened its relations with the Zaidi tribes, whose manpower was essential to a sustained effort against the republic. The secularizing trend, the curbs imposed upon the discretion of the monarch, the dispersal of authority, and al-Badr's obvious dependence upon Saudi largesse all combined to reduce the prestige of the imamate. Religious fervor declined in salience as a motive for political action among the tribes. Nevertheless, their interests remained remarkably constant: preservation of local autonomy; the desire for money and weapons; the opportunity to win distinction in stylized battle; and, finally, the fulfilling of the duties of their faith. The imams had never been able to institute close, direct administration over these tribes, and the royalist regime of 1962-1971 did not do so. The *zakāt* was collected only sporadically, and movement within the territory of the respective tribes took place only on their sufferance. (Traveling from near the Baihān border to 'Amarā for the conference mentioned above, Prince Muḥammad bin Ḥusain was refused passage by the Jawf tribes, and was forced to make a wide detour along the fringe of the desert. The prince named at the same conference to govern the northwestern province was denied access to the territory he was to administer.)

Aside from a tiny nucleus created with much difficulty by Prince Muḥammad bin Ḥusain, the royalists had no regular army, and tribal forces had to be assembled by negotiation with the shaikhs for each contemplated operation of any size. The tribesmen had furthermore to be paid to fight. So long as the Egyptians were in Yemen, the xenophobia of the tribes tended to encourage cooperation with the royalists; when the Egyptians departed, other traditional values asserted themselves: material advantage, and the determination to keep central authority at a distance. The latter contributed in no small degree to the failure of the crucial royalist siege of Sanaa (December 1, 1967–February 8, 1968). One prince explained,

> If the tribesmen had all really been for us, the republicans in Sanaa could have done nothing. But we could never mount a concerted operation against the capital. In January we would have had to throw 20,000 men at least against the city. We had them, and more, but when one tribal chief had agreed, he went away—to rally his men, he said. Meanwhile we would be discussing with another who was to act at the same time as the first. He said yes, but on the day set nothing happened. One had deserted because the republicans bought him off; the other went off and attacked on his own, elsewhere than expected, because he was suspicious. That's the way it has always been.[36]

The tribes changed sides according to practical considerations, as in the past they had allied themselves against Zaidi imams with Ḥamza sharīfs, Yu'firids, Rasūlids, or Idrīsids. The case of one influential shaikh who had been a valued royalist commander suggests some of the motivations. In September 1968, King Faisal gave the Ḥamīd al-Dīn a three-month subsidy at the usual rate, with the warning that no more would be forthcoming unless a decisive victory were won before the end of the year.

> The princes hastened to make economies, and it seems that this is what precipitated their downfall. Some of them considered it prudent not to distribute the usual sums to the tribal chiefs, giving the excuse that the Saudis had not paid. A tribal chief is not so easily deceived. One, Qāsim Munaṣṣar, is said to have declared, "All right, I'll see for myself," whereupon he went off to Nejran, where the Saudis told him that the prince had lied. Instead of returning to demand an accounting, Qāsim Munaṣṣar proceeded to Sanaa and placed himself, apparently definitively, at the side of the republicans.[37]

Only a small minority of the shaikhs conceived and pursued aims transcending age-old tribal concerns and embracing the country as a whole. Of these the most outstanding was 'Abdullah bin Ḥusain al-Aḥmar, who, for reasons we have described, embraced the republic out of hostility toward the Ḥamīd al-Dīn; he rendered signal services to the new regime in senior posts, using his talents and his influence with the Ḥāshid confederation in support of moderate policies. A serious loss to the royalists was the defection of Sinān Abū Luḥūm, shaikh of the strategically located Nahm tribe, who was promptly appointed governor of Hodeida Province by the republicans. However, after the royalist disintegration, even if the tribes had realized that they held the balance of power in Yemen, they still had no country wide goals to achieve through its use. Responding to a correspondent's remark that it was the tribes, in the final analysis, who had won the civil war, the republican leader Muḥammad Aḥmad Nu'mān[38] replied,

> Yes, but they don't know it. . . . The tribal chiefs are strong. They know how to talk to their men and persuade them to fight. But when they have to make political decisions they realize their ignorance. Then they come to us, timidly, asking what they should do. And we, who used to tell ourselves "If it were not for the foreigners the real strength of the country would be the tribes," now hear strange voices, new voices, rising from the true roots of Yemen. "Something has changed in this country," we say; "If they were really so strong, would they break ranks and run?" So we talk with them, and that is how we win in the end.[39]

Thus the royalist regime was undermined by its own inconsistencies and the dilemmas it confronted. Al-Badr did not act like an authentic imam. He rarely led troops in battle, submitted to Sunnī tutelage, exercised little spiritual leadership, and for extended periods was not even physically present in the country. His regime adopted modernizing and secularizing principles, its only hope of wooing support among the Shāfi'ī majority and the urban intelligentsia; but these innovations had little appeal to the Zaidi tribes which were crucial to the prosecution of the royalist effort. The royalist force could be made effective only by means of a hierarchical pattern of authority; but such a system was, as it had usually been, impossible to impose in the tribal areas which were the only territory the royalists were able to occupy. Given the incoherence of their goals, internal rivalries, and practical obstacles, the Ḥamīd al-Dīn princes were unable to mobilize the very substantial energies of the tribes behind one salient, consummatory objective. The survival of the royalists for nearly nine years in contention with Egypt and the republic speaks for the talents of their individual leadership. Their fortunes were finally dependent, however, upon the support of Saudi Arabia, whose motives should be stated briefly.

The Saudi Role

Relations between the royal houses of Saud and Ḥamīd al-Dīn had never been particularly close. They were divided by religious sectarianism, and their conflicting territorial ambitions produced full-scale war in 1933-1934. The Treaty of Taif, in the latter year, established a modus vivendi which preserved a correct atmosphere thereafter. The Saudi monarchs had an understandable repugnance for the violent overthrow of kings. Ibn Saud supported, both materially and morally, the claim of Imam Aḥmad to the Yemeni throne after the Wazīr coup of 1948. King Saud followed the precedent by opposing the 1955 attempt to depose Aḥmad. In 1956 the two regimes joined with Egypt in a basically anti-British pact which, six years later, provided the legalistic excuse for both U.A.R. and Saudi intervention in Yemen. Al-Badr's courting, while crown prince, of President Nasser, and his cultivation of the communist powers, were disturbing to the Saudi royal family, which refrained from any association with communist countries, and feared U.A.R. subversion.

Upon the outbreak of the Yemeni revolution, King Saud's initial, uncharacteristically wise impulse was to hold aloof; Prince Ḥasan's persuasion, however, encouraged Saud's more usual judgment to reassert itself, and he agreed to underwrite the effort to restore the Ḥamīd al-Dīn throne. The decision induced the immediate desertion to Egypt of several Saudi Air Force pilots with their planes; it triggered the build-up of U.A.R. forces in Yemen on a substantial scale; and it encouraged the Nasser regime to consider, and publicly to threaten, the invasion of Saudi Arabia and the extinction of its monarchy. Saudi forces were quite incapable of defending the kingdom's southern border against regular forces, and U.A.R. aircraft made incursions with impunity, to the acute embarassment of Saud's government. A situation soon developed in which the only effective defense of Saudi territory was the ability of the Yemeni royalists to stave off the U.A.R. forces and their Y.A.R. allies. It became the primary aim of Saud, and particularly of Faisal, who succeeded to the throne in November 1964, to remove this threat to the kingdom's security through the evacuation of U.A.R. forces from the peninsula. The interests of the Ḥamīd al-Dīn were consistently subordinated to this objective.

At the Alexandria Arab summit conference of September 1964, Faisal and Nasser discussed the Yemen issue; they stated publicly their common aim of terminating all outside interference, and of allowing the Yemeni factions to decide their country's future among themselves. The Erkowit Conference between royalists and republicans ensued; a ceasefire was arranged, but the national congress envisaged at the meeting failed to come about, as there was little ground between the rigid positions of the opposing sides. The Saudis accordingly supported a renewed offensive by the royalists. This effort made considerable progress because of the growing unpopularity of the Egyptians in Yemen, and of the growing sectarian and ideological cleavages in the republican camp. Nasser and Faisal renewed the attempt at a negotiated settlement in August 1965, when they met at Jidda and concluded a formal disengagement pact, the U.A.R. undertaking to withdraw its forces within ten months of a Yemeni national conference to be held at the town of Ḥaraḍ. (On neither side were the Yemenis consulted.) The meeting convened on November 24, as scheduled; however, the insistence of the Y.A.R. delegates upon preservation of the republican regime during any transitional period deadlocked the discussions from the start, and the conference was shortly disbanded.

The Ḥaraḍ Conference took place just as King Faisal embarked on a program to form a common international front in the name of Islamic solidarity against Nasserist and communist radicalism. Relations rapidly deteriorated between Faisal and Nasser. In February 1966, a vital new policy factor emerged for both leaders when the United Kingdom announced its intention of withdrawing from South Arabia by 1968. Nasser reacted by regrouping his forces in Yemen so as to exploit the situation in the South Arabian Federation, and announced his intention of remaining indefinitely in Yemen. Faisal, alarmed by the prospect of hostile regimes in both Yemen and South Arabia, urgently negotiated with Britain for an emergency air-defense package, pending completion of the elaborate permanent system already contracted for with the United States and the United Kingdom. At the same time, he preserved a moral advantage by keeping the royalists on short rations during the ten-month period after the Ḥaraḍ meeting during which U.A.R. forces were to evacuate Yemen under the Jidda Pact. Meanwhile, he entered into direct contact with Yemeni Third Force leaders, and with Yemeni tribal shaikhs, seeking to promote their cooperation with the Union of Popular Forces (led by Faisal's client Ibrāhīm al-Wazīr) in a common front of all anti-Y.A.R. Yemeni factions. These maneuvers tended to undercut the Ḥamīd al-Dīn, who were meanwhile gradually becoming less vital to Saudi defense, and the royalists made less progress against U.A.R. and Y.A.R. forces than might otherwise have been expected.

The U.A.R. defeat in the Six-Day War of June 1967 made the Egyptian position in Yemen untenable. At the Khartoum Arab summit conference, as a tacit condition of Saudi subsidies, Nasser made firm, and this time sincere, promises to withdraw Egyptian forces from Yemen, which he did in November. Saudi security was not thereby assured. The Soviet Union and revolutionary Arab states—Syria and Algeria—stepped in to fill the arms and money gap in the Y.A.R. At the same time the South Arabian Federation collapsed, well before the British evacuation on November 30, and extreme radicals of the National Liberation Front assumed control of South Yemen. The Saudis financed a final Ḥamīd al-Dīn effort against the Sanaa republican regime. When this failed, the Yemeni royal family, formerly essential to Saudi defense, became increasingly a liability. It was now prudent for Faisal to seek relations with a viable regime in Sanaa of such a nature as to make combined action possible against the N.L.F. in South Yemen. The Yemeni civil war entered a period of stalemate, while the cohesiveness of the Ḥamīd al-Dīn dynasty and its governing apparatus disintegrated. Its strongest figure, Prince Muḥammad bin Ḥusain, resigned as the imam's deputy in March 1969, and abandoned the cause. In May of the following year, with Saudi encouragement, negotiations between royalists and republicans culminated in a reconciliation by which three royalists were allotted portfolios in a combined cabinet; under a unified central government, such administration as the royalists had been conducting continued in the areas under their control. No role in the arrangement was allocated to the Ḥamīd al-Dīn. Two months later, the establishment of normal relations was negotiated between Saudi Arabia and the Yemen Arab Republic.

9
Yemen Reunited

At the Khartoum Summit Conference of August-September 1967 it was agreed that Nasser would withdraw his forces from the Yemen Arab Republic, and that when this was accomplished King Faisal would terminate the Saudi subsidy to the Yemeni royalists. That Yemen should then be left to decide its own destiny untutored was as yet, however, a notion that occurred only to Yemenis. Without consulting either Yemeni royalists or repubicans, the conference established a tripartite commission under the chairmanship of the Sudanese prime minister, Aḥmad Maḥjūb. Its mission was to preside over the formation of a transitional regime and to hold a plebiscite to determine the wishes of the Yemeni people respecting their future government. The clear implication of this plan was that the existing Y.A.R. government lacked legitimacy, and ʻAbdullah al-Sallāl stoutly opposed the commission's coming to Yemen to undertake its task. When it nevertheless arrived at Sanaa, on September 20, it was greeted with violent popular demonstrations, which Egyptian troops endeavored to quell, at some cost of lives on both sides. The commission left Yemen in undignified haste.

The tripartite commission had meanwhile requested, and obtained, from the Egyptian authorities the release of Yemeni political detainees, notably some forty prominent military and civilian figures, both Zaidi and Shāfiʻī, of a wide spectrum of political orientation, who had gone to Cairo in September 1966 in the hope of persuading President Nasser to abandon support of Sallāl and to permit a more representative government to manage Yemen's affairs. Refused access to Nasser, they had been confined for more than a year. Upon their return to Yemen, they were to provide the core of the republic's political leadership for several years. The movement to oust Sallāl began on October 3, with the submission to him by a group of army officers of an ultimatum demanding the formation of a new cabinet that would put an end to corruption, inefficiency, and dictatorial rule. On October 12, the day the Egyptians evacuated Sanaa, Sallāl announced a new council of ministers, retaining the premiership himself. On November 3 he left Yemen, ostensibly to attend the fiftieth anniversary of the Russian Revolution in Moscow; privately, he notified Qāḍī ʻAbd al-Raḥmān al-Iryānī that his actual destination was Iraq and that he would not return to Yemen. One day later, in a quiet military coup, Sallāl was declared deposed. A republican council composed of Iryānī, Shaikh Muḥammad ʻAlī ʻUthmān (a Shāfiʻī with considerable tribal support on Jabal Ṣabr, above Ta'izz), and Aḥmad Muḥammad Nuʻmān assumed the chief-of-state's authority.[1] A new cabinet was headed by Muḥsin al-ʻAynī, an associate of the Baʻth, the regional party that had for several years challenged Nasser's leadership of the Arab left.

In their withdrawal, the Egyptians had taken with them their tanks, armored cars, and aircraft, leaving the new republican government ill equipped to face the continuing royalist threat. Although the U.S.S.R. and Algeria came promptly to its financial support, it was the military units formed, mainly of Shāfiʻī personnel, after the revolution that played the crucial role in defeating the siege of Sanaa. Their high motivation was explained by a Ḥamīd al-Dīn prince:

> These men of the special republican brigades were poor men, newly returned from abroad. For years they had worked as laborers in Djibouti, Kuwait or elsewhere. They had lost their roots; they no longer knew their parents, and had no family or clan with which to take

> refuge if things went badly for them. They had nothing to lose, and knew they were doomed men. So they fought like lions.[2]

Royalist pressure against territory held by the republic gradually eased, and the civil war reached a stalemate. Meanwhile the absence of a consensus within the Y.A.R. regarding the country's objectives became increasingly apparent. The largely moderate leaders embarked on a policy of wooing the Zaidi tribes away from the royalists, while laying the groundwork for eventual conciliation with Saudi Arabia. Compromise with either the Saudi kingdom or the reactionary tribes was regarded by the political left as a betrayal of the revolution. The most bitter opponents to such a compromise were sympathizers of the National Liberation Front in South Yemen, and their enthusiasm was heightened by the N.L.F. accession to power there when the British departed in November 1967. In the Y.A.R., a shooting affray occurred in March 1968 at Hodeida between the militia and personnel of the regular army. To the support of the army, tribal irregulars under Shaikh 'Abdullah al-Aḥmar were summoned from the highlands. At issue was the custody of a shipment of Soviet arms, which the Russians sought to deliver to the militia instead of to the designated authorities of the government.[3] The ideological cleavage extended into the regular army itself. In August it exploded into a full-dress battle in and near the capital, in which nearly two thousand persons were killed and much property was destroyed. Troops commanded by leftist officers were defeated by moderates with tribal backing. The victors were all Zaidis, while the vanquished were Shāfiʿīs, and to assuage the resurgent sectarian polarization, Ḥasan al-'Amrī, the commander in chief, had the leaders on both sides, numbering twenty-four officers, arrested and exiled.

National Reconciliation and the Constitution

Although the Shāfiʿī leadership at one juncture considered a partition of Yemen along sectarian lines, potent factors operated against such a fragmentation of the country. Territorial configurations, although often drawn without regard for ethnic or cultural principles, acquire a mystique. Habituation to the idea of a given geographic area as a discrete entity encourages the belief, among its inhabitants as well as outsiders, that there should be a corresponding political structure. After the work of the pre–World War I Anglo-Turkish boundary commission and the 1934 settlement with Saudi Arabia, "Yemen" was no longer a vague geographical expression equivalent to "southern Arabia," but a reasonably well defined area to which a single government structure ought to correspond. Royalists and republicans alike fought to achieve rule over all Yemen according to their respective lights. Throughout the civil war, contact was preserved between personalities on the two sides, at times on the scale of formal national conferences.[4] The common identification encouraged the evolution of some of the elites on both sides toward attitudes that could form the basis of a single regime. On both sides there were obstacles to be removed. The royalists had to abandon the very symbol of royalism, the Ḥamīd al-Dīn family. The republicans had to suppress the extreme leftists' aspirations toward centralization of authority and social reorganization; to this group any settlement with the royalists on terms other than unconditional surrender was anathema. When the Saudi government felt the need of a friendly regime in Sanaa with which to cooperate in restraining the revolutionary leadership in South Yemen, it was able to mediate between the Y.A.R. and the royalist faction. Curbing any remaining feelings of moral obligation toward the Yemeni dynasty, the Saudis, in March 1970, assisted in arranging a meeting in Jidda between the Y.A.R. prime minister and senior royalist leaders, excluding the Ḥamīd al-Dīn princes. Agreement was reached on a basis for amalgamating the two governments. The ailing and isolated imam gave his permission to the royalist tribes to consider the proposals and arrive at their own decisions, undertaking to be bound by the will of the majority of the Yemeni people.[5] The reign of al-Badr, and the annals of the Zaidi imamate, may be said to end here.

The settlement terms asserted the principle of national unity, and put it into practice by integrating some royalist personnel into the governing structure at all levels. The Republican

Council was expanded to include a royalist; royalists were allocated the cabinet portfolios of justice, *awqāf*, and public works; eight were named to the (appointive) Consultative Council; others received diplomatic appointments. A "tribal and national" conference was to set policy for the unified government. Decentralization of authority was the core of the understanding; administration of areas then under nominal control of the royalists was to be by royalist personnel, and the contemplated conference was to have as one objective the restoration of regional autonomy.

Neither the fact of the agreement nor its terms appealed to some elements on the republican side. Protest strikes among students had to be suppressed, and some radical officers were transferred from posts in which they might have interfered with the arrangements. The mediators' satisfaction with the outcome was reflected in the Saudi press:

> Observers state that the Yemeni agreement will have a salutary moderating effect on the South Arabian situation; that it may pave the way for the liquidation of the communist-puppet minority ruling there; that it may be an incentive toward the unification of all the various Southern organizations and give them the initiative in liquidating the communist regime by armed struggle.[6]

These dispositions provided the framework within which, during the ensuing months, a permanent consitution was drawn up, submitted for public comment, and promulgated. Popular elections, the first in Yemen's history, were held in March 1971, for a Consultative Council.

The Yemeni Constitution,[7] placed in effect on December 28, 1970, patently embodied the thinking of the older generation of Free Yemenis. It sought to establish political procedures that would respect and preserve the hold of Islam over the great majority of the population while erecting effective barriers to autocracy. It declares Yemen to be an Islamic, as well as an Arab, nation, and the *sharīʿa* to be the source of all its laws. A series of provisions seeks to implant the canon law and its interpreters in the administrative structure; members of the

Consultative Council are required to be practitioners of Muslim religious rites; members of the Republican Council must be well versed in the *sharī'a*; a cabinet minister must adhere to Islamic principles; only *sharī'a* scholars may occupy judicial posts; and only eminent canon law jurists are eligible to sit on the Supreme Constitutional Court. In addition to confirming traditional consummatory values, these provisions acknowledge the leadership status of the ulama. A bill of rights, less comprehensive than the 1956 Free Yemeni manifesto, implies that the state treats with each citizen as an individual; this notion is emphasized by the provision that "punishment is individual, and no one shall be made responsible for another's guilt." The foundation of Yemeni society is nevertheless stated to be the family, itself founded on religion, custom, and patriotism. No restructuring of society is thus contemplated, and mention of "custom" in this context appears designed to reassure the tribes that the constitution does not threaten the ordering of their affairs according to long-established procedures.

The constitution's categorical prohibition of "partisanship in all its forms" is rooted in Islam. Unity and harmony are central to the ideal of the Muslim community. As the Prophet had said, "My people will never agree on an error." Divided views necessarily connote the presence of error, and to make of consensus a constitutional obligation is to preserve the community's integrity. Inasmuch as political parties had always been proscribed in Yemen,[8] the provision reflected existing conditions, as laws often tend to do. In practice, of course, parties existed underground, and their surface manifestation was factionalism. Given this rejection of competing approaches to public policy, interaction between rulers and ruled in Yemen tended in reality to be a process of seeking special advantage for sectarian, geographical, economic, or kinship groups, rather than a search for the general public welfare.

Retention of the Republican Council to head the state was designed to prevent concentration of authority in the hands of a single individual. The device had been adopted immediately after the revolution, in reaction to the autocracy of the imams. It had been discarded under the provisional constitutional arrangements of ʻAbdullah al-Sallāl, whose arbitrary rule under U.A.R. supervision stimulated renewed sentiment against autocracy. The dispersion of authority at the top was not in practice approved unanimously by the Y.A.R.'s leading figures. In March 1971, three months after the promulgation of the constitution, Lt. Gen. Ḥasan al-ʻAmrī, himself a member of the Republican Council, proposed that the council be eliminated, the chief of state to be a president or prime minister with suitably restricted powers. The council was conceived, he argued, out of the now outmoded fear that Yemen might again relapse into a dictatorship like Sallāl's, and thus should not be considered a permanent institution. The proposal was effectively resisted, the decisive opposition coming from Shaikh ʻAbdullah bin Ḥusain al-Aḥmar, speaking generally for the tribal chiefs.

The national goals affirmed by the constitution are modest, conservative, and mainly instrumental. While relations are to be strengthened with "our brothers, the Arabs" (as well as with other friends East and West), Arab political unity is not mentioned. The unity of Yemen itself (i.e., including South Yemen) is affirmed, and effort toward its realization is "the sacred duty of every citizen." Social and economic development, however, are the major goals enounced. While industrialization, assumed by many economically backward countries to be a panacea, is not spoken of, the principle of state planning is cautiously endorsed; at the same time, private economic activity is declared to be free, on condition that it does not "violate the interests of the society."

The broad acceptability of this orientation was confirmed by the elections to the Consultative Council held under the new constitution. This first Yemeni experience in choosing representatives by the ballot rather than in face-to-face discussion attracted more popular participation than anticipated by the leaders who conducted it; nevertheless, they were obliged to designate candidates in some constituencies where none came forward. On the other hand, the innovating process attracted as candidates few prominent political leaders. Those elected were, by and large, tribal personalities of traditional outlook. Some left-wing candidates were defeated, as in the case of the former foreign minister and ardent Nasserist Muḥammad Sallām, who ran and lost in Ta'izz Province. The general complexion of the council was well symbolized by its election of Shaikh 'Abdullah al-Aḥmar as speaker. Aḥmad Muḥammad Nu'mān, the elder Shāfi'ī statesman, assumed office as prime minister.

In the most favorable of circumstances it would have been difficult for Yemen to follow the constitutional blueprint faithfully in the conduct of its affairs. In the event, divided counsel and traditional attitudes toward public administration combined with political and economic problems, not all of the country's own making, to retard development of rational, effective government. The new regime faced particularly thorny issues in its relations with the major tribes, with South Yemen, and with Saudi Arabia; it faced great problems in achieving the economic progress promised by its charter.

The peace of 1970 was not profitable to the tribes, who had prospered handsomely during the civil war by auctioning off their loyalties. The Y.A.R. leaders, including the ex-royalists, tried desperately to convince the shaikhs of the benefits of peace, while instituting a system of subsidies, ostensibly to pay the cost of arming and training the tribesmen as irregular forces for the national defense. (These gratuities, which simply lined the shaikhs' pockets, were curtailed only in 1973.) This policy notwithstanding, the government had great difficulty in establishing discipline over the tribes. In mid-July 1970 Gen. Ḥasan al-'Amrī, the commander in chief, attempted to station a military commander in Banī Ḥushaish territory, just northeast of the capital, over the tribe's objection. The result was an uprising extending throughout Bakīl and Khawlān. The following February, an attempt on al-'Amri's life was mounted by Banī Ḥushaish; a number of junior army officers found to be implicated in the plot were summarily dismissed. In May 1971 the Madhḥij tribes around Radā', southeast of Dhamār, interrupted surface communication between the capital and the town of al-Baiḍā', on the South Yemen border. This challenge to government authority impeded the movement of military supplies to the National Unity Front (N.U.F.), a dissident movement in the People's Republic sponsored jointly by the Y.A.R. and Saudi Arabia. The immediate requirement of supplying the N.U.F. was met by an airlift of equipment to al-Baiḍā'.[9] The longer-run problem was dealt with by a major campaign led by al-'Amrī in person; the principal recalcitrant shaikh, Ibn Jir'ūn, was captured and required to surrender hostages and all heavy weapons, including three artillery pieces, in his tribe's possession. The operation required the use of one fourth of the army's total strength of nine thousand. The national police forces were even smaller. By mid-1971 the government had gravitated toward the pre-republican practice of concentrating police strength around the chief urban centers, leaving law enforcement in the rural areas to the tribes themselves. In 1973 regular access to the Jawf and much of Khawlān was effectively denied to Y.A.R. officials, whether military or civilian;[10] a Ḥamīd al-Dīn prince, Yaḥyā bin al-Ḥusain, was even living in the Jawf unmolested.

The regime was able to tolerate decentralized authority in the north without serious detriment to national security. The southern border areas, on the other hand, were vulnerable to a persistent campaign of subversion and at times outright military attack, from the People's Democratic Republic of Yemen (P.D.R.Y.), encouraged and supported by foreign powers. Several factors contributed to the receptivity of many southerners to recruitment by the People's Republic for dissident and terrorist activity. They felt more closely identified with their neighbors to the south than with the Zaidis of the north, whose long history of exploitation was not forgotten. Economic conditions were deteriorating, with increasing demographic pressures on the wealth produced, and for many successive years the monsoon rains failed.[11] Perhaps most important, the quality of local leadership was at best uneven. Minor shaikhs all too often exploited their authority, backed up by military retainers, to plunder the citizens. This situation was aggravated in 1973, when the central government, lacking the personnel and expertise to monitor the frontier and curb internal subversion, formally placed responsibility for public order upon the shaikhs themselves, and threatened retaliation against entire communities where incidents of terrorism and sabotage occurred.[12]

The revolutionary movement headquartered at Aden was aimed not at Yemen alone, but at the entire Arabian Peninsula. It engaged the vital interests of Saudi Arabia, Kuwait, and the United Arab Emirates, the Y.A.R.'s most important potential sources of external aid, as well as of Iran, vitally concerned with the political stability of the peninsula. For these countries, it was not sufficient that the Y.A.R. be able to defend itself against attack and subversion; it should take positive action to promote a change in South Yemen toward a regime of moderate complexion. The Y.A.R. leadership came under pressure to adopt this consummatory objective, to the detriment of its announced instrumental goals.

The tactics used by Saudi Arabia in pursuing its objectives in southern Arabia contributed to incoherence in Y.A.R. policy under the constitutional regime. During the civil war, Saudi policy had been conducted by Prince Sulṭān, minister of defense and aviation, with the assistance of his relatives of the Sudairī family, one of whom governed the border province of Asir. Bypassing the Yemeni royalists, the Saudis frequently dealt directly with shaikhs of the northern Yemeni tribes and paid them subsidies. These operations continued after the Yemeni national reconciliation and the resumption of Saudi relations with the Sanaa government, Shaikh 'Abdullah al-Aḥmar and other influential chiefs being recruited to the list of Saudi clients. At the same time, the Saudi government extended a modest amount of budget support to the Y.A.R. This dual Saudi leverage was applied to encourage conservative, if not reactionary, policies on the part of the Yemeni government; to thwart the efforts of President 'Abd al-Raḥmān al-Iryānī and other moderates to forge a national consensus by accommodation with leftist elements; and to prevent the relaxation of Y.A.R. opposition to the radical regime in South Yemen. Yemen was meanwhile urged toward the left by socialist countries, both Arab and non-Arab, among them some significant suppliers of military and economic aid. The result of these conflicting pressures was the concentration of the Yemeni leadership's energies upon political in-fighting instead of the economic and social development which, as its major published goal, the Yemeni people were entitled to expect.

Problems of Development

There is perhaps no literate Yemeni who is not convinced that the subsurface of his homeland is a vast Aladdin's cave brimming with mineral riches and rare gems. Al-Wāsiʿī devotes ten pages to listing and locating Yemen's mineral deposits, citing the authority of medieval Arab writers and some geological reconnaissance by the American engineer Karl S. Twitchell in the 1920s.[13] If one has the special gifts of a Yemeni Marxist, one can demonstrate that an American petroleum concessionary in the early 1960s struck oil in quantity in the Tihama but failed, for capitalist-imperialist reasons, to proceed with its production.[14] Legends aside, the sad fact is that Yemen's presently known subsoil resources occur in such small deposits that their exploitation can make no substantial contribution to the national wealth.[15] The conviction that Yemen's agricultural production can be readily and indefinitely expanded by irrigating the Tihama is also an article of faith. "Our land was once a model of wealth and fertility," Prime Minister Nuʿmān declared to the Consultative Council on May 24, 1971. "If our agricultural and mineral resources were tapped we would be among the richest countries of the Arab world."[16]

Yemen's economy declined under the Ḥamīd al-Dīn, as we have seen, until their final few years. Much devastation took place in the Zaidi tribal areas during the civil war, and normal activities in republican territory were so disrupted as to reduce agricultural production in both quantity and quality. More importantly, the nature of the economy was modified. With the introduction of a paper currency to replace silver coins as the medium of exchange, the government acquired new capabilities; however, it also had new responsibilities which required sound policies effectively carried out by a disciplined, technically qualified civil service. It was far easier to recruit a large bureaucracy, as was indeed done, than to endow it with skill, integrity, and devotion to the people's welfare.

During the Egyptian presence, budget deficits and exchange shortages were covered by U.A.R. subsidy. Thereafter the weaknesses became apparent. The deficit was less than one million riyals for the first full fiscal year after the U.A.R.

withdrawal; by 1969 it had increased to about 70 million, and the budget introduced by Prime Minister Nu'mān in May 1971 showed a deficit of 90 million riyals, against contemplated expenditures of 170 million ($35 million). The sentiment remained widespread that only the canonical taxes were legal, and the business community tended to avoid all taxes where possible. In practice, the Y.A.R. left responsibility for assessing the *zakāt*, the principal internal tax, in the hands of local shaikhs, ulama, and village headmen, and established no effective penalties for evasion. In fiscal year 1971-1972, the *zakāt* produced revenues of 10,756,000 riyals, as compared to 39,852,000 riyals expended in subsidies to tribal chiefs and related payments. The yield from customs duties, which provided eighty percent of domestic revenue, was limited by inefficient administration and by smuggling. In 1971 Yemen's total foreign trade was estimated at $53 million, of which $35 million was handled by the large merchants. The net capital outflow on trade balance was estimated at $3 million. The Y.A.R. was in debt to foreign governments to the amount of $169 million (of which $93 million had been disbursed by 1971), and was in arrears to most of its creditors: both Germanies, the Soviet Union, several East European states, Italy, and Algeria. Modern industrial enterprise in the public sector was confined to a textile mill built and managed by the Chinese, and a cement plant under construction by the U.S.S.R. Private entrepreneurs had built an aluminum utensils plant, a candy factory, and a soft-drink bottling plant. Industrial expansion was inhibited by the limited capital in both sectors, the scarcity of management skills, the primitive infrastructure and the absence of a large enough market to support import-substitution industries.

These highlights of Yemen's economic and administrative situation give some idea of the obstacles to rapid development in the country, and the inability of the constitutional regime to extract from the society the human and material resources necessary to such development. To some extent foreign assistance, for which the regime could claim credit before the public, could contribute to visible progress, and the Y.A.R. was fortunate in receiving help from a variety of sources in the military, industrial, agricultural, health, education, communications, and finance fields. The use of such aid, however, was as yet haphazard. For more than a decade, beginning under Imam Aḥmad, outside assistance had been pervaded with ideological strife and scandal. The United Nations Development Program had instituted a major operation in the 1950s aimed at self-sufficiency in Yemeni food production. During the Egyptian presence the effort was weakened by corrupt Arab officials, and interfered with by the U.A.R. military. Although by 1971 mostly non-Arab officials were assigned to Yemen by the U.N., its work was still hampered by dissension between communist and Western employees. A "supreme planning council" attached to the Yemeni president's office lacked the power to impose coordination.

Despite these handicaps, a considerable amount of development was actually in train in the form of school and hospital construction, road building, well drilling, and irrigation. Much of this activity was carried on by sections of Yemeni society which were exhibiting a remarkable vitality; the government had the wisdom to encourage and assist this tendency within the limits of its scant resources.

The process may be illustrated by a community development program conducted for several years by the United States Agency for International Development, under the direction of an exceptionally able water resources engineer, Mr. John H. Stewart.[17] The AID role included technical advice in drawing up projects, provision of equipment and hand tools, and assistance in procurement, while the local community furnished the bulk of the capital, labor, and management. One pair of projects involved the improvement of water supplies to two communities in the Ḥujariya area, scarcely forty airline miles from Ta'izz, but isolated by rugged mountain terrain. One of the two localities, al-Turba, a district administrative seat, was reached by a six-hour drive along a primitive motor road from Ta'izz. The second, a cluster of some thirty hamlets centered at Qadas, fifteen kilometers east of Turba, was accessible only by mountain footpaths. It had been dependent upon three wells, of which two ran dry between rainy seasons; some villagers obtained drinking water at the price of a fifteen-kilometer walk. Both communities constructed, on local initiative, landing strips for the Yemeni government's Piper Cub. Only in this way was Stewart's supervision of the water projects made possible.

The Qadas undertaking was a notable feat of organization. A complex "package," it was designed to increase the number of wells, and to provide them with pumps to collect water at a central reservoir. From there water was to be piped as far as possible in the direction of each hamlet. Surplus electrical power from the pumping station was to operate grain mills and to provide the area's first electric lighting. A motor road had to be built into the area to bring in the required equipment and supplies. Initial capital of $32,000 had to be assembled, with the contribution and approval of Qadas villagers working as businessmen in Ta'izz, Sanaa, Aden, and Hodeida. The traditional leadership succeeded in devising a sophisticated technical program, and in mobilizing the human and material resources required to carry it out, with minimum participation by the central government.

These initiatives in Ḥujariya were early, but not unique, examples of development. In many districts and provinces, permanent development cooperatives were being formed to plan and execute projects that the central government lacked the financial and manpower resources to undertake. One of the first, the Ibb Liwā' Cooperative, was atypical in having been instituted on official, rather than private, initiative, although its management was gradually assumed by the citizens. It covers the entire province, one of the most productive in the Yemeni highlands. It began on a small scale in 1966, under the leadership of Hāshim Ṭālib, the provincial governor, and its scope of operations was expanded under his successor, 'Abd al-Laṭīf Ḍayfallah. By 1973 the organization, governed by a council of elected representatives from each of the Liwā''s nineteen *nawāḥī*,[18] had approved an impressive total of 244 projects in the fields of road construction and improvement, water supply and distribution, schools, and public health, at an estimated cost of over 7 million riyals; 38 projects had been completed. In 1973 the cooperative's general council drew up an ambitious five-year plan, estimated to cost over 43 million riyals, and covering the same fields. The organization's funds are derived primarily from a tax of five *buqshas*[19] for each riyal paid by the citizen as *zakāt*. In addition, the central government introduced legislation permitting the allocation to local development boards of one fourth of the *zakāt* collected. Voluntary contributions were anticipated, and financial support from the central government was also hoped for in the future.[20]

By mid-1973 the central authorities saw the need for some coordination and supervision of this burgeoning activity in order to avoid overlapping and conflicts between areas. The existing cooperatives, numbering about sixty, were brought together in a Confederation of Yemeni Development Associations; an army officer already involved in the cooperative movement, enthusiastically if extracurricularly, was elected president. Many cooperatives had feared the loss of their autonomy through formation of the confederation, and Colonel Ibrāhīm al-Ḥamdī, addressing its first general meeting, took particular pains to emphasize the government's sympathy with the movement and to assure the cooperatives that they would remain free to manage their own affairs. "No public cooperative in any province," he declared, "will be affected by the formation of a national union of public cooperatives insofar as its revenue and administration are concerned. It will, on the other hand, profit by planning and coordination, and perhaps by securing additional revenue and facilities in support of its projects."[21]

The relatively impressive scale of development on local initiative was of political relevance in several respects. On one hand, it indicated the presence of a considerable amount of liquid wealth in many parts of the country that the national government was unable to tap effectively through its tax system. The citizens were firmly attached to the preservation of their freedom to mobilize their own resources, and to plan and manage their own projects without interference from the central authorities. Key decisions were made by substructures in the society, reflecting the prevailing pyramidal authority pattern. On the other hand, the success of many of these efforts depended in part upon specialized services that only the national government could provide, directly or through agreements with donors of foreign aid. Schools, clinics, hospitals, and mechanical installations could not function without technically qualified personnel which the cooperatives could not furnish by themselves.

A momentous potential thus existed for the creation of direct links between the people at large and the central government, bypassing the existing local leadership; and for the growth of a new concept of government as a public service instead of an extractive agent, as it had traditionally appeared to be. The attitude of the shaikhs toward the cooperatives varied widely from area to area. In some districts they were the prime movers or enthusiastic supporters; in others they were indifferent to the development movement or deliberately tried to obstruct it as a threat to their own authority. In either case the germ was planted; the shaikh's traditional role as buffer between the people and the exactions of central authority was being redefined. Increasingly, his effectiveness would depend on his ability to secure allocations of goods and services from government, rather than on keeping the government at arm's length. It would require time for such processes to bear fruit. Successive governments under the constitution lacked the resources and administrative effectiveness to furnish the needed personnel and expertise, and the deficiency helped to undermine their legitimacy in the eyes of many citizens.

Failure of the Constitutional Experiment

In an address introducing his government's 1971-1972 budget before the Consultative Council, Prime Minister Aḫmad Nu'mān painted a remarkably frank picture of Yemen's gloomy economic and administrative situation. The country's exports, he said, covered only ten percent of the cost of its imports, and remittances from abroad, which normally filled the gap, had declined with the return of large numbers of emigrants. The treasury had become simply a center for relief of the unemployed and the indigent, and for the enrichment of the greedy. The civil service, he acknowledged forthrightly, lacked the ability to deal with the country's monumental problems. Aging and in precarious health, Nu'mān within a few months admitted his own inadequacy to bring order out of the prevailing chaos, and resigned on July 20.

President Iryānī entrusted the formation of a new cabinet to General Ḥasan al-'Amrī, commander in chief and member of the Republican Council. Al-'Amrī took office on August 24 and at once embarked on plans to seize autocratic power through an army coup. Iryānī, who had received timely intelligence of this intention, was by chance given a means to frustrate them when al-'Amrī rashly murdered a photographer who had affronted him. Al-'Amrī was obliged to resign and leave Yemen on September 4.

Iryānī's choice of Muḥsin al-'Aynī to form the next government was consistent with his long, subtle search for a political balance in Yemen. Of an aristocratic, landed family, and an eminent canon law jurist under the monarchical regime, Iryānī commanded the trust and respect of the Yemeni tribes of both sects. Saudi Arabia had in the past recognized his stature as a religious figure by naming him the Yemeni member of the Islamic World League at Mecca. His was nevertheless not of the conservative orientation that might have been expected from one of such a background. For a decade his considerable diplomatic talents had been devoted to an attempt to create a consensus among the conflicting factions within the Y.A.R, by conciliating the leftists; and to winning external support, both moral and material, for the republic, support which in the existing circumstances could come only from the socialist powers and from the "progressive" Arab states. While seeking correct relations with Yemen's neighbor to the north, he did not consider that Yemen's interest lay in following the Saudi lead unquestioningly. Saudi Arabia's policies, notably an uncompromising posture toward the regime in South Yemen, were being strongly pressed through its Yemeni supporters, including influential members of the Consultative Council. It was logical, therefore, for Iryānī to seek a balance of political forces by choosing a prime minister of leftist reputation.

Al-'Aynī's government, which survived just over a year, was troubled by conservative opposition and by its inability to hit upon a workable policy toward South Yemen. Union of the two territories was the announced objective of both governments, but each envisioned an extension of its own institutions and attitudes over the other. The P.D.R.Y., notwithstanding the leftist flavor of al-ʻAynī's governmnent, intensified its efforts to subvert the Y.A.R. by infiltrating saboteurs and terrorists northward across the frontier. By the summer of 1972, border incidents were engaging substantial units of the regular armed forces of both sides. Mediation by the Arab League led to the signing in Cairo in October 1972 of an agreement between the Y.A.R. and P.D.R.Y. governments to negotiate the terms of unification of the two countries. The goal of union was further confirmed a month later when Iryānī and P.D.R.Y. president Sālim Rubaiʻ ʻAlī, then present in Tripoli for a conference of Arab chiefs of state, signed a further protocol; it was tacitly understood that their Libyan hosts would monitor fulfillment of the undertaking, and extend financial aid to both parties if, and only if, they pursued the goal of unity in good faith. The two governments were to establish a series of joint committees to plan the technical and administrative details of the future merger.

The concept of Yemeni union as thus agreed implied equal legitimacy between the existing governments and their policies. In the Y.A.R. it appealed only to the political left. The tribal leaders were acutely aware that the ruling N.L.F. in South Yemen had liquidated by violence the entire traditional leadership, including the indigenous tribal chiefs; they strongly objected to the nature of the agreement. Opposition, encouraged by Saudi Arabia, found concentrated and effective expression on the floor of the Consultative Council. Cooperation rapidly became impossible between the council and the prime minister, who resigned on December 28, bitterly accusing the council of obstructing plans for union.

Adapting to this demonstration of conservative strength, President Iryānī named Qāḍī ʻAbdullah Aḥmad al-Ḥajrī to head a new government. Al-Ḥajrī's prominence among the Zaidi ulama had won him election to the Republican Council in June 1972, replacing General al-ʻAmrī. A man of unquestioned personal integrity, his political leanings were conservative; he was in sympathy with the policies Saudi Arabia sought to persuade Yemen to follow. Although hard working and devoted, al-Ḥajrī lacked the dynamism necessary to imposc discipline and coordination on the country's administrative apparatus. His predecessor, during three terms of office as prime minister, had staffed much of the bureaucracy with people of leftist views, who worked to obstruct or circumvent the Ḥajrī government's directives. The opposition's effectiveness was considerably enhanced by a long-standing alliance, based on kinship rather than ideology, between Muḥsin al-'Aynī and the Abū Luḥūm family, minor shaikhs of the Nahm tribe. The senior member of the clan, Sinān Abū Luḥūm, had been appointed governor of Hodeida Province during the civil war, upon his defection from the royalists, and had consolidated virtually autonomous rule over it. Holding effective control of Yemen's principal port of entry, he was in a position to influence management of the customs, the country's chief source of domestic revenue, and not all customs receipts found their way to the central treasury. Several of Sinān's relatives held important military posts, including command of the 'Asifa elite force, of an armored brigade, and of the garrison in the sensitive border province of Ta'izz.

Sanaa's influence remained feeble in the Zaidi tribal areas, despite al-Ḥajrī's congenial and moderate orientation. The principal shaikhs tended to view government as a form of personal property, and to think that radicalism could best be contained by doing favors for their friends. As one case in point, Shaikh 'Abdullah al-Aḥmar's position enabled him to secure a sizeable allocation of famine relief commodities, provided by foreign donors to the Y.A.R. government, for distribution at his own discretion. The government's authority was insecure even in the region between Sanaa and Yarīm, normally amenable to rule from Sanaa; in the spring of 1973, work on the Sanaa-Ta'izz road, then being asphalted by the West Germans, was interrupted for an extended period when certain tribes refused to allow members of outside tribes to work in their territory.

The prime minister, educated to the traditional Yemeni methods of rule, did not try to make of his cabinet a coordinated, responsible team; each government department operated as the personal fief of its minister, with little reference to what the others were doing. Corruption and inefficiency were widespread, and the efforts of some Consultative Council members to identify abuses and press for their correction served simply to publicize the government's shortcomings. Another weakness of the leadership was a conflict of personality between the president and the prime minister, who could not work together in harmony. Major decisions often remained pending for long periods, although mediation by the Republican Council's third member, Shaikh Muḥammad 'Alī 'Uthmān, before his assassination by N.L.F. partisans in May 1973, at times moved issues off dead center.

The government was meanwhile unable to devise a policy to deal with subversion, which extended even into the ranks of the ulama. The public trials in the summer of 1973 of dozens of accused saboteurs from the Y.A.R.'s southern provinces demonstrated that ideological considerations were an insignificant factor in recruitment by the P.D.R.Y. for terrorist activity. In most cases, the accused were men of humble station reacting to oppression by the traditional leaders; abuses went unchecked in the absence of central government officials to provide equitable administration. The government's decision to place specific responsibility upon the shaikhs for public order, and its threat to inflict collective punishment on entire communities where acts of terrorism occurred, thus tended to compound the problem, although the device adopted was an ancient one in Yemen. The lack of demonstrable progress either on the southern issue or on economic development stimulated criticism of the Ḥajrī government from the political center as well as from the left.

By early 1974 President Iryānī judged that the deteriorating situation offered an opportunity to reinstate Muḥsin al-'Aynī as prime minister. By so doing, he hoped to deflect leftist criticism; to effect relaxation of the tight Saudi embrace; and to conciliate the P.D.R.Y. In justification of his intent, he declared that it was inconsistent with the Y.A.R. constitution for al-Ḥajrī, a member of the Republican Council, to serve simultaneously as prime minister. (This objection had not been raised in August 1971, when Ḥasan al-'Amrī became premier.) The proposed change was, predictably, supported by the Abū Luḥūm clan and the political left wing, but opposed by most tribal leaders, including 'Abdullah al-Aḥmar; by the conservative sector of the religious establishment; by several Shāfiʿī cabinet ministers, among them 'Abdullah al-Asnag and Aḥmad 'Abduh Saʿīd; and particularly by the Saudis. When the latter threatened to suspend their financial aid unless al-Ḥajrī was retained, Iryānī resorted to the compromise solution of entrusting the formation of an interim government to Dr. Ḥasan Makkī, an experienced Shāfiʿī economist and politician who had occupied numerous ministerial and diplomatic posts; Makkī took office on March 4. The choice was scarcely reassuring to Saudi Arabia, as Makkī had cultivated a reputation as a progressive intellectual, had close connections with the Yemeni left, and had supported the radical wing of the Yemeni army in the clashes of August 1968 so actively as to have sustained physical injury. The new cabinet, needless to say, immediately came under conservative attack, encouraged by the Saudis.

The tolerant posture of the government's leaders toward revolutionary agitation precipitated the debacle of consultative civilian government in Yemen. In early June 1974 documents fell into the government's hands indicating the existence of a well-organized clandestine network, financed by the Iraqi government, which had laid plans to overthrow the constitutional Y.A.R. government and set up a Ba'thist regime in its place. The characteristically mild response of Iryānī was to appoint a delegation to travel to Baghdad to confront President Aḥmad Ḥasan al-Bakr with the evidence. Condemning this reaction as weak and incompetent, Shaikh 'Abdullah al-Aḥmar, with the covert encouragement of 'Abdullah al-Ḥajrī, mobilized a large force of Ḥāshid tribesmen, demanded and received the resignations of the prime minister and the entire Republican Council (then consisting of Iryanī, Ḥajrī, and Aḥmad Nu'mān, who had replaced the late Muḥammad 'Alī 'Uthmān), and announced his intention of occupying Sanaa. Fortuitously, both the army commander in chief, Brig. Muḥammad al-Iryānī, and the chief of staff, Col. Ḥusain al-Miswarī, were then absent from Yemen. The senior officer on the spot, Deputy Commander in Chief Ibrāhīm al-Ḥamdī, backed by the commanding officers of the major units stationed in the capital, declared that the army would defend Sanaa against tribal attack. The Ḥāshid tribes did not take up the challenge. Al-Ḥamdī emerged as head of a military command council that proceeded to a series of measures consolidating itself in authority. Their decisiveness suggests that well-thought-out plans had been prepared for the sort of contingency that had arisen. A state of national emergency was declared. Brigadier Iryānī and Colonel Miswarī were forbidden to return to Yemen, being appointed ambassadors to London and Cairo respectively. The resignations of the prime minister and the Republican Council were confirmed, and that of Hodeida Governor Sinān Abū Luḥūm was elicited. The constitution and the Consultative Council were suspended. The new leaders proclaimed their determination to eliminate chaos and corruption from the government of Yemen and to establish law and organization in their stead.

The Military Regime

The leader of the junta which thus took charge of Y.A.R. affairs was a native of Thulā, Prince Muṭahhar Sharaf al-Dīn's sixteenth century fortress town, and a member of a respected qāḍī family. As mentioned above, he was a prominent leader of the development cooperative movement as well as a successful military officer. His political orientation was squarely in the middle of the road, and his government was consequently subject to attack from both right and left. The successive steps he took during his early months in office to neutralize the principal sources of opposition exhibited a high degree of tactical skill.

Al-Ḥamdī's decision to call upon Muḥsin al-'Aynī to form the first government was an astute and far-sighted one. It served to deflect from the military leadership responsibility for the inevitably unpopular measures necessary to impose discipline on the bureaucracy and the populace. The cabinet al-'Aynī brought together was a colorless one, incorporating several reputed Ba'thists as well as some individuals whose venality was publicly known. The political left was thus maneuvered into a vulnerable position; a further blow to its influence was struck when the resignation of Sinān Abū Luḥūm as governor of Hodeida, tendered in the expectation that he would be immediately reinstated, was allowed to stand. The province passed under Sanaa's direct control.

In October the ruling Command Council was reorganized and expanded. The hard core of the junta had consisted of Ḥamdī as chairman; Col. Aḥmad al-Ghashmī, a member of a Hamdān shaikhly family as the new regime's chief of staff; and Lt. Col. 'Abdullah 'Abd al-'Ālim, a dynamic Shāfi'ī officer, commander of the army's paratroops. An officer of sayyid background, Yaḥyā al-Mutawakkil, acted as deputy chairman. The council was now enlarged to include Prime Minister al-'Aynī and two army officers with close tribal connections: Dirham Abū Luḥūm, military commander in Ta'izz; and Mujāhid Abū Shuwārib, a man of undistinguished family origin but a protégé of Shaikh 'Abdullah al-Aḥmar. He had become the latter's chief lieutenant as leader of the Ḥāshid tribes and governor of Ḥajja Province, and now became titular deputy chairman of the Command Council, relinquishing his governorship. Simultaneously, the Consultative Assembly, under the speakership of 'Abdullah al-Aḥmar, was recalled into session, an act that tended to reconcile the tribes to the military regime and lend it an aura of legitimacy. These two moves sharply enhanced the position of conservative elements, and permitted the gradual removal from positions of command of leftist officers of doubtful loyalty, including members of the Abū Luḥūm clan. The Consultative Assembly, with its rural, conservative complexion, provided a focus for criticism of the al-'Aynī cabinet, whose effectiveness was at an end by January 1975. Al-Ḥamdī dismissed al-'Aynī, pointing out publicly that he no longer commanded the confidence of the Consultative Council, and appointed as his successor the governor of Yemen's central bank, 'Abd al-'Azīz 'Abd al-Ghanī. 'Abd al-Ghanī assembled a cabinet enlisting the country's best available talent in administration and economic management.

As this is written, the regime thus consolidated under Ibrāhīm al-Ḥamdī's firm hand has some solid achievements to show for the period of less than three years during which it has exercised power. It has given Yemen by far the stablest and most effective government the country has had since the 1962 revolution; its single-minded devotion to economic and social development has produced impressive results, and growth seems likely to continue. Considerable progress has been made in placing Y.A.R. relations with South Yemen and with Saudi Arabia on less disruptive and more rational bases than heretofore. External affairs have been managed in such a way as to maximize the flow of outside aid for development. Serious problems nevertheless remain, related both to the changes commonly attendant upon modernization and to the endurance of certain features of Yemen's ancient social and political structure.

The 'Abd al-Ghanī Cabinet

The prime minister, who was born in Ta'izz Province in 1939, holds a master's degree in economics from the University of Colorado. He gained unquestioned expertise in planning and administration in the Yemen Bank for Reconstruction and Development, which he headed before being appointed to his present post. Indifferent to political ideology, hard-working, and painstaking, his considerable energy is applied to ensuring that the Y.A.R.'s bureaucracy functions with efficiency and integrity. The cabinet over which he presides, which has already lasted longer than any of its predecessors, is the first in Yemen's history to operate as a true council of ministers. Lengthy weekly meetings are held; the decisions adopted are binding on all the government departments; and ministers are responsible before their colleagues for the achievement of the goals established, for orderly spending of funds, and for coordination. From the first, the cabinet has embraced a broad political spectrum, from leaders of tribes amenable to government authority to individuals of Ba'thist leanings. Members hold office because of their technical competence, however and ideological debate has been excluded from their official purview.

The shift from nepotism and partisan strife to sound planning and administration has paid off in the quickening pace of development. A three-year development program adopted in 1974 has been substantially completed, and a new five-year plan is in preparation. A major land reclamation project in the Tihama is in successful operation. A basic road network is now in use; additional hundreds of miles of highway are under construction, and many more are planned. The educational base is expanding at the rate of twenty-five percent annually. Many projects completed during the past two years were, to be sure, instituted under previous governments, and the current government cannot claim credit for them all. It nevertheless deserves recognition for their effective management, as well as for accelerating the start of new undertakings. It benefits from the apparent break in the intermittent drought that had afflicted many regions of Yemen since the 1950s, and also from the greatly expanded remittances from migrant workers, in Saudi Arabia and other oil-rich states, which at the end of 1976 were approaching the rate of $800 million annually.

The Southern Question

Al-Ḥamdī took prompt steps to stabilize Y.A.R. relations with its southern neighbor. In October 1974 he began a series of meetings with P.D.R.Y. ministers. Before the end of the year his representatives had participated in an Arab League–sponsored review of progress toward union; a new schedule of meetings of the joint technical committees was drawn up; and the P.D.R.Y. president had visited Ta'izz and Hodeida as guest of the Y.A.R. (In November the Y.A.R. received a commitment of eleven million dollars in aid from Libya, doubtless in recognition of its good faith in executing the November 1972 understandings.) Border incidents continued. The P.D.R.Y., on the other hand, was beginning a gradual relaxation of its campaign to radicalize the other states of the Arabian Peninsula, and by the end of 1976 the border was tranquil. A further step toward normalization occurred in May 1976, when Saudi Arabia established diplomatic relations with the P.D.R.Y.

These measures helped relieve the related problem of disaffection in the Y.A.R. border regions, but the most significant contribution was the constructive policy adopted with the counsel of Lt. Col. 'Abdullah 'Abd al-'Ālim, the paratroop commander, a man of populist outlook and himself a native of the area. He realized that much of the dissidence was due to unrestrained abuse of authority by the local shaikhs, many of whom were reputed to be of remote Zaidi origin. He worked to curb their authority, meanwhile resisting demands by the northern tribal leaders for the dispatch of Zaidi troops to preserve order in the south, as was traditional. The central government has dealt energetically with the authors of terrorist acts; at the same time, its civilian presence in localities difficult of access has been increased, and numerous local projects—roads, schools, wells, clinics, etc.—have been undertaken to encourage the people's loyalty.

Relations with Saudi Arabia

Saudi support of the Ḥamīd al-Dīn during the Yemeni civil war aroused mistrust and resentment on both sides which survived the peace and created residual tension in Saudi dealings with Yemen after the war. Although Saudi Arabia provided an annual contribution to the Y.A.R. budget, it was made painfully clear that this money might be withheld if Yemeni policies displeased the donor. Successive governments under Iryānī's presidency were careful to avoid serious provocation, but none succeeded in reaching a cordial, frank basis of Yemeni-Saudi cooperation. The Saudi practice of paying Yemenis to press its views on the government was a continuing irritant.

A major objective in al-Ḥamdī's foreign policy has been a more satisfactory relationship with Yemen's wealthy neighbor, both to reduce the domestic threat to his freedom of action and to secure increased assistance for Yemen's economic progress. Ḥamdī traveled to Riyad shortly after assuming power, to reassure King Faisal of his government's intentions, a necessary step in view of his appointment of al-'Aynī as prime minister. Patient effort during the ensuing two and one-half years brought results in the form of a reduction (if not an end) in Saudi subsidies to Yemeni tribes and shaikhs, and substantially increased aid to the Y.A.R. government. A joint coordination council has been formed to decide on the scale and form of assistance. The communiqué issued at the close of its third annual meeting, in January 1977, stated the Saudi intention of providing the Y.A.R. with ninety-seven million dollars in budget assistance for the fiscal year 1977-1978, an increase of sixteen million over the current year; and its intention of financing a variety of projects in the fields, among others, of telecommunications, road construction, coffee and fruit cultivation, fisheries, education, and aviation. Saudi Arabia moreover doubled its contribution to the UN Development Program, with the understanding that the increase would be used in Yemen.

Saudi Arabia is also supporting a program, already in the planning stage before the 1974 coup, to modernize the Yemeni armed forces, and shift emphasis from Soviet to American-made equipment. The U.S.S.R. had been the country's principal source of arms since before the 1962 revolution. The Y.A.R. had, however, experienced growing difficulty in obtaining delivery of weapons under successive agreements, the Russians preferring to place their military bets on the P.D.R.Y. Large numbers of Soviet military advisors are nevertheless still present in the Y.A.R., symbolizing the determination of the present regime to maintain freedom of action and to cultivate productive relations with all countries regardless of ideology.

The Northern Tribes

In those areas of Yemen where the Ḥamdī regime has been able to place its policies in full operation, the erosion of the traditional power relationships has accelerated. The greatly increased presence of the national government's administrators and technicians working visibly to enhance the security and prosperity of the citizens has decreased the relevance of the shaikhs' traditional role as buffer between the people and central authority. The clear trend is away from a pyramidal pattern of authority verging on the segmental, and toward increased centralization of decision-making. In the north this process remains largely unaccomplished.

Shaikh ʻAbdullah al-Aḥmar had rendered vital service to the republican cause during the civil war in mobilizing tribal sentiment against the Ḥamīd al-Dīn and for the new regime. As speaker of the Consultative Council, he endeavored to integrate the tribes into the national life, holding out to the northern shaikhs the prospect of material progress, in which the Shāfiʻī south had long since overtaken the north. It was, however, not contemplated that this progress would affect the leadership status of the shaikhs, or diminish the cherished local autonomy of the tribes.

By mid-1975 the Consultative Council, where the shaikhs' collective voice was concentrated, had become the principal restraint on al-Ḥamdī's freedom of action. Its final dissolution left al-Aḥmar without an official position of any kind in the national governing structure. It was anticipated that elections would be held, under a new electoral law adopted before the council disbanded, for a new legislature over which al-Aḥmar would presumably preside; he further made clear that he desired an end of martial law and a thorough purge of leftists from the bureaucracy. As months passed, it became obvious that the military leaders had no intention of meeting these requests with any speed; al-Aḥmar retired to the Ḥāshid headquarters at Khamir, suspending normal intercourse with the government, and trying to approach Saudi officials for help against the Ḥamdī regime. The latter followed the tactic of avoiding armed clash with the tribes, of endeavoring to convince them that they lacked the strength to destroy the national government, and of holding out the promise of liberal aid for their economic progress as a reward for their obedience.

At the end of 1976 (see figure 6), the Sanaa regime was in full control of, and conducting normal governmental operations in, the area south of a line beginning at the Red Sea coast north of al-Luḥayya; passing eastward not far north of Ḥajja, 'Umrān, and Sanaa; and inflecting southeast to a point north of Radā', then east to the P.D.R.Y. border. It also controlled three widely separated enclaves comprising the towns of Ṣa'da, Mārib, and Ḥarīb, and their immediate environs. The territory beyond any effective government influence was a wedge-shaped area with its apex well to the west of Khamir, broadening to the eastward, embracing the entire Jawf, and extending to the undefined Saudi border. The remaining territory was nominally submissive to the central government, but the latter had little or no civilian or military presence there. The Dhū Ḥusain tribe of the eastern Jawf had submitted in principle to Sanaa's authority in 1975, but in practice its various sections were raiding each other, and neighboring tribes, without

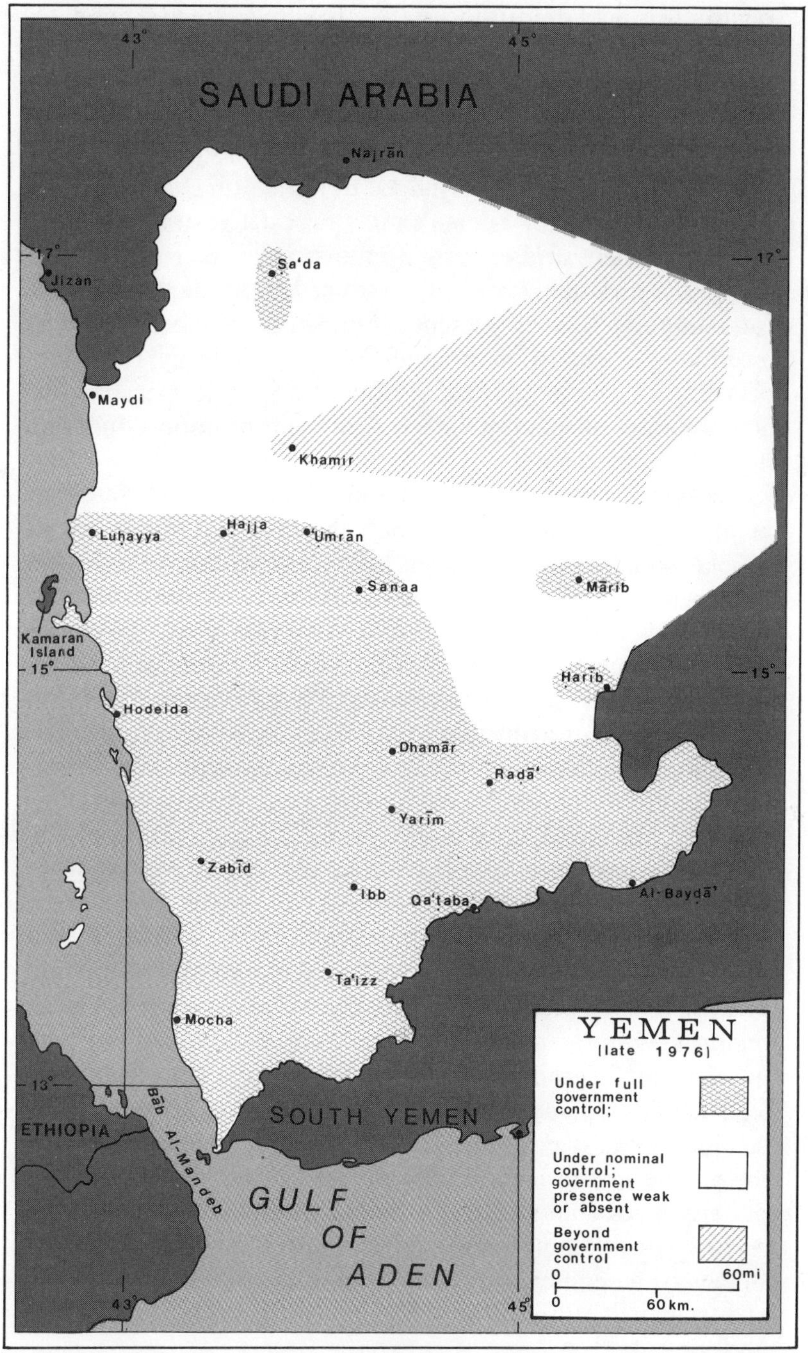
43°
45°
SAUDI ARABIA
Najrān
17°
Jizan
Sa'da
Maydi
Khamir
Luḥayya
Hajja
'Umrān
Sanaa
Mārib
Kamaran Island
15°
Ḥarīb
Hodeida
Dhamār
Radā'
Yarīm
Zabīd
Ibb
Qa'taba
Al-Baydā'
Ta'izz
Mocha
13°
Bāb Al-Mandeb
ETHIOPIA
SOUTH YEMEN
GULF OF ADEN
YEMEN
(late 1976)
Under full government control;
Under nominal control; government presence weak or absent
Beyond government control
0
60mi
0
60 km.

Figure 6

regard for outside authority, as they had always done. A separate Jawf governorate was created on paper in 1975, but the designated governor and his staff had not been able to take up residence there. This situation was of concern to the Ḥamdī regime for two major reasons, aside from considerations of prestige. The Jawf valley is judged by agricultural specialists to be potentially one of Yemen's most productive areas, needing only investment and orderly administration to rival the Ibb region; its produce is needed to reduce Y.A.R. dependence on food imports. Under present circumstances, moreover, it is essentially an extension of Saudi Arabia's economy, not a part of Yemen's, and a substantial flow of imported merchandise enters Yemen through it without payment of import duties to the national treasury.

Tension between the Ḥāshid and the government increased at the beginning of 1977, as the tribesmen halted and seized official vehicles traveling across their territory between ʻUmrān and Ṣaʻda. An attempt at reconciliation was made at the end of January, reportedly with Saudi encouragement. Al-Aḥmar and Abū Shuwārib, at the head of several hundred tribesmen, met with al-Ḥamdī on the outskirts of Sanaa. Speaking for the tribes, Abū Shuwārib stated that they had come to bury the past; abandon disputes; and set about building up the country. On behalf of the government, al-Ḥamdī promised general amnesty; the building of roads, wells, clinics, and hospitals; and the assurance of social justice as advocated by the Koran. As yet it cannot be foreseen whether the tribes and their leaders will, in fact, act in accord with the spirit of reconciliation; one month after the meeting, provocative acts were still occurring. The issue is a decisive one for Yemen and for the present regime's long-range prospects. A fundamental aim of the government is gradually to take power from the traditional leaders and to place it in the hands of new elites possessing the technical skills needed for modernization and enhancement of the people's material and cultural well being. The leadership pattern in northern Yemen, laid down two millennia ago, retains considerable vitality, but is becoming less and less suited to the contemporary era; the open question is whether change in its nature will be evolutionary and orderly, or abrupt and violent.

Epilogue: National Integration

The central role of values in the dynamics of political systems emerges clearly from the examination, in the preceding chapters, of successive regimes in Yemen. The early phase of the ancient Sabean state was characterized by comprehensive agreement among the people of Saba concerning the identity of those entitled to exercise power and the ends, both spiritual and secular, for which it should be employed. The capability of the polity was demonstrated over several centuries of spectacular achievement in engineering and international commerce, and in the imposition of Saba's will upon its neighbors. As the state expanded, it incorporated non-Sabean peoples with other traditions in the ordering of affairs, other secular preoccupations, and other expectations from the use of authority. The range of political values in the more heterogeneous society increased, but the scope of consensus between rulers and ruled shrank, together with the ability of the monarch to enforce his will throughout the country. Eventually, even the Sabean identity of the society vanished; the state became known to Arab tradition by the name of one of the tribes it absorbed, the Ḥimyarites. In the last stages, the rulers adopted consummatory aims responding to the aspirations of only a minority of their subjects; their legitimacy declined to the point where influential segments of the society chose to sever the threads holding the polity together by inviting foreign conquest of their country.

The rise of Islam introduced into southern Arabia a comprehensive system of values embracing not only the spiritual well-being of the individual but also many aspects of his material welfare. The new norms replaced only partially the earlier attitudes toward authority. In particular, the Islamic theoretical ideal of centralized rule entered into permanent tension with the particularism of much of the Yemeni population. Islam failed to establish unmistakably the identity of the individuals entitled to succeed to the secular authority of the Prophet Muḫammad. This ambiguity made it possible for some Muslims to question the legitimacy of any existing regime. It became a continuing factor in the contentions and centrifugal nature of Yemen's politics, and produced a schism that remains an operating factor in its present-day affairs.

The point is well illustrated by the precarious legitimacy of the Ṣulayḫid state. The three sovereigns of the dynasty stand out among Yemen's rulers in their intelligent and beneficent concern for the welfare of their subjects. Remnants are still to be seen of farm-to-market roads constructed by Queen Arwā, and she is affectionately remembered in popular legend. Nevertheless, in the eyes of a majority of Yemenis the Ṣulayḫids were heretics, agents of a foreign anticaliph, the promotion of whose interests was among the Ṣulayḫids' salient concerns. Public attitudes toward Arwā were a curious mixture of veneration for her person and anomic challenge, under orthodox Sunnī leadership, to her authority. Toward the end of her reign, finding no Yemeni she could trust to enforce her will, she felt constrained to call upon the Fatimid court to provide her with an alien minister.

With a broader consensus on political values, the Rasūlids, Sunnīs and Shāfiʿīs like most of their subjects, were able to rule the territory Arwā had controlled, and the Tihama as well, over ten full generations. The sophisticated administrative apparatus they created provided an opportunity for some public voice in decisions; it gave the regime the cohesiveness needed to repel frequent attack by aggressive neighbors, and to withstand the shock of recurrent dynastic struggles for possession of the throne. The structure began to weaken when the mode of authority shifted away from role assignment by merit and achievement toward delegation of power to an aristocracy with ascriptive claims to high status.

The Zaidi imamate was established on equivocal value bases that were never adequately clarified. At its inception, the northern Yemeni tribes sought merely a palliative for the excesses resulting from the segmental authority pattern then prevailing. Zaidi doctrine, by contrast, contemplated a system with a broad scope of authority, tightly centralized, and mobilized for the pursuit of consummatory aims. The two sets of values coexisted in violence-generating tension for a thousand years. The imamate introduced significant social change in the rise of an aristocracy which, by defending moral principle and social justice, served for centuries as the principal continuing link among the various elements of the Zaidi community. The imams were not motivated solely and consistently by the noble tenets of Zaidi doctrine. Repeatedly, consummatory values were set aside for concerns instrumental for themselves and their kinsmen; this led regularly to fragmentation and dispersal of authority, and occasionally to the temporary eclipse of the Zaidi state. On the other hand, foreign challenges periodically induced a reordering of values by which opposition to alien rule became the first concern of both ruler and subject; effective authority could again be exerted to mobilize the society's resources in pursuit of a national goal.

The origin of the twentieth-century Mutawakkilite Kingdom lies in such a struggle by the Yemeni people under Imam Yaḥyā's leadership against the Ottoman occupation. Inconsistency was present in its value system at least from the date of the Da‘‘ān Treaty, which symbolized the imam's willingness to compromise the national goal of freedom from foreign rule. Dynastic interests took on high priority for the rulers; stubborn pursuit of these interests debased the values of the aristocracy, and reduced the area of agreement between the sovereign and various elements of Yemeni society, one by one, until the regime's legitimacy vanished.

These successive polities declined and disappeared not through foreign conquest or other extraneous calamity, but through a failure of national integration. Such integration is essential to the continued viability of a political structure, as well as to the processes of development and modernization. While the concept has many ramifications, it is appropriate to note several basic ones here. It applies to a relatively well defined territory within which, regardless of ethnic, linguistic, or cultural differences, a common sense of nationality exists. There must be a central authority extending into all parts of the territory. Integration implies a consensus between the elites, including the rulers, and the masses concerning acceptable procedures for the resolution of conflict. Certain attitudes must be held in common regarding the social order, standards of justice, national symbols, and goals. Finally, the degree of integration relates to the level at which people are willing and able to combine for coordinated effort toward a common end.

Some ambiguities persist concerning the geographical application of Yemeni nationhood. The unity of the two territories sharing the name has been consistently and authoritatively asserted since Imam Yaḥyā first assumed fully independent rule. Exiled dissidents from the People's Democratic Republic hold high office in the Yemen Arab Republic. The political experience of the two regions has, on the other hand, been diverse; important differences include protracted Western rule of South Yemen's metropolis, and the destruction of the traditional leadership groups during the post-1967 convulsions. The two entities are presently pursuing mutually incompatible sets of values.

At another level, it may be asked whether the Yemenis subordinate their national identity to the more comprehensive Arab one. From some Arab capitals it has been urged upon them that they are the "Arab people in Yemen," rather than Yemenis. The persuasiveness of this thesis to the Yemeni public is placed in doubt by the prompt demise of the U.A.R.-sponsored regime in 1967, and the subsequent pursuit of largely Yemeni goals. The moves toward a national consensus against the U.A.R. presence during the civil war are an indication of some sentiment of national identity. The feeling of identity exists as an operating political value, although its incidence is blurred.

The current regime as yet falls short of exercising effective authority throughout the national territory; its ability to coerce the large tribes is limited. At the same time, there is no higher or alternative authority presently recognized by the tribes. Their posture, which is just beginning to evolve, is to accept the symbolic sovereignty of the republican regime, as they formerly did that of the imams, so long as their freedom to order their local affairs is respected.

Disparate systems of political values exist in contemporary Yemeni society, but there are also some unifying attitudes and aspirations. There is a general sense of national identity and of sharing a common past and future destiny, although myths and symbols to which the whole population can relate remain somewhat implicit. The Yemeni people, while divided along sectarian lines, are solidly Muslim and sincerely devoted to their faith. The insistence of the constitution upon the *sharīʿa* as the criterion of authority is by no means necessarily a retrogressive posture. From the rich Islamic repertory of values it emphasizes those nonsectarian, instrumental ones on which most Yemenis can wholeheartedly agree: social justice and equality, the dignity and freedom of the individual, and the enhancement of his material and cultural condition.

The potency and persistence in Yemen of social solidarity along kinship lines stressed throughout this study is related to the level at which effective integrative action can be undertaken. By contrast with many emerging countries, Yemen did not have the nationally integrating experience of struggle for liberation from Western colonial rule. The campaign against the Ottoman occupation early in the present century is remote in time, and was not carried through to a decisive conclusion. Similarly, the Yemeni consensus was only partial against outside intervention during the internal war of the 1960s; respected national leaders emerged from this Yemeni experience, but no national heroes capable of mobilizing the entire nation. The society does not yet seem capable of sustained and truly integrative action at the national level, although the recently instituted consultative processes, now in suspension, might over time contribute to the development of such a potential. At lower levels of the society, capability for combined action is remarkably strong; it can be, and is, put to use both for purposes consonant with authoritatively established national ends, and for purposes obstructing them.

The pattern of integration in the Yemen Arab Republic is thus quite mixed. It has weaknesses, but also certain strengths. Conflicts exist among various value sets which could promote disintegration: between town and countryside, moderate and radical, lay and cleric, Zaidi and Shāfiʿī, pan-Arab and Yemeni nationalist. If the republic's leaders nevertheless work to encourage the use of local integrative capability along lines consonant with aspirations common to all, the movement should be toward an increasingly cohesive society and a more effective political system.

Notes

Chapter 1

1. W. F. Albright chronology, cited in Wendell Phillips, *Qataban and Sheba* (London: Victor Gollancz, 1955), p. 222.

2. Ibid.

3. Jurjī Zaidān, *al-'Arab qabl al-Islām*, ed. Ḥusain Mu'nis (Cairo: Dār al-Hilāl, n.d.), p. 169.

4. W. F. Albright, *The Archaeology of Palestine* (London: Penguin Books, 1949), pp. 143-145.

5. The South Arabian script, like that of the later Arabic, supplied only consonants and long vowels, and transcribers are free to insert short vowels according to their own linguistic theories. The name of the Sabean god also appears in modern Western writings as 'Almaqa, Ilumquh, etc.

6. Some pioneering students of the South Arabian inscriptions (Glazer, Hommel, etc.) interpreted the term "mukarrib" as denoting intimacy with the deity, and on purely philosophical grounds posited that all Sabean mukarribs preceded all the Sabean kings. This, and other similarly speculative assumptions, made the establishment of South Arabian chronology a singularly difficult task, and stimulated scholarly debates which still continue. The present writer has relied mainly on the work of Mlle. Jacqueline Pirenne, which provides a persuasive synthesis of the available paleographic, numismatic, archaeo-

logical, and literary evidence. Many aspects of the area's remote past remain controversial, however, and some statements made here are subject to review in the light of new data or further analysis by the specialists.

7. The date is in dispute. See Jacqueline Pirenne, *Royaume Sud-Arabe de Qatabân et sa Datation* (Louvain: Publications Universitaires, 1961), p. 167 ff.

8. Dhū Raydān was the fortress at the Ḥimyarite capital of Ẓafār, near present-day Yarīm.

9. Yamnat here probably refers only to the Yemeni Tihama. See Jacques Ryckmans, *l'Institution monarchique en Arabie méridionale avant l'Islam* (Louvain: Publications Universitaires, 1951), p. 211.

10. The precise dates are undetermined. Phillip Hitti proposes 340-378 A.D. in *History of the Arabs*, 9th ed. (New York: St. Martin's, 1967), p. 60. Other scholars would reduce these dates by five years or so.

11. S. D. Goitein, "The Jews in Yemen," in *Religion in the Middle East*, ed. A. J. Arberry (Cambridge: The University Press, 1969), vol. 1, pp. 226-235.

12. The Monophysite congregations, including one at Sanaa and the famous one at Nejran, appear to have been founded a century and a half later. Hitti, *History of the Arabs*, p. 61.

13. Ryckmans, *l'Institution monarchique*, pp. 214-215.

14. All the Ḥimyarite kings are given this title in the Arabic histories. (Plural: *tabābi'a*.)

15. I.e., in this context, "nomads."

16. See Irfan Shahîd, *The Martyrs of Najran: New Documents* (Brussels: Société des Bollandistes, 1971).

17. Ryckmans, *l'Institution monarchique*, pp. 322-325.

18. The Iraqi scholar Jawād 'Alī discusses at length the question of whether Hamdānī and his contemporaries really understood the language of the inscriptions; see *Ta'rīkh al-'Arab qabl al-Islām* (Baghdad: Matba'at al-Tafayyuḍ, 1950), vol. 1, pp. 49-56.

19. *Al-Qaṣīda al-Ḥimyariya*, ed. Sayyid 'Alī al-Mu'ayyad and Qāḍī Ismā'īl al-Jarāfī (Cairo: al-Maṭba'a al-Salafiya, 1958).

20. A notable example is Muḥammad bin 'Alī al-Akwa', *al-Yaman al-Khuḍrā Mahad al-Ḥaḍāra* (Cairo: Maṭba'at al-Sa'āda, 1971). Adopting a chronology now discredited among Western scholars, the author pushes the rise of South Arabian civilization well back into the third millennium B.C. and asserts a Yemeni origin for alphabetic writing and for many features of Sumerian, Egyptian, and other early Middle Eastern cultures.

Chapter 2

1. The term *al-Raḥmān*, "the Merciful," was current in the Arabian Peninsula in reference to the sole deity well before the rise of Islam; it was used, among others, by the Jews in referring to Jehovah.

2. Translation of text in *Middle East Journal* 25, no. 3 (summer 1971): 389-401.

3. W. Montgomery Watt, *Islamic Political Thought* (Edinburgh: The University Press, 1968), p. 96.

4. Ibid., p. 96.

5. Ibid., p. 98.

6. Ibid., p. 98.

7. A. S. Tritton, *The Rise of the Imams of Sanaa* (London: Oxford University Press, 1923), pp. 121-122.

8. "'Umar," in *Shorter Encyclopedia of Islam* (Leyden: E. J. Brill, 1953), p. 601.'

9. Dwight M. Donaldson, *The Shī'ite Religion* (London: Luzac & Co., 1933), p. xxv; Watt, *Islamic Political Thought*, p. 115.

10. The origins of the various traditions are examined in Erling Ladewig Petersen, *'Alī and Mu'āwiya in Early Arabic Tradition* (Copenhagen: Munksgaard, 1964).

11. 'Abdullah bin 'Abd al-Karīm al-Jarāfī, *al-Muqtaṭaf min Ta'rīkh al-Yaman* (Cairo: 'Isā al-Bābī al-Halabī, 1951), p. 48, n. 1.

12. Muḥammad bin Muḥammad Zabāra, *al-Anbā' 'an Dawlat Bilqīs wa Saba'* (Cairo: al-Maṭba'a al-Salafiya, 1956), p. 32, quoting the historian Ibn Athīr.

13. Ibid., p. 31. Zabāra notes that the project is alternatively ascribed to an Abbasid governor.

14. 'Abd al-Wāsi' bin Yaḥyā al-Wāsi'ī, *Ta'rīkh al-Yaman*, 2nd ed. (Cairo: Maṭbā'at Ḥijāzī, 1947), p. 147.

15. Zabāra, *al-Anbā'*, p. 31.

16. Al-Jarāfī, *al-Muqtaṭaf*, p. 48.

17. Zabāra, *al-Anbā'*, p. 31.

18. Al-Wasi'ī, *Ta'rīkh al-Yaman*, p. 148.

19. Ḥasan Sulaimān Maḥmūd, *Ta'rīkh al-Yaman al-Siyāsī fil-'Aṣr al-Islāmī* (Baghdad: al-Majma' al-'Ilmī al-'Irāqī, 1969), p. 98.

20. Watt, *Islamic Political Thought*, pp. 99-100.

Chapter 3

1. A few large urban centers, notably Sanaa and Dhamār, are exceptions.

2. One lucid classification of the Yemeni tribes is given in, 'Abdullah bin 'Abd al-Karīm al-Jarāfī, *al-Muqtaṭaf min Ta'-rīkh al-Yaman* (Cairo: 'Isā al-Babī al-Halabī, 1951), pp. 18-23.

3. E.g., 'Abd al-Wasī' bin Yaḥyā al-Wāsi'ī, *Tārīkh al-Yaman*, 2d ed. (Cairo: Maṭba'at Ḥijāzī, 1947), pp. 15-16.

4. The situation alters eastward from the area we are describing. The Nakha' tribe in the vicinity of Baiḍā', on the present border between Yemen and its southern neighbor, is both well pedigreed and "warlike." Tribalism is (or was until recently) strong throughout the rural areas of the present People's Democratic Republic of Yemen. The Tihama presents a mixed picture in this regard, with a few large tribes and many small communities having no broad kinship links.

5. Ḥusayn F. al-Hamdānī, *On the Genealogy of the Fatimid Caliphs*, School of Oriental Studies Occasional Papers, no. 1 (Cairo: American University, 1958).

6. Ḥusayn bin Fayḍallah al-Hamdānī and Ḥasan Sulaimān Maḥmūd, *al-Ṣulayhiyūn wal-Ḥaraka al-Fāṭimiya fīl-Yaman* (Cairo: Maktabat Miṣr, 1955), p. 31.

7. Al-Qāḍī al-Nu'mān bin Muḥammad, *Risalāt Iftitāḥ al-Da'wa* (Beirut: Dār al-Thāqafa, 1970), pp. 41-42.

8. Not, of course, to be confused with the great port of Aden on the Gulf of Aden, specified by the medieval writers as Aden Abyan, the old name of its hinterland.

9. Ḥasan Suleimān Maḥmūd, *Ta'rīkh al-Yaman al-Siyāsī*

(Baghdad: al-Majma' al-'Ilmī al-'Irāqī, 1969), quoting the manuscript chronicle of Ibn al-Dayba'. The 700 million dirhams reportedly seized from the sultan's treasury would make Ibn 'Alī a wealthy prince indeed.

10. Professor R. B. Serjeant has noted the survival in South Arabia of loose sexual mores into our own times. See "The Zaydis," in *Religion in the Middle East*, ed. A. J. Arberry (Cambridge: The University Press, 1969) vol. 2, p. 291. A thousand years of effort by the Zaidi imams failed to stamp out the manufacture and use of intoxicants in Yemen. In the early 1960s the writer's legation in Ta'izz was able to gauge Imam Aḥmad's current concern with the problem according to the price of raisins, from which brandy was made; it fell sharply whenever the imam moved vigorously against the distillers.

11. The arguments are set forth in Hamdānī and Maḥmūd, *al-Ṣulayḥiyūn*, pp. 39-41.

12. Yaḥyā bin al-Ḥusain, "Anbā' al-Zaman" (Ms.), quoted by Maḥmūd, *Ta'rīkh al-Yaman al-Siyāsī*, p. 172.

13. Al-Jarāfi, *al-Muqtaṭaf*, p. 48.

14. Najm al-Din 'Umāra al-Ḥakamī, *Ta'rīkh al-Yaman*, ed. and trans. Henry Cassels Kay (London: Edward Arnold, 1892), p. 23.

15. Muḥammad bin Muḥammad Zabāra, *A'immat al-Yaman* (Ta'izz: Maṭba'at al-Naṣr al-Nāṣiriya, 1952), p. 93.

16. Ibid., pp. 93-95.

17. The calumnious stereotype of the Ismā'īliya propagated by the Zaidis and Sunnīs was remarkably tenacious. A Zaidi writer at the dawn of the twentieth century tells his readers, "Be advised that the *bāṭinis* (may God Almighty abase them!) did great damage to Islam by their worship of idols. They conceal their thoughts so that they can practice idolatry, while pretending to be Muslims. They are all renegades. . . ." Ḥusain bin Aḥmad al 'Arshī, *Bulūgh al-Marām* (Cairo: Albertiri, 1939), p. 21.

18. 'Umāra, *Ta'rīkh al-Yaman*, p. 19 of Arabic text. Translated by this writer.

19. Ibid., pp. 19-21.

20. "Mecca," in *Shorter Encyclopedia of Islam* (Leyden: E. J. Brill, 1953), p. 373.

21. The *'umra*, or "little pilgrimage," denotes the performance of much of the ritual comprising the *ḥajj*; being performed outside the prescribed season, however, it is a meritorious act rather than fulfillment of the scriptural obligation of pilgrimage.

22. Maḥmūd, *Ta'rīkh al-Yaman al-Siyāsī*, p. 183, quoting the historian al-Fāsī.

23. The clan found outside intervention sufficiently distasteful that they suspended their quarrels long enough to petition 'Alī to name one of their number as ruler. As soon as the Hashimite family was installed, they were attacked by their disgruntled cousins of the Sulaimān branch. The latter were driven south to the coastal plain of present Asir, which thereafter was known as al-Mikhlāf al-Sulaimānī, the "Sulaimānī Province." For the next several centuries they made distinguished contributions to the turbulent and quarrelsome quality of Yemeni history.

24. Hamdānī and Maḥmūd, *al-Ṣulayḥiyūn*, p. 87, quoting the poet al-Qammī.

25. In these times such an army would typically consist of from one to three thousand mounted men, with a similar or larger number of foot soldiers.

26. 'Umāra, *Ta'rīkh al-Yaman*, p. 62.

27. Ibid., p. 62.

28. Ibid., p. 61.

29. Ibid., p. 61.

30. Ibid., p. 63.

31. Ibid., p. 64.

32. Or, rather, his chief minister, Badr al-Jamālī. By this time the caliphs had become, as they were to remain, impotent captives of the vizirs.

33. 'Umāra, *Ta'rīkh al-Yaman*, pp. 68-69.

34. Ibid., pp. 72-73.

35. Ibid., p. 75.

36. The historians differ respecting the circumstances of Ibn Najīb al-Dawla's death. Some state that the conspirators had him assassinated en route to Egypt.

37. 'Umāra, *Ta'rīkh al-Yaman*, p. 66.

38. Joseph Calmette, *le Moyen Age* (Paris: Arthème Fay-

ard, 1948), pp. 78-79.

Chapter 4

1. Al-Qāḍī 'Abdullah bin 'Abd al-Karīm al-Jarāfī, *al-Muqtaṭaf min Ta'rīkh al-Yaman* (Cairo: 'Isā al-Bābī al-Ḥalabī, 1951), p. 103.
2. Ibid., pp. 103-104.
3. Ibid., p. 22.
4. Maḥmūd Kāmil, *al-Yaman Shimāluhu wa Janūbuhu* (Beirut: Dār Beirut lil-Ṭabā'a wal-Nashr, 1968), p. 145.
5. Cornelis van Arendonk, *les Débuts de l'imamat zaidite au Yemen*, trans. Jacques Ryckmans (Leyden: E. J. Brill, 1960), p. 134.
6. Dwight M. Donaldson, *The Shī'ite Religion* (London: Luzac & Co., 1933), pp. 113-117.
7. Van Arendonk, *les Débuts de l'imamat*, pp. 36-37.
8. Ibid.
9. In this respect, Zaidism is more exclusive than the early Kaisaniya sect, which considered eligible 'Alī's progeny by any of his wives; less so than the orthodox Shī'a whose imams are all descended from 'Alī and Fāṭima's son Ḥusain (after their elder son, Ḥasan).
10. 'Alī bin Muḥammad bin 'Ubaidallah al-'Abbāsī al-'Alawī, *Sīrat al-Hādī ilā al-Haqq Yaḥyā bin al-Ḥusain* (Beirut: Dār al-Fikr, 1972), p. 28 (referred to hereafter as *Sīra*).
11. Amīn al-Rīhānī, *Mulūk al-'Arab*, 3d ed., 2 vols (Beirut: Maṭābi' Ṣādir al-Rīḥānī, 1951), vol. 1, p. 141.
12. Van Arendonk, *les Débuts de l'imamat*, p. 30.
13. Al-'Alawī, *Sīra*, p. 51.
14. Ibid., p. 52.
15. Van Arendonk, *les Débuts de l'imamat*, p. 256.
16. Al-'Alawī, *Sīra*, pp. 48-49.
17. Ibid., pp. 44-47.
18. Ibid., p. 62.
19. Ibid., p. 61.
20. Van Arendonk, *les Débuts de l'imamat*, p. 261.
21. Al-'Alawī, *Sīra*, pp. 73-78.
22. Ibid., pp. 146-148.
23. Yaḥyā bin al-Ḥusain al-Yamanī, *Anbā' al-Zaman fī*

Akhbār al-Yaman, ed. Mohamed Madi (Berlin: Walter de Gruyter, 1936), pp. 19-50.

24. Al-'Alawī, *Sīra*, pp. 89-91.

25. Yaḥyā bin al-Ḥusain, *Anbā' al-Zaman*, p. 17.

26. Muḥammad bin Muḥammad Zabāra, *A'immat al-Yaman fī al-Qurn al-Rābi' 'Āshir lil-Hijra* (Cairo: Maṭba'at al-Salafiya, 1956), p. 25.

27. Najm al-Din 'Umāra al-Hakamī al-Yamanī, *Ta'rīkh al-Yaman*, ed. and trans. Henry Cassels Kay (London: Edward Arnold, 1892), pp. 79-80.

Chapter 5

1. Taqī al-Dīn Aḥmad bin 'Alī al-Maqrīzī, *Kitāb al-Sulūk li-Ma'rifat Duwal al-Mulūk*, ed. Muḥammad Muṣṭafā Ziyāda (Cairo: Lajnat al-Ta'lif wal-Tarjama wal-Nashr, 1956), vol. 1, pt. 1, p. 52.

2. Ibid. 'Umāra's ambiguous motives led to his execution by Saladin, who suspected him, perhaps justly, of implication in a conspiracy to restore the Fatimid regime.

3. The Ayyūbids, and after them the Rasūlids, carried to an extreme the inflation of nomenclature introduced by the Abbasids. To give this particular Ayyūbid prince his full due we should have to refer to him as "the Sultan, the Exalted Monarch, Sun of the Faith, Turān Shāh, Son of the Sire of Kings, Star of the Faith, Ayyūb Son of Shādī, Son of Marwān, the Kurd." For simplicity's sake we shall usually refer in this chapter to individual Ayyūbids by their titles, except where their given names are familiar to the general reader. We shall use a title for the Rasūlid princes, since all are usually thus identified by the historians, and their surviving monuments are thus known (e.g., two Ta'izz mosques: the Muẓaffariya, built by Sultan al-Muẓaffar Yūsuf, and the Ashrafiya, a work of Sultan al-Ashraf II Ismā'īl bin 'Abbās).

4. Upon Saladin's death in 1192, control of Egypt passed to the family of his son al-'Ādil Abū Bakr, while another son, Khuḍr, held Aleppo. The latter attempted to perform the pilgrimage in 1213; "When he approached Mecca, retainers of al-Mālik al-Kāmil Muhammad, son of 'Ādil, prevented him from performing the *ḥajj*, saying, "You have come only to seize

the territory of Yemen.' He said, 'O kinsmen, bind me if you will, but let me perform the pilgrimage rites.' They replied, 'We have no orders save to turn you away.' So he returned to Syria without accomplishing the *ḥajj*, which saddened the people." (al-Maqrīzī, *al-Sulūk*, p. 178.)

5. Ibn al-Mujāwir, *al-Mustabṣir*, as quoted in Abū Muḥammad Bā Makhrama, *Ta'rīkh Thaghr 'Adan*, ed. Oscar Lofgren (Uppsala: Almqvist & Wiksells Boktryckeri AB, 1950), p. 65. As of the early 1950s, the medieval dinar was roughly appraised at $2.40.

6. Al-Maqrīzī, *al-Sulūk*, vol. 1, Part 2, p. 397.

7. Muḥammad bin Muḥammad Zābara, *A'immat al-Yaman*, (Ta'izz: Maṭba'at al-Naṣr al-Nāṣiriya, 1952), p. 112, citing Khazrajī, Janadī, and other historians.

8. One eccentric and probably demented monarch, al-Mu'izz Ismā'īl (1197-1202), posed as God himself before retreating to the only somewhat less extravagant claim to be an Umayyad caliph. Ismā'īl is also credited with exotic culinary preferences: he was a cannibal. 'Abd al-Wāsi' bin Yaḥyā al-Wāsi'ī, *Ta'rīkh al-Yaman*, 2d ed. (Cairo: Maṭba'at Hijāzī, 1947), p. 182.

9. I.e., to the Zaidi imam.

10. Zabāra, *A'immat al-Yaman*, p. 142.

11. Ibid.

12. 'Alī bin al-Ḥasan al-Khazraji, *al-'Uqūd al-Lu'lu'iya* (Cairo: Maṭba'at al-Hilāl, 2 vols., 1911 and 1914). Trans. Sir J. W. Redhouse as *The Pearl-Strings* (London: Luzac, 2 vols., 1906-1907). Vol. 1 of trans., p. 90.

13. Ibid., vol. 1 of trans., p. 89.

14. Surely a slip of the pen for "my father."

15. Al-Khazrajī, *Pearl-Strings*, vol. 1, p. 89.

16. Ibid., p. 117.

17. The Rasūlid princesses are modestly known by the name of the eunuch who kept their respective households. This lady's title appears in the annals as *Dhāt al-Sitār al-Rafī' al-Dār al-Shamsī:* "Mistress of the Elegant Curtain, al-Shamsī's Abode."

18. On the site of present al-Ḥusainiya, in the Tihama midway between Zabīd and Bait al-Faqīh.

19. Al-Khazrajī, *Pearl-Strings*, vol. 1, p. 119.

20. Ibid., vol. 2, pp. 120-121.
21. Ibid., vol. 1, p. 119.
22. Ibid., p. 109.
23. Claude Cahen and R. B. Serjeant, "A Fiscal Survey of the Medieval Yemen," *Arabica* 4, no. 1 (1957): 23-30.
24. Ibn al-Mujāwir, *al-Mustabṣir*, p. 56 ff.
25. Al-Khazrajī, *Pearl-Strings*, vol. 1, p. 171.
26. E.g., the collection in Bā Makhrama, *Ta'rīkh Thaghr 'Adan*, pt. 2, pp. 2-260.
27. Al-Khazrajī, *Pearl-Strings*, vol. 1, p. 295.
28. Ibid., vol. 2, p. 273.
29. Ibid., vol. 1, p. 245.
30. Ibid., vol. 2, p. 156.
31. The dirham here is not a coin but a unit of weight equivalent to 3.12 grams. The original measure was thus about 750 grams. The peasant was taxed, as we have seen, according to a fixed average yield. This was stated in terms of a standard measure. If the size of the latter was increased without a corresponding revision of the assessment on his plot, the peasant's taxes increased proportionately, whether paid in kind or in cash.
32. Al-Khazrajī, *Pearl-Strings*, vol. 2, p. 159.
33. Ibid., pp. 159-160.
34. Ibid., p. 135.
35. Ibid., vol. 1, pp. 138-139.
36. Ibid., p. 122.
37. Ibid., pp. 229-230.
38. Ibid., vol. 2, pp. 138-139.
39. Ibid., vol. 1, p. 313.
40. Ibid., p. 313.
41. Ibid., vol. 1, p. 298.
42. Ibid., vol. 2, pp. 65-66.
43. Al-Khazrajī died in 1409.
44. Al-Khazrajī writes that the Qāḍī "hated the Ashā'ira and persecuted them harshly because of their partiality for the Qāḍī Jamāl al-Dīn Muḥammad bin Ḥassān, the minister. Qāḍī Shihāb al-Dīn was furthermore of Ghassānid descent, and was never moved by any compassionate sentiment." (*al-'Uzūd,* vol. 2 of Arabic text, p. 94.) Qāḍī Jamāl al-Dīn was deputy gov-

ernor at Ḥaraḍ beginning in 1369, and it is possible that Qāḍī Shihāb al-Dīn was jealous of his reputation, apparently well merited, for sound and humane administration. Qāḍī Jamāl al-Dīn was named minister after the incidents mentioned here, and succeeded Qāḍī Shihāb al-Dīn at Fashāl in 1373.

45. On the site of modern al-Manṣūriya, one day's march north of Bait al-Faqīh.

46. His mother, Jihat Ṣalāḥ, a lady of no mean ability and determination, reassembled the scattered army, led it back to Yemen, and governed effectively as al-Mujāhid's regent until his release.

47. Al-Ashraf I died of natural causes in 1296, after a reign of less than two years; he was succeeded by his brother al-Mu'ayyad.

Chapter 6

1. The "official" historian of the subsequent Ottman expedition of Sinān Pasha attributes the appeal to Muẓaffar Shah. Quṭb al-Dīn Muḥammad bin Aḥmad al-Nahrawālī, *al-Barq al-Yamānī fil-Fatḥ al-'Uthmānī* (Riyad: Dār al-Yamāma, 1967), p. 19. As the reign of Muẓaffar II extended from 1511 to 1526, the first Mameluke expedition must have taken place during the time of his father and predecessor, Maḥmūd II.

2. Also known as Salmān al-Rayyis.

3. *Al-Faḍl al-Mazīd 'alā Bughyat al-Mustafīd fī Akhbār Madīnat Zabīd*, quoted in al-Nahrawālī, *al-Barq al-Yamānī*, p. 17.

4. Al-Nahrawālī, *al-Barq al-Yamānī*, p. 20.

5. Ibid., pp. 80-81; Yaḥyā bin al-Ḥusain bin al-Qāsim, *Ghāyat al-Amānī fī Akhbār al-Qaṭr al-Yamānī*, ed. Sa'īd 'Abd al-Fattāḥ 'Ashūr, 2 vols. (Cairo: Dār al-Kitāb, 1968), vol. 2, p. 684.

6. That is, from about 1526.

7. Al-Nahrawālī, *al-Barq al-Yamānī*, pp. 91-92.

8. Al-Sayyid Muṣṭafā Sālim, *al-Fatḥ al-'Uthmānī al-Awwal lil-Yaman* (Cairo: Arab League Institute for Arab Research and Studies, 1969), pp. 187-195.

9. Al-Nahrawālī, *al-Barq al-Yamānī*, p. 441.

10. Ibid., pp. 128-129.

11. Aḥmad bin Muḥammad bin Abī Bakr al-Yāfiʿī, an astrologer and *sharīʿa* judge in the Shawāfī region around Ibb and Jibla, had repeatedly told the people that, should both the sun and the moon be eclipsed during a month of Ramadan, the Ottoman state would collapse. This coincidence did occur in 1567. Ibid., p. 171.

12. Shams al-Dīn died in 1555, predeceasing his father, the imam, by two years.

13. Yaḥyā bin al-Ḥusain, *Ghāyat al-Amānī*, vol. 2, p. 745.

14. Ibid., pp. 743-840.

15. Originally adopting the title al-Manṣūr, he styled himself later al-Hādī, then al-Mahdī. He is popularly known as Lord of Mawāhib, the palace he built near Dhamār.

16. We may recall that physical fitness was among the essential qualifications for the imamate.

17. Qāḍī ʿAbdullah bin ʿAbd al-Karīm al-Jarāfī, *al-Muqtaṭaf min Ta'rīkh al-Yaman* (Cairo: ʿĪsā al-Bābī al-Ḥalabī, 1951), p. 166.

18. Ibid., p. 167.

19. Ibid., p. 166.

20. Ibid., p. 180.

21. The paramount shaikhs of Ḥāshid still come from the al-Aḥmar family.

22. Jarāfī, *Al-Muqtaṭaf*, p. 181.

23. Ibid., p. 182.

24. Of Bakīl, this tribal grouping, also called Duhma, is one of two wings of the Awlād Shākir; its two major subdivisions are Dhū Muḥammad and Dhū Ḥusain. In neither occupation did the Turks even attempt to administer them, and the imamate's control of them was never any better than tenuous. Al-Jarāfī, *al-Muqtaṭaf*, pp. 182-183; Muḥammad bin Muḥammad Zabāra, *A'immat al-Yaman bil-Qarn al-Rābiʿ ʿAshr lil-Hijra* (Cairo: Maṭbaʿat al-Salafiya, 1956), pp. 24-26.

25. Al-Jarāfī, *al-Muqtaṭaf*, pp. 185-186.

26. Ibid., p. 197.

27. Carsten Niebuhr, *Travels Through Arabia and Other Countries in the East*, trans. Robert Heron, 2 vols. (Edinburgh: 1792; reprinted Beirut: Librairie du Liban, n.d.).

28. Ibid., vol. 2, p. 47.

29. Ibid., pp. 51-52.
30. Ibid., pp. 87-88.
31. Ibid., pp. 103-104.
32. 'Abd al-Ḥamīd al-Baṭrīq, *Min Tārīkh al-Yaman al-Ḥadīth*, (Cairo: Arab League Institute for Arab Studies and Research, 1969), p. 81. This work gives a well-documented account of Muhammad 'Alī's occupation of Yemen.
33. Muḥammad bin Muḥammad Zabāra, *A'immat al-Yaman*, Part I (Ta'izz: Maṭba'at al-Naṣr al-Nāṣiriya, 1952) pp. 422-424.
34. Al-Jarāfī, *al-Muqtaṭaf*, p. 202.
35. The memory among Turks of the dreadful cost remained alive in the 1960s. The Honorable Parker T. Hart, American ambassador in Ankara 1965-1968, informed me that his Turkish friends declared there was hardly an Anatolian family that did not lose at least one son in Yemen. (Conversation in June 1971.)
36. 'Abd al-Wāsi' bin Yaḥyā al-Wāsi'ī, *Ta'rīkh al-Yaman*, 2d. ed. (Cairo: Maṭba'at Ḥijāzī, 1947), pp. 372-373.
37. Ibid., pp. 373-374.
38. Ibid., pp. 304-309.
39. Yaḥyā's father, al-Manṣūr Muḥammad, had been in correspondence with 'Abd al-Raḥmān al-Kawākibī (d. 1903), Muḥammad 'Abduh (d. 1905), and other leaders of the Islamic reform movement. Qāḍī 'Abdullah bin 'Abd al-Wahhāb al-Mujāhid al-Shamāhī, *al-Yaman: Insān wa Ḥaḍāra* (Cairo: 'Ālam al-Kutub, 1972), p. 164.
40. Text in al-Wāsi'ī, *Ta'rīkh al-Yaman*, pp. 375-376.

Chapter 7

1. Qāḍī 'Abdullah bin 'Abd al-Wahhāb al-Mujāhid al-Shamāḥī, *al-Yaman: al-Insān wal-Ḥaḍāra* (Cairo: 'Ālam al-Kutub, 1972), p. 170.
2. An ardent Arab nationalist as well as a perceptive and critical observer, Rīḥānī visited Yemen for the purpose of negotiating a treaty between Imam Yaḥyā and Sharīf Ḥusain, then king of Hijaz.
3. Amīn al-Rīḥanī, *Mulūk al-'Arab*, 3d ed., 2 vols. (Beirut: Maṭābi' Ṣādir al-Rīḥānī), vol. 1, p. 81.

4. Ibid., p. 82.

5. Then a province governor, later the leader of the abortive 1948 coup in which Imam Yaḥyā was murdered.

6. Al-Rīḥānī, *Mulūk al-'Arab*, vol. 1, pp. 111-112.

7. Ibid., p. 117.

8. G. Wyman Bury, *Arabia Infelix, or the Turks in Yemen* (London: Macmillan, 1915), pp. 115-116.

9. U.S. Department of State Despatch No. 52, from Harlan B. Clark, American Consulate at Aden to the Secretary of State, April 23, 1945, p. 29.

10. Harold F. Jacob, *The Kings of Arabia* (London: Mills and Boon, 1923).

11. Al-Sayyid Muṣṭafā Sālim, *Takwīn al-Yaman al-Ḥadīth* (Cairo: Arab League Institute for Higher Arab Studies, 1963), p. 250.

12. Ibid.

13. Al-Rīḥānī, *Mulūk al-'Arab*, vol. 1, pp. 263-264.

14. The town's population had increased to an estimated 15,000 by the early 1950s. Qāḍī 'Abdullah bin 'Abd al-Karīm al-Jarāfī, *al-Muqtaṭaf min Ta'rīkh al-Yaman* (Cairo: 'Isā al-Bābī al-Ḥalabī, 1951), p. 247, n. 3.

15. Al-Rīḥānī, *Mulūk al-'Arab*, vol. 1, p. 265.

16. During the plebiscite the Hodeidans received evidence of what they might expect under an Idrīsid regime. The sayyid issued a decree demanding a loan from the Hodeida merchants in the amount of £30,000 secured by the port's customs receipts. Ibid., p. 261.

17. Clark, Despatch 52, p. 6. British writers interpret the events differently.

18. The sayyid had the five Hodeida spokesmen kidnapped and deported to Jizan. They were released after seven months confinement, against payment of a substantial ransom, or the furnishing of their children as hostages. Rīḥānī, *Mulūk al-'Arab*, vol. 1, p. 262.

19. 'Abd al-Wāsi' bin Yaḥyā al-Wāsi'ı, *Ta'rīkh al-Yaman*, 2d ed. (Cairo: Maṭba'at Ḥijāzi, 1947), p. 341.

20. The writer was assured by informed Yemenis in 1961 that several hundred Zarānīq leaders were cast into the Ḥajja dungeons without food or water, and perished. As a conse-

quence, the tribe was left without effective leadership, and remained docile for a considerable time thereafter.

21. Aḥmad Muḥammad al-Shāmī, *Imām al-Yaman, Aḥmad Ḥamīd al-Dīn* (Beirut: Dār al-Kitāb al-Jadīd, 1965), p. 233.

22. Ibid., pp. 67-68.

23. Al-Rīḥānī, *Mulūk al-'Arab*, vol. 1, p. 123.

24. Al-Shamāḥī, *al-Yaman: al-Insān wal-Ḥaḍāra*, pp. 168-169, 281-302.

25. This Qāḍī family is not to be confused with the great sayyid family of the same name.

26. Al-Shāmī, *Imām al-Yaman*, p. 136.

27. Ibrāhīm 'Alī al-Wazīr, *Bain Yaday al-Ma'sāt* (Beirut: Dār al-Andalus, 1963), pp. 51-54.

28. Even the imams studied with a number of scholars, and obtained their licenses.

29. An indictment of Shī'ism in Yemen was published in Cairo in the name of the Shāfi'ī ulama in Lower Yemen in 1970: 'Abdullah al-Muwāfiq, *al-Shī'a fī al-Yaman* (Cairo: Maṭba'at al-Salafiya, 1970).

30. The Maria Theresa thaler, called locally the riyal. This beautiful coin, first minted in Austria in 1780, achieved great popularity in Arabia and the Horn of Africa, and continued to be struck with the original date. It became the standard currency of Yemen until after the 1962 revolution. Its value fluctuated with local supply and demand, and with the world price of silver. It was worth $0.7392 in 1945, and in 1962 approached parity with the U.S. dollar.

31. Clark, Despatch 52, p. 68. Professor R. B. Serjeant, to whom I am indebted for many constructive observations on an early version of the present work, puts this remuneration in proper perspective by pointing out that it coincided exactly with the pay scale of the Yemeni army at the time.

32. Muḥammad Sa'īd al-'Attār, *al-Ta'akhkhur al-Iqtiṣādī wal-Ijtimā'ī fil-Yaman* (Algiers: Dār al-Ṭalī'a lil-Ṭabā'a wal-Nashr , 1965), p. 80.

33. *Mulūk al-'Arab*, vol. 1, pp. 130-139.

34. Clark, Despatch 52, p. 87.

35. *Mulūk al-'Arab*, vol. 1, p. 160.

36. Clark, Despatch 52, p. 77.
37. *Bain Yaday al-Ma'sāt*, p. 65.
38. Ibid., pp. 71-72.
39. Ibid., p. 81.
40. I observed during my service in Cairo, 1957-1959, that the indignation of some members of the Yemen Legation staff at these student invasions was rather pro forma.
41. Al-Wazīr, *Bayn Yaday al Ma'sāt*, pp. 84-85.
42. Nazīh al-'Aẓm, *Riḥla bi Bilād al-'Arabiya al-Sa'īda*, quoted in Sālim, *Takwīn al-Yaman al-Ḥadīth*, pp. 421-423. Al-'Azm visited the country as interpreter for the American engineer Karl S. Twitchell, whose philanthropic efforts to promote Yemen's economic progress were ultimately thwarted by the imam's caution.
43. Al-Rīḥānī, *Mulūk al-'Arab*, vol. 1, p. 205.
44. Ibid., p. 152.
45. Notably, agreements with Italy (1928), USSR and China (1955), Czechoslovakia (1957). Other ties were formed for the purposes of asserting the legitimacy of the imams' regime in the international community, and of enlisting political support against the British position in Aden.
46. One representative example: ". . . these ardent youths returned with the light of civilization in their blood-cells, the radiance of right guidance, their hearts filled with enlightened thoughts and penetrating judgments, with alert minds, a consciousness demanding more knowledge and culture, their eyes wide open to everything transpiring in their country." Wazīr, *Bain Yaday al Ma'sāt*, pp. 67-68.
47. Al-Sayyid 'Abd al-Razzāq al-Ḥasanī, *Ta'rīkh al-Wizārāt al-'Irāqiya*, 6 vols. (Ṣaida: Maṭba'at al-'Irfan, 1953), vol. 4, pp. 211-212.
48. Sālim, *Takwīn al-Yaman al-Ḥadīth*, p. 64, n. 1. The guard was, of course, a senior Ḥāshid shaikh.
49. Ibid., p. 430, n. 1.
50. Clark, Despatch 52, p. 86.
51. Ibid., p. 86, n.
52. In mid-1962 my staff in Ta'izz were informed by local businessmen that many farmers refused to plant winter crops, on which the tax incidence was higher than on the main-season

crop. Many villagers had sold most of their animals, as taxation had rendered stock-raising unprofitable. Exports of coffee and hides had declined sixty percent and forty-five percent respectively over the preceding two decades.

53. *Bain Yaday al Ma'sāt*, p. 90.

54. Clark, Despatch 52, enc. 1.

55. Al-Wazīr, *Bain Yaday al Ma'sāt*, pp. 75, 91-92.

56. William Harold Ingrams, *The Yemen: Imams, Rulers and Revolutions* (London: John Murray, 1963), p. 74.

57. As early as 1922, Rīḥānī observed, "whatever may be said of Imam Yaḥyā's abundant justice and perfect clemency, the Shāfi'īs under his rule are discontented, and those in his armed forces fight their brother Shāfi'īs reluctantly." *Mulūk al-'Arab*, vol. 1, p. 149.

58. Ingrams once saw a telegram which the imam addressed to his son, beginning, "O Aḥmad, the people are tired of your cruelty." *The Yemen*, p. 72.

59. Sometimes with a grim humor. In August 1961, Imam Aḥmad ordered the governor of Ta'izz Province boarded up in his offices for five days with his entire staff; the governor had, to the great inconvenience of the citizenry in the outlying districts, centralized graft-producing functions theretofore performed at the district level.

60. For example, 'Abd al-Raḥīm 'Abdullah, *al-Yaman, Thawra wa Thuwwār* (Cairo: Dār al-Naṣr, 1967), pp. 82-83; 'Attār, *al-Ta'akhkhur*, p. 302.

61. Dr. Ḥasan Mekkī, later foreign minister and prime minister of the Yemen Arab Republic.

62. American Legation, Ta'izz, Despatch No. 50, November 16, 1960.

63. Sayyid 'Abd al-Raḥmān 'Abd al-Ṣamd Abū Ṭālib, a casualty of the 1962 revolution.

64. American Legation, Ta'izz, Despatch No. 15, August 31, 1960.

65. *An-Naṣr*, Sanaa, 16 Shawwāl, 1381 (March 22, 1962).

66. Ibid.

67. A cogent account appears in Manfred W. Wenner, *Modern Yemen 1918-1966* (Baltimore: Johns Hopkins Press, 1967). A version varying in some details is given by Shamāḥī,

al-Yaman: al-Insān wal-Ḥaḍāra, pp. 306-313.

68. Conversation with the writer in May, 1971.

69. Al-Rīḥānī, *Mulūk al-'Arab*, vol. 1, p. 161.

70. American Legation, Ta'izz, Telegram No. 119, April 20, 1960.

71. Sukhna: the site of mineral springs in the foothills inland from Hodeida, where Imam Aḥmad held his court for several months after his return from abroad in 1959.

72. American Legation, Ta'izz, Telegram No. 109, March 15, 1960.

73. Hugh Scott, *In the High Yemen*, 2d ed. (London: John Murray, 1947), p. 131.

74. Aḥmad Ḥusain Sharaf al-Dīn, *al-Yaman 'abr al-Ta'rīkh* (Cairo: Maṭba'at al-Sunna al-Muḥammadiya, 1963), pp. 343-352.

Chapter 8

1. E.g., Muḥammad Sa'īd al-'Aṭṭār, *al-Ta'akhkhur al-Iqtiṣādī wal-Ijtimā'ī fīl-Yaman* (Algiers: Dār al-Ṭalī'a, 1965), p. 286; Aḥmad Ḥusain Sharaf al-Dīn, *al-Yaman 'abr al-Ta'rīkh* (Cairo: Maṭba'at al-Sunna al-Muḥammadiya, 1963), p. 324.

2. Aḥmad Ḥusain Sharaf al-Dīn, *al-Yaman 'abr al-Ta'rīkh* (Cairo: Maṭba'at al-Sunna al Muḥammadiya, 1963), p. 324.

3. Qāḍī 'Abdullah bin 'Abd al-Wahhāb al-Mujāhid al-Shamāḥī, *al-Yaman: al-Insān wal-Ḥaḍāra* (Cairo: 'Ālam al-Kutub, 1972), pp. 177-182.

4. Ibid., p. 199.

5. Ibid., pp. 179-180.

6. Solidarity among full brothers within Arab dynasties vis-à-vis their half-brothers can often be of political importance, as it is currently in the ruling family of Saudi Arabia.

7. Ibn Saud's animosity toward Aḥmad dated from the latter's able military campaign in 1934 against forces commanded by Crown Prince Saud, who suffered a humiliating defeat. Imam Yaḥyā, anxious for peace with Ibn Saud, had the utmost difficulty in obliging Aḥmad to disengage, and to surrender Nejran to the Saudis.

8. Al-Shamāḥī, *al-Yaman*, p. 189.
9. Ibid., p. 190.
10. The imam, with good reason, had become so suspicious of their loyalty that he had relieved the Iraqi-trained officers of troop command, and made them pensioners of the court without meaningful functions.
11. Al-Shamāḥī, *al-Yaman*, pp. 222-223.
12. The leader of the murder squad was 'Alī Nāṣir al-Qarda'ī, shaikh of the Murād, a Zaidi tribe of the Madhḥij group, located south of Mārib. Years before, Yaḥyā had divested the Qarda'ī of administration of their home area, and sent the tribe on a humiliatingly abortive military mission against Shabwa. According to Shamāḥī (*al-Yaman*, p. 225) the assassination was delayed for a day because Shaikh 'Alī demanded, and received from 'Abdullah al-Wazīr, a certificate absolving him in the eyes of God from guilt for Imam Yaḥyā's murder. The rank and file of the assassination party were tribesmen of Banī Ḥushaish, whose territory just northeast of Sanaa includes Wādī Sirr, the site of the Wazīr family estates.
13. Amīn Sa'īd, *Al-Yaman, Ta'rīkhuhu al-Siyāsī mundhu Istiqlālihi fīl-Qurn al-Thālith lil-Ḥijra* (Cairo: 'Īsā al-Bābī al-Ḥalabī, 1959), pp. 141-142.
14. 'Abdullah bin 'Abd al-Karīm al-Jarāfī, *al-Muqtaṭaf min Ta'rīkh al-Yaman* (Cairo: 'Īsā al-Bābī al-Ḥalabī, 1951), p. 262.
15. Al-Shamāḥī, *al-Yaman,* p. 238.
16. E.g., Sharaf al-Dīn, *al-Yaman 'abr al-Ta'rīkh*, p. 384 ff.; Sa'īd, *al-Yaman*, pp. 258-265; Sir Tom Hickinbotham, *Aden* (London: Constable & Co., 1958), pp. 177-181; Ṣalāḥ al-'Aqqād, *Jazīrat al-'Arab fīl-'Aṣr al-Ḥadīth* (Cairo: Arab League Institute for Arab Research and Studies, 1969), pp. 83-85; al-Shamāḥī, *al-Yaman,* pp. 281-305.
17. Al-'Aṭṭār, *al-Ta'akhkhur*, pp. 298-299.
18. Carl Leiden and Karl M. Schmitt, *The Politics of Violence: Revolution in the Modern World* (Englewood Cliffs, N.J.: Prentice-Hall, 1968), pp. 44-45.
19. Al-'Aṭṭār, *al-Ta'akhkhur*, p. 300.
20. 'Abd al-Raḥīm 'Abdullah, *al-Yaman, Thawra wa Thuwwār* (Cairo: Dār al-Naṣr, 1967), pp. 33-35.

21. American Legation, Ta'izz, Airgram No. 66, January 26, 1963.

22. Sallāl and other top Y.A.R. leaders assured me fervently that the Egyptians had been invited solely because of intervention which had already occurred both from Saudi Arabia and from the federation. They had excellent political reasons for endeavoring to convince me of this. On the other hand, British authorities could turn up no evidence at the time confirming any action from the south, and the idea that Saudi forces could at this time have penetrated Yemeni territory in effective numbers is simply laughable. (They did, of course, supply arms to the royalists.) One must conclude that from the first the republican regime felt it could not maintain itself by its own resources. As late as 1966, U.S. officials estimated that, of the overall Yemeni military potential, the northern tribes possessed about ninety percent and the Y.A.R. armed forces the remaining ten percent. (Conversation with Harlan B. Clark, May 1971.)

23. In the early engagements where Y.A.R. army units fought beside Egyptian units, the former were as likely to fire at the U.A.R. troops—foreigners—as at the supposedly common royalist enemy. U.A.R. commanders soon learned that their units were safer when operating independently.

24. According to reports I received at the time, the Egyptians demanded the liquidation of a number of sayyids whom they considered unsympathetic to the Nasser regime.

25. Notable examples were Sayyid Muḥammad 'Abd al-Quddūs al-Wazīr, who was detained for several years; and Sayyid Yaḥyā al-Kibsī, arrested and detained for two years upon being observed in conversation with me in a Sanaa street. (I was seeking to lease a building owned by the Kibsī family to house a projected Sanaa branch of our Ta'izz embassy.)

26. The exception, Aḥmad Mirwanī, had been a fellow student of Sallāl at the Iraqi Military Academy. He served briefly as Y.A.R. minister of education.

27. The text is reprinted in 'Abdullah al-Muwāfiq, *al-Shī'a fīl-Yaman* (Cairo: Maṭba'at al-Salafiya, 1970), pp. 69-80.

28. The limited degree to which the rank and file of tribesmen were moved by abstract principle was brought home to me

in 1973, when I talked with a group of Hamdān al-Yaman, far up Wadi Ḍahr, not far from Sanaa. Asked which side they were on during the civil war, they replied with a fine wit, that they had been republicans during the day (when Y.A.R. and Egyptian forces moved about), and royalists at night (when the imam's sympathizers enjoyed complete freedom of movement). It was clear that these Hamdān would have been well satisfied had all those carrying arms and claims on their property and loyalty simply gone, and stayed, away.

29. The principal Nasserists were the army faction headed by President 'Abdullah al-Sallāl and including 'Abdullah Jizailān, 'Abd al-Laṭīf Ḍayfallah, Muḥammad Ahnūmī, and 'Abd al-Raḥīm 'Abdullah. Originally associated with the group, Ḥasan al-'Amrī broke with them in 1966 and moved toward the "reform" position.

30. Imam Aḥmad once complained to me that all the Yemenis who went to study in the United States came back communists.

31. The figure fluctuated widely, and its maximum is a controversial question. Final authority is not claimed for the stated number, attributed to General Ḥasan al-'Amrī by Claude Deffarge and Gordian Troeller, *Yemen '62-'69* (Paris: Robert Laffont, 1969), p. 249.

32. It was reliably reported to me in 1962 that Imam Aḥmad had given his son a list of about two hundred Yemenis, with the advice, "When I die, if you execute these people, you will have a quiet reign."

33. On one such visit in 1961, Ḥasan made a "progress" between Sanaa and Ṣa'da in the course of which the tribesmen collected for him a purse of 50,000 riyals. (He prudently turned the money over to Imam Aḥmad.)

34. Dana Adams Schmidt, *Yemen: The Unknown War* (New York: Holt, Rinehart and Winston, 1968), p. 209.

35. King Faisal, who attended, was interested in ending the bickering among the Ḥamīd al-Dīn, which was reducing the effectiveness of royalist military and administrative operations.

36. Deffarge and Troeller, *Yemen '62-'69*, p. 264.

37. Ibid., p. 268.

38. Son of Aḥmad Nu'mān, founder of the Free Yemeni Party; foreign minister in the al-Ḥajrī government (1972-74), he was assassinated in Beirut in 1975, reportedly by N.L.F. sympathizers.

39. Deffarge and Troeller, *Yemen '62-'69*, p. 265.

Chapter 9

1. Ill, and perhaps doubtful of the republican regime's prospects, Nu'mān did not return to Yemen at this time. He resigned his seat on the council on November 23, being replaced by Gen. Ḥasan al-'Amrī, the army commander in chief.

2. Prince Muḥammad bin Ismā'īl, quoted in Claude Deffarge and Gordian Troeller, *Yemen '62-'69* (Paris: Robert Laffont, 1969), p. 263.

3. Deffarge and Troeller (*Yemen '62-'69*, p. 261) give a different account of the incident, attributed to "a leftist Yemeni" (unidentified), according to which the governor of Hodeida, Shaikh Sinān Abū Luḥūm, obstructed delivery of the weapons to the militia because he wanted them for his Nahm tribesmen. My version follows intelligence reports available to me at the time at Jidda.

4. E.g., the Khamir and Taif conferences of 1965, as distinct from the Erkowit and Ḥaraḍ meetings stemming from U.A.R.-Saudi initiatives.

5. *Al-Jazīra* (Riyad), May 26, 1970.

6. Ibid.

7. "The Permanent Constitution of the Yemen Arab Republic," *Middle East Journal* 25, no. 3 (summer 1971); 389-401.

8. Except for the abortive attempts in 1962 and 1966 to form a single political organization along the lines of the U.A.R.'s Arab Socialist Union. A similar project in 1972-73 did not proceed beyond the cadre stage.

9. Al-'Amrī briefly jailed the entire management and staff of Yemen Airlines who were reluctant to fly the equipment to al-Baiḍā', where the airport was believed still sown with mines laid during the civil war. The mines proved less fearsome than the commander in chief's jails.

10. This was frustrating to archaeologists, among others, who were unable to visit the important ancient site of Barāqish.

11. In 1973 most of the mature trees in the al-Baiḍā' area, which had for several years been annually defoliated by desiccation, finally died.

12. Robert W. Stookey, "Social Structure and Politics in the Yemen Arab Republic," *Middle East Journal*, 28, nos. 3 and 4 (summer and autumn, 1974): 248-260, 409-418.

13. 'Abd al-Wāsi' bin Yaḥyā al-Wāsi'ī, *Ta'rīkh al-Yaman*, 2d ed. (Cairo: Maṭba'at al-Ḥijāzī, 1947), pp. 88-98.

14. Muḥammad Sa'īd al-'Aṭṭār, *al-Ta'akhkhur al-Iqtiṣādī wal-Ijtimā'ī fī al-Yaman* (Algiers: Dār al-Talī'a, 1965), pp. 217-218.

15. Exceptions are the large rock-salt deposits at Ṣalīf (a high-bulk, low-value commodity); and limestone near Bājil, used in a cement plant recently built by the U.S.S.R.

16. Foreign Broadcast Information Service, Middle East File, June 2, 1971, p. B 1.

17. Mr. Stewart was frequently asked by Yemenis in the rural areas for advice on where to dig new wells. Often, excavation at the spot he recommended uncovered an already existing well constructed in Ḥimyarite times and later buried by the elements. The account in the text is taken from reports by Mr. Stewart to Chargé d'Affaires Harlan Clark dated February 25 and March 11, 1966, kindly made available to me by Mr. Clark.

18. Sing. *nāḥiya*. In Yemen the province (*liwā'*) is divided into districts (*qaḍā'*), then townships (*nāḥiya*), and finally into villages (*qāriya*) or rural localities (*'azla*).

19. Forty *buqash* (sing. *buqsha*) equal one riyal.

20. *Al-Thawra* (Sanaa), March 6, 1973.

21. Ibid., June 26, 1973.

Bibliography

Primary Sources in Arabic (some translated)

Abū Muḥammad ‘Abdullah al-Ṭayyib bin ‘Abdullah bin Aḥmad Bā Makhrama. *Ta'rīkh Thaghr ‘Adan ma‘ Nakhb min Tawārīkh ibn Majāwir wal-Janadī wal-Ahdal.* Edited by Oscar Lofgren. Uppsala: Almqvist & Wiksells Boktryckeri, 1950.

_____. *History of the Yemen at the Beginning of the 16th Century [Qilādat al-Nahr fī Wafāyāt A‘yān al-Dahr].* Edited and translated by Lein Oebele Schuman. Amsterdam: 1960.

‘Alī bin Muḥammad bin ‘Ubaidallah al-‘Abbāsī al-‘Alawī. *Sīrat al-Hādī ilā al-Haqq Yaḥyā bin al-Ḥusain.* Edited by Dr. Suhail Zakkār. Beirut: Dār al-Fikr, 1972.

‘Alī bin al-Ḥasan al-Khazrajī. *al-‘Uqūd al-Lu'lu'iya fī Ta'rīkh al-Dawla al-Rasūliya.* 2 vols. Cairo: Matba‘at al-Hilāl, 1911 and 1914. Also as *The Pearl-Strings: A History of the Resūliyy Dynasty of Yemen.* Translated by Sir J. W. Redhouse. 2 vols. London: Luzac & Co., 1906 and 1907.

Jamāl al-Dīn Muḥammad bin Sālim bin Wāṣil. *Mufarrij al-Kurūb fī Akhbār Banī Ayyūb.* Edited by Dr. Jamāl al-Dīn al-Shayyāl et al. Cairo: Ministry of Culture, 1957-72.

al-Ḥasan bin Aḥmad bin Ya‘qūb al-Hamdānī. *Geographie der Arabischen Halbinsel. Sifat Jazīrat al-‘Arab.* Edited by

David H. Müller. Amsterdam: Oriental Press, 1968 (first published in Leiden, 1884-1891).

_____. *Kitāb al-Iklīl*. Edited by Muḥammad bin 'Alī al-Akwa'. Part I. Cairo: Maṭba'at al-Sunna al-Muḥammadiya, 1963.

Najm al-Dīn 'Umāra al-Yamanī al-Ḥakamī. *Yaman—Its Early Medieval History. [Ta'rīkh al-Yaman].* Edited and translated by Henry Cassels Kay. London: Edward Arnold, 1892.

Nashwān bin Sa'īd al-Ḥimyarī. *Mulūk Ḥimyar wa Aqyāl al-Yaman*. Edited by al-Sayyid 'Alī bin Ismā'īl al Mu'ayyad and Ismā'īl bin Ahmad al-Jarafī. Cairo: al-Maṭba'a al-Salafiya, 1959.

al-Qāḍī Nu'mān bin Muḥammad. *Risālat Iftitāḥ al-Da'wa*. Edited by Wadād al-Qāḍī. Beirut: Dār al-Thaqāfa, 1970.

Quṭb al-Dīn Muḥammad bin Aḥmad al-Nahrawālī al-Makkī. *al-Barq al-Yamānī fī al-Fatḥ al-'Uthmānī*. Riyad: Dār al-Yamāma, 1967.

Tāj al-Dīn 'Abd al-Bāqī bin 'Abd al-Majīd al-Yamanī. *Ta'rıkh al-Yaman al-Musammā Bahjat al-Zaman fī Ta'rīkh al-Yaman*. Edited by Muṣṭafā Ḥijāzī. Cairo: Mukhaimar, 1965.

Tāqī al-Dīn Ahmad bin 'Alī al-Maqrīzī. *al-Dhahab al-Masbūk fī Man Ḥajja min al-Khulafā' wa al-Mulūk*. Edited by Dr. Jamal al-Dīn al-Shayyāl. Cairo: Maktabat al-Khānjī, 1955.

_____. *Kitāb al-Sulūk li-Ma'rifat Duwal al-Mulūk*. Edited by Dr. Muḥammad Muṣṭafā Ziyādah. Vol. 1, pts. 1, 2. Cairo: Lajnat al-Ta'līf wa al-Tarjama wa al-Nashr, 1956 and 1957.

Yaḥyā bin al-Ḥusain bin al-Manṣūr al-Qāsim bin al-Mu'ayyad al-Yamanī. *Anbā' al-Zaman fī Akhbār al-Yaman*. Edited by Muḥammad Madi. Berlin: Walter de Gruyter, 1936. Events of years 280-322 A.H. only.

_____. *Ghāyat al-Amānī fī Akhbār al-Qaṭr al-Yamānī*. Edited by Dr. Sa'īd 'Abd al-Fattāḥ 'Ashūr. 2 vols. Cairo: Dār al-Kitāb, 1968.

Secondary Sources in Arabic

'Abdullah, 'Abd al-Raḥīm. *al-Yaman, Thawra wa Thuwwār.*

Cairo: Dār al-Naṣr, 1967.
ʻAlī, Jawād. *al-ʻArab Qabl al-Islām*. 7 vols. Baghdad: Matbaʻat al-Tafayyud al-Ahliya, 1952.
al-ʻAqqād, Dr. Ṣalāḥ. *Jazirat al-ʻArab fī al-ʻAṣr al-Ḥadīth*. Cairo: Arab League Institute for Arab Research and Studies, 1969.
al-ʻArshī, al-Qāḍī Ḥusain bin Aḥmad. *Bulūgh al-Marām fī Sharḥ Misk al-Khitām fī man Tawallā Mulk al-Yaman min Malik wa Imām*. Edited by Father Anastase-Marie de St.-Elie. Cairo: Louis Sarkis, 1939.
al-ʻAṭṭār, Muḥammad Saʻīd. *al-Ta'akhkhur al-Iqtiṣādī wa al-Ijtimāʻī fī al-Yaman*. Algiers: Dār al-Ṭalīʻa, 1965.
al-Baṭrīq, Dr. ʻAbd al-Ḥamīd. *Min Ta'rīkh al-Yaman al-Ḥadīth*. Cairo: Arab League Institute for Arab Studies and Research, 1969.
Fakhrī, Dr. Aḥmad. *al-Yaman Māḍīhā wa Ḥāḍiruhā*. Cairo: Maṭbaʻat al-Risāla, 1957.
al-Ḥaddād, Muḥammad Yaḥyā. *Ta'rīkh al-Yaman al-Siyāsī*. Cairo: ʻĀlam al-Kutub, 1976.
al-Ḥasani, al-Sayyid ʻAbd al-Razzāq. *Ta'rīkh al-Wizārāt al-Irāqiya*. 2d ed., vol. 4. Sidon: Maṭbaʻat al-ʻIrfān, 1953.
al-Jarāfi, Qāḍī ʻAbdullah bin ʻAbd al-Karīm. *al-Muqtaṭaf min Ta'rīkh al-Yaman*. Cairo: ʻĪsā al-Bābī al-Ḥalabī, 1951.
Kāmil, Maḥmūd. *al-Yaman Shimāluhu wa Janūbūhu Ta'rīkhuhu wa ʻAlāqātuhu al-Duwaliya*. Beirut: Beirut Printers and Publishers, 1968.
Maḥmūd, Dr. Ḥasan Sulaimān. *Ta'rīkh al-Yaman*. Cairo: Maktabat Miṣr, 1957.
———. *Ta'rīkh al-Yaman al-Siyāsī fī al-ʻAṣr al-Islāmī*. Baghdad: al-Majmaʻ al-ʻIlmī al-ʻIrāqī, 1969.
al-Muwāfiq, ʻAbdullah. *al-Shīʻa fī al-Yaman*. Cairo: Maṭbaʻat al-Salafiya, 1970.
al-Rīḥānī, Amīn. *Mulūk al-ʻArab*. 2 vols. Beirut: Maṭābiʻ Ṣādir al-Rīḥānī, 1951.
Saʻīd, Amin. *al-Yaman Ta'rīkhuhu al-Siyāsī mundhu Istiqlālihi fī al-Qurn al-Thālith lil-Hijra*. Cairo: ʻĪsā al-Bābī al-Ḥalabī, 1959.
Sālim, al-Sayyid Muṣṭafā. *Takwīn al-Yaman al-Ḥadīth*. Cairo: Arab League Institute for Higher Arab Studies, 1963.

———. *al-Fatḥ al-'Uthmānī al-Awwal lil-Yaman*. Cairo: Arab League Institute for Arab Research and Studies, 1969.

al-Shahārī, Dr. Muḥammad 'Alī. "Tarīq al-Thawra al-Yamaniya." Kitāb al-Hilāl, no. 188 (1966).

Shalabī, Aḥmad. *Fī Qusūr al-Khulafā' al-'Abbāsiyīn*. Cairo: Anglo-Egyptian Publishers, 1954.

al-Shamāḥī, Qāḍī 'Abdullah bin 'Abd al-Wahhāb al-Mujāhid. *al-Yaman: al-Insān wa al-Ḥaḍāra*. Cairo: 'Ālam al-Kutub, 1972.

al-Shāmī, Aḥmad Muḥammad. *Imām al-Yaman Aḥmad Ḥamīd al-Dīn*. Beirut: Dār al-Kitāb al-Jadīd, 1965.

Sharaf al-Dīn, Aḥmad Ḥusain. *al-Yaman 'abr al-Ta'rīkh*. Cairo: Maṭba'at al-Sunna al-Muhammadiya, 1963.

Surūr, Dr. Muḥammad Jalāl al-Dīn. *al-Nufūdh al-Fāṭimī fī Jazīrat al-'Arab*. 2d ed. Cairo: Dār al-Fikr al-'Arabī, 1957.

Tāmir, 'Ārif. *Arwā bint al-Yaman*. Cairo: Dār al-Ma'ārif, 1970.

Tarcici, Dr. 'Adnān. *al-Yaman wa Ḥadārat al-'Arab*. Beirut: Dār Maktabat al-Ḥayāt, n.d.

al-Wāsi'ī, 'Abd al-Wāsi' bin Yaḥyā. *Ta'rīkh al-Yaman*. 2d ed., enl. Cairo Matba'at Hijazi, 1947.

al-Wazīr, Ibrāhīm 'Alī. *Bain Yaday al-Ma'sāt*. Beirut: Dār al-Andalus, 1963.

———. *Likay lā namḍī fī al-Ẓalām*. Beirut: Dār al-Andalus, 1958?

Zabāra, al-Sayyid Muḥammad bin Muḥammad. *A'immat al-Yaman*. Ta'izz: Maṭba'at al-Naṣr al-Nāṣiriya, 1952.

———. *A'immat al-Yaman bil-Qurn al-Rābi' 'Āshir lil-Hijra*. Cairo: al-Maṭba'a al-Salafiya, 1956.

———. *al-Anbā' 'an Dawlat Bilqīs wa Saba'*. Cairo: al-Maṭba'a al-Salafiya, 1956.

———. *Nayl al-Waṭar*. 2 vols. Cairo: al-Maṭba'a al-Salafiya, 1929, 1932.

Zaidān, Jurjī. *al-'Arab qabl al-Islām*. Edited by Dr. Ḥusain Mu'nis. Cairo: Dār al-Hilāl, n.d.

Documents

Reports by John H. Stewart, U.S. Agency for International Development to Chargé d'Affaires, American Embassy,

Ta'izz:
1. "Four Weeks in the Community Development Program," February 25, 1966.
2. "A New Miracle at Kadas," March 11, 1966.
Despatch No. 52 dated April 23, 1945, from American Consul, Aden, to U.S. Secretary of State.

Yemen Central Planning Organization. *Statistical Year Book, 1972*. Sanaa: 1973.

_____. *Preliminary Report on the Socio-Demographic Survey in Sanaa City*. Sanaa: 1973.

_____. *Tashrī'āt wa Anẓimat al-Jihāz al-Markazī lil-Takhṭīṭ*. Publication no. 1. Sanaa: 1972.

Works in Western Languages

Albright, William Foxwell. *The Archaeology of Palestine*. London: Penguin Books, 1949.

Arberry, Arthur J., ed. *Religion in the Middle East*. 2 vols. Cambridge: The University Press, 1969.

Be'eri, Eliezer. *Army Officers in Arab Politics and Society*. New York: Praeger, 1970.

Bethmann, Erich W. *Yemen on the Threshold*. Washington, D.C.: American Friends of the Middle East, 1960.

Boals, Kathryn. *Modernization and Intervention: Yemen as a Theoretical Case Study*. Ph.D. dissertation, Princeton University, 1970.

Bowen, Richard LeBaron, Jr., Albright, Frank P., et al. *Archaeological Discoveries in South Arabia*. Baltimore: Johns Hopkins Press, 1958.

Bury, G. Wyman. *Arabia Infelix or the Turks in Yemen*. London: Macmillan Co., 1915.

Coulson, N. J. *A History of Islamic Law*. Edinburgh: The University Press, 1964.

Deffarge, Claude, and Troeller, Gordian. *Yemen '62-'69*. Paris: Robert Laffont, 1969.

Donaldson, Dwight M. *The Shī'ite Religion*. London: Luzac, 1933.

al-Hamdani, Husayn F. School of Oriental Studies Occasional Papers, no. 1. *On the Genealogy of the Fatimid Caliphs*. Cairo: American University, 1958.

Hansen, Thorkild. *Arabia Felix. The Danish Expedition of*

1761-1767. Translated by James and Kathleen McFarlane. New York: Harper and Row, 1964.

Hickinbotham, Sir Tom. *Aden*. London: Constable & Co., 1958.

Ingrams, William Harold. *Arabia and the Isles*. 3d ed. New York: Praeger, 1966.

_____. *The Yemen: Imams, Rulers and Revolutions*. London: John Murray, 1963.

Macro, Eric. *Yemen and the Western World since 1571*. New York: Praeger, 1968.

Niebuhr, Carsten. *Travels through Arabia and Other Countries in the East*. Translated by Robert Heron. 2 vols. Beirut: Librarie du Liban, n.d.

O'Ballance, Edgar. *The War in the Yemen*. Hamden, Conn.: Archon Books, 1971.

Petersen, Erling Ladewig. *'Alī and Mu'āwiya in Early Arabic Tradition*. Copenhagen: Munksgaard, 1964.

Philby, H. St. J. B. *Arabian Highlands*. Washington, D.C.: Middle East Institute, 1952.

_____. *Sheba's Daughters, Being a Record of Travel in Southern Arabia*. London: Methuen & Co., 1939.

Phillips, Wendell. *Qataban and Sheba*. London: Victor Gollancz, 1955.

Pirenne, Jacqueline. *Paléographie des inscriptions sud-arabes: Contribution à la chronologie de l'Arabie du Sud antique*. Brussels: Paleis der Academiën, 1956.

_____. *le Royaume Sud-Arabe de Qatabân et sa datation*. Louvain: Publications Universitaires, 1961.

Reilly, Sir Bernard. *Aden and the Yemen*. London: Her Majesty's Stationery Office, 1960.

Rihani, Ameen. *Arabian Peak and Desert: Travels in al-Yaman*. Boston and New York: Houghton Mifflin Co., 1930.

Ryckmans, Jacques. *l'Institution monarchique en Arabie méridionale avant l'Islam*. Louvain: Publications Universitaires, 1951.

Sanger, Richard H. *The Arabian Peninsula*. Ithaca, N.Y.: Cornell University Press, 1954.

Schmidt, Dana Adams. *Yemen: The Unknown War*. New

York: Holt, Rinehart, and Winston, 1968.

Scott, Hugh. *In the High Yemen.* 2d ed. London: John Murray, 1947.

Serjeant, Robert B. "The Two Yemens: Historical Perspectives and Present Attitudes." Lecture to the Royal Central Asian Society, November 1, 1972.

_____. *The Saiyids of Ḥaḍramawt.* London: University of London School of Oriental and African Studies, 1957.

_____. *The Portuguese off the South Arabian Coast.* Oxford: The Clarendon Press, 1963.

Shahîd, Irfan. *The Martyrs of Najran: New Documents.* Brussels: Société des Bollandistes, 1971.

Shoufani, Elias S. *al-Riddah and the Muslim Conquest of Arabia.* Toronto and Buffalo: University of Toronto Press, 1973.

van Arendonk, Cornelis. *Les Débuts de l'imamat zaidite au Yemen.* Translated by Jacques Ryckmans. Leyden: E. J. Brill, 1960.

von Horn, Maj. Gen. Carl. *Soldiering for Peace.* New York: David McKay, 1967.

Watt, W. Montgomery. *Islamic Political Thought.* Edinburgh: The University Press, 1968.

Wenner, Manfred W. *Modern Yemen 1918-1966.* Baltimore: Johns Hopkins Press, 1967.

Index